2022

Land Politics

Land Politics examines the struggle to control land in Africa through the lens of land titling in Zambia and Senegal. Contrary to standard wisdom portraying titling as an inevitable product of economic development, Lauren Honig traces its distinctly political logic and shows how informality is maintained by local actors. The book's analysis focuses on chiefs, customary institutions, and citizens, revealing that the strength of these institutions and an individual's position within them impact the expansion of state authority over land rights. Honig explores common subnational patterns within the two very different countries to highlight the important effects of local institutions, not the state's capacity or priorities alone, on state building outcomes. Drawing on evidence from national land titling records, qualitative case studies, interviews, and surveys, this book contributes new insights into the persistence of institutional legacies and the political determinants of property rights.

Lauren Honig is an assistant professor of political science at Boston College. Her research on property rights, citizen-state linkages, customary authority, and informal institutions in Africa has been published in numerous journals. She has received fellowships and grants from the National Science Foundation, Social Science Research Council, and Fulbright Association, among others.

Land Politics

*How Customary Institutions Shape
State Building in Zambia and Senegal*

LAUREN HONIG
Boston College

CAMBRIDGE
UNIVERSITY PRESS

University Printing House, Cambridge CB2 8BS, United Kingdom

One Liberty Plaza, 20th Floor, New York, NY 10006, USA

477 Williamstown Road, Port Melbourne, VIC 3207, Australia

314–321, 3rd Floor, Plot 3, Splendor Forum, Jasola District Centre, New Delhi – 110025, India

103 Penang Road, #05–06/07, Visioncrest Commercial, Singapore 238467

Cambridge University Press is part of the University of Cambridge.

It furthers the University's mission by disseminating knowledge in the pursuit of education, learning, and research at the highest international levels of excellence.

www.cambridge.org
Information on this title: www.cambridge.org/9781009123402
DOI: 10.1017/9781009129183

© Lauren Honig 2022

This publication is in copyright. Subject to statutory exception and to the provisions of relevant collective licensing agreements, no reproduction of any part may take place without the written permission of Cambridge University Press.

First published 2022

A catalogue record for this publication is available from the British Library.

ISBN 978-1-009-12340-2 Hardback

Cambridge University Press has no responsibility for the persistence or accuracy of URLs for external or third-party internet websites referred to in this publication and does not guarantee that any content on such websites is, or will remain, accurate or appropriate.

Contents

List of Figures		*page* vii
List of Tables		ix
Acknowledgments		xi
1	Introduction: Land Titling as State Building	1
2	Plot by Plot: Customary Authority and the Incremental Expansion of State Property Rights in Africa	38
3	Why Institutions Matter: A Theory of Collective Costs and Customary Constraints in Land Titling	83
4	The Institutional Foundations of Land Authority in Zambia and Senegal	109
5	The Unofficial Differences among Official Chiefs in Zambia: Vertical Accountability and Patterns of Land Titling	155
6	Holding Ground in Senegal: Horizontal Accountability, Institutional Legacies, and the Continuation of Customary Property Rights	202
7	Exit or Engagement: How Status within Institutions Impacts Smallholder Titling	244
8	Conclusion: The Resilience of Customary Institutions and Property Rights, Beyond State Design	278
Appendices		293
References		327
Index		353

Figures

2.1	The gap between trust in chiefs and state actors, from largest to smallest	page 47
2.2	The percentage of customary land per country in 2015	51
2.3	Subnational differences in land authority in four African countries	61
2.4	Evidence of local-level institutional pluralism in property rights in nineteen African countries	64
3.1	Predictions of the hierarchy framework	105
3.2	Predictions of the customary privilege theory	106
4.1	British map of precolonial polities in Zambia	113
4.2	French map of precolonial polities in Senegal	114
4.3	Hierarchical institutions in Zambia in the colonial era	123
4.4	Hierarchical institutions in Senegal in the colonial era	127
5.1	Locations of Bemba and Bisa chiefdoms, northern Zambia	172
5.2	Map of the rates of land titling per district in Zambia through 2012	184
5.3	Land titling by institution type, Zambia	186
5.4	Effect of hierarchy on predicted rates of titling in Zambia	188
5.5	Comparing land titling among the three types of official chieftaincy systems in Zambia	189
5.6	Predicted rates of land titling by land values and hierarchy in Zambia	192
6.1	Locations of Dagana and Podor districts, northern Senegal	218
6.2	Map of rates of land titling per district in Senegal, 2007–2013	233
6.3	Effect of hierarchy on predicted rates of titling in Senegal	235

6.4 Predicted rates of land titling by land values and hierarchy in Senegal — 238
6.5 Evaluating the strength of customary property rights in districts with and without hierarchy in Senegal — 241
7.1 Modes of land access, by country — 251
7.2 The effect of customary privilege on smallholder land titling at different levels of income, education, and land values in Zambia — 264
7.3 The effect of customary privilege on tenure security in Zambia and Senegal — 269
8.1 The inverse relationship between trust in chiefs and engagement with the state — 284
8.2 The inverse relationship between trust in the state and engagement with chiefs — 284

Tables

1.1	Comparing Senegal and Zambia	*page* 30
2.1	Key differences between customary and state property rights in Senegal and Zambia	58
5.1	Chieftaincy systems in Zambia	167
5.2	Summary of attributes of Bemba and Bisa institutions in 2013	172
5.3	Effects of hierarchy on smallholder land titling in Zambia	196
7.1	Comparing households with and without titles	252
7.2	Correlates of smallholder land titling in Zambia	260
7.3	Correlates of smallholder land titling in Senegal	265
7.4	Evaluating support for alternative models of land titling	273
A.1	Chapter 5: Zambia land titles data set: Summary statistics and variable descriptions	294
A.2	Chapter 6: Senegal land titles data set: Summary statistics and variable descriptions	296
A.3	Chapters 5 and 7: Zambia smallholder data set: Summary statistics and variable descriptions	299
A.4	Chapter 7: Senegal smallholder data set: Summary statistics and variable descriptions	302
B.1	Chapter 5: Land titling and hierarchy with alternative specifications in Zambia	306
B.2	Chapter 5: Balance statistics for probability weighted analyses of hierarchy and smallholder land titling	308
B.3	Chapter 6: Land titling and hierarchy with alternative specifications in Senegal	310
B.4	Chapter 6: Land rental markets, titling, and hierarchy in Senegal	312

B.5	Chapter 7: Customary privilege and tenure security in Zambia	313
B.6	Chapter 7: Customary privilege, tenure security, and resistance in Senegal	315
B.7	Chapter 8: Analyses of the relationship between trust in chiefs and engagement with the state	316
C.1	Differences among brotherhood communities in sample	322
C.2	The impact of customary privilege in relation to Islamic marabouts in Senegal	323

Acknowledgments

This book is about the very local decisions that determine the expansion of state authority and the resilience of customary land institutions within the modern state. It draws upon insights shared by thousands of Senegalese and Zambian citizens who took the time to participate in surveys, focus groups, and interviews. I express my deep appreciation to the smallholder farmers, customary authorities, and bureaucrats in these two countries who contributed in a variety of ways to this project. The book would not have been possible without their willingness to share with me their experiences with land rights and customary institutions. Further, members of civil society organizations, nongovernmental organizations, and government agencies working in the domains of land and agriculture generously shared their time, shapefiles, reports, databases, and expertise. Confidentiality was a condition of these interactions, particularly given that land was a highly sensitive topic at the time in these two countries. I have preserved their anonymity in these pages but recognize that their contributions made this research possible.

In Zambia, I was lucky to have the support of two excellent research institutions. I express my deep appreciation to Hon. Chance Kabaghe and Thom Jayne for welcoming me to the Indaba Agricultural Policy Research Institute (IAPRI). Colleagues at IAPRI contributed to this project in large and small ways; special thanks to Jordan Chamberlin, Mwamba Chishimba, Cardinal Hachikona, Munguzwe Hichaambwa, Stephen Kabwe, Nicky Mason-Wardell, Brian Mulenga, Eustensia Munsaka, Nick Sitko, and Ballard Zulu. I am also grateful to have been part of the research community created by the Southern African Institute for Policy and Research (SAIPAR). I am thankful to Jessica Achberger,

Marja Hinfelaar, and Manenga Ndulo of SAIPAR for sharing their wisdom and networks. In addition, SAIPAR's Zambia Legal Information Institute database was an important resource for this project. In Zambia, Webster Chewe, Obino Paul Mulenga, Heather Musariri, and Rave Suzah provided excellent research assistance. I am grateful to have partnered with Caritas Kasama for the research in Northern Province. Dr. Patrick Manda shared his personal library and deep knowledge of Zambia's customary authority systems. The National Archives of Zambia and the University of Zambia provided invaluable documentary resources. Further, I acknowledge the contributions of representatives of the Zambia Land Alliance; the Ministry of Local Government and Housing; the Zambia Wildlife Authority; the Ministry of Land, Natural Resources, and Environment; the Ministry of Agriculture and Cooperatives; the Ministry of Chiefs and Traditional Affairs; the House of Chiefs; the Central Statistics Office; USAID; Zambia Development Agency; the Zambia Law Development Commission; and the Zambia National Farmers Union, among others.

In Senegal, the West Africa Research Center (WARC) was my home base. I am grateful to the WARC director, Ousmane Sène, and to Mariane Yade for building this community of scholars and for sharing their expertise. I am indebted to Fodé Sarr for his collaboration with data collection. I thank Mamadou Coulibaly, Mamadou Diagne, Mame Diarra Diop, Ndèye Astou Fall, Cherif Kandji, Ousmane Mbaye, Amadou Tidiane N'Diaye, Mamadou Ndiaye, Ibrahima Niasse, and Fatimata Soumare for their assistance with survey enumeration. Joanna Sherif also provided invaluable research assistance in Senegal. I spent many hours in the National Archives of Senegal (ANS) and acknowledge the contributions of the ANS team to this project. A number of land experts in Senegal shared their expertise and guidance in the early stages of this project, including Iba Mar Faye and Ibrahima Almamy Wade. I also gratefully acknowledge the contributions of staff and experts at the Centre de Suivi Ecologique; La Société d'Aménagement Delta; La Direction Générale des Impôts et des Domaines; USAID; MCA; the ANSD; ANIDA, PDIDAS, PDMAS; L'Agence pour la Promotion des Investissements et des Grands Travaux; La Direction de l'Agriculture; ESRI Senegal; ENDA-Pronat; and the Initiative Prospective Agricole et Rurale, among others.

This book began as a dissertation project at Cornell University. I recognize the many ways in which the training and encouragement to explore that I received at Cornell's Department of Government contributed to this project. I owe a great intellectual debt to my dissertation committee, who provided constructive criticism and enthusiastic support for this project: Nic van de Walle, Ron Herring, and Tom Pepinsky. Ken Roberts shared invaluable feedback as an external reader. Kevin Morrison encouraged me to explain the causes of plural land rights before tackling its consequences. It is a great sorrow that I cannot share the finished project with him. Elsewhere on the Cornell campus, I was fortunate to engage with interdisciplinary communities of scholars focused on land and issues related to African development. The land team at the Institute for the Social Sciences, particularly Wendy Wolford and Chuck Geisler, pushed me to think about this project in new ways. Muna Ndulo offered guidance and facilitated a weekly seminar that kept me connected with regional issues. Friends and colleagues in Cornell's Department of Government provided feedback on grant applications, prospectuses, and chapters that became part of the book. Thank you to Amanda Cheney, Aileen Cardona, Seb Dettman, Aaron Gavin, Triveni Gandhi, Mariana Giusti-Rodríguez, Erin Hern, Don Leonard, Natalie Letsa, Mariano Sánchez-Talanquer, Greg Thaler, and Martha Wilfahrt.

Many others have contributed to this project along the way. I was incredibly fortunate to receive feedback on the entire manuscript from Kate Baldwin, Cathy Boone, Clark Gibson, and Lily Tsai during a book workshop hosted at Boston College (BC). I am grateful to my BC colleagues who participated in this workshop, Jennie Purnell and Jerry Easter, and to Selene Campion and Shirley Gee for their support. Special thanks are due to other BC colleagues who have provided feedback and guidance, particularly Jennifer Erickson, Michael Hartney, Peter Krause, Jonathan Laurence, and Thibaud Marcesse. I also thank the BC students who helped out with research on this book: Aiche Ba, Riley Casadei, Colin Cross, Theodora Danias, Aissata Diallo, Christi Goff, Sydney Koehler, Stephen Michaels, Jess Podgurski, Victoria Pouille, and Brianna Stonick.

This book also builds upon feedback from and thoughtful conversations with Sarah Andrews, Mariana Candido, Jessica Chu, Chipo Dendere, Bob Dowd, Karen Ferree, Hernán Flom, David Glovsky, Gary Goertz, Mai Hassan, Mike Hoffman, Stuart Kirsch, Kathleen Klaus, Karrie Koesel, Jen Lazuta, Tina Lee, Emily Lieberman, Ellen Lust, Aditi Malik, Dan Mattingly, Anne Meng, Nichola Minott, Ken Opalo, Jeff Paller, Jessie Pinchoff, Rachel Beatty Riedl, Amy Erica Smith, Liz Sperber, Maggie Triyana, and Brian Valente-Quinn. Jaimie Bleck and

Sean McGraw provided comments on the entire draft at key moments. In addition, this study benefited from the feedback of audiences and workshop participants at Boston University, Northwestern University, and Notre Dame University, as well as the American Political Science Association, Midwest Political Science Association, and African Studies Association annual conferences.

I am also grateful to team at Cambridge University Press. Sara Doskow quickly and enthusiastically ushered this book through the beginning of the publication process; Jadyn Fauconier-Herry and Rachel Blaifeder guided its completion. I am overwhelmed with appreciation for the two anonymous reviewers who provided detailed, thoughtful, and constructive feedback on the entire manuscript during a global pandemic. This book is much stronger thanks to these reviews. In addition, I gratefully acknowledge the editorial support of Catherine Rae and Tom Mowle, as well as Chris Soldt's assistance with creating images for the final manuscript. Keith Jenkins at Cornell and Awanti Acharya at BC provided guidance with GIS mapping. Earlier versions of the material in Chapter 7 were published in the article "Selecting the State or Choosing the Chief? The Political Determinants of Smallholder Land Titling," *World Development* 100, 94–107 (December 2017) and portions of Chapter 2 were published in "Traditional Leaders and Development in Africa" in *The Oxford Research Encyclopedia of Politics*, Oxford University Press (2019). I am thankful to Elsevier and Oxford University Press for permission to reproduce this material.

I recognize all of the funding that makes an undertaking such as this possible. Fieldwork in Senegal and Zambia from 2013 to 2015 was funded by generous financial support from the Social Sciences Research Council International Dissertation Research Fellowship, the National Science Foundation Doctoral Dissertation Improvement Grant, and a Fulbright-IIE research grant for Zambia. Research trips to Senegal and Zambia in 2011 and 2012 were supported by the Institute for Social Sciences, the Einaudi Center for International Studies, and the Department of Government at Cornell University. In addition, I had a year-long visiting research fellowship at the Kellogg Institute for International Studies at the University of Notre Dame, which provided me with time to write and a rich intellectual community. I also gratefully acknowledge the funding from Boston College that facilitated various elements of research and manuscript preparation.

My final debt is to the family and friends who have sustained me, inspired me, and unconditionally supported me over the years. I gratefully acknowledge the friends who have shared my successes and failures, and provided balance during the long process of completing this book. Thank you. My deepest appreciation goes to my family, who have always encouraged me to chart my own path. To Kim, thank you for championing my choices and being a model of persistence. I am so lucky, and so is Miles. Many thanks to Sam and Karen who fed me and kept me laughing throughout. To my father, whose fundamental belief in the power of education structured my childhood. To my mother, who shared her love of learning and fostered our curiosity. With gratitude to my family for laying a strong foundation.

I

Introduction

Land Titling as State Building

In recent years, the question of who controls land in African countries has grown increasingly contentious. Violent protests, accusations of land grabbing, and heated debates over land rights occur across the continent. Soaring demand for land, from both global and domestic markets, fuels these conflicts. Foreign investors purchase vast tracts of land for commercial agriculture; growing cities encroach on peri-urban areas; and members of the urban middle class seek rural plots of land as investments for the future. Simultaneously, millions of subsistence farmers and pastoralists depend on secure access to fertile land, which is threatened by land degradation, climate change, and population growth. This high demand has provoked the expansion of state property rights – land titles – on vast areas of land previously governed by customary authorities and local communities.

Land titling is deeply political. In Zambia and Senegal, the focal countries in this book, titling permanently transfers land from customary to state control. Each new title shifts the distribution of power over land rights toward the state. Land titling is therefore a process of expanding state power over land, not merely part of an inevitable evolution toward formality or a product of economic development. Titling codifies and maps land rights that were previously outside direct state control. In doing so, it makes land and its users legible to the state.[1] This extends the state's territorial reach within boundaries inherited from colonial rule and increases its interactions with citizens. Further, land

[1] Scott 1998.

titling makes it easier for the state to distribute and tax land, building the state's revenue base and capacity to extract.[2] Given these linkages between land and political authority, states have long employed land rights as an essential technology of state building.[3] Strong states use top-down campaigns, such as forced collectivization schemes or compulsory mass land titling, to weaken alternative systems of property rights and land authority. However, land registration is now the most common form of land reform in African countries.[4] From Benin to Mozambique to Madagascar, governments have established frameworks for "piecemeal" land titling, in which individual agents – citizens, bureaucrats, and investors – register customary land as new state titles.[5] This allows state control over property rights to grow, plot by plot, during an era of high demand for African land.

There is reason to expect that land markets and the state's interests will dictate where land titling occurs. Investors and regular citizens alike should seek titles on more valuable and desirable land, where the economic benefits of formal property rights are the highest. State property rights should therefore develop first in areas with higher population density, fertile land, and infrastructure access.[6] Further, states are powerful; they have the resources to encourage or compel titling on any land within their territorial boundaries. In Zambia, all land is vested in the president. In Senegal, land without titles is "owned" by the nation. These states have thus laid the legal groundwork for politicians who are motivated to facilitate lucrative land markets or to fulfill strategic political agendas to determine where titling occurs. In addition, it is costlier for the state to project authority over geographic distances; therefore, state control of land should expand first in areas closest to seats of bureaucratic

---

[2] For example, Zambia's minister of finance introduced the country's 2014 budget to parliament with a speech extolling the importance of land titling to increase government revenue and "bring sanity in land administration." See: The 2014 Budget address by Hon. Alexander B. Chikwanda, Minister of Finance, Delivered to the National Assembly on October 11th, 2013.

[3] Migdal 1988; Fisiy 1992; Scott 1998; Boone 2007; Lund 2008.

[4] Sikor and Müller 2009, 1308.

[5] Countries with piecemeal titling or registration policies include Angola, Benin, Botswana, Burkina Faso, Burundi, Cameroon, Cape Verde, Central African Republic, Chad, Côte d'Ivoire, Democratic Republic of Congo, Ghana, Equatorial Guinea, Eritrea, Gabon, Guinea-Bissau, Guinea, Kenya, Liberia, Lesotho, Madagascar, Malawi, Mali, Mozambique, Mauritania, Namibia, Niger, Nigeria, Republic of Congo, Senegal, Sierra Leone, Somalia, South Africa, South Sudan, Sudan, Tanzania, The Gambia, Togo, Uganda, Zambia, Zimbabwe.

[6] Boserup 1965; North 1990; Platteau 1996; Alston et al. 1999; Miceli et al. 2001.

power and transportation networks.⁷ The standard wisdom thus anticipates that demand from state actors and individuals embedded in land markets determines patterns of land titling. It suggests that land remains in the customary domain because it is low in value or state actors are disinterested in titling it.

However, two examples illustrate the limitations of top-down and structural approaches to land titling. The first is from Zambia, where customary authorities or "chiefs" are legally recognized as the custodians of customary land. In practice, any new titles require written consent from an official chief. When the government needed land to expand a program of resettlement schemes in 2012, it therefore turned to the chiefs. Bureaucrats traveled throughout the country to the rural homes of customary authorities to beg for tracts of customary land to title, bearing gifts to show respect. They brought them groceries, goats, or chickens; some greeted the chief with cash tucked into the palm of their hands.⁸ The bureaucrats' goal was to convince the chiefs to cede a parcel of land, in order to start the process of permanently converting it to state land title.

Chiefs reacted very differently to the government's demands for land. Some consented upon first request. One offered the program a very large area of land while telling the bureaucrats to spread the word to investors so that they would seek land in his chiefdom.⁹ Some chiefs dictated the location and the size of the land for the government's resettlement project. A few indefinitely delayed the negotiations. Others explicitly refused to transfer any land out of the customary domain, even after repeated visits from the state's representatives. From the perspective of bureaucrats seeking land in Zambia, "Chiefs have the upper hand in which area they will give up for government development."¹⁰ Through their responses to these land negotiations, customary authorities determined which land, if any, was transferred to the state's formal control.

A second example, from Senegal, highlights the agency of regular citizens in the expansion of state authority over land. Even within the same communities, some citizens dismiss the opportunity to adopt a state land title, while others welcome it. Senegalese farmers with small plots of customary land have the option of titling their land. Without titles, they

---

[7] Herbst 2000.
[8] Interviews with bureaucrat (BUR-641), Lusaka, Zambia, September 20, 2013; with bureaucrat (BUR-656), northern Zambia, January 8, 2014; with bureaucrat (BUR-609), northern Zambia, February 20, 2014.
[9] Interview with bureaucrat (BUR-620), northern Zambia, January 8, 2014.
[10] Interview with bureaucrat (BUR-648), Lusaka, Zambia, August 29, 2013.

rely on customary rights. They retain access to land through their connections to the community and to Senegal's unofficial chiefs – customary authorities who do not have state-recognized land authority. These citizens' customary property rights may include complex systems of secondary rights, such as seasonal usage arrangements, that serve as a form of risk-sharing within the community.[11] Following the government's efforts to make formalization more accessible, some customary landowners eagerly pursue land titling in order to gain ownership rights in the eyes of the state. They apply to rural councils to have the boundaries of their land documented and their land rights written into the state's land registries. Other citizens decline the opportunity to convert their customary property rights to titles, reporting that it is unnecessary or that they feel secure on the land of their grandparents.[12] As these examples illustrate, customary authorities and citizens have vastly different reactions to land titling in their communities, which impacts how and to what extent state control of land grows.

Understanding this contemporary state-building process requires paying greater attention to the responses of these two sets of actors: chiefs and citizens. Why do some chiefs encourage land titling in their domains and others thwart it? Why do some citizens with customary land rights in a community seek a state title while others do not? More generally, how do customary land regimes survive, despite powerful economic interests and state efforts to title land?

Zambia and Senegal provide the foundation for answering these questions. The two countries feature different colonial histories, geographies, and official roles for customary authorities. Nevertheless, they are both part of a broader global pattern in which governments have courted land markets and facilitated land titling, allowing formal state property rights to progressively replace customary land tenure. Examining a similar process in these diverse countries provides greater insight into the determinants of the local decisions that constrain and facilitate the growth of state control over land.

This book will show that customary land is not idly waiting to be titled; rather, it is actively maintained by the actors that gain power from its informality. Moreover, it reveals that the customary institutions in which these chiefs and citizens are embedded shape how they respond to land titling. I argue that both the strength of the institution and the

---

[11] For examples, see Toulmin and Quan 2000a; Meinzen-Dick and Mwangi 2009.
[12] Author's Senegal smallholder survey, 2014.

individual's status within it impact these local decisions. As a result, communities with stronger customary institutions – those with hierarchical legacies in these two countries – are better able to retain control of land. In addition, by structuring social and political relations within communities, customary institutions also condition whether citizens engage with the state by seeking titles for their own plots of land. Consequently, these institutions impact when and where customary land tenure endures, contributing to the resilience of customary authority and shaping patterns of state building within the territory. Before elaborating upon this institutional argument, the following section situates this debate over land rights within an era of increasing land scarcity and competition for land.

1.1 LAND POLITICS

The struggle for authority over land has high stakes for the state, customary authorities, and citizens. The question of who controls land is deeply political, in part, because land holds multiple forms of value. It is the most important factor of production for agricultural economies: Millions of citizens in African countries depend on secure access to land for their livelihoods. Yet the significance of land extends beyond its material value. Land often holds social importance, as a connection to one's ancestors and community.[13] This makes it harder and more contentious to reallocate it among potential land users. Such non-commodity values mean that, unlike bags of maize, land cannot be easily bought and sold for a fixed price. Further, the long history of elites exploiting land as a political resource shapes its contemporary role in politics.[14] Current debates over land rights reflect political grievances about past policies and practices related to land. While the key issues are specific to each country, land is ubiquitous as a political fault line.

As a result, land has played a role in nearly all conflicts in the region. Contested land claims contributed to Côte d'Ivoire's recent civil war and Kenya's 2008 electoral violence.[15] In the Democratic Republic of Congo's protracted conflict, militias have fought to control prime land.[16] The Rwandan genocide was exacerbated by extreme land scarcity and

---

[13] Fisiy 1992.
[14] For examples, see Kanyinga 1998; Chauveau 2000; Klopp 2000; Babo 2013; Médard and Golaz 2013.
[15] Boone 2014; Klaus and Mitchell 2015.   [16] Autesserre 2010.

inequality of access.[17] Rural citizens throughout the continent have been impacted by small-scale land conflicts, which are often associated with divisions based on ethnicity, migration status, and agricultural livelihood (e.g., farmers or pastoralists). In urban areas too, land disputes have become commonplace. There, the combination of high demand for land and unsettled systems of property rights translates into conflict over multiple allocations of the same land parcels and protest over abruptly razed informal settlements.[18] Control of land is a source of power and wealth, making land rights a central issue in contentious politics.

This book examines issues of political authority over land in an era when the stakes of land control and access are rapidly increasing. Pressure on land in Africa is growing, exacerbating existing political cleavages. African cities are the sites of technological innovations and gleaming skyscrapers, yet the majority of the population in sub-Saharan Africa practice agriculture.[19] Given the predicted doubling of the continent's populations in the next thirty-five years,[20] the number of people dependent on land for their livelihoods will continue to rise. Climate change and land degradation decrease the stock of arable land, pushing households to move or extend their areas of crop production. Well-intentioned conservation efforts sequester major areas of land for carbon trading and animal protection.[21] As the cost of land in cities rises with urbanization, African middle classes are increasingly looking to regional capitals and rural areas to buy land. These compounding sources of stress on land challenge the stability of the current systems of land authority. This intense pressure is magnified by demand for land from global investors.

Investors from a range of both Global North and Global South countries participated in feverish efforts to accumulate African agricultural land in the first decades of the twenty-first century. Global interest in African land was prompted, in part, by concerns about national food security and volatile food prices, and interest in new arenas for investment following the 2008 financial crisis. In 2009 alone, there were an estimated 39.7 million hectares (ha) of investment deals in African land; this

---

[17] Prunier 1995; André and Platteau 1998; Bigagaza, Abong, and Mukarubuga 2002.
[18] See, for example, du Plessis 2005; Ocheje 2007.
[19] Approximately 65 percent of the labor force in sub-Saharan Africa was engaged in agriculture in 2014. World Bank, "Human Capital for Agriculture in Africa." *Science, Technology, and Skills for Africa's Development* (Washington, DC: World Bank Group, 2014).
[20] UNICEF, *Generation 2030/AFRICA* (UNICEF, August 2014).
[21] See Gibson 1999; Unruh 2008.

contrasts with an average of 1.8 million ha per year from 1961 to 2007.[22] Large commercial land deals and state farms are not new, but they have increased rapidly across the continent and developing countries, more generally.[23] They have the potential to fundamentally transform land values in African countries, as land has become increasingly scarce and potential investors abundant.[24]

International and multinational land deals have impacted most countries in Africa, provoking deeply political debates over how land should be used and governed. In Madagascar, President Marc Ravalomanana's attempt to lease 3.2 million ha of land to the South Korean company Daewoo triggered protests and contributed to the fall of his regime in 2009.[25] Liberia's Nobel Peace Prize–winning president, Ellen Johnson Sirleaf, was denounced for having allocated a third of the country's land to international investors between 2006 and 2011, much of it for biofuel production.[26] Sudan, Ethiopia, Madagascar, Mozambique, Tanzania, and Sierra Leone had the greatest number of land deals between 2000 and 2012.[27] The large land deals in Zambia and Senegal described in Chapters 5 and 6 are typical of a phenomenon that is widespread across Africa.

The vast majority of multinational land deals occur on customary land, which is treated as an inexpensive resource by investors and state actors alike.[28] States have promoted and defended land deals as a means of diversifying the national economy and attracting foreign direct investment. Further, these global land markets have roused domestic land markets, as elites and middle classes claimed their own shares in response to the rapid decrease in the supply of customary land. Both private citizens and commercial investors have sought to formalize their rights to new areas of customary land through titling. As a result, markets for customary land have transformed existing systems of land tenure and state–customary relations.

Governments made this possible by establishing legal frameworks to facilitate titling, designed to allow markets to determine the speed and

---

[22] Deininger and Byerlee 2011, 9.   [23] Alden Wily 2012.
[24] Collier and Venables 2012, 3.   [25] Thaler 2013.
[26] Silas Kpanan'ayoung Siakor and Rachel S. Knight, "A Nobel Laureate's Problem at Home," *New York Times*, January 20, 2012.
[27] In order of territorial size of land deals by international investors as described in Moyo, Jha, and Yeros 2019, 12–13.
[28] Moyo, Jha, and Yeros 2019, 14. The authors estimate that 80 percent of land deals constituted new alienations of customary land.

location of changes in land rights regimes. These policies empower both public and private actors with influence over where state property rights develop, through "voluntary, purposeful, and sporadic registration," also known as piecemeal or incremental land titling.[29] Initiatives to advance land titling accelerated in the 1990s, inspired by highly influential narratives of informal property rights as impediments to economic development.[30] Further, international financial institutions and donors have championed titling as a necessary tenure reform.[31] For example, a 2013 World Bank report estimated that only 10 percent of the land in sub-Saharan Africa had been registered in individual land rights and recommended an increase to 50 percent of land within ten years.[32] Governments and international institutions have promoted land titling as a foundation for land markets, tenure security, and economic growth, even as scholars challenged the claim that customary land tenure in Africa is insecure[33] and researchers debated whether titling led to improvements in productivity or investment.[34] By courting global markets and encouraging land titling, governments have accelerated the expansion of state authority over land.

The local politics of land titling thus merit further scholarly analysis for three key reasons. First, the incremental adoption of land titles is a tremendously important pathway for the growth of state control of land in the contemporary era. Since independence, in 1960 (Senegal) and 1964 (Zambia), the land under the state's direct authority has grown from 5 to 6 percent to more than 40 percent of the territory, according to the governments' own records.[35] Thousands of negotiations for small and large plots of land have replaced customary tenure with state titles. Beyond Zambia and Senegal, this model of incremental

---

[29] Place, Roth, and Hazell 1994, 25. This differs from top-down divisions of land between customary and state rights, such as policies of "compulsory and systematic registration" in which everyone in a given area obtains a land title, adjudication schemes, and the colonial dual land tenure divisions described in Chapter 4 (Place, Roth, and Hazell 1994, 25).

[30] Most notably, de Soto 2000.   [31] Manji 2006. See also, Obeng-Odoom 2020.

[32] Byamugisha 2013.

[33] Sjaastad and Bromley 1997; Musembi 2007; Goldstein and Urdy 2008; Banda 2011.

[34] Lund 2001; Higgins et al. 2018.

[35] Customary land tenure governed an estimated 95 percent of land at independence in Senegal (see M. C. Diop 2013, 242). In Zambia, 94 percent of the territory was customary land at independence (see Northern Rhodesia, "Ministry of Land Annual Reports" 1935–1946, Shelf 16/Box 93A, Government Series, National Archives of Zambia).

and demand-driven land registration has become "the new orthodoxy" of land titling[36] and has been implemented in nearly every country in sub-Saharan Africa.[37] Second, examining the incremental process of land titling reveals the local politics that sustain customary property rights regimes. It shows why customary land tenure endures, despite policies that have been described "as a systematic effort to dislodge or displace indigenous tenure in order to replace it with registered or state-administered land."[38] Third, investigating this very localized process of land titling reveals why changes in property rights regimes cannot be divorced from struggles over political authority and the control over a vital resource. Land titling provides a window into how political authority is constructed and negotiated in modern states, particularly those grappling with colonial legacies.

1.2 THE ARGUMENT

The central premise of this book is that we cannot understand how state power over land grows without examining the institutions that it replaces. We know that transformations in property rights regimes have always been political; they are a product of distributional bargaining that can shift political relations in communities and create winners and losers.[39] Yet, we have few theoretical frameworks to help us understand the role of local institutions. I offer new insights into the political and social determinants of land titling with a theory of collective costs and customary constraints. I argue, first, that customary institutions can impact the expansion of state power over land by shaping the decisions of their members – chiefs and citizens. Even if there are compelling benefits to titling for these actors, customary institutions can create incentives for members to prioritize the collective costs of losing control over land. Second, customary institutions vary in their capacity to shape members' decisions. However, strong institutions have features that help members slow the erosion of customary land tenure, even on in-demand land. As a result, subnational variation in the strength of customary institutions helps explain broader patterns of state building. It is not merely undesirable or peripheral areas that remain in the customary domain.

This theory highlights the influence of a set of customary institutions that govern social, political, and economic interactions. These institutions

---

[36] Coldham 2000, 71. [37] See footnote 5. [38] Diaw 2005, 49.
[39] Bates 1989; Libecap 1989; Plateau 2000b, 96–107.

generate communities that share norms, beliefs, expectations, and practices. The term "customary" indicates that they gain legitimacy from custom or tradition: Members of the institution understand its processes and rules to be rooted in historical precedents. The main customary institutions examined in this book trace their origins to political communities that formed prior to the creation of the colonial state. However, "customary" does not mean static or unchanging. As Hubert Ouedraogo has explained, "customary" signifies principles that are perceived to be endogenous and local by the community, even as members have creatively adapted these rules over time.[40]

The leaders of these customary institutions are customary authorities, also known as chiefs.[41] Chiefs are an important set of political actors in many African countries.[42] They are officially and unofficially involved in a variety of governance functions, including land management and conflict adjudication.[43] In addition, they serve as intermediaries between citizens and the state.[44] Studies of customary institutions have often treated the chief as synonymous with the institution because of the important role of chiefs in enforcing and interpreting these sets of social and political rules. However, chiefs and customary institutions are not one and the same. Chiefs are individual elites embedded within institutions. These institutions continue to exist in the absence of any one chief.[45] By separating institutions as "the rules of the game in society" from the actors that implement them,[46] we gain new insight into how institutions can shape or constrain the behavior of chiefs. To underscore this point, I refer to both customary authorities and regular citizens as members of the institution.

---

[40] Ouedraogo 2011.

[41] This terminology was introduced by the colonial state. Some scholars prefer the terms "traditional authority" and "traditional leader" or to preface these terms with "neo-" to emphasize how "tradition" has been reinterpreted and created. I opted to use the terms "customary authority" and "chief" to represent leaders within customary institutions because they are common parlance in Senegal and Zambia, respectively.

[42] See Chapter 2 for comparative data.

[43] Boege 2006; Chiweza 2007; Logan 2013; Baldwin 2016, chapter 2; Aiyedun and Ordor 2016.

[44] Boafo-Arthur 2001; Fanthorpe 2006; Fokwang 2009; Muriaas 2009; Bado 2015; Koter 2016; Dionne 2018, chapter 6.

[45] If the institution did not exist in the absence of any one customary authority, the book's framework would regard it as an extremely weak institution and anticipate an unconstrained chief.

[46] This is consistent with classic political economy approaches to institutions. See North 1990.

All of these members can gain a variety of concentrated benefits from participating in land titling. Scholars have highlighted the rewards that chiefs receive for facilitating land titling, ranging from political favor with state representatives to significant material gifts.[47] Studies show that citizens report seeking titles in anticipation of increases in tenure security, access to credit, and to facilitate inheritance, among other potential personal benefits.[48] Existing research that examines local responses to titling has focused on these individual inducements, which are undoubtedly important. In the absence of any anticipated benefits, we would not expect chiefs or citizens to facilitate land titling.

However, titling decisions are political because they have implications for the community as a whole. Even if members would gain persuasive individual benefits from titling, they may resist it because of collective costs to the institutions in which they are embedded. Land is a key power base for the customary institutions featured in this book. These institutions govern complex systems of informal property rights[49] on untitled land and derive influence from their control over such customary land. Customary institutions determine who can farm or set up a shop; on which land they can do so; whether these rights can be inherited; and how long an individual can retain landownership without actively using it. They also establish processes for adjudicating conflicts over land among community members through, for example, seeking an audience with a hereditary chief or a local council. Further, an institution's governance of property rights reinforces its political authority in other domains. Members have incentives to comply with directives from other institutional processes to help secure their land rights. Consequently, controlling this valuable economic resource can also be a source of group power in relation to the state, which must engage with leaders of customary institutions for both access to land and influence over local populations. Land

---

[47] Fisiy 1995; Boafo-Arthur 2001; Nolte 2013; Chitonge 2019.

[48] See Ghebru, Koru, and Taffesse 2016; Schmidt and Zakayo 2018; Harris and Honig 2022; and Gochberg 2021 for examples from Ethiopia, Tanzania, Uganda, Zambia, and Malawi of why individuals reported that they wanted land titles.

[49] Drawing on Helmke and Levitsky (2004, 731), informal institutions are understood here as rules that are "created, communicated, and enforced outside of public channels"; they include the norms and social codes that guide the behavior of public officials, such as bureaucrats and Supreme Court justices. Thus, regardless of whether a chief has official recognition as a land authority, rules that govern different land usage and ownership arrangements that were not created by the state are informal property rights. Consistent with this approach, in this book "formalization" of property rights is not the process of documenting land rights alone, but of transforming them into statutory property rights.

is therefore a material basis for the institution's power in citizens' lives and within the modern state. Furthermore, the institution's power is the power of its members, including its chiefs. Preserving the institution's control over land is thus an example of a "collective goal" or "institutional interest."[50] These terms (used synonymously here) refer to objectives that are shared by actors within the institution, as a function of their membership. They are, however, not shared equally among members.[51]

Customary institutions matter for land titling outcomes because they impact how members perceive and are held accountable to a collective goal of retaining control over land. When maintaining customary land tenure has group benefits, decisions facilitating titling are a defection from a collective goal. A collective action framework is therefore a useful foundation for understanding how customary institutions impact a very complex set of decisions. Collective action models examine why individuals opt to contribute to publicly beneficial outcomes, given private gains from defecting. A rich literature has identified informal community institutions as a solution to this tension between collective and individual benefits, because institutions determine individuals' expectations of others, their incentives, and their ability to be punished.[52] Explaining how customary institutions impact land titling thus builds upon a core insight gleaned from collective action approaches: Customary institutions can influence individual behaviors by shaping whether actors are more responsive to concentrated benefits or collective costs. From here, we can begin to consider different ways in which customary institutions influence the decisions of their members in favor of retaining customary control over land.

Customary institutions may impact land titling outcomes by creating incentives for chiefs and citizens to reinforce the institution's power over land. As described earlier, chiefs can thwart or facilitate titling in their zones; they may organize resistance to new land titles on customary land or choose to partake in a process of changing land tenure. Citizens'

---

[50] This is conceptually parallel to my discussion of "state interests." The state is not a unified actor but a set of institutions. Representatives of the state's institutions, or state actors, advance state interests.

[51] As Chapters 3 and 7 detail, those with greater power within the institution should be more invested in advancing institutional goals. The collective benefits from membership in an institution are unevenly distributed.

[52] Ostrom 1990; Tsai 2007; Akinola 2008; Xu and Yao 2015; Magaloni, Díaz-Cayeros, and Ruiz Euler 2019.

actions are also consequential, including their decisions to engage with the state's systems of property rights by seeking titles. However, customary institutions can moderate the agency of chiefs and citizens by inducing these actors to prioritize a collective interest in retaining customary control over land.

One way that customary institutions slow the erosion of customary land tenure in their zones is by establishing processes to hold leaders accountable to institutional goals. Some, but not all, customary institutions generate internal forms of accountability.[53] Customary institutions can create an extra check on chiefs' decisions and deter them from opting for individual benefits at the expense of the institution's long-term power base. Later chapters illustrate two institutional accountability mechanisms in Senegal and Zambia: vertical systems of punishment and coordinated horizontal constraints. Vertical accountability is the result of internal processes that allow elites to sanction other elites at different levels of hierarchy. However, even in the absence of clear vertical lines of authority between chiefs, institutions can create horizontal accountability among elites through institutional elements that create forums for establishing shared expectations and opportunities for social sanction. Horizontal accountability mechanisms can generate checks and balances among customary authorities within a customary institution, analogously to processes of horizontal accountability in a government's political institutions.[54] They create constraints on the "nearly unlimited discretion of rulers,"[55] allowing institutions to shape chiefs' behaviors. Consequently, by generating constraints on individual chiefs, customary institutions can influence land tenure outcomes.

Another way that customary institutions impact land titling is by shaping citizens' preferences for converting their own land to statutory titles. Customary institutions structure social relations, distributing status within the institution and therefore different levels of privilege within the community. Citizens who have more privilege in their local customary institution gain social and political benefits from its continued power. In this book, I argue that citizens will be more likely to prioritize the collective goal of retaining customary power over land when they gain

---

[53] See, for examples, Bates 1987, 41–42; Dia 1996, 39–41; Ayittey 2010; Baldwin and Holzinger 2019; Nathan 2019. Note that Acemoglu, Reed, and J. Robinson (2014) also consider variation in the "constraints" on chiefs' power, which they conceptualize as political competition among multiple ruling families.
[54] O'Donnell 1998; Signé and Korha 2016.   [55] Diamond 2008, 300.

greater benefits from it. Such advantages may include expectations of more secure customary property rights or better outcomes in community courts. These benefits are tied to the continuing power of the customary institution. In contrast, individuals who face exclusion or low status within the institution have greater incentive to seek the protections offered by state property rights. Consequently, the political costs and benefits of titling within a given customary institution should vary depending on the customary privilege of each citizen. Although titling one's own land is often understood as an economic decision, it is also a political choice to exit from the customary institution's control over land rights.

Customary institutions, however, are not equally capable of shaping members' behaviors and preventing defections that threaten their power bases. Even within the same country, there is enormous diversity in organizational capacity among customary institutions. Enforcement and stability, defining characteristics of institutional strength among formal institutions, also apply here.[56] Stronger customary institutions have organizational elements that increase compliance with the institution's rules and norms. Clear lines of authority and dense social networks facilitate this. Further, while customary institutions are adaptable by nature, stronger institutions have a stable influence in members' lives and benefit from longer time horizons. Weak customary institutions, by contrast, are sets of rules that can more easily be ignored. The heterogeneity among customary institutions should affect whether members are, in fact, constrained.

In Senegal and Zambia, the historical origins of customary institutions impact their contemporary strength. This is the final piece in my argument. In particular, I focus on the differences among hierarchical and nonhierarchical legacies. Customary institutions with hierarchical legacies trace their roots to powerful precolonial states with hierarchical authority structures that withstood the colonial conquest. These institutions had a distinctly high organizational capacity at the end of the nineteenth century. This contrasts with the customary institutions with nonhierarchical legacies in these two countries, which either had hierarchical structures that were razed during colonial territorial conquest or, more commonly, never endogenously developed hierarchy. As later chapters will explain in greater detail, the diverse origins of these institutions set them on different trajectories, producing variation in the

---

[56] Levitsky and Murillo 2009.

contemporary strength of customary institutions within each country. Historical institutional structures thus contribute to patterns of state building through their impact on the contemporary strength of customary institutions.

The theory and empirical evidence presented in the rest of this book expand upon the argument that customary institutions shape the state's expansion of power over land by influencing how chiefs and citizens respond to titling. The next three sections of this introductory chapter introduce the explanatory variable, outcome of interest, and broader implications of this study. First, I situate my theory within the scholarship on customary institutions and precolonial legacies. Next, I introduce why my outcome of interest, land titling, is a form of fragmented state building. I then explain what my approach, which highlights the differences among the institutions in which chiefs and citizens are embedded, teaches us about state–society relations in the postcolonial state. The final sections of this chapter provide the empirical approach and roadmap to the book.

1.3 EXPLANATIONS GROUNDED IN CUSTOMARY INSTITUTIONS AND HISTORICAL LEGACIES

Understanding politics in contemporary African states requires us to seriously consider the political systems that preceded the colonial intervention. This insight guides the explanatory framework of this book. As I describe in Chapter 4, precolonial, colonial, and independent state institutions all contribute to the current status of land and political authority in Zambia and Senegal, a common feature of former colonies. Customary institutions with roots in the precolonial period were undoubtedly transformed in a variety of ways by colonial and subsequent independent government policies.[57] Yet, many remained resilient even as states attempted to weaken them. Despite significant change over time and heterogeneity across precolonial institutions, historical legacies continue to impact contemporary politics. This book builds upon scholarship that has examined the long-term legacies of customary institutions through the study of their institutional structures. As I will show, contemporary state building and the roles of customary authorities reflect this institutional heterogeneity.

---

[57] See Ajayi (1968) for a discussion of African institutions' continuity and adaptation in the colonial era.

African political institutions prior to colonization featured varying degrees of organizational complexity.[58] Some precolonial political institutions were states that developed through long processes of war-making and state-making. Such precolonial state building mirrors what we understand of the development of states elsewhere in the world: The need to provide protection under threat of war generated systems of law, taxation, and identity nationalism.[59] These polities developed complex institutional structures with multiple levels of authority, known as hierarchy or centralization. For example, Cheikh Anta Diop's foundational work on precolonial Africa describes the Cayor of Senegal and the Mossi of Burkina Faso as constitutional monarchies, with kings governing through ministries, bureaucrats, and militaries in the nineteenth century.[60] The Lozi kingdom in Zambia had the administrative apparatus to organize mass labor campaigns for major infrastructure projects, multiple levels of authority, governance councils, and a powerful military.[61] In Cameroon, the Bafut precolonial state used spiritual power, as well as control over trade routes and military might, to exercise centralized authority.[62] Robert Bates' comparative study of precolonial state formation highlights a set of key indicators of centralized political institutions: national armies, bureaucracies, and monarchs. His findings suggest that these precolonial states were also more likely to have developed aristocracies, commoner councils, and the capacity to provide public goods such as roads or bridges.[63]

Other precolonial political institutions governed communities without state-like structures. These political communities never developed centralized authority above the village level, resulting in their label as stateless societies.[64] The Kikuyu of Kenya, for example, had established systems of conflict resolution and age-grade societies for community governance, but power was highly decentralized within the polity.[65] In northern Ghana, each village in the Chakali institutions had its own political leaders, spiritual leaders, and councils of elders who functioned independently of authorities in other villages.[66] Such nonhierarchical institutions are sometimes termed decentralized, segmentary, or acephalous (headless) institutions.[67] Scholars use the terminology of hierarchical/

---

[58] Ki-Zerbo 1972; Ayittey 1991; Nabudere 2004.
[59] Carneiro 1970; Hintze 1975; Tilly 1990; Spruyt 2002; Thies 2004. [60] C. Diop 1960.
[61] Mainga 1973. [62] Asombang 1999. [63] Bates 1987. [64] Ayittey 1991.
[65] Kenyatta 1938. [66] Daannaa 1994.
[67] Fortes and Evans-Pritchard 1940; Geschiere 1993; Mahoney 2010; Yaro 2013.

1.3 Explanations Grounded in Customary Institutions

nonhierarchical, state/stateless, and centralized/decentralized to represent this foundational difference among institutional structures.

Political economists have advanced the study of such institutional legacies by identifying patterns that result from variation in the precolonial structures. In cross-national quantitative studies, hierarchy is correlated with improved development outcomes. For example, Philip Osafo-Kwaako and James Robinson showed that hierarchy was associated with economic institutions that contribute to public goods provision and economic development, such as credit access, transportation routes, security services, and market exchange.[68] Stelios Michalopoulos and Elias Papaioannou found that areas that were ruled by hierarchical precolonial institutions now have greater nighttime light density, a proxy for economic activity and infrastructure access; Marcella Alsan's research replicated this finding.[69] This effect is independent of a number of potentially confounding variables, such as population density and geographic endowments. Similarly, Nicola Gennaioli and Ilia Rainer showed that precolonial hierarchy predicts a set of improved health and education outcomes, as well as an increase in paved roads.[70] These are signs of greater public goods investments in zones with hierarchical institutions, which suggests systematic patterns related to institutional heterogeneity.

Within-country comparisons of historical institutional structures have also identified the long-term effects of hierarchy. For example, Sanghamitra Bandyopadhyay and Elliott Green showed that Ugandan citizens living in areas with hierarchical customary institutions were wealthier than fellow citizens in areas with nonhierarchical institutions.[71] However, in Nigeria, some of the poorest regions have hierarchical legacies. Belinda Archibong has argued that hierarchical institutions with leaders who rebelled against the state lost the ability to lobby for public goods, leading to long-term differences in infrastructure access.[72] This scholarship connecting institutional structure to developmental outcomes illustrates clearly that these legacies impact contemporary politics. However, these works have generally focused on establishing the correlation between historical structure and contemporary outcomes. In response, scholars have called for increased attention to the mechanisms that generate these differences between institutions and how

---

[68] Osafo-Kwaako and J. Robinson 2013.
[69] Michalopoulos and Papaioannou 2013; Alsan 2015.   [70] Gennaioli and Rainer 2007.
[71] Bandyopadhyay and Green 2016.   [72] Archibong 2019.

these differences reinforce themselves over time.[73] This book takes on these tasks.

Existing literature has emphasized three important mechanisms that connect hierarchy to contemporary political outcomes. First, hierarchy can increase the bargaining power of customary leaders.[74] As Catherine Boone has described, hierarchical structures raised the credibility of rural elites' "threats/promises to control peasants and mobilize collective action (through the use of persuasion or coercion)."[75] A hierarchical structure allows leaders to influence more citizens than a decentralized institution could, which may increase the leader's leverage against the state. Central to this mechanism is the distribution of power: A leader in a hierarchical customary institution has concentrated control over a larger number of people. Second, chiefs in hierarchical institutions may have stronger ties of loyalty and obedience with their citizens.[76] Much like the bargaining power that results from having more followers, increasing the strength of these ties also increases the chief's political influence within the state. Customary authorities with more obedient followers can more effectively and quickly mobilize them, for example, to protest or vote in a certain way.

Third, hierarchical customary institutions may also impact contemporary politics through their ability to generate legitimacy for state institutions. Pierre Englebert theorized that a territorial overlap with a hierarchical customary institution makes it easier for state politicians to consolidate power without relying on patronage.[77] The Tswana customary institution of Botswana provides an example of this dynamic. Scholars studying Botswana's political and economic successes (and its evasion of the dreaded resource curse) have argued that the spatial overlap between state boundaries and the hierarchical Tswana customary institution is a source of increased state capacity and accountability among leaders.[78]

My research builds on these studies by exploring how hierarchical institutions can facilitate the pursuit of collective interests over the autonomous interests of individual chiefs, to retain a source of power: control of land. In contrast to mechanisms that emphasize how hierarchy strengthens leaders, I demonstrate that in a context in which the

---

[73] Holzinger, Kern, and Kromrey 2016, 475.
[74] Boone 2003; Baldwin 2014; Archibong 2019.   [75] Boone 2003, 29.
[76] Koter 2016.   [77] Englebert 2000a, 2000b.
[78] Englebert 2000b; Acemoglu, Johnson, and J. Robinson 2003; Samatar 2005; Hjort 2010.

institution's interests and the state's interests are at odds, hierarchy can weaken individual leaders. Hierarchical institutions have a greater capacity to generate checks on the autonomy of elites through stronger internal ties of accountability. Chiefs who are not embedded in hierarchical institutions are, by contrast, freer to respond to their individual interests. Contemporary institutions in Senegal and Zambia illustrate how variation in the strength of internal accountability functions as a hierarchy mechanism. Specifically, I use comparative case studies of customary institutions to show that within each country, chiefs in hierarchical institutions are more constrained than their neighbors in nonhierarchical institutions. Further, I explain why the capacity to influence the outcomes of individual decisions that would undermine an institutional power base is part of a dynamic process of reinforcing the differences in strength among institutions. In doing so, the theory and findings in this book contribute new analysis of hierarchy mechanisms and suggest how such legacies are replicated.

There is much to be learned from African political systems about how local institutions impact the state and retain influence over time. Customary institutions are a key subtype of political institutions. They draw on claims of legitimacy that are independent of the state. Such institutions are particularly influential in countries with weak state structures and boundaries formed by colonialism, but customary institutions vary considerably across many dimensions. This creates a challenge for identifying systematic patterns that are generalizable across contexts. Drawing broad theoretical conclusions from this diversity of institutions requires a degree of abstraction. This has, in part, led to the growth of studies described previously that rely on a binary of hierarchical or nonhierarchical institutions. Such a binary categorization can be a useful analytical tool for identifying systematic patterns. However, it is not comprehensive of the many sources of variation that impact the ways in which customary authorities and institutions functioned in the contemporary era or prior to colonization. The statistical analyses in this book rely on the simplified binary categorization of institutions as hierarchical or nonhierarchical, while qualitative analyses in Senegal and Zambia provide comparative case studies that detail a sliver of the diversity among customary institutions today. This approach seeks to balance breadth and specificity in the study of hierarchical legacies and contemporary customary institutions. It highlights the impact of these institutional legacies on one specific outcome: the expansion of state control over land.

1.4 LAND TITLING AS FRAGMENTED STATE BUILDING

State building throughout the world has been a process of replacing competitors to the state's authority over property rights. As states struggled to formalize land rights in the seventeenth-century British countryside and in nineteenth-century Japan, they strengthened the rule of state law and built their tax bases. When the United States replaced settler land rights in the nineteenth-century American frontier, it established its monopoly of authority over citizens. Indeed, the enforcement of property rights and control of territory are central to our understanding of the modern state.

However, the state's expansion of authority over land has never been an easy or linear process. Shifts to state property rights challenge existing social and political structures. As the state gains authority over a valuable resource, another set of elites loses authority; resistance to state-led land reform is therefore embedded in broader struggles over political authority. For example, in Stalin's Russia, the state's collectivization schemes targeted landowners and village-level political institutions. These produced thousands of incidents of protest and "mass disturbance" against the state in 1930 alone.[79] In Switzerland, the state's attempt to exert control over the nation's forests through a series of new laws in the nineteenth century provoked resistance from community groups that perceived this transfer of authority over valuable natural resources as a threat to their political power.[80] Today, similarly contentious transformations of land rights are occurring in African states, where governments have actively promoted land titling to reform existing systems of land tenure. In this context, customary authorities are the set of elites whose power wanes as the state's grows. The responses of customary authorities and communities to land titling reflect these broader historical patterns of state building.

Land titling is a tool of state building that serves four main purposes. First, land titling increases the geographic reach of the state's institutions within its defined territory. In postcolonial states, the state's presence in the everyday lives of citizens varies spatially, particularly between rural and urban populations, or the core and periphery of the country.[81] State administrative offices, health clinics, and schools are generally concentrated in densely populated areas. As a result, in more peripheral regions,

---

[79] Viola 1996, 137.   [80] Zimmermann 1994.
[81] See, for example, Hydén 1980; Bierschenk and Olivier de Sardan 1997; Herbst 2000.

citizens have fewer regular interactions with the state's services, institutions, and agents. Following Michael Mann's classic framework, one of the defining features of a state is its territoriality. Spatial disjunctures in the state's authority represent a challenge to the infrastructural power of the state, understood as the state's ability to "penetrate" society and implement its agendas "throughout the realm."[82] The state builds its infrastructural power through institutions and technologies that increase the "territorial reach" of the state.[83] The expansion of physical infrastructure increases the visibility of the state in the citizens' lives. Consistent with this conceptualization of state building, Jeffrey Herbst and others have treated variation in the density of infrastructure, such as roads, as an indicator of the state's power and capacity.[84]

Land titling similarly expands the territorial or spatial reach of state power. It spreads state property rights institutions to places where they did not previously exist. It formally transfers the responsibility for enforcing citizens' property rights from a customary authority to the state. This strengthens the exchange between state and citizen, as citizens must comply with state directives such as taxation in order to secure their rights. Land titling also increases the visibility of the state in the citizen's life through interactions with civil servants who map land and process new titles, creating a document that is a new physical representation of the state's authority in the citizen's life. By establishing new links between citizen and state, titling increases the state's penetration in the daily lives of citizens, even in otherwise peripheral areas.

The second state-building function of land titling is to increase the legibility of land and of the citizens using that land. Legibility is the degree to which information can be comprehended, collected, and counted, in this case, by the state. Put simply, the state cannot control its citizens or their land without information about them. As James Scott argued, land titling standardizes complex systems of customary land ownership, creating a unified system of individual ownership that the state can understand.[85] It converts the system of land management from locally understood land tenure rules that are informal, unwritten, and regularly changing to a "rational" statutory system. This parallels other legibility processes such as standardizing languages and systems of weights and

---

[82] M. Mann 1984, 189.   [83] Soifer 2008.
[84] Herbst 2000; Thies 2009; Acemoglu, García-Jimeno, and J. Robinson 2015; Müller-Crepon, Hunziker, and Cederman 2021.
[85] Scott 1998.

measures within the state's territory.[86] Increasing the legibility of land and citizens, sometimes termed "informational capacity," is critical to certain state functions. Information about individual residents strengthens the state's ability to monitor citizen behavior and enforce its own laws.[87] As a result, scholars have treated population censuses as indicators of state capacity[88] and identified voter registration as a means of expanding state power.[89]

The third state-building function of land titling is to increase the rule of state law. As Sandra Joireman has suggested, the very existence of plural systems for the enforcement of property rights in African states indicates the weakness of the rule of law: The state lacks a monopoly of authority in this domain.[90] Customary institutions feature different sets of rules for accessing and using land than those of the state. Despite attempts by the colonial states to codify what they termed "customary law,"[91] the rules of customary property rights vary widely over time and among different customary institutions. Customary property rights are not understood or executed by the state; rather, they are enforced by customary authorities. Further, the control of land undergirds the power of customary institutions in other domains of citizens' lives. This includes, for example, the alternative systems of justice and conflict resolution that customary institutions provide.[92] The presence of alternatives to the state's institutions creates opportunities for citizens to avoid the state's laws when they are unsatisfactory or unenforceable. For example, Thomas Bierschenk and Jean-Pierre Olivier de Sardan described how a citizen in rural Benin has multiple arenas for seeking conflict resolution in the case of a theft, including both customary and statutory forums.[93] Marco Gardini argued that citizens in Togo engage with customary authorities for dispute resolution as an alternative to "the savagery of the State."[94] This can be an effective adaptation strategy for citizens, who have opportunities to seek the governance outcomes they desire without engaging with the state. However, from the perspective of the rule of state law, the existence of institutions that are not subsumed under state authority but instead function in parallel to the state, is a challenge to its domination.[95]

---

[86] Weber 1976; Scott 1998.   [87] D'Arcy and Nistotskaya 2017; Lee and Zhang 2017.
[88] Centeno 2002; Brambor et al. 2020.   [89] Slater 2008.   [90] Joireman 2011.
[91] Snyder 1981; Chanock 1985; Moore 1986.
[92] Boege 2006; Oba 2011; Bennett et al. 2012; Aiyedun and Ordor 2016; de Juan 2017.
[93] Bierschenk and Olivier de Sardan 2003, 158.   [94] Gardini 2013, 254.
[95] See Holzinger, Kern, and Kromrey 2016 for an overview of parallelism and institutional dualism.

1.4 Land Titling as Fragmented State Building

Consistent with this logic, Ilia Murtazashvili and Jennifer Murtazashvili framed the absence of legal titling as "anarchy."[96]

Titling is the legal process that replaces alternative rules for land access with the state's rules. Correspondingly, it can increase the rule of law by weakening alternatives to the state's authority over land. This can have broader impacts on the rule of state law by removing control over property rights as a source of political authority for chiefs. As a result, land titling can be understood as a softer alternative to the "building armies mechanism" of state building,[97] in which the state weakens challenges to its rule by increasing the size of its security apparatus and eliminating alternative authorities through sheer force. Land titling allows a state to increase its political authority without relying on the expansion of the state's coercive abilities. As Christian Lund has explained, control over landed property rights is central to both the formation and exercise of political authority.[98] Land titling thus builds the monopoly of state authority.

Expanding state control over property rights also impacts the state's fiscal capacity, which is the fourth state-building function of land titling. Fiscal capacity is the state's ability to generate and collect revenue, which states need to provide public goods and security, among other basic roles of the state. The ability to tax is so central to a state's ability to fulfill its agenda that taxation is often used as an indicator of state power.[99] Land titling is the first step in expanding the state's ability to extract revenue from land. Customary land cannot be taxed by the state, as it has not been mapped, measured, and attributed to an individual user. The state can tax the citizens who use customary land for their agricultural inputs and production, but it cannot extract taxes for land use itself until customary land has been registered in state property rolls. In Zambia and Senegal, the moment the land transfers from customary to state rights, it is subject to land taxes or ground rents.[100] A parcel with state property rights remains within the state's tax base, even if the owner of the title changes. For example, if the state revokes an individual's title for unpaid taxes or lack of development on the land, the state can then allocate the land to another user, who would again be subject to taxes. As a result, each hectare of land that shifts from customary to state expands the state's

---

[96] Murtazashvili and Murtazashvili 2015. Note that their argument is that anarchy in land governance should be considered as an efficient policy option.
[97] Taylor and Botea 2008. [98] Lund 2008.
[99] Centeno 2002; Thies 2004, 2009; Besley and Persson 2010. See also Lieberman 2002.
[100] While the law is clear, the enforcement of these land taxes is far from consistent.

potential revenue base. This increases the state's fiscal capacity by making it possible for the state to extract revenue from a resource that was previously untaxable, regardless of whether the state does so at any given moment.

Analyzing land titling as a state-building process in the current era reveals a surprising consequence of global land markets: They can strengthen the state's authority. At this writing, land is treated as the last frontier in globalization by multinational investors, governments, and carbon traders, among others. While scholars have argued that globalization "eclipses" state power or undermines public institutions,[101] examining contemporary land titling processes demonstrates that global land markets catalyze state building by accelerating the conversion of land from customary to state property rights. Counter to their other effects on state power, global markets increase the state's authority in African countries by breaking down the institutional alternative to the state: customary property rights. Through changes in property rights regimes, this aspect of globalization in Africa is not "softening" the state's sovereignty but rather is strengthening it. In this case, markets and states are not in opposition: State building occurs *through* the extension of land markets.

Land titling is thus a substantial step toward greater state capacity, which constructs the state's authority. It creates new opportunities for state actors to exert state power by expanding the state's territorial reach; increasing the legibility of land; weakening alternatives to its rule of law; and enlarging the state's revenue base. However, state actors choose to use their power in different ways. They may opt for "forbearance" from enforcing laws for political reasons[102] or because the costs of exercising their power are high. State capacity and state performance are conceptually distinct, as capacity is a tool that may be used toward different ends.[103] Therefore, although state capacity is necessary for the effective provision of social services and security, state capacity can also be used to oppress and dominate citizens. Perhaps most prominent among African countries is the case of Rwanda's extremely high state capacity, which facilitated the genocide of hundreds of thousands of civilians.[104] Land titling increases the state's ability to implement its agenda, yet it uproots existing social structures and systems of land ownership. The development of state capacity is therefore costly to different social actors.

---

[101] For a discussion of these arguments, see Evans 1997.   [102] Holland 2017.
[103] Centeno, Kohli, and Yashar 2017.   [104] J. Robinson 2002; Straus 2013.

1.5 RECONSIDERING HOW SOCIETY IMPACTS THE STATE

Consequently, the immediate impacts of titling on the average citizen are mixed – they are highly dependent on who the citizen is and how the state manages titled land. As a result, this book examines land titling and increasing state capacity not as a panacea for development, but instead as issues of power and control.

1.5 RECONSIDERING HOW SOCIETY IMPACTS THE STATE

Land titling is an interaction between states, citizens, and customary authorities. Thus, in addition to being a process of contemporary state building, titling is the outcome of interest for this study because of what it reveals about state-society relations. There is a long history of states employing land policy to reorganize society. Colonial authorities used land to fragment social groups and prevent challenges to the state.[105] Governments have initiated land reforms and redistributions to placate or punish certain constituencies.[106] Further, state land laws and practices create the boundaries and content of citizenship.[107] Land is a means for the state to impact society, yet this book highlights that it is also a forum in which social actors impact the state. My approach thus echoes Joel Migdal's analysis of rural elites' ability to thwart the government's attempts to consolidate social control in Egypt, by providing new examples of how "the society shapes the state even as the state deeply influences society."[108] Examining the politics of land titling generates new insights into an important set of intermediaries between the state and its citizens in African countries, and how customary institutions shape these interactions.

Customary authorities fascinate observers of African politics because of their influential and complicated relationships with the state. In both the colonial and contemporary states, governments have tried to harness the influence of customary authorities to implement the state's agenda. An extensive body of scholarship on customary authority in Africa has examined collaboration or hybridity between chiefs and the state[109] and the ways in which the state has molded customary authority.[110] Colonial

---

[105] Migdal 1988. [106] Albertus 2015.
[107] Kuba and Lentz 2006; Boone 2007; Lund 2011. [108] Migdal 1988, 181.
[109] Bayart 1989; Logan 2009; M. Williams 2010.
[110] For examples, see Colson 1949; Chanock 1985; Moore 1986; Mamdani 1996.

governments used chiefs to collect taxes and mobilize forced labor; more recently, incumbent politicians have relied on customary authorities to broker votes in elections.[111] In contemporary African states, chiefs often assist in administrative tasks and state governance. Where the state is weak, governments depend on customary authorities to help implement their policies, thereby empowering chiefs as intermediaries. As a result, the boundary between state and customary is often blurred.

There is ample evidence that chiefs are strategic political actors who have used their connections with the state to increase their own power and wealth. In South Africa, for example, chiefs align with the political parties most likely to provide legal power and benefits.[112] Customary authorities have used their control over natural resources for short-term gains, particularly by selling land previously held in the customary domain. Kwame Boafo-Arthur, for example, described Ghanaians feeling betrayed after the loss of a community resource by "the decadent traditional authority who, for want of personal wealth, dubiously and treacherously sold the Lagoon for peanuts."[113] Scholars also have recounted the ways in which customary authorities were compromised by the colonial encounter and corrupted by their interactions with the post-independence state.[114] In many of the prevailing scholarly narratives, customary authorities in Africa have been treated as colonial creations lacking agency outside of the state's interests or as unconstrained big men.

Mahmood Mamdani's highly influential work reinforced the idea of chiefs as individual "despots," divorced from the institutions that undergird their local power. His "decentralized despotism" approach to customary authorities hinged on the claim that colonial states undermined internal institutional constraints and removed the meaningful differences among these customary institutions. Mamdani explained that the heterogeneity among the internal institutions of precolonial kingdoms and stateless societies (which became "administrative chieftainships") affected how the leaders of precolonial institutions made decisions, governed, and controlled populations.[115] He then argued that these differences among customary institutions were erased by the colonial state, which preferred

---

[111] Koter 2013; Baldwin 2016; Gottlieb 2017; Nathan 2019.
[112] de Kadt and Larreguy 2018. See also Hendricks and Ntsebeza 1999.
[113] Boafo-Arthur 2001, 8.
[114] van Rouveroy van Nieuwaal 1996; Ali, Fjeldstad, and Shifa 2020.
[115] Mamdani 1996, 37–48.

1.5 Reconsidering How Society Impacts the State

to have the same type of customary institutions throughout the territory. In his terms, "the point about colonialism was that it generalized both the conquest state and the administrative chieftainship, and in doing so it wrenched both free of traditional restraint."[116]

However, the colonial state's strategy of homogenizing customary institutions was not sufficient to generate its intended outcomes. As Sara Berry and others have emphasized, the colonial regimes "rarely exercised enough effective control to accomplish exactly what they set out to do."[117] This book probes the continuing sources of variation among customary institutions and chiefs in Zambia and Senegal. It suggests that the colonial state did not have the resources to completely erase the important differences among the institutions underpinning individual chiefs, which, in some cases, had been built over centuries. Colonial states changed the roles and incentives of chiefs through, for example, the use of indirect rule and attempts to reify customary law. Differences in a customary institution's internal organization were more difficult for a colonial or postindependence state to transform. These include the internal accountability mechanisms that can constrain the chiefs. By focusing on the real and historically rooted differences among the institutions in which chiefs are embedded, we gain further insight into the variation in the roles and behaviors of these political actors within the state. Among other implications, my institutional approach highlights that "retraditionalization policies"[118] within any given country empower a set of actors with very different institutional constraints. The continuing heterogeneity among customary institutions impacts how chiefs govern and how they mediate the relationship between citizen and state.

Further, examining the local politics of land titling demonstrates how chiefs who benefit from the power of the state retain their ability to independently challenge it. Customary authorities gain legitimacy from their interactions with the state and with customary institutions, making them a "hybrid" authority.[119] Citizens, for their part, are embedded in overlapping statutory and customary institutions. They draw on them creatively and strategically, in a process known as institutional syncretism.[120] Studying interconnected and, at times, collaborative forms of

---

[116] Mamdani 1996, 40. [117] Berry 1992, 330. See also Spear 2003.
[118] Kyed and Burr 2007. On the wave of policies that empowered chiefs, see Englebert 2002; Chiweza 2007; Muriaas 2009; Nuesiri 2014.
[119] Logan 2009; M. Williams 2010; Goodfellow and Lindemann 2013; Bauer 2016; Albrecht 2017.
[120] Galvan 2004.

authority is challenging, but land titling provides a window into how members preserve an institution's autonomy from the state. For customary authorities in Senegal and Zambia, titling is more costly than other forms of collaboration because it is a permanent, unidirectional change. Land cannot be "unregistered" from state property rights, even if its owners change. Titling involves a legal transfer of authority over resources, not an easily revoked or fluid status. Thus, land titling is closer to a zero-sum interaction between state and customary authority; unlike a decision to broker votes or facilitate policy implementation, the state's gain is the customary institution's loss. Probing circumstances in which customary and state interests differ provides new insight into the hybrid and autonomous nature of these authorities. It reveals how customary institutions can generate and facilitate the pursuit of interests separate from those of the state, despite their integration.

Studying the relationship between customary institutions and land titling also illustrates how these local institutions influence citizens' relationships with the state. I focus on land titling in this book because it is a forum for investigating why citizens choose to engage and disengage with different political institutions. My theory builds upon the insight that citizens seek new forms of property rights after weighing the existing system relative to alternatives. They evaluate the social and political costs of this change, in addition to economic considerations. In the case of land titling, citizens are turning toward the state and away from exclusively relying on customary authorities to protect their land claims. As a result, through these decisions, citizens act as agents who construct the state's power. Thus, customary institutions impact a citizen's decision to interact with the state by creating or reducing demand for new property rights. This is consistent with research that shows how institutions that serve as an alternative to the state can shape citizen engagement with the state in other domains. For example, citizens may decide among customary and state conflict resolution forums, selecting the ones that provide the best outcomes for their profiles[121] and choosing the state's agents when the customary system no longer efficiently provides justice.[122] Examining individuals' demand for state property rights reveals how local institutions shape their decisions to engage with the state as well as why customary institutions retain their influence.

---

[121] Sandefur and Siddiqi 2013. [122] Ensminger 1992, chapter 6.

1.6 EMPIRICAL APPROACH

The expansion of state authority over land through titling is occurring in countries across the continent. The motivating logic of the case selection for this book was to represent a key difference in systems of customary authority in African countries: official and unofficial chiefs. In Senegal, chiefs have local legitimacy in their oversight of customary land but no statutory role in land governance. Other countries, including Zambia, follow a model of official customary authority. There, the state recognizes chiefs as the custodians of customary land. Such official status for customary authorities provides chiefs with more direct channels for influencing state policy. It can also tame them, by "co-opting" them or strengthening their ties to the state apparatus.[123] Further, it may hold implications for representation of citizens; for example, Fred Hendricks and Lungisile Ntsebeza suggested that it may reinforce ethnic divisions in South Africa.[124] Official and unofficial status is a critical and representative difference among forms of customary authority in Africa.[125] In Zambia and Senegal, the variation in the legal status of customary authorities reflects the legacy of British and French colonial rule, respectively. Colonial powers laid the groundwork for the modern legal frameworks in African states. Following independence, the governments of Zambia and Senegal maintained the colonial scaffolding of the state's integration of customary authority.

Zambia and Senegal therefore function as most-different cases within a set of basic scope conditions. The two countries feature distinct types of customary authority, colonial histories, agricultural systems, and geographies. Zambia is a landlocked country in southern Africa with an economy that has been based on copper extraction since the 1920s. As a result, the Zambian economy rises and falls with international copper prices. To mitigate this vulnerability, state actors have tried to diversify the economy through commercial agriculture, with particular attention to promoting the staple crop, maize. By contrast, Senegal's economy is based on fishing and smallholder agriculture. Its primary exports have long been groundnuts and fish, while millet and rice are the staple crops for subsistence farmers. Mining is limited. In addition, Senegal is located on the

---

[123] Herbst 2000, 183. Henn (2020) makes a similar argument that chiefs with constitutionally recognized powers become complements to the state, while chiefs without state recognition function as competitors in relation to public goods provisions.
[124] Hendricks and Ntsebeza 1999, 100.   [125] Kyed and Buur 2007.

TABLE 1.1. *Comparing Senegal and Zambia*

Subregion	Senegal West Africa	Zambia Southern Africa
Regime Type (Polity IV Score)[126]	Democracy (7)	Democracy (7)
GDP Per Capita USD (2013)[127]	1,263	1,620
Population Size (2013)	14 million	15 million
Population Engaged in Agriculture % [128]	50%	63%
Land Mass	193,000 sq km	743,000 sq km
Geographic Position	Coastal	Landlocked
Colonial Power	France	Britain
Statutory Recognition of Customary Authorities as Land Authorities	No	Yes

West African coast and is a major regional power; historically, it was the seat of the federation of French colonies. However, the two countries also share key scope conditions. They fit within the set of African states that have not experienced protracted civil wars or major White settlement, factors that have the potential to radically transform rural social structures. They are both democracies. While the theoretical argument is not a priori limited to such cases, setting these scope conditions allows for a clearer comparison of the relevant factors at work. Table 1.1 presents key points of comparison between the two countries.

The questions that guide this study relate to the subnational politics of land titling: How do customary institutions influence local responses to land titling? Why does the expansion of state control of land occur more rapidly in some areas than others? Yet investigating similar processes of state building within such different countries uncovers important trends in the continuing power of customary institutions. It reveals that strong customary institutions can impact land titling outcomes in countries with

---

[126] Monty G. Marshall, Ted Robert Gurr, and Keith Jaggers, "Polity IV Project, Political Regime Characteristics and Transitions, 1800–2015," Center for Systemic Peace, 2016.

[127] GDP per capita, Population Size, Land Mass data from World Bank, *World Development Indicators* (Washington, DC: World Bank Group, 2021).

[128] In Zambia and Senegal, 63 percent of the population and 50 percent of all households rely on agriculture, respectively. Central Statistics Office, 2012, "2010 Census of Population and Housing: National Analytical Report," Lusaka, Zambia: Government of the Republic of Zambia; Agence Nationale de la Statistique et de la Démographie (ANSD), 2014, "Rapport Définitif-RGPHAE 2013," Dakar, Senegal: Government of the Republic of Senegal, 151.

and without official chiefs, and with legacies of British or French land policy. My approach to answering these research questions triangulates multiple methods, levels of analysis, and sources of evidence. I use statistical analyses of national–level land tenure data sets to identify broad patterns in land titling and hierarchical legacies. At the local level, comparative case studies of institutions in each country clarify the mechanisms at work. In addition, individual-level survey data shed light on the effects of status within an institution. Finally, the foundation for understanding these issues is a wealth of insights gleaned from interviews and primary documents.

The best measure of the expansion of statutory rights over land is the state's own record of titles. In both countries, government agencies shared land titling records that I used to create national data sets of the amount of customary land that had transferred to statutory titles in every district of the country. These data are a product of the state-building process itself, which reflects the state's capacity to collect data on land titling, in addition to being an aggregated measure of land titling outcomes. If customary institutions do impact local responses to land titling, these patterns should be evident at the national level. These data sets also facilitate analyses that adjudicate among the other factors that should impact the development of state property rights, described at the start of this chapter (and detailed in Chapter 2): land values, land quality, infrastructure access, population density, and distance to the capital city. This approach allows me to examine whether the strength of customary institutions has an impact that is independent of alternative (and additional) explanations for land titling related to geography and land markets.

Determining how customary institutions shape actors' behavior is more difficult than isolating statistical patterns in outcomes. The internal rules of customary institutions are informal and generally unwritten. They are also dynamic: Political procedures that have been documented in the past may have changed. Instead, it is the contemporary practices within these institutions that are most relevant to land negotiation outcomes. Comparative case studies illuminate some mechanisms through which customary institutions influence land titling. Each country chapter includes a comparison of neighboring customary institutions that have different historical structures but fall in the same agricultural zone. This approximates a most-similar case selection, which helps isolate the differences in the institutions while maximizing similarities related to geography and land. This lessens concerns that land quality and agricultural practices are determining the variations among institutions and in customary authorities' responses to land allocation requests. These local-level case studies illustrate how customary institutions generate constraints on their leaders.

This project also relies on two individual-level surveys to examine how customary institutions impact the likelihood that citizens who are smallholder farmers[129] engage in land titling. These surveys identify who has titles for their small plots of land in rural communities and how this relates to their position within the local customary institutions. The two surveys in this book are designed to be complementary. The Zambia survey is an excellent agricultural census collected by the Indaba Agricultural Policy Research Institute (IAPRI) in Lusaka.[130] It includes every province of the country, representing a range of customary institutions. The Senegal survey is an original survey that I fielded with a team of enumerators and designed to be representative of rural communities within two districts. Both are geocoded at the household level, which allowed me to identify household attributes that are not part of the survey, including distance to infrastructure. Analysis of these surveys helps identify how institutions can impact citizens' decisions to title their land, while accounting for relevant individual characteristics such as wealth, geographic location, and education. Combined, the surveys from two different countries suggest generalizable effects of privilege within the customary institution on the likelihood smallholders title their land. Further, the large, nationally representative sample of smallholder farmers in Zambia provides an additional opportunity to investigate the relationship between hierarchy and titling, using an individual-level data set.

All three empirical strategies depend heavily on interviews, focus groups, and other qualitative data collection. This includes 81 interviews with customary authorities in Zambia and Senegal; 15 focus groups with smallholder farmers in Zambia; open-ended survey questions from an original survey of 1,001 smallholder farmers in Senegal; and 98 interviews with local council members, bureaucrats, and agricultural investors. These findings rely on additional primary evidence in the form of documents from government ministries and investors, as well as historical land

---

[129] Smallholders (or small-scale farmers) are defined as households using less than 20 ha of land. The average agricultural household in the Senegal and Zambia smallholder surveys used between 2 and 3 ha of land. In this book, titles ranging in size from 100 ha to 200,000 ha are considered large.

[130] Author's institutional host during fieldwork.

records, correspondence, and reports from colonial archives. Newspaper articles also play a role in this research; they help triangulate reported land deals and allow me to quote what public figures say in the press without violating the confidentiality of my research interviews.

Interviews were also critical for identifying where there is demand for land titles and where land negotiations fail. Quantitative data sets of land titles reflect successful conversions from customary to state property rights, but they do not show how many attempts were unsuccessful. This issue is only partially mitigated by including measures that approximate demand, such as land value. As a result, my interviews focused on reconstructing specific land negotiations and identifying the causes of failed negotiations. Customary authorities shared how often they had been approached for large-scale land titles in the past five years and explained the logic of their responses. Interviews with state bureaucrats and investors probed how they had selected land before they approached any customary authorities. The insights gleaned from these interviews establish the interests of state actors, customary authorities, and citizens in the land negotiations described in the pages that follow.

1.7 PLAN OF THE BOOK

The expansion of state power through titling is shaped by the systems being replaced and customary institutions have an important role in this process. The rest of the book elaborates these points. Chapter 2 provides an overview of the contemporary context of customary authority and control over land in Africa, while situating Zambia and Senegal within broader cross-national trends. It shows that institutional pluralism in land rights at the local level is widespread and provides necessary background on the key mechanism driving incremental shifts in the control over land: piecemeal land titling. The chapter traces the titling process in Zambia and Senegal, including how customary authorities use unofficial and official channels to exert agency over it. In addition, Chapter 2 presents two alternative explanations for the uneven expansion of state control over land. One approach highlights the state's capacity and interests, suggesting that land remains in the customary domain where the state lacks administrative capabilities or is disinterested in expanding its authority over property rights. Other explanations emphasize the importance of structural processes of induced institutional change (IIC) in property rights, such that customary land tenure continues due to low land values and limited competition for land. However, without frameworks that examine the agency of citizens and customary authorities, and the ways in which institutions shape their decisions, our understanding of this fragmented state-building process is incomplete.

Chapter 3 lays out a new theoretical model, which highlights the tensions between collective costs and concentrated benefits that make land titling political. Institutions matter because they impact how members perceive and are held accountable to these collective costs, including to the institution's power base. After elaborating mechanisms by which institutions influence the decisions of chiefs and citizens, the chapter introduces the second element of the framework, that historical legacies impact the contemporary strength of customary institutions in Zambia and Senegal. This theory helps explain why two chiefs would have different responses to the same land deal as a result of the institutions in which they are embedded. Similarly, it shows why citizens with high or low privilege in an institution would have different evaluations of titling. This framework creates expectations about how institutions impact aggregate patterns of land titling, which are elaborated and tested in Chapters 5–7.

However, we cannot proceed to the contemporary context of customary institutions, state power, and land rights in Zambia and Senegal without examining the institutional interplay that generated it. This book is not about precolonial legacies alone. Precolonial institutional endowments were shaped by the colonial and independent states, which contributed to the unofficial or official status of their leaders today. Chapter 4 provides an overview of three layers of superimposed political institutions in Zambia and Senegal. It places particular emphasis on the differences between the British and French colonial era institutions. These colonial institutions established distinct legal foundations for the independent states. The Zambian and Senegalese governments responded to the existing institutional frameworks. As a result, the difference between the two countries in the official role of chiefs in land governance remains, despite active domestic debates about land policy reform.

This comparison of colonial institutions is essential to one of the book's conclusions: The impact of customary institutions on land titling is not confined to countries where chiefs exercise unofficial influence and can therefore claim independence from the state apparatus. Nor is it uniquely an attribute of countries where chiefs are officially recognized as custodians of customary land. This comparison demonstrates that neither French nor British colonial rule erased the ability of the leaders of customary institutions to retain autonomy from the state; nor did they eradicate the variations in internal mechanisms that allow members of customary institutions to advance their power interests. Despite the many differences between Senegal and Zambia, the comparison reveals a fundamental similarity in the impacts of customary institutions on state building through titling.

Chapters 5 and 6 turn to the role of customary authorities in the contemporary era. Each chapter examines how customary institutions shape land titling through their influence on a powerful set of decision makers – their own chiefs. Customary institutions impact titling: (1) despite the state's interest in expanding control of land and facilitating global land markets; and (2) because chiefs have real agency in the piecemeal land titling process. Customary authorities are not merely responding to the state's will, but weigh different considerations in their responses to titling. Chapters 5 and 6 begin by addressing each of these two points within Zambia and Senegal, respectively. They continue with comparative case studies that illustrate mechanisms through which customary institutions can constrain their own leaders and hold them accountable to collective goals. Each chapter then presents a similar subnational pattern of land titling, which supports the hypothesis that institutions with hierarchical legacies slow the erosion of customary control over land today.

Chapter 5 examines the influence of customary institutions on land negotiations in Zambia, where, as in many former British colonies, chiefs are recognized by the state as custodians of land. The state's recognition endows individual customary authorities with highly concentrated power over the decision to convert land to titles. Some chiefs accept the compelling individual incentives to cede customary land and are unfettered in their decisions. However, some institutions can generate ties of vertical accountability among their chiefs. Superior chiefs can monitor, punish, and reward inferior chiefs, creating checks on their decisions. A comparison of two customary institutions with different historical structures that share a language group and climactic zone illustrates this mechanism. Statistical analyses of the national–level and individual–level land titling data sets provide support for the argument that customary institutions shape titling outcomes in Zambia. Examining the amount of land that has been titled by district reveals that areas with nonhierarchical institutions have greater overall rates of land titling, all things being equal. Further, living in a zone with hierarchical institutions also decreases the likelihood that a smallholder farmer has a land title. This chapter includes analyses of two distinct land titling data sets to support the argument that hierarchical institutions make it harder to access title in their domains.

The parallel approach in Chapter 6 identifies how customary institutions in Senegal shape land titling in the era of global land markets and piecemeal titling policies. In Senegal, customary authorities have unofficial influence over land, which allows horizontal ties of accountability to more effectively constrain chiefs. To illustrate how institutions in Senegal facilitate horizontal constraints among their leaders, this chapter examines a land deal attempted in two neighboring institutional zones. It shows how the negotiations over land differed as a result of the distinct historical structures of the customary institutions in these communities. The chapter then turns to patterns of land titling and customary institutions throughout Senegal. As in Zambia, I find that land titling is slower to replace customary property rights in zones with hierarchical customary institutions. These results are independent of important alternative explanations including the value of land, distance to the state's capital, and group size.

Chapter 7 shifts focus to the citizen level in both countries, revealing how customary institutions impact smallholder land titling. It shows that titling is not an economic decision alone; it is also a strategic choice between engaging with the customary institution or the state. This updates conventional approaches to land titling, which assume that all citizens want state titles but are constrained by a lack of financial resources. First, the chapter introduces the argument that replacing one's customary property rights with state title is a form of exit, and that an individual's decision to exit is informed by the privilege afforded to them by their local institution. Second, it reveals a common pattern within the diverse customary institutions in Zambia and Senegal, that smallholders with customary privilege are less likely to have titles. This is the case even among citizens with otherwise similar profiles, who have accessed land through inheritance and with the same levels of education. The statistical analyses then probe two related mechanisms connecting privilege and titling: increased tenure security and concern for collective costs. These results illustrate that customary institutions shape citizens' engagement with the state by structuring privilege within the community and impacting access to land titles.

Chapter 8 concludes by examining the implications of these findings for the role of customary institutions in the modern state; for the political determinants of property rights; and for policy design. This book explores how customary institutions, citizens, and chiefs impact the expansion of state control over land, determining how state capacity grows and why it is spatially uneven. It shows that, by influencing how chiefs and citizens weigh competing incentives in their decisions, customary institutions can divert the outcomes intended by state policy or predicted by market forces. Local power dynamics and the agency of members of customary institutions are thus critical to understanding both the resilience of customary land tenure regimes and the continuing influence of customary institutions in citizens' lives.

2

Plot by Plot

Customary Authority and the Incremental Expansion of State Property Rights in Africa

In Zambia and Senegal, the countryside is a patchwork of state and customary property rights. As a result, the state's knowledge of the land and control over its users varies significantly, even within a region. From the perspective of the state, its expansion of control over land is incomplete. The partial reach of the state is apparent even within the same small communities, where some citizens are subject to the state's land authority and others are outside of it, securing land rights through customary authorities. This scenario of plural, mixed, and contested property rights is ubiquitous within Africa, as customary land exists in nearly every country on the continent. Also ubiquitous is the push to replace customary control of property rights with state authority. Policy frameworks encourage these changes, yet state power over land does not expand smoothly in response to market forces and governmental prerogatives. Instead, the resulting patterns of state building are uneven and reveal much about the role of customary institutions in structuring interactions between state and citizen.

This chapter lays the groundwork for understanding how property rights shift from customary to statutory authority and why customary institutions matter. Although the book's main focus is on Zambia and Senegal, this case selection has implications for countries in Africa more generally. In this chapter, I situate these two countries within the context of broader regional trends in customary authority and land control. The roles of chiefs and the rules of customary tenure vary widely across and within countries, yet they are features of most African countries. This is the result of common histories of colonial institutions imposed upon preexisting political communities and relatively recent independent statehood. Thus, situating Zambia and Senegal in the context of diverse African countries sheds light on similarities and differences within the continent. However, the scope of this chapter is limited to the contemporary context. I reserve discussion of the historical background on chiefs and land tenure in Zambia and Senegal for Chapter 4.

The chapter is divided into three sections. First, I introduce customary authorities and the institutions in which they are embedded. These local authorities have multiple roles within citizens' daily lives and within the modern state. They are also elite members of customary institutions that exist beyond the personality of any individual chief. Customary authorities and institutions are the central focus of this book because of their influence over land and citizens.

Second, this chapter provides an overview of the complex and dynamic systems of land authority in African countries. It maps the cross-national extent of land that is outside of the state's direct control – customary land. It describes the robust systems of property rights that govern access to such land and provides evidence of the considerable subnational variation in the types of property rights that citizens use to secure land access. Understanding the state's partial and changing authority over land also requires attention to the mechanics of land titling. Thus, in this section, I also introduce the specific channels through which customary authorities influence land tenure outcomes in Senegal and Zambia. This local-level process of negotiating for and adopting titles is critical to the aggregate patterns of land control that are explored in this book.

The third section of the chapter introduces two prominent frameworks for understanding where state authority over property rights develops. State-centric approaches to land tenure emphasize how the state's interests in titling certain areas of land vary depending on geography, political strategies, and fiscal calculations. They examine the state's priorities but do not fully account for the agency of a wider array of actors in incremental titling processes. Market-centric approaches focus on structural factors, particularly those contributing to land values, that induce actors to seek titles in some areas but not others. These explanations anticipate a similar pattern of land titling: Geography and infrastructure affect the value of land, and the value of land affects the economic benefits of titling. However, we would observe different patterns if customary institutions mediate how chiefs and citizens evaluate prospective land titles. This final section explains why we need new frameworks that examine how customary institutions shape the expansion of state property rights.

2.1 CUSTOMARY AUTHORITY AND INSTITUTIONS IN CONTEMPORARY AFRICA

Customary authorities are influential political actors in most African countries. They are best understood as a set of elites who derive legitimacy from tradition, culture, and spirituality. Many customary authorities have hereditary claims to power and shared ethnic ties within their communities.[1] They reinforce their political power through narratives of common origin and spiritual rituals that reflect a connection with group ancestors.[2] However, it is worth repeating that the reference to custom and tradition is not indicative of static or unchanging roles. Instead, it represents a "mode of legitimization."[3] Custom can be a political tool that symbolizes separateness from the state, in addition to a connection to the past.[4] It allows chiefs to position themselves as an alternative type of leader that is independent of the state, despite the long history of chiefs engaging with the administrations of colonial and independent states.

Although this set of elites is defined by a shared connection to tradition, customary authorities are highly heterogeneous – even within the same country. Recognizing that chiefs are actors embedded within a diverse set of customary institutions is critical to understanding this heterogeneity. Customary institutions are sets of rules and processes that regulate multiple political, economic, and social domains of members' lives; they bind together communities governed by the institution. The customary institutions featured in this book establish the rules of access to land, marriage, and political participation. They define appropriate social behavior and the norms of inclusion in the community. They are the foundation for customary systems of justice. Further, castes and clans gain their meanings from customary institutions.[5] Like their leaders, customary institutions obtain legitimacy from their connection to shared historical or identity narratives, mythologies of common origin, spiritual beliefs, and other references to custom. Although members of customary institutions often share common lineages or ethnicities, customary institutions are not, by definition, ethnic institutions.[6] Customary institutions

---

[1] Logan 2009, 104; Baldwin and Holzinger 2019.   [2] Swidler 2013; Nuesiri 2014, 51.
[3] Holzinger, Kern, and Kromrey 2016, 470.   [4] Willis 2013, 220.
[5] See, for example, the discussion of castes in Senegal in A.-B. Diop 1981; Mbow 2000.
[6] See also the discussion of why traditional leaders are not ethnic leaders in Baldwin 2016, 44–48.

may be multiethnic and members of the same ethnic group may be governed by different customary institutions.

Among other functions, customary institutions decide how power is distributed within a political community, including who has which rights of participation and voice. They designate who can be a chief and who has the right to select the leader. In some institutions, these rules are highly complex and constraining. In others, they may be straightforward or weakly enforced. In Zambia, for example, there are recurring cases of contested successions based on claims that the leader did not follow the institution's established rules. In Senegal, the customary institution in urban Dakar had two paramount leaders for years because of succession disputes. These institutions are an arena in which politics occur; the existence of rules and norms does not mean they are always followed. Further, like other political institutions, customary institutions adapt in response to changing political circumstances to retain relevance and power. Thus, scholars such as Francis Nyamnjoh have compared Africa's customary institutions to European monarchical systems to help explain the continued relevance of such historical political institutions within modern democratic states.[7]

Importantly, these customary institutions exist outside of their leaders. While some governments, researchers, and customary authorities themselves have framed the relationship between the two with the logic of "*l'état, c'est moi*,"[8] chiefs and customary institutions are not the same. Individual chiefs are special members of the institution. They are unique, first, because they have a disproportionate ability to alter it. The institution generates rules, but individual leaders can uphold, manipulate, and selectively ignore them. Their interpretations of rules and executive decisions can change the norms of the customary institution if repeated over time. They can weaken the institution by neglecting its regulations or ceding its power resources. Second, customary authorities depend on the customary institution to rule. They derive legitimacy from their institutions. For example, customary institutions shape what citizens see as appropriate leadership behavior and when they need to comply with customary governance. This creates opportunities for the institution to impact the behavior of chiefs. As a result, the relationship between individual chiefs and customary institutions is dependent but not constitutive. Customary authorities influence how the institution functions, but

---

[7] Nyamnjoh 2014.
[8] This concept is rooted in the likely apocryphal statement of King Louis XIV of France.

the institution is greater than any individual chief. Leadership can change. The customary institution does not die with the chief.

In addition to being embedded in customary institutions, chiefs are embedded in – and gain power from – the state. Throughout Africa, there is a long history of governments engaging with customary authorities to maintain social stability, mobilize votes, organize labor, and collect taxes in colonial and independent states. Chapter 4 explains how colonial rule laid the foundation for the integration of chiefs within the contemporary states in Zambia and Senegal. In brief, colonial regimes relied on customary authorities for local governance, to varying degrees and in different ways. The colonial era created opportunities for customary authorities to define their roles within the state, both as a result of colonial policy and as entrepreneurial political agents. Some colonial regimes strengthened the power of customary authorities in relation to local populations through land policies and "native" court systems that centralized power in the hands of an individual chief.[9] They also exiled or attempted to disempower customary authorities who challenged their authority too strongly and rewarded collaborators. The colonial era established the initial frameworks of state-customary relations in each individual country.

After independence in the 1960s, many African states passed laws to abolish customary authority in a wave of socialist and nationalist reforms. However, customary authorities retained their popular influence despite government policies designed to curtail their power. Thus, in the 1990s and 2000s there was a countervailing trend of increased statutory power for chiefs.[10] Scholars have attributed the wave of pro-customary authority policies to the combination of democratization and the low legitimacy of the African state.[11] Notably, chiefs gained more statutory recognition of their power in democracies.[12] For example, Ghana's 1992 constitution guaranteed the existence of chiefs, customary law, and traditional councils while mandating the noninterference of the state in installing or dethroning chiefs. It also gave chiefs oversight in the appointment of 30 percent of district assembly members. In 2005, the government of South Africa introduced a new law that recognized the powers of chiefs and their councils over communal land.[13] Mozambique's customary leaders had their authority over a variety of rural governance

---

[9] For examples of these transformations, see Crowder 1964; Migdal 1988; Daannaa 1994; Beall and Ngonyama 2009; Banda 2011.
[10] Englebert 2002; Kyed and Buur 2007; Baldwin 2016.   [11] See Nuesiri 2014.
[12] Baldwin 2016.   [13] Beall and Ngonyama 2009, 10.

2.1 Customary Authority and Institutions

duties legally recognized in 2000. Their newly codified responsibilities ranged from taxation, land management, and administering justice to upholding "local customs, uses, and cultural values."[14] Other forms of statutory power include official advisory roles in Houses of Chiefs in Côte d'Ivoire, Namibia, Zambia, Liberia, South Africa, Ghana, and Botswana.[15] In some countries, including Zambia, customary authorities gain a salary or other direct benefits from the state.

Outside of official roles, customary authorities are tied to the state through informal relationships and practices. State actors depend on the local influence of customary authorities to realize their bureaucratic and political aims. In many countries, officials treat chiefs as the gatekeepers to local populations. The homes of customary authorities are often the first stop for government agents visiting a community. State actors may find it necessary to treat the chief as an intermediary for both social and practical reasons, relying on them, for example, to help distribute public goods such as fertilizer and NGO donations.[16] Further, politicians commonly engage with customary authorities as vote brokers and political patrons in elections.[17] Chiefs are effective brokers because their regular interactions with citizens provide ample opportunities for them to organize voting blocks and influence voting behavior. Customary authorities can thus gain power and material benefits from their relationships with state actors.

Customary authorities, therefore, combine dual sources of legitimacy, from both the state and custom. As a result, they exercise a great deal of influence in the everyday lives of citizens in many African countries. Often, they are closer to local populations than state authorities. For many citizens, a chief is the first authority they contact when they have governance issues. Among more than 40,000 sub-Saharan African citizens in twenty-six countries surveyed by the Afrobarometer in 2016, 34 percent had reached out to a customary authority in the last year to discuss a problem or express an opinion. This connection between citizens and chiefs is not exclusively a rural phenomenon: 21 percent of urbanites in the sample had contacted a customary authority in the previous year. By contrast, only 12 percent of the full sample had

---

[14] Buur and Kyed 2005, 14.
[15] See van Binsbergen 1987 on the House of Chiefs in Zambia.
[16] Swidler and Watkins 2017, 10.
[17] Boafo-Arthur 2001; van de Walle 2007; Beck 2008; Fokwang 2009; Bado 2015; Koter 2016; de Kadt and Larreguy 2018.

contacted a government official, and 23 percent had contacted a local councillor.[18] In Benin, Burkina Faso, Burundi, Cameroon, Côte d'Ivoire, Eswatini, Lesotho, Madagascar, Mali, Mozambique, Niger, Sierra Leone, Togo, Zimbabwe, and – notably – Senegal and Zambia, citizens were at least three times more likely to report contacting a customary authority than a government official.

As local political authorities, chiefs have three interconnected governance functions: conflict resolution, organizing collective action for local public goods, and land allocation. In many countries, including Senegal and Zambia, chiefs adjudicate cases of petty crimes, family quarrels, and land disputes. For example, in an interview, one chief in the Dagana district of northern Senegal reported his role in conflict resolution as follows:

> When there is a conflict, I resolve it ... If there is a problem in the village, I don't like the gendarme, I don't like the police. For me, my preference is to resolve it. It is often required. Even yesterday, I resolved a small problem ... I call the elders and the mothers. We get together and we resolve the situation. Up to present, we haven't had any problems [with this approach].[19]

Similarly, in Zambia, customary authorities hold regular meetings to hear the cases of disputes among community members and then offer resolutions in the form of punishments or other directives. In some circumstances, customary systems of conflict resolution can be more consensus-based and attentive to the need to restore social peace.[20] At the same time, in adjudicating conflicts, customary authorities can reinforce political and social divisions. For example, one group of citizens in northern Zambia lamented during a focus group interview that their chief's decisions were biased by his personal relationships, offering the example of a thief who received a light punishment because he was close to the chief.[21] Such influence in the domain of local conflict resolution and security provision is not uncommon: Cross-nationally, conflict adjudication was the most commonly reported role for customary authorities.[22]

A second major role of chiefs is organizing local public goods within communities. They do so by mandating collective contributions of labor or money for community projects, such as repairing wells and roads. This function is particularly important in contexts where the state does not, or

---

[18] Afrobarometer 2016.
[19] Interview with customary authority (CA-164), northern Senegal, December 11, 2014.
[20] Boege 2006; Oba 2011.
[21] Interview with smallholder farmers (FFG-547), northern Zambia, February 4, 2014.
[22] Afrobarometer 2008. Based on a nineteen-country sample.

2.1 Customary Authority and Institutions 45

cannot, provide many of the public goods that aid development. For example, Shittu Akinola described how customary authorities facilitated collective action to construct water projects, bridges, and roads in oil communities of the Niger Delta that felt neglected by the state.[23] Asiyati Lorraine Chiweza discussed how chiefs in Malawi mobilized village residents to create bricks and provide materials for development projects.[24] In Sierra Leone, Richard Fanthorpe has suggested that residents participated in community labor, albeit begrudgingly, because they believed that the chief was more likely to protect their interests than bureaucrats or politicians.[25] Examples of local public goods organized by chiefs in Senegal include *"set/setal"* campaigns to clean the public spaces in the village[26] and efforts to mobilize contributions to needy residents after the harvest.[27] Promoting hygiene campaigns;[28] regulating sustainable forest use;[29] and organizing labor for "self-help" school construction through making bricks and drawing water were cited as examples of this role in Zambia.

Control over land strengthens customary authorities' powers in conflict resolution and in the coordination of local public goods. As detailed later in the chapter, customary authorities hold a range of responsibilities in relation to property rights on customary land. In some communities, the chief's main role is to enforce customary rules by adjudicating land disputes among lineage-based owners. In other communities, the customary authority is understood as the principal owner of all of the land. The chief's ability to revoke or weaken a household's land rights is a key point of leverage over local populations. In extreme (and uncommon) cases, a severe violation of the chief's regulations could lead to expulsion from land. Customary authorities' influence over land is an important source of political power that adds weight to their directives, even in other domains of governance.

Thus, customary authorities can influence local populations through both coercive power and moral authority, relying on legitimacy from custom and their relationships with the state. The broad cross-national trend is that citizens' evaluations of their chiefs are complex and varied, as we might expect of other types of political authority. In Zambia and

---

[23] Akinola 2008. [24] Chiweza 2007. [25] Fanthorpe 2006.
[26] Interview with customary authority (CA-106), northern Senegal, December 9, 2014.
[27] Interview with customary authority (CA-168), northern Senegal, December 11, 2014.
[28] Interview with smallholder farmers (FFG-551), northern Zambia, February 10, 2014.
[29] Interview with customary authority (CA-537), central Zambia, October 16, 2013.

Senegal, the citizens I interviewed were far more likely to criticize their specific chief than the system of customary authority as a whole. They often reminisced about good chiefs and how a chief should ideally behave. Similarly complicated perspectives on the chieftaincy were present in Ghana, where Janine Ubink found that citizens' support for the chieftaincy was independent of their evaluations of the chiefs' performance on specific tasks.[30] Emmanuel Nuesiri has suggested that citizens trust chiefs and legitimize their power over land as "a practical judgement ... irrespective of whether they like the chief or do not like the chief, or whether they consider the individual on the throne as the rightful heir, usurper or state crony."[31] This helps explain the broader trend across Africa of citizens expressing positive feelings about customary authority as a whole. The majority of African citizens within the countries surveyed by Afrobarometer in 2008–9 reported that they trust their customary authorities and would like to see their influence increase.[32]

Figure 2.1 examines the differences among countries in trust in chiefs, relative to trust in state actors. It charts the gap between trust in state actors and customary authorities, from a high gap (Madagascar) to a low gap (South Africa). Predictably, trust in both state actors and chiefs differs widely across countries. In South Africa, where chiefs were associated with the Bantustan system of the apartheid regime,[33] citizens express nearly equal trust in customary authorities and state authorities. On the other end of the spectrum are Madagascar and Sierra Leone, where there is considerably higher trust in chiefs than in the state, which may be in part due to these countries' histories of political upheavals and conflict. Among African countries, Zambia and Senegal feature mid-level gaps in trust between state and customary actors. While citizens express considerably higher trust for chiefs than the state in both countries, in Senegal there is both higher overall trust in customary authorities and a greater gap between customary and state actors than in Zambia. This is consistent with the greater association between chief and state that accompanies official state recognition in Zambia. However, despite the variation across

---

[30] Ubink 2007.   [31] Nuesiri 2014, 51–52.
[32] Overall, 58 percent of respondents preferred increase. By country, preferences for increased influence for "traditional leaders" were 50 percent or above in Benin, Botswana, Burkina Faso, Ghana, Kenya, Lesotho, Liberia, Malawi, Mali, Mozambique, Namibia, Nigeria, Senegal, Uganda, Zambia, and Zimbabwe. Preferences for increased influence for traditional leaders were below 50 percent in Madagascar, South Africa, and Tanzania. See Logan 2013.
[33] See Ntsebeza 2005; M. Williams 2010.

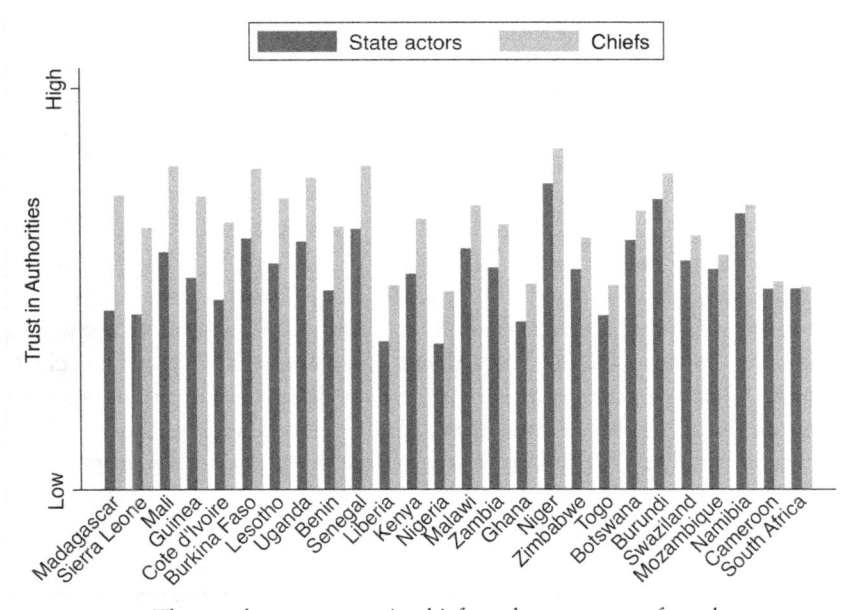

FIGURE 2.1. The gap between trust in chiefs and state actors, from largest to smallest
Notes: Figure displays responses to the question: "How much do you trust each of the following, or haven't you heard enough about them to say?" Trust in state actors combines reported trust in president, legislature, electoral commission, tax department, local government council, police, army, and courts. Trust in chiefs is reported trust in traditional leaders.
Source: Afrobarometer 2016.

countries, a general pattern emerges from these survey responses: Citizens report higher trust in their customary leaders than in their state leaders.

Unofficial and Official Customary Authorities in Senegal and Zambia

Zambia and Senegal are meaningful cases for the study of customary authority in Africa because of their differences. Most importantly, they feature two distinct types of relationships between customary authorities and the state in the arena of land governance. Zambia's official chiefs have state-recognized control over land. Senegal's customary authorities exercise informal influence in this domain. As Chapter 4 will elaborate, the differences between the two systems derive from their colonial histories. The British in Zambia and the French in Senegal had different philosophies about land tenure and African political authority. Both European powers, however, designed their approaches to chiefs in coordination with their approaches to land. These domains reinforced each other and created the foundation for contemporary state–customary relations in each country. In Zambia, official recognition produced a system of customary authority that is more standardized than it is in Senegal. These differences are detailed in Chapters 5 and 6. The following is a preview of these different systems of customary authority.

In countries with official chieftaincy systems, the state registers and recognizes customary authority. Such constitutional recognitions are more common in former British colonies.[34] For example, in Malawi, Botswana, Ghana, and Zambia, each chiefdom has a legal status within the state. In Zambia, the government has recognized 286 official chiefdoms.[35] The boundaries of each of these chiefdoms were initially mapped and codified by the colonial state, and later adopted by the Zambian government. Each official chief governs a clearly defined territory. They earn salaries from the government, which increase depending on whether the chief is officially a paramount chief, senior chief, or chief. These official chiefs rely on a network of village headmen and headwomen for day-to-day governance in their domains, however the village heads do not have formal status from the state or salaries in Zambia. Their authority is largely determined by the individual chief, the community, and the rules of the institution. Some chiefs select the heads, while others leave the decision to the village or a lineage within the village. In some chiefdoms, the village heads are organized by groups or zones, or under a hierarchical structure with a senior head. For the average citizens on customary land in Zambia, chief and village head are the most important customary authorities in their lives. Additional unofficial customary authorities exist in some institutions, including subchiefs, customary elders or councillors, and queen mothers. However, only the 286 chiefs have state-recognized authority over the land in their jurisdictions. These chiefs – and only these chiefs – must document their consent for new land titles. This system provides Zambia's chiefs with a high concentration of power.

In other African countries, customary authorities have no official power over land or conflict resolution, but are nevertheless influential in citizens' lives. Senegal is an example of a country with diverse systems of customary authority that are outside of state codification. This is also the

---

[34] Holzinger et al. 2019.
[35] During the writing of this book, President Michael Sata increased the number to 288.

case among Senegal's Sahelian neighbors Mali and Burkina Faso. In these contexts, there are no fixed boundaries for chieftaincies or official hierarchical titles.[36] Chiefs in these countries may gain power from the state informally, when state politicians visit their homes or comply with their advice, but they draw no state salaries and have no constitutionally recognized land authority. In Senegal, customary authorities include elders collectively recognized as the "masters of the village," village chiefs with inherited power, and lineage heads, among others. Senegal notably features a set of customary authorities that derive legitimacy from both custom and a global religious doctrine: Islamic marabouts. While these religious leaders and the institutions in which they are embedded are not a main focus of this book, Appendix C addresses their role in historical and contemporary land titling politics.

Zambia and Senegal illustrate the differences between living in a country with official chiefs and one with unofficial chiefs. In Zambia, the state identifies citizens as subjects of a specific chief who governs dozens of villages, based on where they live or were born. In Senegal, citizens who are asked whether there are any customary authorities in their communities will list a variety of local elites with titles and roles that vary based on the customary institution. In Zambia, citizens' responses to this question produce a shorter list of customary authorities, reflecting the standardizing influence of an official chieftaincy system. In an official system, the state strengthens and circumscribes the chief's power; in an unofficial system a chief's influence is more reliant on citizens' recognition of their authority and participation in the customary institution.

These two sections have described the important presence of customary authorities in citizens' lives and within the modern state. The official and unofficial roles that chiefs occupy vary widely; however, as I argue throughout the book, we should conceptualize all customary authorities as actors embedded with diverse customary institutions. That some of these institutions are extremely weak and others very strong is meaningful for a wide range of outcomes. The following section examines one domain in which customary institutions and authorities exert influence: land governance. They determine access to land in the absence of statutory property rights, a role that is particularly critical to their political power.

---

[36] The government does, however, register the name of the village chief (*chef de village*) as the head of the lowest administrative unit, the village.

2.2 LAND AUTHORITY AND PROPERTY RIGHTS IN AFRICA

The Cross-National Extent of Customary Land

The state has asserted its control over all land within its boundaries in constitutions and land laws throughout Africa. On paper, the state is the "owner" of the land in Sudan, Gabon, Guinea, Mauritania, and Democratic Republic of Congo. All land is "vested" in the state or the presidents in Zambia, Malawi, Namibia, and Nigeria. In Senegal, Mali, Burkina Faso, Madagascar, Cameroon, Côte d'Ivoire, and Ghana, the state is the "manager," "guardian," or "administrator" of the land within its boundaries.[37] However, the reality of land authority in these countries contrasts sharply with these assertions because of the prevalence of property rights enforced by non-state authorities. In practice, the state's control of land is partial.

Customary land is outside of the state's direct control. Instead, property rights on customary land are governed by customary authorities, who determine how the land should be distributed and who can use it. State land, by contrast, consists of land registered under statutory property rights, such as titles, as well as other areas overseen directly by the state, including national parks or forests. Customary land lacks these statutory rights. Consequently, customary land in Africa is often defined and measured as land without registered land titles.[38] The changes in direct land authority that accompany land titling are thus central to this definition of customary land.

Figure 2.2 illustrates the approximate extent of customary land in each African country, based on data compiled by Fabrice Dubertret and Liz Alden Wily.[39] A few trends are clear from this map. First, nearly every country in Africa has some customary land, with the notable exception of Rwanda.[40] Customary land is known as "tribal land" in Botswana; "communal land" in South Africa and Namibia; "traditional land" in Equatorial Guinea and Mauritania; and "community land" in South Sudan and Kenya. In Senegal, customary land is called "national domain land," legally defined as all land that remains unregistered (*non-immatriculée*) in the government's records. This terminology is shared with other former French colonies such as Mali and Niger. In the former British colonies of

---

[37] Diaw 2005; Alden Wily 2015.   [38] Colin and Woodhouse 2010, 3.
[39] Dubertret and Alden Wily 2015. For a description of the underlying data, see Alden Wily 2015.
[40] Rwanda's population density and state capacity are exceptionally high within Africa. Between 2009 and 2013, the government registered all of the land in the country. The state's land tenure regularization (LTR) campaign replaced customary property rights with more than 11 million statutory land titles. See Nkurunziza 2015.

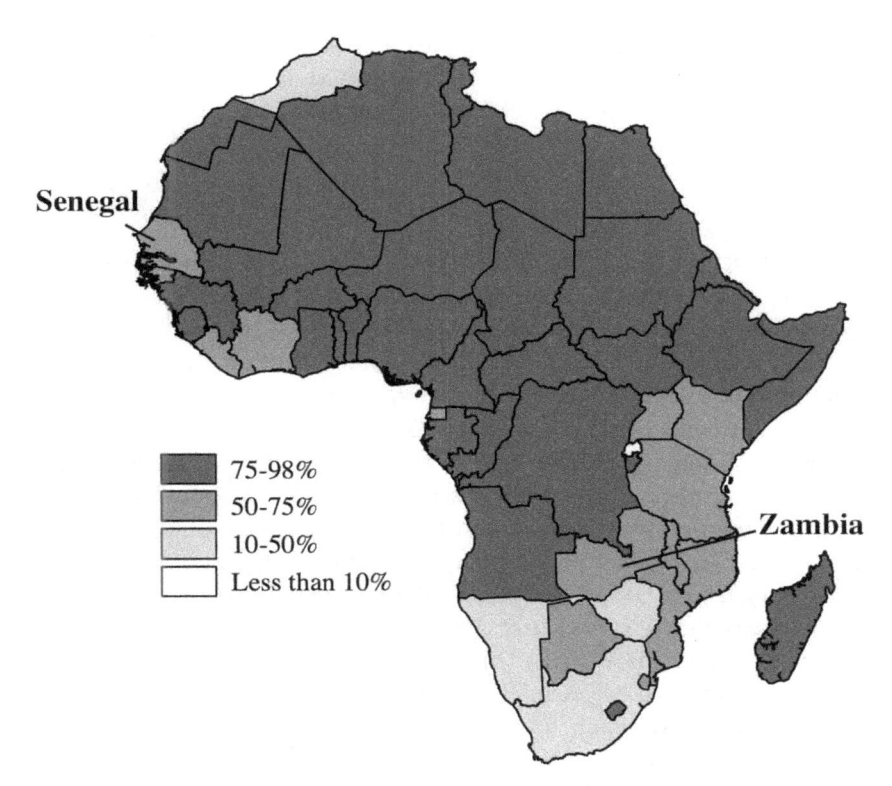

2.2 Land Authority and Property Rights in Africa

FIGURE 2.2. The percentage of customary land per country in 2015
Notes: Shading in the map represents the variable "Total percentage of indigenous and community lands in the country."
Source: Dubertret and Alden Wily 2015.

Zambia and Malawi, "customary land" is the official name for land that is governed by customary property rights.

Second, Figure 2.2 also shows the proportions of customary land within each country, highlighting the overall scarcity of direct state control over property rights within Africa. In almost all countries in 2015, most land was customary. Within sub-Saharan Africa (and excluding Rwanda), the only countries where less than half of the land is customary are Namibia, Zimbabwe, and South Africa, the three former settler colonies with histories of White minority rule. Colonial rule had a more disruptive impact on customary land tenure regimes in these countries, as the colonizers expropriated large areas of land from Africans for White settlers.[41] Elsewhere,

---
[41] Herbst 2000, 188.

customary land tenure has remained predominant. Zambia and Senegal fall within the middle range of amounts of customary land, with an estimated 60 percent of their land under customary control.

What Are Customary Property Rights?

A wide range of non-statutory property rights determines access to customary land. A comprehensive account of the different land tenure systems on customary land would be impossible to provide here, as the diversity of the societies (and corresponding institutions) in which land relations are embedded generates great variation in the rules of access to land.[42] Further, customary land tenure is notably dynamic and was shaped by colonial and independent state policies, among other sources of change. Instead, this section discusses the similarities in customary property rights across Zambia and Senegal, two geographically distant countries, each composed of many institutions and local systems of customary land tenure.[43] Examining the commonalities among customary property rights regimes in the two countries helps illuminate broader patterns on customary land. This section considers primary ownership rights over land first before introducing the importance of secondary land rights on customary land.

In some customary land tenure regimes in both countries, individual families hold primary ownership rights to the land that they use. Many of these families trace their land claims to ancestors who first cleared the land or settled in the community. These rights were then passed through matrilineal or patrilineal inheritance to future generations; consequently, they are known as lineage-based land rights. For example, in Senegal, the Wolof terms the "master of fire" (*borom daye*) and the "master of the ax" (*borom n'gadio*) describe property rights derived from being a member of a lineage with historically rooted land claims in the community, in reference to processes of clearing previously unused land.[44] In addition,

---

[42] Okoth-Ogendo 1989.
[43] A large literature addresses the internal dynamics of different customary land tenure systems within each country. On Zambia, see Colson 1966; Palmer 2000; Gordon 2001; Kajoba 2002; Chitonge 2019. On Senegal, see Blundo 1996; Tine and Sy 2003; Galvan 2004; Billaud 2009; Dahou and Ndiaye 2009; Hesseling and Eichelsheim 2009; Kaag, Gaye, and Kruis 2011.
[44] Inheritors of the right of fire are known as *lamanes* in Wolof and Serer languages, translated as "master of the land" (Gellar 2005, 19). See also Goundiam 1965; M. Diop 1972.

individual families can gain customary ownership rights if they purchase or are given land by previous landowners or customary authorities. Newcomers can also access land through systems of borrowing or sharecropping from landowning lineages. In contexts where individual family lineages are understood to be the primary landowners, customary authorities protect and enforce these rights.

Alternatively, customary authorities may be perceived to be the primary holders of ownership rights for all of the land in their communities. In this type of customary tenure regime, individual families are understood to have usage rights to land that is owned by a customary authority. This may be the case even for family lineages that have used the same plots of land for generations. In this customary authority-as-owner model, newcomers can be incorporated into the community as tenants or clients of the customary authority, maintaining their access to land through continued recognitions of this relationship. More generally, all land users rely to varying degrees on ties with the customary authority in order to continue accessing land in this system. This may resemble a patron–client relationship or require compliance with the chief in other community governance domains. Where customary authorities are owners of the land, the citizen's access to customary land is not merely *protected by* the chief but *derived from* the chief.

These two understandings of customary land ownership within Zambia and Senegal reflect patterns elsewhere on the continent. In a review of customary land tenure in twenty-two African countries, John Bruce found that tenure regimes could be characterized as "lineage-based" or "monarchical" systems.[45] These divisions also correspond with Jean Ensminger's categories of "lineage-controlled" and "chief-controlled" land tenure.[46] In my interviews in both Zambia and Senegal, some customary authorities claimed to be the owners of all land in their communities. Others reported that individual families are the owners of the land, but that customary authorities serve as the custodians of these rights. However, these two categories are ideal types that are not always clearly differentiated or agreed upon, particularly because "ownership" holds different meanings in different land tenure systems. A customary authority may say that lineages own the land, while the citizens say that the chief owns the land, or vice versa. Similarly, citizens within the same community may disagree on the relative strength of lineage

---

[45] Bruce 1998, 8–9. [46] Ensminger 1997, 169.

rights in relation to customary authorities. The question itself is political. The strength of the chief's claims thus varies on a spectrum between customary authority-as-owner and lineage-as-owner within the customary tenure regimes in these countries.

Customary land tenure is more likely to fall into the customary authority-as-owner category when the state has recognized a chief's authority over land. In Zambia, chiefs are legally the custodians of customary land, and the government has largely treated them as the primary owners of the customary land in their jurisdictions. Thus, in Zambia, it was more common to hear that the chief was the owner of all of the land than it was in Senegal. Yet some official chiefs in Zambia reported that individual lineages "own" their customary land, suggesting that state recognition has not entirely eroded the system of lineage-based rights. Nevertheless, citizens in Zambia described accessing land through a chief at higher rates than in Senegal. As detailed in Chapter 7, 87 percent of the smallholders in the Senegal survey reported family inheritance as their mode of accessing land; only 14 percent reported "being allocated" their land by a customary authority. By contrast, in Zambia, 40 percent indicated that they accessed land through family inheritance, while 46 percent held land that was allocated to them by a village head or chief. These differences reflect the prevalence of the lineage-controlled customary tenure system in Senegal and the cohabitation of customary authority-as-owner and lineage-as-owner systems in Zambia.

An important feature of customary tenure is that it accommodates a wide range of other land rights, beyond the community's interpretations of primary land ownership. Property rights over natural resources are often understood as a bundle of entitlements. On customary land in Africa, the different entitlements in this bundle may include the right to use the land; to keep revenue or profits from the land; to modify or improve the land; to rent it out; to alienate or sell it; and to pass it on to one's children through inheritance.[47] For any given plot of land, each of these rights could be held by different actors. For example, an elder may be the only individual who has the right to sell the plot, but his nephew may have the right to keep profits from crops produced on the land. Similarly, a woman and her husband may have the right to use the land, but her brother holds the rights to rent it out. Groups within the same community or individuals within the same family can have different

---

[47] Colin, Le Meur, and Léonard 2009, 11.

types of rights over any given piece of land. As a result, customary property rights may include complex systems of secondary usage rights, in which multiple actors have rights to use the land in specific ways, even if they are not the primary owner.

Customary land in Zambia and Senegal features a variety of different arrangements of secondary land rights. For example, one lineage may own a plot of land, but all community members have usage rights to a passageway within it for access to a water source. In some customary tenure systems, community members with cattle are permitted to graze on individuals' agricultural plots after their harvests. Such secondary rights can be mutually beneficial: The cattle fertilize the farmers' land, while the herders gain fodder for their livestock. Other common sets of secondary rights in the two countries are areas of shared usage such as floodplains for short-term agriculture or forests for collecting wild plants, animals, and insects. Customary property rights include a far greater diversity of different types of rights than standard land titles allow.[48] The incompatibility of individual state land titles with customary "property notions," or the content of the bundle of property rights, is thus one of the major critiques of land titling.[49] (On the other hand, individualizing land rights is also one of the key arguments in favor of titling).[50]

The principles that guide customary land rights are not static laws but dynamic and adaptable interpretations of institutional rules by customary authorities. There are many examples of how these land tenure rules have changed over time in African countries, as a result of state policy, land markets, new crops, and demographic shifts. In some cases, the commercialization of agriculture and increasing population densities have led communities to discard specific land use practices, such as women-owned fields.[51] An institution's secondary group rights, such as shared grazing land, may become more exclusive or transform into private, individual customary land rights.[52] Alternatively, new crops can increase the value of land, changing rules of land access and increasing the importance of kinship ties.[53] A customary institution's land tenure norms may change,

---

[48] Systems of secondary rights also include land usage rights established by gender and marital ties. See Gray and Kevane 1999; Toulmin and Quan 2000a; Meinzen-Dick and Mwangi 2009.
[49] Ng'ong'ola 1982, 119.
[50] For examples, see the review of the individualization of tenure argument in Obeng-Odoom 2020, chapter 3.
[51] Kevane and Gray 1999.   [52] Ensminger 1990, 667–69.   [53] Moore 1978.

as a result of both broad structural forces and the agency of local actors (such as chiefs) who implement these rules.

Common across the range of customary land regimes is one defining feature: Customary authorities enforce property rights. Customary property rights are sets of decisions made by customary authorities with reference to the institution's rules or "customary principles."[54] Different institutions may have different rules, but customary property rights share a procedural logic that favors negotiability and social networks because they are interpreted by customary authorities who are part of the communities they govern.[55] In both customary authority-as-owner and lineage-as-owner land tenure, chiefs execute property rights. Where lineage rights are stronger, the customary authorities' roles are interpreting and protecting these rights. In a customary authority-as-owner system, chiefs have more power to allocate and reallocate land rights in response to social welfare concerns or economic opportunism. However, in both systems, chiefs interpret the existing land tenure rules and enforce systems of property rights by adjudicating land disputes.

As a result, the chief as enforcer on customary land parallels the state's role on state land. Land titles are a contract with statutory authorities; customary property rights are a contract with customary authorities. In his book, Ato Kwamena Onoma helps illustrate this point by applying the same framework to both chiefs and state leaders. He shows that, within their realms, each type of authority is an actor who responds to political and structural conditions to provide weak or strong property rights.[56] The chief overseeing customary rights and the government administering statutory land titles are both enforcers within their domains.

How are customary land rights understood in state law? On customary land in Senegal and Zambia, individual rights to land are not legible to the state. Instead, customary landowners are only recognized as having usage (or "usufruct") rights. This makes it exceedingly difficult for state authorities to adjudicate land conflicts on customary land. In practice, citizens cannot easily apply to the state if, for example, they are dissatisfied with the customary authority's ruling on a dispute over the inheritance of customary land. Treating customary rights as usage rights also allows the state to evade responsibility for the tenure security of these populations. For example, when state projects or land deals displace customary landowners, they are offered compensation for their investments on the land, but not the land

---

[54] Lavigne Delville 2000, 99. [55] Chauveau 1998, 72–73. [56] Onoma 2009.

2.2 Land Authority and Property Rights in Africa

itself. From the perspective of the state in Senegal and Zambia, customary landowners have no ownership rights to land if they do not have a title.

Statutory property rights, in contrast, are land rights that are directly overseen by state authority. This book uses a broad definition of land titles: A land title is a written recognition of statutory rights. It is a contract, which acknowledges the state's responsibility for overseeing property rights on that land. Different forms of statutory rights fall under the umbrella of land titles. These include long-term leases and permits or certificates of occupancy. A key component of the land titling process is recording these statutory rights in a land registry; land registration, titling, and formalization are, consequently, parallel terminologies for the expansion of state property rights. Critical to the state-building function of land titling is that it codifies land ownership in a statutory document, making it possible for the state to enforce property rights. However, while land titling allows the state to enforce property rights, this does not mean that it reliably does.

Enforcement determines the security of any property right, regardless of whether it is a state title or a customary claim. Table 2.1 summarizes the key differences between customary and statutory property rights. It categorizes the security of tenure for both types of rights as "varied" because efficient and equitable enforcement may be lacking (or present) in either rights regime. Whether citizens have confidence in their customary property rights depends on the chiefs involved and the customary institutions in which they are embedded. For example, some customary institutions effectively stave off displacements from large-scale land deals and can generate strong property rights for community members. Yet even institutions that protect citizens from threats to their customary land rights that originate outside of the community may leave citizens feeling vulnerable to threats from within their communities. Their leaders may make enforcement decisions that are biased against certain groups or are generally extractive. Relatedly, state property rights may be ineffectively enforced due to low state capacity or the political incentives of state agents.[57] As Lund has suggested, titles may be less secure than other types of land tenure if they are illegitimate among local populations; tenure security requires social consensus that the property right is legitimate.[58] Similarly, Ron Herring observes that state property rights are not effective if the state – and its representatives – are not perceived to be legitimate at

---

[57] See Platteau 1996; Gibson, Lehoucq, and J. Williams 2002; Smith 2003; Onoma 2009; Murtazashvili and Murtazashvili 2015.
[58] Lund 2001, 157–59.

the local level.[59] Therefore, neither customary nor statutory property rights can be categorized, in a general way, as more or less secure.[60] The security of either type of property right is contingent on the individual landowner, and on the nature of the institutions in which she is embedded.

TABLE 2.1. *Key differences between customary and state property rights in Senegal and Zambia*

	Customary Property Rights	Statutory Land Titles
Authority Responsible for Enforcement	Customary authority	State authority
Types of Rights	Plural or Singular: • Individual, group, collective, secondary rights	Singular: • Individual or (rarely) corporate
Legibility to State	Low • Known to local communities	High • Registered in state records
Enforcement and Tenure Security	Varied	Varied
Sources of Legitimacy	• Ancestry and lineage • Patron–client ties with customary authorities • Social networks • Compliance with local norms • Rental or sharing agreements	• State law • Formal documents • Compliance with administrative requirements related to usage of land or tax payments

Land titling is the process of formalizing property rights and expanding the state's land domain – it does not necessarily change usage or access. In some circumstances, land titling coincides with major transformations in how land is used, but in other cases, it is just the authority over property rights that changes.[61] Further, it is important to

---

[59] Herring 2002, 275.
[60] See also Jacoby and Minten 2007; Musembi 2007; Banda 2011; Obeng-Odoom and Stilwell 2013; Simbizi, Bennett, and Zevenbergen 2014.
[61] An excellent stream of literature within anthropology, geography, and political science establishes the importance of access as distinct from property rights. See Ribot 1998; Ribot and Peluso 2003; Sikor and Lund 2009.

acknowledge the complexity and fluidity of these rights on the ground. Chiefs can have an unofficial role overseeing customary property rights on land that has a title, particularly on land that has been abandoned by its legal owners. Similarly, citizens can choose to obtain titles for their plots and also comply with any land governance directives of local customary authorities to maintain positive relationships in the community. Therefore, the division between customary and state land rights is not absolute and depends on the state's interest in and capacity to enforce. However, registration of land rights is a necessary step for the state to exert direct control over land. Titling fundamentally transforms the legal status of a plot of land, which impacts the long-term power of states – and customary authorities.

Institutional Pluralism within Countries and Communities

How are state and customary rights distributed within countries? As Figure 2.2 illustrated, neither the state nor customary authorities have complete control over landed property rights in any African country (except Rwanda). Rather, there is significant subnational variation in state control of land.[62] We might imagine that land titles are an urban or peri-urban phenomenon while citizens in more isolated rural villages exclusively rely on customary rights. Or that there are clearly bounded domains of communities with either customary or statutory rights. Instead, these systems intermingle within African countries. The patchwork of state and customary property rights in African land tenure regimes is a form of institutional pluralism, as multiple institutions can regulate land access within a given country and within a given community.[63] For example, neighbors in a village in central Uganda may derive their land rights from customary authorities, landlords, or state land titles.[64] In some communities in Mozambique, customary "régulos" allocate land; in others, this is the role of the party secretary.[65] Citizens in Mali's western Kayes Region are more likely to report that customary authorities manage land than those in Gao to the east, but both types of property rights are present in both regions.[66]

---

[62] D. Williams 1996; Herbst 2000; Boone 2003; Baldwin 2014.
[63] See Toulmin and Quan 2000a, 2; Meinzen-Dick and Pradhan 2002; Young 2002.
[64] Place and Otsuka 2002. [65] Pitcher 2002; de Sousa Santos 2006.
[66] Afrobarometer 2008.

Such institutional pluralism differs from the conventional understanding of "dual land tenure." Colonial governments created dual land tenure regimes through the top-down partitioning of land between zones of customary and state land. Chapter 4 provides examples of this process. In many countries, including Zambia, colonial governments prohibited access to land titles on customary land. These land tenure divisions were explicitly racialized in colonies such as Southern Rhodesia (now Zimbabwe) and South Africa. Consequently, the term dual land tenure often implies a separation of land between *homogeneous zones* of either state or customary authority. However, there is far more spatial heterogeneity in the current context of property rights in African countries. As a result of incremental land titling, property rights are often mixed within the same localities: Some citizens rely on the state and others on customary authorities for their access to land. These citizens are subject to different rules, and these rules are executed by authorities with distinct sources of legitimacy. Institutional pluralism at the very local level is unlikely to occur when top-down decision-making, by state actors, is the primary determinant of land tenure regimes. Instead, this phenomenon suggests that there is local agency in facilitating and thwarting the expansion of land titling on customary land.

Figure 2.3 illustrates the extent of institutional pluralism within four African countries. These countries represent the book's two focal cases and two nearby countries with similar colonial legacies, Malawi and Burkina Faso. Zambia and Malawi are former British colonies with official chiefs. Burkina Faso and Senegal are former French colonies with unofficial chiefs. The figure maps citizens' beliefs about de facto authority over land in their communities using Afrobarometer survey data.[67] The darkest shading signifies that the majority in the sampled communities agreed that customary authorities "actually" manage land. The lightest shading represents the inverse: majority recognition of the state's authority. However, the most common situation is an intermediate level on the spectrum, indicating that respondents in the sampled localities disagree on who has authority over land. Both types of authorities govern land within that community.

---

[67] The shading represents the percentage of rural respondents who reported either customary or statutory control over land within the sampled enumeration area(s) in that district or region. They provide an indication of the extent of subnational variation in land authority within each country, but may not be representative of the entire district or region in which the sampled community was located.

2.2 *Land Authority and Property Rights in Africa* 61

(a)

Senegal
Dioulacolon, Kolda

Tapoa

Burkina Faso

Authority over Land
☐ State
▲ Customary

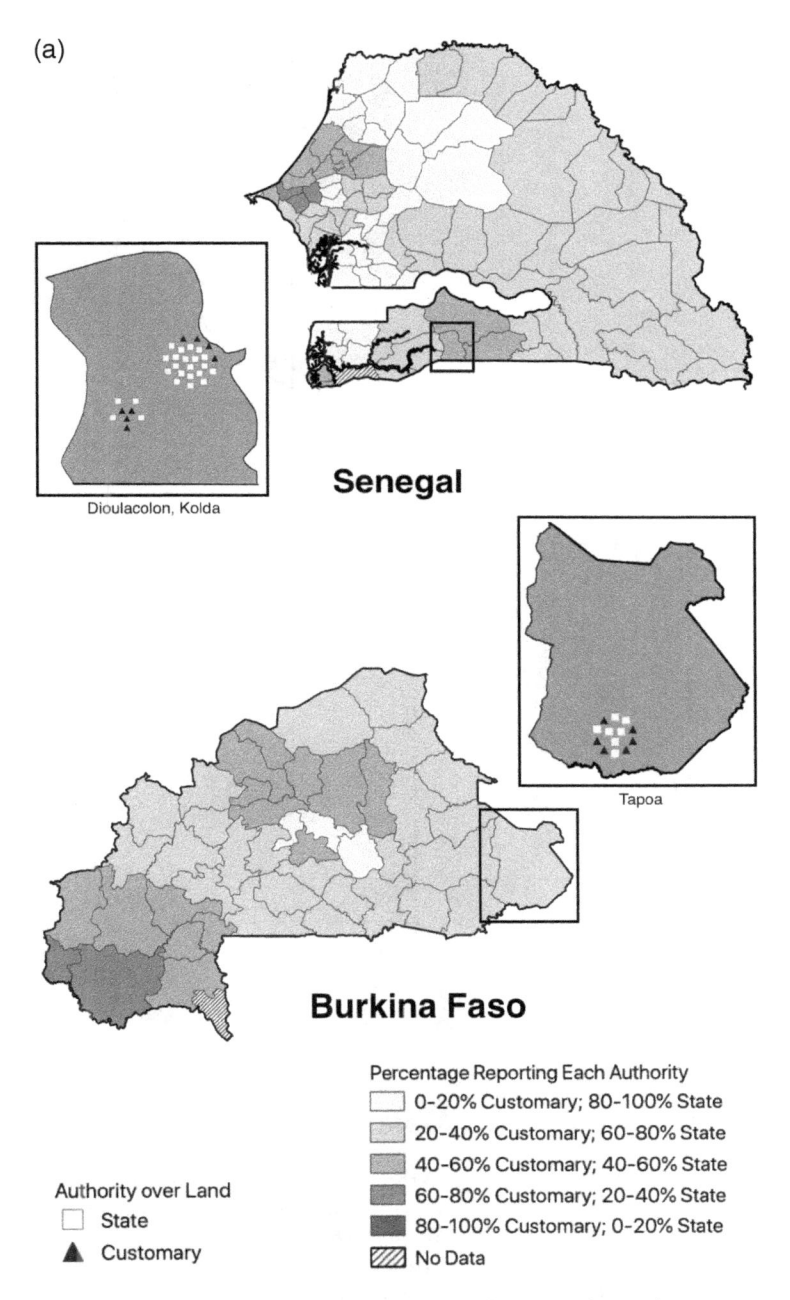

Percentage Reporting Each Authority
☐ 0-20% Customary; 80-100% State
☐ 20-40% Customary; 60-80% State
☐ 40-60% Customary; 40-60% State
☐ 60-80% Customary; 20-40% State
☐ 80-100% Customary; 0-20% State
▨ No Data

FIGURE 2.3. Subnational differences in land authority in four African countries
Notes: Figure reports the percentage of rural respondents within localities (enumeration areas) reporting that customary or state authorities govern land allocation.

(b)

Zambia

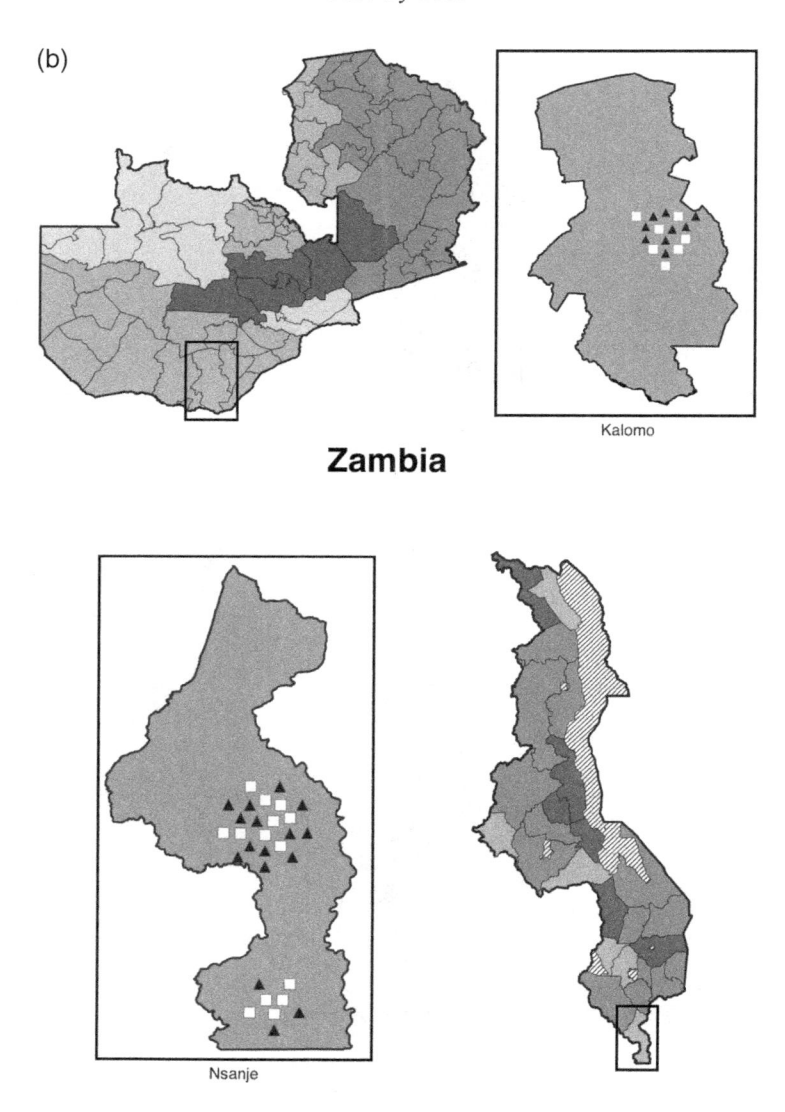

Kalomo

Nsanje

Malawi

FIGURE 2.3. (*cont.*) Inset panels map the individual survey responses within localities. Based on the question: "Who do you think actually has primary responsibility for managing each of the following tasks: Allocating Land." Response options were collapsed into a dichotomous indicator of: customary (options "traditional leader" and "community members") or state (options "central government," "state government," and "local government").
Source: Afrobarometer 2008.

The inset maps illustrate individual survey responses at the community level.[68] Black triangles represent individuals who reported customary authority over land; white squares signify an individual response of state authority over land. Each cluster depicts a random distribution of all of the responses in one GPS point, which represents one locality. The inset maps are thus visualizations of the cohabitation of both types of customary property rights at the hyper local level. Even within these small enumeration areas (or villages), authority over land is mixed: Neighbors believe that different types of authorities govern access to land.

The four maps in Figure 2.3 reveal some fundamental similarities among two former British colonies and two former French colonies. Institutional pluralism exists at the local level in all four countries, despite their differences in official chieftaincy systems and colonial land tenure policies. Regardless of former colonial power, the state's authority over land is geographically mixed within each state. On the other hand, respondents in the two former British colonies were overall more likely to report customary authority over land than respondents in the two former French colonies. As we might anticipate, de facto customary land authority is greater in the two countries with official chiefs.

Figure 2.4 examines these cross-national patterns of institutional pluralism among a larger set of African countries. The graph illustrates the percentage who reported customary control over land, disaggregated at the lowest available subnational administrative unit in nineteen countries sampled by the Afrobarometer. The values on the X-axis reflect citizens' (dis)agreement on who oversees property rights. The values of 0 and 100 represent complete agreement within the locality on which type of authority was responsible for land allocation. The gray box reports the middle 50 percent of the data, with the median marked in the center of the box. With a few exceptions, these boxes are clustered in the middle of the distribution, indicating a common pattern of disagreement about who controlled land within each locality. Some citizens' experiences led them to believe it was the state; others believed it was a customary authority. This highlights that customary and state authority over land are mixed even at the local level in each country.[69]

---

[68] Border districts were selected for the inset maps for clarity of the figure.

[69] Combined responses within the nineteen-country sample were traditional leaders (32%); local government (31%); central government (27%); community members (7%); state government (2%). N = 15,175. Figures 2.3 and 2.4 include "community members" in the indicator of customary land governance to represent non-statutory allocations of land. This includes village councils and other leadership that respondents do not consider to be

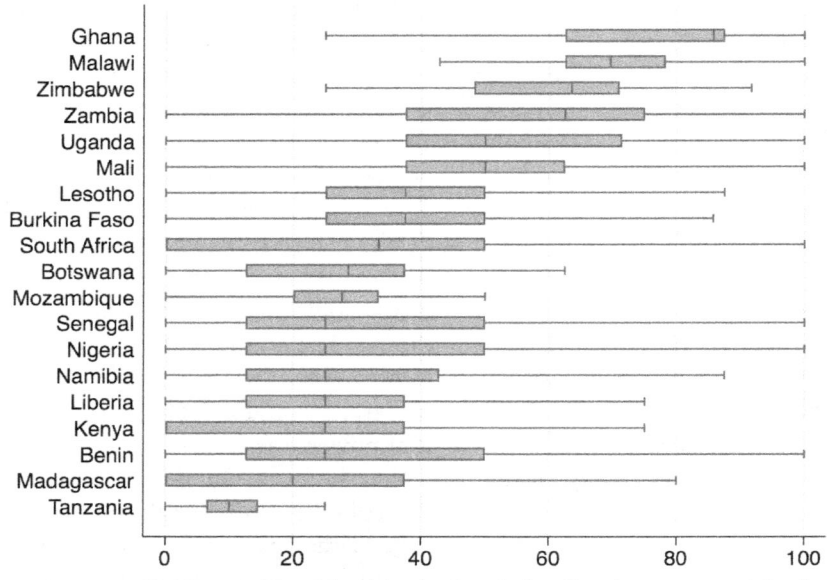

FIGURE 2.4. Evidence of local-level institutional pluralism in property rights in nineteen African countries
Notes: Figure reports the percentage of rural respondents per locality (enumeration area) reporting that customary authorities govern land allocation. Countries arranged from highest to lowest median reported customary control of land per locality. Based on the question: "Who do you think actually has primary responsibility for managing each of the following tasks: Allocating Land." Response options were collapsed into a dichotomous indicator of: customary (options "traditional leader" and "community members") or state (options "central government," "state government," and "local government").
Source: Afrobarometer 2008.

Across countries, the extremes prove the rule: Local institutional pluralism is present even in the countries with the highest and lowest customary control over land. Figure 2.3 arranges each country from highest to lowest median customary control of land per locality. Ghana has the strongest customary authority over land in this data set. There, the majority of respondents in most sampled communities of the country reported that customary authorities govern land access. Notably, the five countries with the highest median customary control of land are all former British colonies, an indication that the British colonial system of

---

part of the local government. For example, Madagascar has a very high response rate of "community members" (18%), in reference to their *fokonolona* councils of village notables and elders.

land tenure described in Chapter 4 impacted the role of customary authorities beyond the Zambia case. Nevertheless, there are British colonies at both ends of the spectrum, signalling the importance of the independent governments' institutions as well. Among the countries in this sample, Tanzania has the lowest reported customary influence over land. After independence in this former German and British colony, President Julius Nyerere's government weakened customary institutions by physically moving people through forced villagization programs, among other policies.[70] Yet even on the extremes of this nineteen-country spectrum, property rights are spatially uneven and mixed. In Ghana, some citizens reported state authority over their land rights, even if the majority in their locality relied on customary authorities. In Tanzania, one in ten respondents in the median enumeration area reported that it is not the local or central government but a non-state authority who governs land, consistent with the broader regional trend of institutional pluralism.

Situated in the middle of the distribution, Zambia and Senegal represent typical cases among the surveyed countries. As Figure 2.2 also illustrated, Zambia had greater reported customary control of land than Senegal, consistent with the official role of Zambia's chiefs in land governance. Figure 2.3 shows that 25 percent of citizens reported that customary authorities control land in the average locality in Senegal, in contrast to 61 percent in Zambia. Further, both countries feature considerable spatial variation in the extent of the state's land authority (represented by their 0–100 ranges). In some localities in each country, all sampled citizens agreed that customary authorities control their land and in others, all citizens reported that the state is the land authority. However, overall, institutional pluralism within localities was the most common scenario in both Zambia and Senegal.

Piecemeal Land Titling

Understanding these property rights patterns and the limited reach of the state requires attention to the mechanics of altering land authority. One driver of institutional pluralism in property rights is the incremental and piecemeal expansion of land titling. Each new title on customary land shifts the proportion of land under customary or state authority within a

---

[70] See Hydén 1980; Moore 1986; Lal 2015. In addition, British indirect rule did not begin in Tanzania until 1926; Tanzania's colonial chiefs were never empowered to the same degree as in other former British colonies, including Zambia.

country; for all of the reasons described in Chapter 1, titling land builds the state's authority. However, it is also expensive and it would require high state capacity to register all of the land in a country. Titling involves labor from bureaucrats and land surveyors to document land rights and adjudicate competing claims, among other costs. As a result, most countries in Africa have established legal frameworks for piecemeal land titling, in which applicants on customary land can register their land rights and access titles where none existed before, as demand arises. These policies generate a fragmented but unidirectional process of expanding state authority over land. Due to this type of titling, property rights regimes are not only mixed, but they are continually changing.

Piecemeal land titling is not a recent phenomenon in African countries. As Clement Ng'ong'ola described, President Hastings Banda of Malawi advocated increased land titling to parliament in 1967 by arguing that, with customary tenure, "No one is responsible... for the uneconomic and wasted use of land because no one holds land as an individual... everybody's baby is nobody's baby at all."[71] However, land titling in African countries became an even greater policy priority toward the end of the twentieth century. Processes of democratization and economic liberalization in the 1990s were accompanied by renewed attention to the potential benefits of land titling. Policymakers and researchers lauded titling as a means of increasing individual rights over land and facilitating land markets. They argued that both small-scale and large-scale investment required commodification of the land. For example, Hernando de Soto's *Mystery of Capital* helped advance the claim that increasing access to land titles was the key to economic development.[72] He argued that the world's urban and rural poor could not leverage their most important asset – their land – without titles. This narrative established informal land rights as the key barrier to economic development, much like President Banda's claims in 1967. International institutions and consultants promoted the doctrine of land titling, with references to the World Bank's 1975 Land Reform Policy Paper, which encouraged replacing customary land tenure with formal, fully commoditized land rights. The recommendation to low-income countries globally was to implement market-oriented land reforms.[73] This was and continues to be an influential approach to land tenure reform.

---

[71] Ng'ong'ola 1982, 115.   [72] de Soto 2000.
[73] For analysis of the World Bank's role in promoting the doctrine of land titling, and how its approach has changed, see Deininger and Binswanger 1999; Manji 2006. For critiques of this approach, see Musembi 2007; Bromley 2009.

In this period, governments across the continent reconsidered and debated their land policies, motivated by the goal of increasing land registration. In Zambia and Senegal, piecemeal land titling was available before 1990. However, both countries conformed to regional trends by streamlining (in Zambia)[74] and decentralizing (in Senegal)[75] the process. Policy reforms elsewhere expedited bottom-up (piecemeal) land registration. This included policies designed to encourage land titling in Benin (1993 and 2007); Burundi (2011); Cameroon (2005); Guinea (1992 and 2001); Kenya (2012); Madagascar (2005); Mali (2000); and Rwanda (2004). Such reforms reflect state priorities; in practice, plenty of bureaucratic and political obstacles to land registration remain. However, such laws make it possible for individual actors to initiate land titling, in contrast to an exclusively state-led or top-down process. Laws that encourage piecemeal land registration facilitate state building while allowing demand from private and public actors to dictate which areas of land are titled first.

These national policies expedite piecemeal land titling, but local-level politics determine which land transfers to state authority and which remains in the customary domain. In both Zambia and Senegal, land titling begins at the local council. These councils are a combination of elected councillors and bureaucrats tasked with technical assistance.[76] Applicants for land titles must deliver a set of documents to the local council and pay administrative fees, including costs for mapping and surveying land. Each council then meets to deliberate and vote on all of the land titling applications submitted in a given period. Some applications are scrutinized only insofar as they have submitted all required documents; title applications for larger and more contentious land deals generally receive more discussion and debate. The documents the councils generate are the first step in the titling process. In Senegal, the local council's document is an extract of proceedings (*extrait de délibération*). The equivalent document in Zambia is known as the district council recommendation letter.

---

[74] Republic of Zambia. *Lands Act*, 1995.
[75] Republic of Senegal. *Loi 96-06 du 22 mars 1996 portant Code des collectivités locales*, 1996.
[76] Zambia's elected district councils were established in 1991 through the *Local Government Act* and *Local Government Elections Act*. See Chikulo (2009) for analysis of this decentralization process. In Senegal, the rural council system began in 1972 and gained increased authority over land governance in 1996 through laws *Loi 72-25 du 19 avril 1972 relative aux communautés rurales* and *Loi 96-06 du 22 mars 1996 portant Code des collectivités locales*.

The local council's approval is the first stage for titles on customary land of all sizes and initiated by all actors. Both farmers titling their small plots of customary land and multinational corporations or urban elites seeking titles for large commercial agriculture investments seek approval at the local council. Similarly, public sector actors initiating titling to service the government's development agenda, such as resettlement schemes and state farms, pass through the same titling process as private deals.

Following approval from local councils, titling applications advance through the state bureaucracy. In Zambia, they proceed to the Ministry of Lands and Natural Resources. In Senegal, land registration and titling are functions of the Ministry of Finance; land governance is explicitly linked to the state's fiscal revenue.[77] Applications move slowly through this multistage process. As a result, citizens often use early stage statutory documents to reinforce their property claims, prior to obtaining the final documents. Most titles in these countries are leasehold titles, which the government issues to applicants after registering the parcels of formerly customary land in the state's property regime.[78] These leases can be sold and used as credit in the banking system. Yet both states also reserve the right to revoke a long-term lease if land taxes are unpaid or the land is left undeveloped for years. Regardless of whether the individual owners of the leasehold change, the shift in legal status of the land remains. The local council is thus a key step in the expansion of state land authority through incremental titling.

Opportunities for Local Agency in Land Titling

The bureaucratic procedure for translating demand for titles into statutory land documents may appear straightforward on paper, but in practice, it is highly uneven, as local actors have the opportunity to thwart or facilitate these shifts in property rights. In Senegal and Zambia, customary authorities can exert significant agency in the land titling process before the council issues a written decision on an application. However, their capacity to influence diminishes once the application passes through

---

[77] This section reflects the process in each country in 2014. Names of ministries are prone to changing.
[78] Freehold titles, with complete rights to a private individual in perpetuity, are no longer available to applicants. Since 1994 in Senegal, agricultural land can only be leased. In Zambia, The Land (Conversion of Titles) Act of 1975 transformed all freehold titles into ninety-nine-year leases.

this preliminary stage in the conversion process. Therefore, the key opportunities for customary authorities to intervene are during and prior to the councils' deliberations.

In Zambia, chiefs have an official role in determining whether the local council grants a title, as each application to register customary land requires the written consent of the chief. In some cases, this documented consent is in the form of the chief's thumbprint, but it is most often a letter or map signed by the chief. Zambia's chiefs can, and often do, refuse to consent to new land titles in their zones. When they do so, the land titling process stops there. This mechanism for chiefs to exert influence on titling is fairly straightforward because it is codified and then reinforced in practice. However, a second means through which customary authorities intervene in titling requires greater elaboration: informal influence over councils.

Even without official veto rights over applications for new titles on customary land, chiefs can impact the adoption of land titles through their influence on council members or other official decision makers. They can advise councillors against granting a title or maneuver to elect representatives of their customary institutions to the council. Senegal provides an example of unofficial channels for influencing land titling. In Senegal, chiefs have no legal authority to block a land application that they find displeasing. Councils may call upon customary authorities during their deliberations to provide oral testimony of the current land usage in their zones. However, this role is only consultative, as councils have the statutory right to approve titling requests for any land users in the community and for large land buyers who promise to develop the land, regardless of the consent of customary authorities. Thus, the council has the legal authority to ignore the recommendations of chiefs, but, in practice, a chief's approval or disapproval can weigh heavily on their decision.

Council members in Senegal described being beholden to the consent of customary authorities for land titling applications due to the chief's local legitimacy and social power. They reported the fear of social backlash as a reason for denying land titling applications that did not have the customary authority's support. When asked if they could give a title without the approval of the village chief, council presidents responded that they "wouldn't dare ... nothing can move forward without his consent"[79] and "it's impossible."[80] For their part, customary authorities

---

[79] Interview with rural council member (RC-151), central Senegal, October 29, 2014.
[80] Interview with rural council member (RC-109), northern Senegal, September 23, 2014.

reported that this could never happen because "it's the village chief who declares the truth of the property rights of the applicant. Therefore, the rural council president cannot do anything without him."[81] Customary authorities are thus "unavoidable" in the council's politics of land allocations.[82] They can use their local influence and knowledge of the community to impact how the council interprets the state's land laws and who it deems qualified to access a land title.

The phenomenon of customary authorities exerting influence over the council's land titling decisions is not universal throughout Senegal, but it is common. Local councillors refer to the practice of abiding the recommendations of customary authorities with the Wolof language word *masla*.[83] This term represents making decisions based on social expediency or moral relativism, even if it diverges from the law.[84] For example, one council president invoked the concept to explain his obligation to follow the advice of customary authorities, saying that:

The masla is a strategy for preserving social peace. Instead of applying the law the way it is supposed to be, you apply the spirit of the law ... it's a way of contributing to social cohesion because if you must apply the law precisely, it will mean that there will be a lot of social problems. That's the masla: what you need to do but you avoid doing it so you don't disappoint or create problems.[85]

This idea represents the practical constraints of decentralized local councils in Senegal and the reality that they are embedded in societies structured by customary institutions. Conforming to the expectations of customary authorities helps them function more effectively. As Abdourahmane Ndiaye has argued, these elected councils gain legitimacy "by carefully avoiding rupture with local customary laws."[86] Ngone Diop Tine and Mouhamadou Sy described this difference between law and practice at the local level as a product of "socio-cultural inertia."[87] Decentralized governance structures such as Senegal's councils have the potential to empower local populations with more decision-making

---

[81] Interview with customary authority (CA-149), northern Senegal, September 5, 2014.
[82] Plançon 2009, 847.
[83] Interviews with rural council member (RC-108), northern Senegal, September 16, 2014; with rural council member (RC-127), central Senegal, October 27, 2014.
[84] For other examples of masla (or massla), see Alissoutin 2008, 56–57 and "Sénégal: Laxisme, 'Masla' et Gestion Informelle de l'Etat: le Cpc Tient Me Wade pour Premier Responsable," *Sud Quotidien*, October 15, 2002.
[85] Interview with rural council member (RC-127), central Senegal, October 27, 2014.
[86] A. Ndiaye 2019, 149.   [87] Tine and Sy 2003, 219.

2.2 Land Authority and Property Rights in Africa

power. Yet councils can also serve as an extension of the customary institution or an individual chief.[88]

The potential to be rejected by the local council due to the official or unofficial disapproval of customary authorities makes prior negotiations for land titles exceedingly important. These early discussions are additional opportunities for customary authorities to impact which land shifts to state property rights. Savvy investors, bureaucrats, and citizens meet with chiefs before submitting applications to the council. They negotiate with customary authorities, attempting to obtain their official or unofficial recommendations. When customary authorities generate high barriers or costs to obtaining a title in one location, applicants may seek out different zones of customary land. Such negotiations allow customary authorities an additional opportunity to influence where land titling takes place.

Finally, customary authorities exert agency over piecemeal land titling outcomes through the provision of information. In addition to their ability to consent to or refuse land titling attempts, chiefs can determine whether local populations believe that titling is suitable or available to them. Citizens turn to chiefs for information about land governance, including information on how to obtain a land title. In my Senegal survey, 60 percent of the sample population of smallholder farmers reported that a customary authority was their source of information about land titling; 34 percent reported that they obtained information from the council.[89] Chiefs have the opportunity to discourage or encourage land titling in their domains, in their role as a source of information. For example, some chiefs in Zambia reported warning local citizens that the state will expropriate their land for unpaid taxes if they title it.[90] Customary authorities, consequently, have agency in the titling process through their ability to impact both the decisions of councils and potential applicants for land titles.

This chapter has so far introduced a key set of actors and institutions that govern land in the absence of state property rights in African countries. It has provided an overview of the meaning and prevalence of customary property rights. It has also introduced three key property rights patterns present in many African countries, including Zambia and

---

[88] Such capture of decentralized structures by customary authorities has been observed elsewhere. See Chiweza 2007 for descriptions of how political decentralization empowered customary authorities in Malawi.
[89] Author's Senegal smallholder survey, 2014.
[90] Interview with customary authority (CA-556), northern Zambia, January 14, 2014.

Senegal. First, the state's control over property rights is partial. Second, there are a mix of property rights institutions, even at the hyper local level. Some land has been mapped and registered in state titles, while other land is governed by informal rules administered by customary authorities. Third, the proportions of customary and state land are continually changing as a result of piecemeal land titling. The percentages of customary land per country depicted in Figure 2.2 and citizens' reports on land authority in their communities (Figures 2.3 and 2.4) are, consequently, snapshots of one moment in time because the state's land authority grows with each new title. The final section of this chapter examines major theoretical approaches for understanding the expansion of state power over land through titling.

2.3 WHERE DO LAND TITLES DEVELOP FIRST? ALTERNATIVE EXPLANATIONS FOR THE UNEVEN EXPANSION OF STATE CONTROL OVER LAND

The division of land between state and customary control is not static. Whereas more than 90 percent of the land in Zambia and Senegal was customary land at independence, state land authority has been steadily growing. Fifty years later, the proportions of customary and state land control are on the cusp of being equal in both countries.[91] What might explain where statutory land titles develop first and where customary control of land is resilient? This section examines existing explanations for this fragmented state-building process. State-centric approaches highlight the state's interests in titling certain areas of land in states with limited capacity to directly govern all land rights. In addition, market-centric approaches emphasize how changing land values induce demand for new property rights, such that titling occurs first on the most desirable land. In response to these approaches, Chapter 3 elaborates a new theoretical framework that centers the role of customary institutions in shaping how states and markets expand land titling.

State Capacity and Interests

To understand where land titling occurs, the first place to look for an explanation is the state, which has the power to compel titling and an

---

[91] See Chapter 1, footnote 35 for historical data. See Chapters 5 and 6 for contemporary estimates in Zambia and Senegal, respectively.

interest in implementing their stated agendas. States promote land titling due to its long-term effects on state power and capacity (as described in Chapter 1). However, state authorities also have shorter-term interests in advancing land titling, particularly when their policy agendas hinge on the ability to title customary land. In Senegal and Zambia, these policies include agricultural and land-intensive schemes intended to bring national economic and social benefits, such as zones of irrigated state land for smallholders; resettlement projects to promote urban–rural migration; and other schemes for state-supported farming. Similarly, state policies to diversify the economy by increasing agricultural investment and commercial farming also require land to shift from customary to state control. Such policies increase the state's opportunities to tax investors for their exports and for the use of land that was previously not revenue generating. Governments hope for a variety of additional benefits from facilitating commercial agriculture, including increased employment and infrastructure investments. However, in order to implement such policies, the state needs to be able to access customary land and convert it into titles. Without this ability, the state is weak – unable to translate its preferences into actions.[92]

The state is not only important because of its interests in facilitating titling; it also has the resources and power to register any area of customary land. The state has the legitimacy as a sovereign entity to do what it sees fit within its boundaries and can apply the principle of eminent domain to compel land conversions. Further, it benefits from the widespread narrative that land titling and agricultural investment are imperative for development. National and local developmental goals justify compulsory titling for small plots in rural, urban, or peri-urban areas, as well as for large land deals and state programs. Importantly, the state has a security apparatus to support its agenda, including by forcibly removing resistant communities.

Finally, the state's interests are also relevant to land tenure outcomes because its representatives – politicians and bureaucrats – have individual interests in translating demand into new titles. Politicians can derive personal benefits from successfully facilitating land deals as brokers between investors or state agencies and the community. They can demonstrate their political influence and gain financially from titling land in the name of the state's development agenda. Further, officials in the agencies tasked with agricultural

---

[92] Geddes 1994, 14.

development and investor support are under pressure to implement state projects. In Senegal and Zambia, projects are frequently planned in offices in the capital city, and then bureaucrats are tasked with accessing the required land. Failure by individual state agents to title a new area of customary land for a project or investor can have career repercussions, so state representatives also have a personal interest in implementing this state-building project.

Given the high stakes of land titling for the state, a state-centric approach emphasizes how the state's interests in certain areas of land should determine tenure outcomes. In states without the capacity to title all land at once, state actors will prioritize titling in some areas over others. If there were no local agency in the expansion of land titling, the state's interests would explain which land remains in the customary domain and where land transfers to state control. The geographic, political, and fiscal models that follow all provide insight into which land the state should try to title first.

Geographic models of state building focus on the increasing costs of expanding state power across space. Herbst elucidates a core-to-hinterland (or periphery) model in which state power expands from central nodes of political authority, such as capital cities and administrative centers, to rural hinterlands.[93] State authority weakens at greater distances from the bureaucratic core because the costs of exercising state power are higher. In this framework, it is easier to project state power in closer proximity to the core and more difficult in topographic peripheries. These costs of broadcasting authority in the hinterlands are exacerbated by difficult geographies and lower population densities; infrastructure development, such as roads and railways, decreases these costs of projecting state power. This core-to-hinterland framework has clear implications for the expansion of state power over customary land within countries.[94]

There is reason to believe that the expansion of state land authority would follow a similar pattern as other forms of authority, spreading from core to hinterland. The higher costs of projecting state authority at greater distances from the seat(s) of state power also apply to land tenure. Converting customary land to titles requires multiple interactions with the state. Individuals seeking titles must visit state offices to process their applications. Often, the surveyors who map the new state property rights on customary land are based in capital cities and government agencies.

---

[93] Herbst 2000.
[94] Herbst's own discussion of land tenure examines cross-national differences in the state's ability to weaken chiefs' influence.

2.3 Where Do Land Titles Develop First?

Similarly, the bureaucrats identifying customary land to title for state projects must visit the land in question; targeting land that is farther from their offices requires more time and resources. Further, the costs of projecting state power from core to hinterland may also reduce actors' incentives to seek titles on more distant land. Potential title applicants may anticipate that it would be harder for the state to enforce state rights in geographic peripheries.

Consequently, one implication of a state capacity model is that titling should develop first in core areas. It should be easier (or less costly) to replace customary rights on land that is closer to infrastructure and administrative offices. As a result, customary land tenure should endure in hinterland areas because they are farther from the seat of state power. A state capacity approach suggests that customary control of land is most resilient where there are geographic and structural challenges to projecting state authority. In addition, as the land within the same localities and districts has similar proximity to the seats of state power, this approach would anticipate limited local-level variation in titling.

A second model of the uneven expansion of state power emphasizes political considerations rather than distance. Not all land is equally desirable to the state. The state's priorities for where land titling develops first may reflect its political calculations. Land titling builds the state's capacity, yet state actors may have incentives to limit their capacity or to not invest in it.[95] State politicians may prefer to have weaker local bureaucratic and security institutions so they can increase their opportunities for clientelism[96] or reduce voters' expectations of them.[97] Similarly, states might circumscribe where individuals access land titles as a strategic political choice. This was a cornerstone of British colonial land policies, which were designed to reinforce the chiefs' power, as discussed in Chapter 4. Further, as Boone has described, states in the late colonial and post-independence periods implemented different strategies of territorial administration in response to variation in rural social structures.[98] In her framework, the state was most likely to choose a strategy of "usurping" customary institutions that were economically independent of the state and hierarchically organized; there, the state's interests in

---

[95] Besley and Persson 2010.
[96] Acemoglu, J. Robinson, and Santos 2013; Fergusson, Larreguy, and Riaño 2018.
[97] Gottlieb 2016.   [98] Boone 2003.

expanding land titling should be highest.[99] Kate Baldwin expanded upon this framework to show that state politicians built multiethnic electoral coalitions by increasing chiefs' power over land.[100] These approaches highlight that the state's representatives should have greater interest in expanding titling in some zones to weaken challengers to their authority and lesser interest in titling in other zones to reward collaborators. Further, they emphasize how strategic political logics have impacted where land titling is most desirable for the state: For both state actors and chiefs, land is a political resource.

The control of land is also an economic resource for the state. This suggests a third key factor shaping which land is more desirable to the state: revenue opportunities. The fiscal benefits to the state of titling an area or plot of land vary. Titling has administrative costs, such as boundary surveys, verifications of rights, and record keeping.[101] As described earlier, states rely on the piecemeal model of land titling when they do not have the resources to title all land within their boundaries simultaneously. The state may decree that it has legal authority over all land in the territory, but titling land is a lower priority unless the state has a particular taxation opportunity or project in mind. For example, titling the land of a subsistence farmer who has not sought title and lacks the resources to pay taxes and administrative fees for mapping the land yields fewer immediate benefits for the state.[102] The state has far more to gain when it facilitates titling for a parastatal company seeking to grow maize for export on a large parcel of customary land, for example.

These three models highlight that all land within the territory is not equally desirable to the state. The costs of extending power over geographic distances, political strategies, and fiscal calculations may all impact where the state's representatives would like titling to expand first. However, the process of titling land in Zambia and Senegal described earlier in this chapter reveals why examining the variation in state interests alone is insufficient for understanding land tenure outcomes in these countries. First, chiefs have agency, including the capacity to resist attempts by state actors to title land in their zones. Second, private actors

---

[99] The framework generates predictions about the state's institution-building strategies, but the book's case studies underscore that the strategies are not always successful due to local resistance.
[100] Baldwin 2014. [101] Bromley 1989; Murtazashvili and Murtazashvili 2015.
[102] Relatedly, Andrews, Pritchett, and Woolcock (2017, 57) described Afghanistan's attempt to title all land as "premature load bearing" for a fragile state.

also initiate land titling, so the state's interests are not always paramount. The following paragraphs expand upon these two points.

The state's interests in titling certain areas of land may not translate into land tenure conversions because their attempts may be resisted or rejected in local negotiations. State actors must balance their interests in implementing their titling agendas with calculations related to maintaining social stability and, in democracies such as Zambia and Senegal, winning elections. Recall from earlier in the chapter that state actors often rely on customary authorities to assist in local governance. Further, chiefs can encourage their followers to comply with the state's directives or to resist and protest a government initiative. For this reason, politicians openly court customary authorities during their campaigns. For example, in the lead-up to the contentious 2012 elections, Senegal's incumbent president, Abdoulaye Wade, provided lavish per diems to village chiefs for attending a conference. He also promised them salaries, which, if executed, would have been a first for Senegal's government.[103] In Zambia, the ruling party provided cars, on loan, to nearly half of the country's chiefs six months before the 2008 elections.[104] An angry customary authority can impede a governance initiative or cost political parties an election. Particularly when the state has lower capacity, bureaucrats and politicians must consider the need to maintain social peace.

The popular influence of chiefs makes titling land by brute strength alone an unappealing strategy for the state. Instead, state actors have incentives to comply with a process of local negotiations over customary land in which customary authorities and other local actors can refuse titling attempts. Although the creation of a new title is almost always in the state's long-term interest, in the context of low-density agricultural land, expropriating land from resistant customary authorities is also costly to the state. Consequently, state actors may prefer to look elsewhere for land to title than to force a land deal on a resistant customary authority. That attempts to title land by state actors do fail highlights the limitations of a state-centric approach. State interests may determine where the state's representatives attempt to expand power over land through titling, but they do not explain where they succeed.

---

[103] Note that these salaries were promised but never realized. See "Le Président Wade Annonce un Statut pour le Chef de Village," *Agence de Presse Sénégalaise*, July 19, 2011.

[104] "Govt. Hands over 150 Vehicles to Chiefs," *Lusaka Times*, May 11, 2008. This is also discussed in Baldwin (2016, 48–49).

Second, the state's interests in certain areas of land cannot fully explain where state property rights develop because the state is not the sole actor initiating titling in contexts with piecemeal titling policies. Such land titling policies encourage citizens, investors, and individual bureaucrats to initiate the process of titling land. In contrast to colonial patterns of state-initiated land divisions or compulsory land titling, piecemeal titling policies have allowed for bottom-up processes to build the state's land authority. They weaken the state's ability to engineer which land has customary or state property rights. Further, as demand for land, and therefore state revenue opportunities, increases in the era of booming land markets in Zambia and Senegal, it has become increasingly costly to tactically weaken the state's capacity to directly exert control over land in certain parts of the territory for political gains. This suggests the need for greater attention to explanations that model the expansion of land titling at the local level.

Markets and Land Values

Individuals opting to seek titles (or not) also impacts where state control over land develops. A second major explanatory framework for the subnational variation in titling focuses on how land values and competition shape demand for new forms of property rights. In this approach, shifts in the control over land are not the result of the state's choice of land to title, but of structural factors that induce individuals to seek titles. While state-centric approaches emphasize variation in the benefits of titling an area of customary land for state actors, market-centric approaches highlight variation in the value of titling for land users. The factors that increase the desirability of titling a parcel of land for the state and for private actors are often the same, but the two frameworks emphasize different sets of decision makers and processes of institutional change. In particular, scholars of induced institutional change (IIC) emphasize the bottom-up drivers of land titling. They focus on why private actors would pursue changes in property rights from complex, informal, and customary rights to individualized, formal rights that are legible to the state and markets. Given that private actors can initiate land titling under the piecemeal titling polices present in Zambia, Senegal, and most African countries, the IIC approach is an important framework for understanding where statutory rights develop first.

Induced institutional change approaches emphasize the effects of scarcity and land values on titling. Scholars studying "evolutionary" or incremental property rights transformations focus on changing factor values (or scarcities) that create demand for new institutions.[105] These frameworks rely on the logic that competition over more valuable land weakens the existing systems of property rights, pushing individuals to seek formal, statutory property rights. The higher the land value, the greater the incentive to adopt property rights institutions that generate exclusive and documented ownership.[106] Competition, scarcity, and value should consequently increase the likelihood of land titling.

One source of increasing land scarcity is population growth. Ester Boserup's work on demographic change is the foundation for many modern studies of land titling.[107] She argued that increasing population densities in agricultural communities prompt technological innovations, including the shift toward private property rights adjudicated by state authority. Other formulations of the IIC approach have highlighted a larger set of factors that can increase the value of land, such as technology, the commercialization of crops, and better transportation networks.[108] For example, John Bruce, Shem Migot-Adholla, and Joan Atherton interpreted patterns of greater individualization of land rights in zones of high population density in Ghana and high commercialization of agriculture in Rwanda as evidence in support of the induced institutional change hypothesis.[109]

Another branch of the IIC framework examines the expansion of titling as a product of the transaction costs of obtaining titles for populations living on customary land.[110] This is the central logic of Jean-Philippe Platteau's depiction of the "Evolutionary Theory of Land Rights." He explained that when land is abundant and conflicts between neighbors are infrequent, the costs of titling are high, relative to any benefit. However, this calculation shifts as population density and the commercialization of agriculture increases. Consequently, higher land values should render customary property rights increasingly insecure, prompting actors to turn to the state for the protection of individual property rights. Similarly, studies of land titling by Thomas Miceli, C. F. Sirmans, and Joseph Kieyah, as well as by Lee Alston, Gary Libecap, and

---

[105] Ahmad 1966; North and Thomas 1973; Ruttan and Hayami 1984. For a critical summary, see Grabowski 1988.
[106] Anderson and Hill 1975.   [107] Boserup 1965.   [108] Deininger and Feder 2001.
[109] Bruce, Migot-Adholla, and Atherton 1994.   [110] Platteau 1996, 2000b.

Bernardo Mueller, have modeled demand for land titles as a function of the costs of land registration relative to the value of land. In these two studies, factors that decrease the transaction costs of land registration, such as literacy and proximity to administrative centers, increase the likelihood that an individual seeks a title. Likewise, these frameworks predict increased titling on land with proximity to markets, greater agricultural suitability, and a higher monetary value because they increase the relative benefits of title.[111]

The same characteristics of land that induce institutional change among its current users should also make land more desirable to actors participating in global or domestic land markets. Wealthy investors and powerful politicians acquiring and titling customary land should first seek land that is more valuable, all things being equal. Actors responding to markets should prioritize customary land that is closer to urban areas, to state services, and to the infrastructure necessary for marketing agriculture. Consequently, explanatory frameworks based on land values and core-to-hinterland state building make similar predictions that titling should develop first in proximity to capital cities and transportation infrastructure. This book's empirical analyses will treat such structural factors, which impact land values and state reach, as alternative explanations for understanding where land titling occurs, testing their implications against those of the theory elaborated in Chapter 3.

However, individuals' evaluations of land values and the costs of adopting new property rights may also reflect the social and political relationships in their communities. Proponents of the IIC approach have proposed that ideology, vested interest groups,[112] and economic heterogeneity[113] affect the speed of institutional change. Further, shared, informal norms within a community can influence how land markets function. For example, Kathryn Firmin-Sellers argues that culture shapes the actors' "choice set" for the individualization of land tenure by dictating what the community accepts as fair.[114] Ensminger similarly highlights how concepts of fairness and justice influence citizen interest in new property rights in ways unanticipated by the classic IIC approach.[115] This suggests the need for further exploration of how local institutions condition

---

[111] Alston, Libecap, and Mueller 1999; Miceli, Sirmans, and Kieyah 2001.
[112] Ruttan and Hayami 1984. [113] Baland and Platteau 1999.
[114] Firmin-Sellers 2000a. [115] Ensminger 1992, chapter 5.

whether land values, population density, and transaction costs translate into demand for change.

Finally, even if individuals are highly interested in land titling in a given zone, customary authorities can influence whether this shift occurs and at what cost. Neither the market-centric IIC model nor the state-centric model sufficiently accounts for the agency of chiefs embedded in customary institutions, who impact how demand translates into outcomes. The state-centric and market-centric frameworks help us to identify which land the state should want to be successfully titled and where citizens should have the greatest interest in adopting titles, respectively. Yet, local agency in land negotiations impacts whether the land targeted by the state and private actors actually converts from customary to statutory property rights.

Therefore, understanding where state control over land develops requires further attention to the forces that influence local responses to titling. When state policies and land markets promote the expansion of land titling, how do customary institutions condition land tenure outcomes? Chapter 3 answers this question. It elaborates a new theory to help explain how customary institutions shape customary authorities' and citizens' evaluations of potential changes in the control of land. These actors' decisions produce – or prevent – the expansion of state property rights.

2.4 CONCLUSION

This chapter has covered a broad terrain. It has introduced the customary authorities, institutions, and property rights that are present in countries throughout Africa. It has challenged the image of dual land tenure as clearly divided, homogeneous zones of either customary or statutory land control, instead emphasizing the prevalence of institutional pluralism, in which property rights are mixed and regularly changing within communities. This is evidence of the patchy process of contemporary state building; future research should explore its myriad other potential consequences. For now, the focus is on how this situation came to be, and, therefore, why the expansion of state authority is uneven. This chapter has also introduced a key mechanism of change in property rights – piecemeal titling – and illustrated that there are multiple opportunities for local actors to impact where titling occurs in Zambia and Senegal. Attention to local agency, and the institutions that constrain these agents, has important implications. It suggests that state control of land is not partial and mixed by design. Instead, approaching this state-building process by investigating the decisions of local agents highlights how institutional pluralism is actively maintained and cultivated at the local level. Customary authorities and the institutions in which they are embedded have a profound influence on how state property rights develop and where customary tenure remains. The pages that follow describe why this is the case.

3

Why Institutions Matter

A Theory of Collective Costs and Customary Constraints in Land Titling

Heated protests over the loss of customary land rights periodically arise in developing countries throughout the world. These became more frequent in African countries in the first two decades of the twentieth century, due to increased pressure from global and domestic land markets. African citizens have mobilized against large-scale land deals initiated by state actors and state-backed investors, condemning them as land grabs from rightful owners. In Malawi, for example, community members carried hoes, knives, and signs stating "the land belongs to us; we will not allow anyone to grab our land" to protest the lease of a large area of land allocated by a chief to a politician.[1] In northern Uganda, dozens of elderly women stripped in front of government ministers, police, and hundreds of community members to protest a land lease on customary land. They chanted "our land" while drawing on cultural taboos against nudity to highlight the severity of the encroachment.[2] In Senegal, citizens plastered posh areas of Dakar with graffiti saying "No to agribusiness that grabs our land" and protesters rallied against land deals on customary land with posters proudly declaring "our land, our soul." Populations in Zambia have similarly mobilized against land deals in public demonstrations with signs asserting "Land is life. Leaders find alternative land for our families."[3]

---

[1] Steve Chirombo-Mana, "Communities March against 'Land-Grabber' Ex-minister Khembo," *Nyasa Times*, August 4, 2017.
[2] Catherine Byaruhanga, "The Ugandan Women Who Strip to Defend Their Land," *BBC Africa*, June 1, 2015.
[3] E. C. Hatimbula, "Land Is Life, Let's Protect It!" (Zambia Land Alliance Presentation, SIDA Conference, Lusaka, Zambia, November 10, 2010).

Such protests are popular reactions to changes in the control and use of land. They involve a wide range of actors and grievances, which vary considerably by country. However, two key themes are recurrent. First, they show just how important land is to local communities, as a social good (i.e., "our soul") as well as an economic resource. Land deals are highly political because land is more than a vital factor of production. For many, it is also a tie to community and ancestry. Put differently, the value of land is multidimensional. Second, these protests reveal frustrations with the process of transforming land control and, in particular, the distribution of the benefits of these deals. Citizens lament the loss of customary land that is currently in use or is needed for future generations. Moreover, they mobilize protests against political elites and structures that have excluded ordinary members of local communities from the benefits of such deals, particularly those that are large and visible. Land frequently exits the customary domain quietly, as a form of "silent privatization"; regular community members may not be aware that customary land has been titled until after the new registration is complete.[4] Citizens rally because the collective costs to such land deals are not accompanied by collective gains.

These protests reveal local dynamics that are critical for understanding shifts in authority over land more generally. They encourage us to focus on the potential costs of land titling, even those that are diffuse or unquantifiable. This includes costs to the customary institution's continuing power. Shifts in authority over property rights create political winners and losers. These institutional costs ground the theoretical approach of this book.

This chapter introduces a new framework to explain how customary institutions impact the expansion of land titling. It provides an alternative to the prevailing approaches, which focus on the state's capacities or interests in extending control over land and how land values induce actors to seek statutory rights. As the previous chapter described, negotiations with chiefs and local populations are pivotal to land tenure outcomes in processes of incremental land titling. Accordingly, we need new theoretical models to understand the forces that impact local agency in land negotiations. The theory proposed here examines how customary institutions shape chiefs' responses to land titling attempts and citizens' evaluations of titling for their own land. In doing so, it contributes new insight into the political relations that structure changing property rights regimes.

---

[4] Chitonge et al. 2017.

A basic collective action scenario helps illustrate when and why customary institutions become salient for land titling decisions. On the one hand, there are collective benefits to retaining customary control over land for members of the institution: It conserves existing norms of resource use, access to land for members, and/or the institution's power base. On the other hand, there are also compelling individual benefits to facilitating titling, such as material gains and political rewards for chiefs or the ability to eschew customary land use norms for citizens. Given these concentrated benefits, members acting in their own self-interest will erode the customary institution's power over land. However, customary institutions can shape members' incentives and make them less likely to pursue land titles, thereby preserving the institution's land authority. Customary institutions can generate mechanisms to hold chiefs accountable to collective goals of maintaining customary control over land. They can also reduce citizens' demands for statutory property rights by providing them with reasons to invest in the long-term survival of the institution's power base.

This model establishes how customary institutions can induce members to prioritize a collective goal of retaining customary land control, given individual benefits. However, customary institutions are not all equal: Stronger institutions are better able to constrain the individual choices of their members– and, of course, institutions that are better able to constrain the choices of their members become relatively stronger. Attention to this dynamic process over time reveals how historical legacies can continue to shape contemporary outcomes, through differences in institutional strength. In Senegal and Zambia, institutions that independently developed hierarchical structures were endowed with a stronger organizational capacity. Their ability to slow the loss of institutional power reinforces the contrasts between strong and weak institutions. Land titling, consequently, provides a window into the persistence of legacies of hierarchy in these countries.

The chapter proceeds by describing these two components of my theoretical framework. First, it explains how customary institutions can shape individual incentives for members when there are trade-offs between collective costs and individual benefits. Second, it identifies the importance of the variation in an institution's ability to do so. Combined, these two components predict how customary institutions impact their leaders' responses to land titling. They also reveal why we would expect a citizen to respond differently to the opportunity to title his or her land in the absence of a customary institution that structures privilege in the community. The final section of the chapter summarizes the observable implications of this theoretical framework, which will be examined throughout the book.

3.1 COLLECTIVE COSTS AND CUSTOMARY CONSTRAINTS: HOW CUSTOMARY INSTITUTIONS IMPACT LAND TITLING

Why do customary authorities agree to cede customary land to state property rights? Why do regular citizens replace their customary rights with titles? Land titling offers clear benefits to local actors – customary authorities receive personal economic and political rewards for participating in large land deals; citizens seek titles when they expect it will improve their personal circumstances. When these two sets of actors respond positively to land titling opportunities, state control over land expands. Yet land titling attempts that would be privately beneficial regularly fail, even on land that is used seasonally or extensively (i.e., non-intensively). To understand these outcomes, we must consider the potential for both concentrated benefits and collective costs to changes in the control over property rights.

The Foundations for Collective Action in Land Titling

Concentrated Benefits for Customary Authorities
The concentrated benefits for customary authorities of agreeing to land titling are evident to even the most casual observer of land politics in Senegal and Zambia. As described in Chapter 2, these local elites wield a great deal of influence in the land conversion process. State representatives, investors, and smallholder farmers pursuing land titles seek their official or unofficial consent. Customary authorities, in turn, have the power to decide under what conditions to agree to land titling. Each negotiation over land presents an opportunity for customary authorities to benefit personally from the conversion of customary land.

The material benefits to individual chiefs are one key reason why they do agree to land conversions. These payments can be significant, particularly for customary authorities living at the same economic level as smallholder farmers in their communities. First, applicants offer money and in-kind gifts as compensation directly to the chief.[5] For large-scale

---

[5] For examples, see Brown 2005.

land deals, in-kind material benefits may include livestock, groceries, homes, and cars. For smallholder titling, customary authorities often gain "tribute" in the form of small cash gifts, chickens, and portions of the harvest. Second, as representatives of their communities, chiefs may also accept benefits earmarked to be distributed to the entire community. Thus, they can negotiate with investors or state actors for cash gifts as compensation for the loss of customary land and become personally responsible for allocating it within the community.

Customary authorities may also facilitate land titling in hopes of gaining political favor. As Chapter 2 described, chiefs derive power from their interactions with the state. Customary authorities may anticipate that building personal relationships and goodwill with politicians by agreeing to land titling requests will generate dividends in the future, such as responsiveness to their requests for state expenditures, favor in disputes, and empowering policies. Much like the calculations that undergird decisions to collaborate with politicians as vote brokers, customary authorities may opt to cooperate with the state-building project for material and political benefits. Consequently, the political advantages of being perceived as a cooperative chief (and the disadvantages of being seen as uncooperative or "difficult") are also key incentives for customary authorities to agree to cede control over land. Political favor should be particularly motivating in a system of official chieftaincy such as Zambia's, in which the state endows chiefs with official salaries and can take them away.

In short, customary authorities are encouraged to consent to titling by a variety of concentrated benefits. Although it is standard for investors seeking large plots of land to pledge community contributions such as creating jobs and building infrastructure, these promises of collective gains for the loss of customary land are difficult to enforce after the land has been titled.[6] They consequently have low credibility. Instead, with rare exceptions, the immediate benefits of land conversions are privately captured. For customary authorities who control this vital factor of production, these individual benefits are a compelling reason to agree to cede customary land to title.

Concentrated Benefits for Citizens

Much like the casual observer who would tell us that to explain a chief's willingness to cede customary land to title we should look at how much

---

[6] For examples of the gaps between promised and realized benefits, see Ng'ombe and Keivani 2013, 40; A. Ndiaye 2019.

cash was in the envelope he received, the conventional explanation for why a citizen seeks a title to her own plot of customary land is that she wants to increase her tenure security. A basic definition of tenure security is: the perception that one's land will not be expropriated now or in the future.[7] Security has a number of developmental implications. For example, citizens with high tenure security should be more likely to invest in their land, in part because they can capture the future returns on any investments they make.[8]

For individuals seeking a title to their land, anticipated improvements in tenure security are key concentrated benefits driving their decisions. Titling as a means to increase tenure security is the foundation for the induced institutional change (IIC) framework, as described in Chapter 2. The basic argument is that individuals seek new property rights when their current rights are insecure. They rationally opt for the statutory alternative as an improvement upon their existing customary property rights. There are a number of reasons why citizens might doubt the security of their customary land holdings. For example, individual chiefs differ in whether they provide strong or weak property rights.[9] In addition, citizens may perceive that the customary system is biased against them or unable to protect them from land expropriations by family members, neighbors, or well-heeled investors. Individuals seek land titles because it frees them from dependence on the customary institution for securing their property rights.

A title itself is written evidence of a formal, individualized land right. Some citizens are motivated to register their land rights because it produces a legal document, which holds greater weight in the banks that provide credit and in state courts than unwritten customary claims. By making land rights legible to those outside of the customary institution, titles can potentially increase a citizen's ability to invest in his land or to legally sell it. Further, citizens may seek titles because it allows them to assert individual ownership and prevent any encroachments or shared access to their land.

The concentrated benefits to citizens of obtaining an individual land title may be both economic and political, and can be broadly understood as anticipated improvements in the ability to continuously profit from and use one's land. Recall from the previous two chapters that land titling

---

[7] For in-depth conceptualizations of tenure security, see van Gelder 2010; Obeng-Odoom and Stilwell 2013; Simbizi, Bennett, and Zevenbergen 2014.
[8] See, for example, Goldstein and Udry 2008.   [9] Onoma 2009.

does not universally increase tenure security. However, *among citizens who take the initiative to seek a title for their plot of customary land*, this is a key individual benefit driving the decision.

These concentrated benefits to customary authorities and citizens are critical for understanding why local actors would facilitate land titling. Concentrated material and political benefits induce chiefs to consent to land titles that reduce the resources under their control. Citizens seek titles in anticipation of individual benefits in the form of increased tenure security or legible land rights. There are clear and compelling incentives at the individual level to facilitate titling. Yet, these concentrated benefits are not the only considerations for members of a customary institution.

Collective Costs to Members
Land titling replaces the customary institution's power over land with the state's authority. By definition, it reduces the amount of land within the customary land tenure system. This shift is permanent in Senegal and Zambia. Once the land is registered in the state's systems, it cannot then revert to being outside of state property rights. As a result, land titling is costly to two related collective goals: (1) maintaining long-term institutional power and (2) retaining the customary land domain for current and future generations of community members. The collective costs of reductions in customary land authority are shared by members of institutions (including customary authorities and citizens), but they are not distributed evenly among them. Expectations related to the distribution of these collective costs within an institution will be discussed later in the chapter.

The first immediate cost to community members to consider in a model of land titling decision-making is the loss of land that had previously been part of the customary land tenure system. Land titles for large-scale deals are the most visible example of this, as they involve land used by many households. However, titles of any size reduce the customary domain. Large-scale land deals may displace community members, pushing them to inferior land.[10] Local populations may lose the land they and their ancestors farmed for generations, as well as access to areas that are not actively cropped but are still central to their livelihoods, for accessing water, collecting firewood, and pasturing livestock. Even without displacement, transfers of land out of the customary domain may generate

---

[10] For examples, see Brown 2005, 93; Ansoms and Hilhorst 2014.

concern among members of the institution that future generations will need to compete with domestic and global land markets for access to land, or pay land usage fees to the state.[11]

Titling can also interfere with the complex systems of secondary land rights governed by customary institutions. A common complaint from citizens about both large- and small-scale land titling in their communities is that it "produces fences." Titling establishes private, individual rights to a plot of land, and can therefore replace any preexisting secondary or group rights that existed on the land, such as passages to waterways, shared grazing lands, and spiritual sites. Exclusive rights are, of course, useful to individual farmers (see "concentrated benefits for citizens"), but they can be harmful to the community's systems of risk management and secondary land rights.[12] Changes to the community's land use systems and available stocks of customary land are two widely referenced collective costs of titling to members.

These immediate costs coincide with reductions in the institution's long-term power and, therefore, the power of its members. Titling encroaches on the institution's influence over land governance and reduces the quantity of land under the institution's direct control. It diminishes the institution's jurisdiction by replacing it with the state's rules. For example, Moussa Djiré drew attention to these power implications in reference to statutory titling in Mali, arguing that "registering land ownership is not merely a technical operation. It is a key land policy option that perpetuates the colonial policy of securing a state takeover of land management."[13] Titling reduces the authority of customary institutions over a critical resource and its users.

Land titling can also be understood as being costly to the institution's power base because it decreases the number of people who exclusively rely on the institution for access to land. On customary land, citizens secure their land rights by complying with institutional processes and norms. Customary property rights are ties of dependence between land users and customary authorities (as well as other community members). This dependence may include obeying the directives of chiefs, headmen, elders, large landowners, and customary land councils, among others. In some institutions, it involves paying informal land taxes or tributes.[14] Further, the institution's control over land may also strengthen compliance with institutional obligations beyond those related to land, such as

---

[11] Chitonge 2019. [12] Bruce 1993. [13] Djiré 2007, 1.
[14] See, for example, Bierschenk and Olivier de Sardan 2003, 155.

abiding norms of appropriate behavior within a community. Land authority is thus a source of power for the institution's rules, processes, and authorities in multiple areas of governance and community life.

The control of land can also provide leverage for customary authorities and communities in relation to the state. The institution's ability to influence citizen behaviors, including contentious or electoral political participation, increases its representatives' bargaining powers with state actors and politicians. As a result, controlling the land of more people creates opportunities for members to lobby the state to further group (and personal) interests. This includes, for example, customary authorities brokering access to national public goods, such as roads and schools.[15] Beyond influence over populations, control over a resource desired by the state and private actors can also increase members' power. Members can gain tangible benefits from being part of a more powerful customary institution, as well as pride. Thus, in addition to reinforcing the influence of the customary authorities and elites that exercise power within a community, the institution's power over land can be a source of group power for citizens.

Members may also rely on the institution's continued control over land for revenue, by way of short-term and negotiable rental agreements on customary land. As a result, titling may also be perceived to be collectively costly due to its effects on how members profit from their land ownership. This is what Parker Shipton found when he investigated why land registration proceeded more slowly in regions with Luo institutions than in other areas of Kenya. He described how the "land patrons" within the institution were concerned about temporary users gaining permanent rights through titling. Further, "land elders" focused on the implications of registration for losses of both wealth and authority.[16] The institution's power over property rights may allow members to retain absolute ownership rights that they interpret as being inalienable – regardless of usage – and ancestral; viewed from another perspective, members may be committed to maintaining the customary tenure regime because it allows them, their fellow community members, and their descendants to continue to extract wealth in perpetuity as land patrons.

A few additional potential collective costs to land titling relate, again, to the institution's power. Introducing a new form of property rights into a community can reduce confidence in the existing land rights regime.

---

[15] Fokwang 2009; Baldwin 2016.   [16] Shipton 1998, 105.

When individuals title their land, they may create doubt about the value of customary property rights by endorsing its institutional competitor, state property rights. Further, the expansion of state property rights introduces competing forums for the adjudication of land rights conflicts. This can generate uncertainty, as the customary institution no longer has a monopoly on conflict resolution. For example, Doreen Nancy Kobusingye, Mathijs van Leeuwen, and Han van Dijk described how such "institutional multiplicity" slowed and undermined settlements of land disputes in Uganda.[17] While titling may increase tenure security for individual beneficiaries, it can render the customary property rights of other community members less secure.[18]

Titling also has the potential to change the "social fabric" of the community by introducing new modes of protecting land rights.[19] Customary institutions establish rules and systems of conflict resolution within the community. They facilitate collective action for local public goods provision, such as residents contributing labor or materials for repairing schools. However, citizens may gain greater autonomy from community obligations once they gain a title from the state.[20] As a result, the weakening of the institution's ties with the local population can impact social order within the community more generally. Of course, some community members may be happy to see this social fabric change. As with other consequences of weakening the customary institution, its costliness to members should be contingent upon their status with the institution. However, for the institution's power, reducing the strength of the community's ties to its leadership is undoubtedly corrosive.

Collective costs to land titling trigger the institutional responses described in the following section. Explanations for local responses to land titling have often highlighted the concentrated benefits that chiefs and citizens as individual agents stand to gain. Indeed, there are significant incentives for facilitating titling. A narrow focus on these individual benefits would lead to predictions that citizens are equally eager to title their own land but merely constrained by the material costs of accessing titles, or that customary authorities cede land any time a powerful politician or wealthy investor asks. However, these actors are embedded in customary institutions. The institutional costs to title make these calculations more complex.

---

[17] Kobusingye, van Leeuwen, and van Dijk 2016.
[18] Dickerman et al. 1989; Quan 2000, 37; Musembi 2007.   [19] Chitonge 2019, 219.
[20] Kajoba 2002.

The tension between collective costs and concentrated benefits of title is therefore the starting point for understanding how customary institutions impact the decisions of chiefs and citizens. These costs and benefits will vary greatly with each proposed conversion of land from customary property rights to state titles. For example, the collective costs for customary institutions are amplified in the case of large-scale and more visible land deals because they magnify the loss of institutional power and group access to resources. Titles for small plots of land initiated by citizens are less immediately costly to customary institutions, but they may nevertheless impact the power of the institution and the strength of everyone else's customary property rights. These costs to the institution's power base are why land titling is a political act, and not merely an inevitable evolution toward formalization.

Customary Institutions and the Challenge of Land Titling

Customary institutions retain their power over land when local actors prioritize the collective costs of titling, even in the presence of attractive concentrated benefits. Given that new land titles chip away at the customary land domain, each individual decision to facilitate a title can be understood as a defection from the goal of protecting an institutional power base. By examining shifts in land authority through a collective action frame, in which there are trade-offs between group goals and individual interests, we gain new insight into the survival of customary institutions and their ability to shape the expansion of the state apparatus.

Collective action theories describe the conditions under which individuals cooperate to further group goals. The central challenge in organizing collective action is the incentive for individuals to defect from advancing the group's interest. When benefits are collective and diffuse, individuals are prone to free riding.[21] A number of institutional solutions follow from this core insight. In particular, the domains of land and natural resource management have been a fruitful arena for understanding how institutions help communities overcome collective action problems to promote group interests. Elinor Ostrom and her collaborators have demonstrated how informal and local institutions allow members to manage shared natural resources, preventing the "tragedy of the commons."[22] More generally, their collective action approaches have illustrated that local,

---

[21] Olson 1965.
[22] Ostrom 1990; Gibson, McKean, and Ostrom 2000. See also Runge 1986. On the tragedy of the commons, see Hardin 1968.

non-state institutions greatly impact how community members respond to concentrated benefits and collective costs.

However, the land titling model proposed here differs from the classic collective action framework for natural resource management in two key ways. First, the collective outcome of interest is continued control over land, not sustainable resource use.[23] The collective good threatened by defections is the power of the customary institution, which has a variety of practical benefits for its members. Second, this land titling model relaxes the assumptions of a true collective action dilemma, in which everyone's interests are best served by the collective good outcome. This assumption reflects a game-theoretic prisoner's dilemma, but in reality, land titling outcomes are more complex than the classic dilemma model accommodates. Even in cases with high collective costs to the loss of customary land, the collectively optimal outcome and the individually optimal outcome may not be the same for land titling. The central insight from this scholarship, that local institutions can prevent defections from a group interest, is nevertheless important for identifying the role of customary institutions in shaping the individual choices that reduce the institution's power over land.

Customary institutions that cannot resolve this collective action problem risk the loss of power. Members' responses to titling attempts are therefore a source of bottom-up institutional change for the customary institution. Whether the institution remains influential depends on the choices of their members; as James Mahoney and Kathleen Thelen have described, institutions weaken when "institutional supporters of the old system prove unable to prevent defection to the new rules."[24] Land titling replaces the customary institution as the salient source of property rights rules. Thus, to retain power, the institution's representatives must prevent the new rules – state land titles – from encroaching on their domain, by making it harder or costlier to access titles there. This slows a bottom-up process of institutional weakening and increases the resilience of the institution's power.

Mechanisms of Accountability and Institutional Resilience

How do customary institutions resolve collective action problems and retain power? The collective action problem described here relates to the

---

[23] Relatedly, land in customary tenure regimes in Africa is generally not a true common pool resource.
[24] Mahoney and Thelen 2009, 16.

specific question of loss of control of land, as members respond to compelling incentives to transfer land out of the customary domain. However, scholars have illustrated that customary institutions are an important solution to other types of collective action dilemmas due to institutional characteristics that facilitate effective cooperation.[25] For example, collective action is more likely among groups that have regular, repeated interactions, which can generate trust and strengthen the bonds between members. Further, shared culture and traditions can increase prosocial norms and reciprocity.[26] They allow members to coordinate the group's expectations of each other's behaviors.[27] In addition, members of customary institutions are often relatively homogeneous economically and socially, which can decrease the temptation to free ride from collective goals. Groups with denser networks, such as co-ethnics, can more easily sanction and monitor collective behavior.[28] Finally, self-organized groups, with rules that are "locally devised," are better able to prevent defections from the collective interest.[29]

In the model of local responses to land titling described here, the actors with the greatest power to change the institution's resource base are its customary authorities. Customary authorities are special members of a customary institution; as leaders, they have more influence in the land titling process and therefore more opportunities to prevent or facilitate defections. One established institutional solution to collective action problems is for a leader (or hegemonic authority) to initiate cooperation and sanction "rational egoists" for deviating from a collective goal.[30] Chiefs can function as such hegemons by forestalling other members from replacing customary land control with land titles. However, to retain institutional power over land, members must also prevent defections from leaders. This is a significant challenge, given the individual benefits available to chiefs for large and small land conversions.

Many customary authorities wield power in relation to their communities without institutional constraints and can freely respond to the personal benefits of agreeing to convert large areas of customary land. Examples of such unconstrained behavior are plentiful. For example, Franklin Obeng-Odoom has suggested that "tribal chiefs frequently act

---

[25] Akinola 2008; Xu and Yao 2015; Goist and Kern 2018; Magaloni, Díaz-Cayeros, and Ruiz Euler 2019.
[26] Baland and Platteau 1996; Koopmans and Rebers 2009.   [27] Greif 1994.
[28] North 1990; Greif 2006; Habyarimana et al. 2009.
[29] Ostrom 1990; Baland and Platteau 1996; Agrawal 2001.
[30] Bianco and Bates 1990. See also, the Leviathan solution in Ostrom 1990.

in ways that enhance their material position."[31] Jesse Ribot described community frustration with chiefs in eastern Senegal who were "bought for a few sacks of rice."[32] Cyprian Fisiy identified customary authorities in Cameroon who "perceive the land registration process as a means of enriching themselves."[33] And in Zambia, Horman Chitonge found that "some chiefs have just fallen prey to the egoistic lure of money and the politics of patronage."[34] By ceding customary control over land, these chiefs weaken the very institutions from which they derive their authority.

Not all customary authorities are unconstrained, however. Customary institutions can generate accountability among their leaders by creating incentives for chiefs to comply with overarching institutional rules and interests. They can shape how customary authorities make decisions, pressuring them to consider group priorities. They do so by broadening the range of individuals who are involved in a customary authority's decision-making. This makes it harder for the customary authority to make autonomous decisions that are divorced from institutional interests. Establishing opportunities for the leader's decisions to be vetoed by other actors is a means of increasing institutional checks and balances. Such institutions create "constrained chiefs," who face institutional incentives to prioritize group interests. By contrast, "unconstrained chiefs" make decisions with greater autonomy from their institutions. Such accountability mechanisms are internal to the institution, and, given their informality, are easily overlooked.

Accountability among Elites

Institutions can constrain their leaders through entrenched rules and practices that generate ties of horizontal or vertical accountability. For an internal mechanism to change the behavior of leaders and create a constrained chief, it needs to increase the actor's incentive to comply with the institution's goals rather than pursue his or her personal interests. Two mechanisms for generating accountability among networks of elites and customary authorities within an institution are illustrated in this book: vertical systems of punishment and rewards and the horizontal coordination of constraints.

Institutions generate vertical accountability through hierarchical ties among elites, at different levels of authority, that can sanction individual leaders. Institutional features such as superior councils or clearly defined

---

[31] Obeng-Odoom 2012, 168.   [32] Ribot 1999, 36.   [33] Fisiy 1995, 60.
[34] Chitonge 2019, 217–18.

ranks among customary authorities facilitate monitoring and judging an individual leader's behavior. Institutions can provide clear and regularized procedures for such superior authorities to consider cases against chiefs or enforce punishments, including the right to dethrone him or her. Through hierarchical ties among chiefs, institutions can thus create "local accountability."[35] An institution that generates systems of punishment and rewards among upper and lower tier customary authorities is particularly effective at shaping a chief's behavior because its sanctions come from within the rules and procedures of the institution. When the leader's right to rule arises from the same set of regulations that has produced a punishment, it makes it harder for an individual chief to resist or delegitimize the sanction. An internally legitimate threat of sanction by other actors in the institution can create checks on a chief's decisions.

Even in the absence of functional hierarchies, customary institutions can shape leaders' incentives by creating ties of horizontal accountability. Customary institutions generate constraints on chiefs through entrenched expectations of consultation and information sharing. Institutional processes can broaden the set of actors who influence the customary authority's decisions by facilitating interactions among those who can effectively pressure him or her. In addition, they can foster group interest formation and the transmission of such interests to the chief. Institutional features such as consultation practices in which specific lineage elders or community actors regularly advise or challenge the leader promote horizontal accountability. Similarly, by establishing forums for regular public or group discussions,[36] institutions cultivate opportunities for members to communicate collective priorities to chiefs, to monitor chiefs' behaviors, and then to respond to chiefs' actions. Institutions can increase the number of actors with a voice in decision-making to counterbalance the power of an individual customary authority.

Further, horizontal accountability stems from an institution's capacity to facilitate the sanctioning of chiefs. Institutions help constrain chiefs by creating opportunities for social sanctioning from other members, which might include threats, harassment, or ostracism of a customary authority who defies the group interest.[37] The same institutional features that promote the communication of information and interests also encourage

---

[35] Gennaioli and Rainer 2007.
[36] A noted example of this type of public assembly is the Kgotla established by the Tswana customary institutions in Botswana. See Ngwenya and Kgathi 2011.
[37] For example, Valsecchi (2003) documents a case in which a paramount chief in Ghana was confronted and accused of wrongdoing by a gathering of several hundred elders, fifteen divisional chiefs and queen mothers, and citizens.

these forms of social sanctions. Notably, the ability to enforce horizontal accountability may be highly unequally distributed within the institution and the institution's own rules establish which members have greater influence over the chief's decisions. Customary institutions can thus generate social pressures and consultation processes that make it more difficult for the chief to ignore a collective interest, creating accountability without a vertical system of rewards and punishments. These institutional processes impact the decisions of customary authorities; in their absence, we would expect different responses to land titling opportunities.

An additional consideration is that state context impacts how customary institutions function today. The government's laws, policies, and practices shape how customary authorities and institutions mediate between citizens and the state. Official chiefs gain more power from outside of their customary institutions than unofficial chiefs, allowing official customary authorities to retain office with limited support from the local population. Further, Zambia's system of state recognition endows individual customary authorities with nearly complete official authority over decisions to cede land out of the customary domain. This generates a highly unequal power distribution within the institution, which undermines the customary institution's ability to coordinate horizontal accountability vis-à-vis a chief. However, as Chapter 5 illustrates, a strong internal system of vertical accountability can counter the concentrated power of an official relationship with the state. In contrast, in contexts with unofficial customary authorities, who are less protected by the state, horizontal accountability can more effectively constrain chiefs. If the continuing influence of customary authorities is highly dependent on their institutions and their members, social pressure and entrenched expectations of consultation should have a stronger effect on their decision-making. The chapters on Zambia and Senegal provide examples of these mechanisms in context. Importantly, even if chiefs have official (or formal) power, the institutional rules and processes that shape their behavior are internal to the institution. They should consequently be understood as informal institutional constraints.

Recognizing that some customary institutions can hold their leaders accountable, but others cannot, challenges both the romantic view of customary institutions and the narrative of chiefs as decentralized despots. Such accountability mechanisms were described in historical and anthropological analyses of African political institutions,[38] but have

---

[38] See Dia 1996, 39–41; Ayittey 2010 for additional examples and an overview of different systems of accountability within customary institutions in Africa.

received less attention within research that emphasizes how states created chiefs and manipulated customary institutions for political ends. However, recent scholarship has started to examine variations in political accountability in contemporary customary institutions, in part because it helps illuminate the persistence of citizen support for customary authority. For example, Kate Baldwin and Katharina Holzinger found that 30 percent of the traditional institutions in their global sample have mechanisms to dethrone a leader.[39] Their research also revealed additional accountability mechanisms actively in use, such as institutions that sanction their customary authorities by forcing them to apologize for misdeeds or justify their actions to the group.

There are thus several ways in which customary institutions can generate accountability to group goals, even among powerful chiefs tempted by concentrated benefits. However, the accountability at the heart of this framework is to the power prerogatives of the institution. Constrained chiefs are not necessarily downwardly accountable to regular citizens, particularly those without a voice in institutional political processes. Instead, these accountability mechanisms help explain how institutions prevent defections by individual chiefs that reduce its power base, which is a vested interest of elites and higher status members.

The Privileges of Membership: Increasing the Costs and Decreasing the Benefits of Title

This chapter has so far proposed that customary institutions affect the expansion of state property rights by shaping how local actors weigh the collective costs and individual benefits of potential titles. Yet the benefits of long-term customary power over land are not evenly distributed among members of the customary institution. The leaders who derive their authority from the institution should have a higher motivation to maintain its power. However, the unequal distribution of benefits from the continuation of customary control over land should influence other members' decisions as well.

Customary institutions impact whether citizens seek titles for their own land by shaping their perceptions of the collective costs of land titling. They can dampen a member's demand for new forms of property rights by making those collective costs more directly costly to the individual. This insight echoes the concept of asymmetrical benefits in Mancur

---

[39] Baldwin and Holzinger 2019.

Olson's classic collective action framework: When the collective good is not evenly distributed, those with higher rewards should be more motivated to contribute.[40] It follows that members who derive greater benefits from the institution's continuing power should be more invested in preventing the erosion of its control over land.

Which members stand to lose more from weakening customary institutions? To answer this question, we must examine the distribution of power within communities. Customary institutions structure social and political relations among citizens. These social structures may be exclusionary and inegalitarian.[41] A consequence of these structures is that customary institutions generate different levels of privilege based on features such as ethnicity, gender, age, marital status, caste, duration of residency, and lineage. Privileged members gain benefits that might include increased political power, social influence, and even land tenure security. The institution's role in shaping customary privilege produces asymmetry in the distribution of the collective costs of land titling. Privileged members have more to gain from the continued power of the institution, and more to lose when state property rights replace customary tenure, because their privileged status is tied to the institution's power. This, in turn, should impact individuals' evaluations of land titles.

Seeking title for one's plot of customary land is a form of exit from the customary institution's system of property rights. Individuals deciding whether to adopt a land title must compare the costs and benefits of exit. Customary privilege impacts these calculations by generating noneconomic costs (and benefits) to land titling. Individuals who would be negatively affected by a decrease in the institution's power base should be less likely to respond favorably to the opportunity to title. By contrast, exit from customary property rights is a welcome change for those who experience few benefits from the continuation of customary control of land. Chapter 7 expands this discussion with examples of customary privilege and the noneconomic costs of individual titling from rural Zambia and Senegal.

Examining the effects of the uneven distribution of privilege suggests that customary institutions decrease the likelihood of actors engaging in behaviors that weaken the institution's power base by generating greater

---

[40] Olson 1965.
[41] For examples, see Hilhorst 2000; Tripp 2004; Joireman 2011; Ouedraogo 2011, 91. For a discussion of the importance of recognizing inequality and social processes of exclusion within customary land tenure systems, see Peters 2004.

benefits to membership. They can thus create committed members who are invested in the long-term power of the institution because they more directly profit from it. This component of the framework has additional implications for the members who gain the most from the institution's power: customary authorities. In the short term, they can gain concentrated benefits by agreeing to land titling. However, they stand to lose the most from land titling in the long term because their privileges, and those of their family members, are tied to the institution's power. As a result, high levels of privilege should also provide disincentives for chiefs to jointly defect by ceding customary land.

Contemporary Institutional Strength

Customary institutions impact land titling decisions when there are trade-offs between group costs to the institution's control over land and individual benefits to members. They can create incentives for individuals to prioritize the continuation of customary tenure, by making defections costlier through the allocation of privileged membership. Customary institutions can also facilitate ties of accountability that prevent leaders from defecting from the collective goal, although the efficacy of different accountability mechanisms varies depending on the state context.

However, customary institutions do not have the same capacity to generate these tools of institutional resilience, ultimately contributing to subnational variation in the state's control over land. Some institutions are better at creating incentives for leaders and citizens to prioritize preserving the institution's power base. Others are too weak to constrain their chiefs or foster real ties of accountability. Heterogeneity among institutions is thus critical to understanding how they impact members' decisions. In particular, contemporary institutional strength helps explain the variation in local responses to land titling. In the cases of Zambia and Senegal, this strength has historical determinants.

The contemporary customary institutions in Zambia and Senegal trace their origins to two very different types of historical structures, which endowed them with distinct organizational capacities. As described in Chapter 1, some institutions underwent a long process of precolonial state building to develop the stratification of hierarchy above the village level. They endogenously developed state-like bureaucracies and complex political systems. This process generated nationalism, leaving them with strong group identities that reference symbols and mythologies of kingdoms or states. The residue of a long precolonial state-building process contributes to the strength among institutions born out of hierarchy relative to other customary institutions. Even as colonial and postindependence state regimes legislated changes in the power of customary authorities, the institutions in which these actors were embedded retained their heterogeneity, in part because the differences between strong and weak institutions are self-reinforcing. As a result, scholars including Jean-François Bayart have concluded that the colonial era more successfully weakened nonhierarchical ("acephalous") institutions than hierarchical ("centralized") institutions and social structures.[42]

In the countries examined here, the start of colonial rule is the appropriate benchmark for examining the legacy of hierarchy. The European conquest of Africa destroyed some precolonial power structures, while halting wars among precolonial polities and fixing the boundaries of new states. As described in Chapter 4, the aggressive campaigns of French conquest in Senegal were successful at razing existing power structures in some cases, although the strongest hierarchies survived this conquest. By contrast, the British in Zambia neither seriously attempted, nor succeeded, in radically reconfiguring the structures of strong precolonial institutions; their goal was to co-opt them. After the major exogenous shock of conquest, the start of colonial rule "locked-in" customary institutional endowments, contributing to differences in internal organization and institutional strength that were reinforced over time.[43] Further, also addressed in Chapter 4, the independent governments in Zambia and Senegal retained the status quo of land tenure and customary authority policies from the colonial era, thereby creating a fertile environment for these initial endowments to persist.[44]

The collective action model described earlier suggests a dynamic model of institutional strength. The historical structure of customary institutions is sticky because the initial differences in an institution's organizational capacity were difficult to overcome. Strength begets strength, as stronger institutions are better able to generate compliance with individual decisions that reinforce the institution's power. In doing so, they increase the value of membership in the institution and facilitate the increasing returns that contribute to institutional stability.[45] By contrast, the loss of

---

[42] Bayart 1989, 179.   [43] See Ikenberry 1994.
[44] For examining similar phenomena in countries outside of Zambia and Senegal, selecting the appropriate benchmark for the origins of institutional legacies requires attention to exogenous shocks that dramatically reconfigured institutional power and locked-in institutional endowments.
[45] Pierson 2000.

customary power and the weakening of customary property rights is a form of continued decreasing returns. Institutions that have a lower capacity to prevent defections should continue to get weaker, as the defections further reduce the benefits of membership. This shortens the time horizons of citizens and chiefs, who should perceive fewer long-term benefits to maintaining customary power over land. For them, reinforcing the institution's power base should become less valuable than immediate concentrated benefits of new titles. This decreases members' incentive to prevent defections from the institution. The inverse is true of strong institutions. Members of a strong institution should be more motivated to protect the institution's domain because it is stronger, as a consequence of other members also having a greater commitment to its continued power. In this way, the initial differences among institutions become self-reinforcing.

This is an argument for the stickiness of historical institutional legacies. Yet we also know that customary institutions are not static. For example, as described in Chapter 2, land tenure rules are prone to change over time as new crops and state policies are introduced. This also applies to an institution's authority structures: Even customary institutions that no longer have functioning structures of hierarchical authority benefit from the legacy of hierarchy. The process of precolonial state building provided an initial endowment of institutional strength that distinguishes these institutions from others. Despite changes in the rules within the institution, the legacy of hierarchy (or not) contributes to heterogeneity among contemporary customary institutions. Stronger institutions have greater capacity to prevent defections from their own rules, even as they adapt within the modern state. Focusing on variation in strength helps explain why hierarchical legacies have consistent impacts on contemporary outcomes in cross-national studies, despite the profound differences among countries in both the state's integration of chiefs and the functions of customary institutions.[46] The heterogeneity in the relative strength of these institutions should persist in the absence of dramatic exogenous shocks, as historical institutional endowments establish the trajectories of these institutions.

These self-reinforcing dynamics among institutions within the same country are particularly notable in the case of a fixed power resource such as land. This framework explains that stronger customary

---

[46] Gennaioli and Rainer 2007; Michalopoulos and Papaioannou 2013; Osafo-Kwaako and J. Robinson 2013; Bandyopadhyay and Green 2016.

institutions make it harder to acquire land in their domains, increasing the costs of titling for state agents, investors, and citizens. Since they are not reducing overall market demand for land within the country, this implies that stronger institutions push land deals (and migrating citizens seeking land to title) to zones with weaker institutions. The power bases of weaker institutions should therefore erode more quickly than those of stronger institutions. This reinforces the relative differences among customary institutions that share the same national context.

3.2 OBSERVABLE IMPLICATIONS FOR LAND TITLING

This theoretical framework produces a few observable implications about changes in land authority in Zambia and Senegal. It suggests that constrained chiefs should be more likely to prioritize institutional power in negotiations over land. They should thus be more likely to respond to attempts to title customary land with tactics such as outright refusals, protracted negotiations, demands for high payments, and the imposition of substantial conditions. Internal accountability does not imply that constrained chiefs block every potential land title, only that they make it more difficult for land to exit the customary domain. Constrained chiefs should increase the costs of titling in their areas relative to areas where chiefs are unconstrained, all things being equal. These higher costs will tend to result in a lower rate of land titling in areas where chiefs are constrained than in zones with weaker institutions.

Figure 3.1 illustrates this first observable implication of the theory of collective costs and customary constraints. The historical institutional endowment shapes the contemporary strength of the institution, which in turn impacts the institution's ability to constrain chiefs. Thus, even when new land titles offer concentrated benefits, these leaders face accountability to the potential collective costs. Further, chiefs in stronger institutions also have greater incentive to invest in the long-term power of the institution than chiefs in weaker institutions, who have shorter time horizons. This contributes to differences in land tenure outcomes: The theory predicts that there will be lower rates of land titling in zones with customary institutions with hierarchical legacies.

This pattern defies the predictions of the induced institutional change approach elaborated in Chapter 2. IIC models anticipate land titling will advance in high-demand areas, which might occur if the state's claims of de jure sovereignty over all land (with or without titles) reflected the on-the-ground reality of land authority. Policies in Zambia and Senegal

3.2 Observable Implications for Land Titling

Historical institutional endowment		Contemporary institutional strength		Capacity to generate internal accountability		Expected titling outcomes
Hierarchical	→	Stronger	→	Greater	→	Lower rates of land titling
Nonhierarchical	→	Weaker	→	Lesser	→	Higher rates of land titling

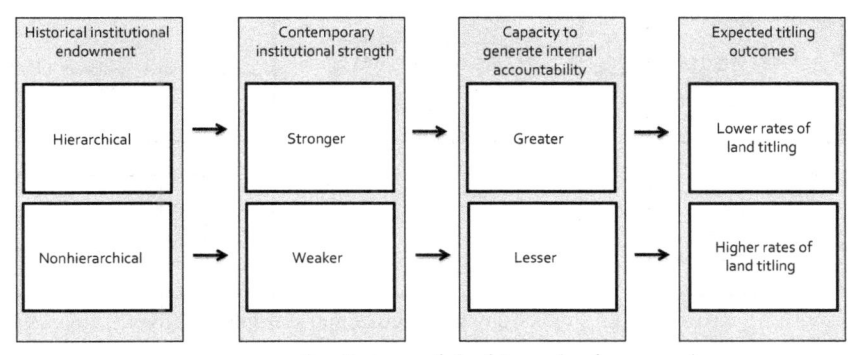

FIGURE 3.1. Predictions of the hierarchy framework

clearly establish the state's interest in allowing demand for titles to translate into the expansion of state control over land. However, when state property rights instead develop on less desirable land and community members describe active resistance to shifts in land authority, it highlights that the state is not all-powerful, and it therefore must engage with influential social forces – members of customary institutions and their leaders – in order to fulfill its agenda. This theory predicts that customary institutions can create outcomes that challenge the state's interests in formalizing land tenure.

Second, this theory has observable implications for variations in land titling within communities. Figure 3.2 illustrates what we should see if customary institutions impact the decisions of regular citizens with small plots of land. I have argued that institutions impact citizens' demand for new forms of property rights by shaping how they benefit from the local customary institution's continued power over land. For those who gain limited benefits from the institution, the costs of exit are lower and they can more easily defect from the goal of sustaining institutional power. This act of low confidence in the customary institution weakens it, making the citizen an important contributor to variations in the resilience of customary institutions. This theory predicts that citizens who are advantaged within their institutions will be less likely to adopt land titles. It implies, for example, that households with different levels of customary privilege would have distinct perceptions of the collective costs of title. The economic costs and benefits of titling may be the same for two households, but the household with customary privilege has reason to prioritize the collective costs because those more acutely affect it. All things being equal, citizens who derive little privilege from the institution

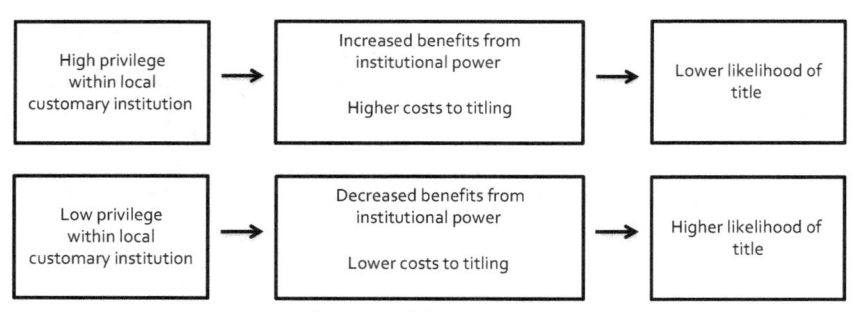

```
┌─────────────────┐     ┌──────────────────────┐     ┌─────────────────┐
│  High privilege │ ──▶ │ Increased benefits   │ ──▶ │ Lower likelihood│
│   within local  │     │ from institutional   │     │    of title     │
│customary        │     │       power          │     │                 │
│  institution    │     │ Higher costs to      │     │                 │
│                 │     │      titling         │     │                 │
└─────────────────┘     └──────────────────────┘     └─────────────────┘

┌─────────────────┐     ┌──────────────────────┐     ┌─────────────────┐
│  Low privilege  │ ──▶ │ Decreased benefits   │ ──▶ │Higher likelihood│
│   within local  │     │ from institutional   │     │    of title     │
│    customary    │     │       power          │     │                 │
│  institution    │     │ Lower costs to       │     │                 │
│                 │     │      titling         │     │                 │
└─────────────────┘     └──────────────────────┘     └─────────────────┘
```

FIGURE 3.2. Predictions of the customary privilege theory

will be more likely to adopt statutory property rights. This prediction contrasts with IIC approaches that model transaction costs such as time, money, and the accessibility of titles, but neglect to account for how being a member of a community might impact the individual's calculations. Figure 3.2 depicts the expectations of my argument.

We can also extend this framework to identify a number of other explanatory factors and observable implications of the theory that are beyond the scope of the empirical investigations in this book but are nevertheless interesting. Notably, outside of the two country cases, contemporary institutional strength may have different origins. In that case, contemporary strength (the second stage in Figure 3.1) would be the starting point for generating expectations about the comparative impacts of customary institutions on statutory land titling.

Further, other factors that impact members' incentives to invest in the long-term power of the institution should also shape local responses to land titling, according to this theory. For example, members should be more likely to prioritize individual gains over institutional power if they anticipate an impending threat to the institution's land authority from, for example, a mass displacement due to a state mining project. Even in a stronger institution, an event that prompts members to expect that it will soon weaken should alter how they evaluate the costs and benefits of titling.

Similarly, institutional constraints are not the only factors that structure how chiefs weigh personal gains and collective costs. Other personal and institutional characteristics should also affect a customary authority's incentives to prioritize the long-term costs to the institution's power base, such as age, alternative financial opportunities or professional activities, the security of the leader's rule, and whether a child or extended family member inherits power. We might anticipate patterns related to these characteristics in a data set with chiefs as the unit of analysis. Similarly, we might examine additional factors that are endogenous to the strength of the institution's rules and processes, such as the frequency of disputed successions, which should also shape how chiefs respond to potential titles that feature trade-offs between immediate benefits and long-term costs to the institution's power base.

Finally, if status within the institution impacts a citizen's choice to engage or exit, we should see a parallel dynamic with status in state institutions. In short, characteristics that generate privilege within state institutions, such as ruling party affiliation, education, language skills, and wealth, should also shape titling decisions. This is discussed to some extent in Chapter 7, but a full exploration of how status in state institutions impacts land titling remains for future study.

3.3 CONCLUSION

The theory presented in this chapter suggests a path dependence in land tenure regimes that results from an institution's ability to reinforce its power. Even if customary tenure is not the most desirable outcome for the state, it continues because it is a critical resource for those who control it. Members of customary institutions gain social legitimacy, economic rents, and political power from control over land and consequently have incentives to slow the conversion of customary land to state titles. Similarly, customary property rights may not be the best option for all; however, for select groups, they are preferable. It is those who stand to lose the most in material resources and status who should be most committed to maintaining the customary system, making the development of state authority over land a process of political change and resistance. Of course, this framework is not intended to be exhaustive of all potential explanations for titling decisions. Rather, it explains how the heterogeneity among the customary institutions on the ground impacts titling, thereby creating spatial differences in the state's expansion of control over land.

This chapter has provided the theoretical framework that will be elaborated throughout the book using evidence from Senegal and Zambia. These countries represent two very different state contexts for customary authority in Africa, of official and unofficial chieftaincies. This, in turn, shapes how customary authorities interact with state actors and informs the mechanisms available to customary institutions to constrain leaders. In Zambia and Senegal, the colonial administrations established the scaffolding for this divergence between official and unofficial chieftaincy systems. Despite the many similarities among colonial regimes, the differences between the British and French philosophies of colonial state domination profoundly impacted the modern systems of land tenure and customary authority in these two African countries. The next chapter introduces the three layers of institutions that generated the current status of chiefs and land authority in Zambia and Senegal.

4

The Institutional Foundations of Land Authority in Zambia and Senegal

The contemporary systems of customary authority and land rights in Zambia and Senegal are a composite of layers of institutions. Like a kaleidoscope with three lenses, we must consider all three institutional layers to see the full picture. The first layer is the political institutions that preceded the colonial intervention. These precolonial institutions established citizenship in large and small political communities and structured political, economic, and social interactions between and within these communities. The second layer is the political institutions that were imposed during the colonial intervention. The European colonial regimes erected new boundaries, merging some preexisting political communities into colonial states and splitting others. Despite more than seven decades of official colonial rule, during which colonial governments attempted to weaken precolonial institutions and instituted new laws regulating daily life for Africans, the first layer did not disappear. The third layer is the political institutions created by the governments of independent states. After independence, these governments added institutions to replace, reform, or reinforce the colonial institutions they had inherited. All three of these layers contribute to the current state of land politics and customary authority.

Each of these layers is, of course, composed of multiple and dynamic rules and processes. Precolonial states gained and lost power; colonial regimes adapted their strategies of domination over time; ideologies such as nationalism, socialism, and liberalism shaped the policies enacted by successive independent governments in Zambia and Senegal. Yet it is nevertheless important to examine each layer as a component of the current image. This chapter provides an overview of each layer, with the heaviest emphasis on the colonial institutions, which are not explored elsewhere in the book. It begins by describing the precolonial polities that existed in the territories that would become Zambia and Senegal. Some of these were hierarchical states, while others were more loosely organized communities. All of these hierarchical customary institutions survived into colonial Zambia, but the French successfully destroyed some of them in Senegal, leaving only the strongest intact. The next section of the chapter examines the significant differences between the British and French colonial institutions in these two countries. In Senegal, the French colonial regime emphasized the rights of the victor, claiming that it had replaced all existing forms of sovereignty. By contrast, the British model in Zambia depended on recognizing existing political authority structures and, where no strong political institutions were found, attempting to build new ones. Land policies that reinforced these colonial narratives followed. The differences among these British and French colonial approaches led to the system of official chiefs in Zambia and unofficial customary authorities in Senegal. This chapter concludes with an overview of the most important land and customary authority policies enacted between 1960 and 2012 in the two independent countries.

4.1 AFRICAN POLITICAL INSTITUTIONS ON THE EVE OF COLONIZATION

Prior to European colonization in the nineteenth century, a heterogeneous mix of political institutions governed the territories that would become Senegal and Zambia. Both territories featured a range of political structures, which scholars have categorized as kingdoms, dynasties, bureaucratic states, autonomous villages, centralized chieftaincies, communities ruled by elders, independent groups, loosely organized chieftaincy systems, and stateless societies.[1] These polities featured institutions that established the boundaries of their political communities by determining who was a citizen; what their political obligations were; and how newcomers could be integrated into society.[2] They each had their own rules for land access and different forms of resource rights. These institutions also determined how power was distributed in the political community. For example, in some institutions the authority to create and enforce laws was shared among family heads within the community; in others,

---

[1] C. Diop 1960; Ki-Zerbo 1972; Phiri 1988; Gould 2010. See also Brelsford, William Vernon. *The Tribes of Zambia*. 1956. Lusaka, Zambia: Government Printer.
[2] For detailed examples, see Diagne 1967.

legislative power was concentrated in a supreme monarch and council.[3] The political institutions that governed just prior to colonization would gain the moniker of "customary institutions" when the colonial state was imposed. This terminology distinguished them as having a separate source of legitimacy from the statutory institutions created by the colonial state, even as the colonial authorities attempted to incorporate them, use them to serve their agendas, and change them.

Zambia

One of the many differences among the precolonial political institutions was their organizational structures, which would impact their ability to retain influence following colonization. In Zambia, there were four hierarchical institutions on the eve of colonization: the Bemba, Chewa, Lozi, and Ngoni polities.[4] The Lozi kingdom was located on the western boundary of the subsequent Zambian state, the Chewa and Ngoni in the east, and the Bemba in the north. These polities had developed state-like structures with militaries, bureaucracies, systems of taxation, and multiple levels of hierarchy through a process of endogenous state building. For example, the leadership of the Chewa state had strengthened its hierarchy of tributary kings, chiefs, and lineage-based councillors by collecting and distributing wealth obtained from control over trade routes, particularly through the ivory trade.[5] The neighboring Ngoni built their kingdom through military conquest and subsequent integration of captured populations into its hierarchy of authority.[6]

These four hierarchical polities did not, however, rule all of the land that would become Zambia. Elsewhere in the territory, nonhierarchical institutions governed the political, economic, and social lives of local populations. Historical records described the structures of the Mambwe institutions of northern Zambia as individual villages with autonomous systems of administration, security, and conflict resolution, which were

[3] Kouassigan 1966, 31–32.
[4] The Lunda was a powerful precolonial state in the eighteenth century that was headquartered within the boundaries of the contemporary Democratic Republic of Congo and controlled territory in northern Zambia. By the end of the nineteenth century it had been significantly weakened by internal disputes and external attacks. By most measures, its hierarchical structure had eroded before colonization (Kay 1967). Nevertheless, in Chapter 5, I include analyses that categorize Lunda as a hierarchy as robustness checks. On the Lunda state, see also Roberts 1976; Gordon 2001.
[5] Langworthy 1971.   [6] Lukhero and Barnes 1999.

united into a larger community through kinship ties among their leaders.[7] Similarly, the Ila community of south-central Zambia was organized into independent chieftaincies and with clan-based succession.[8] In the south, the population now known as the Tonga was a loosely connected ethnic group without any unifying organization beyond small village clusters.[9] And, in the north, the Lungu institutions were bound together by alliances among male and female leaders with a heterogeneous mix of clan and lineage-based authority.[10] Further, many of the nonhierarchical precolonial political institutions in Zambia at the time were internally fragmented because their members had migrated to evade conflict with militarized precolonial kingdoms.[11] The map in Figure 4.1 portrays the distinct precolonial political communities in Zambia, as drawn by the colonial authorities. Note that this figure also includes native reserve boundaries, a colonial land tenure category that is detailed in the next section of the chapter.

Senegal

As in Zambia, a mix of hierarchical and nonhierarchical political institutions governed populations and territory in precolonial Senegal. Figure 4.2 depicts these precolonial states and political communities, as understood by the French colonizers in 1861. In the northwest corner of the territory was the small Waalo kingdom (spelled on the map as Oualo).[12] Three centuries earlier, this independent polity had broken off from the large Djoloff empire. To the east of the Waalo was the powerful Fouta Toro theocratic state, which was divided into six provinces that governed a large area in the north of Senegal's territory.[13] In the south-central region, the Sine kingdom had developed a state-like structure over generations of conquests that began in the fourteenth century. It was headed by a king who governed through layers of authority from provincial leaders to village nobles. The kingdom had an organized military apparatus, and a royal council made governance decisions for the entire territory.[14] Its leadership was allied with the neighboring Saloum kingdom; the royal lineages in these kingdoms, but not all of the governed

---

[7] Watson 1958.   [8] Brelsford 1956, 66.   [9] Colson 1948.   [10] Watson 1976.
[11] Meebelo 1971, 7.   [12] Barry 2012, 131.
[13] D. Robinson 1975. On the precolonial Fouta Toro institution, see also Wane 1966; Diagne 1967; Kane 2004.
[14] Also spelled as Siin. Galvan 2004, 50–59.

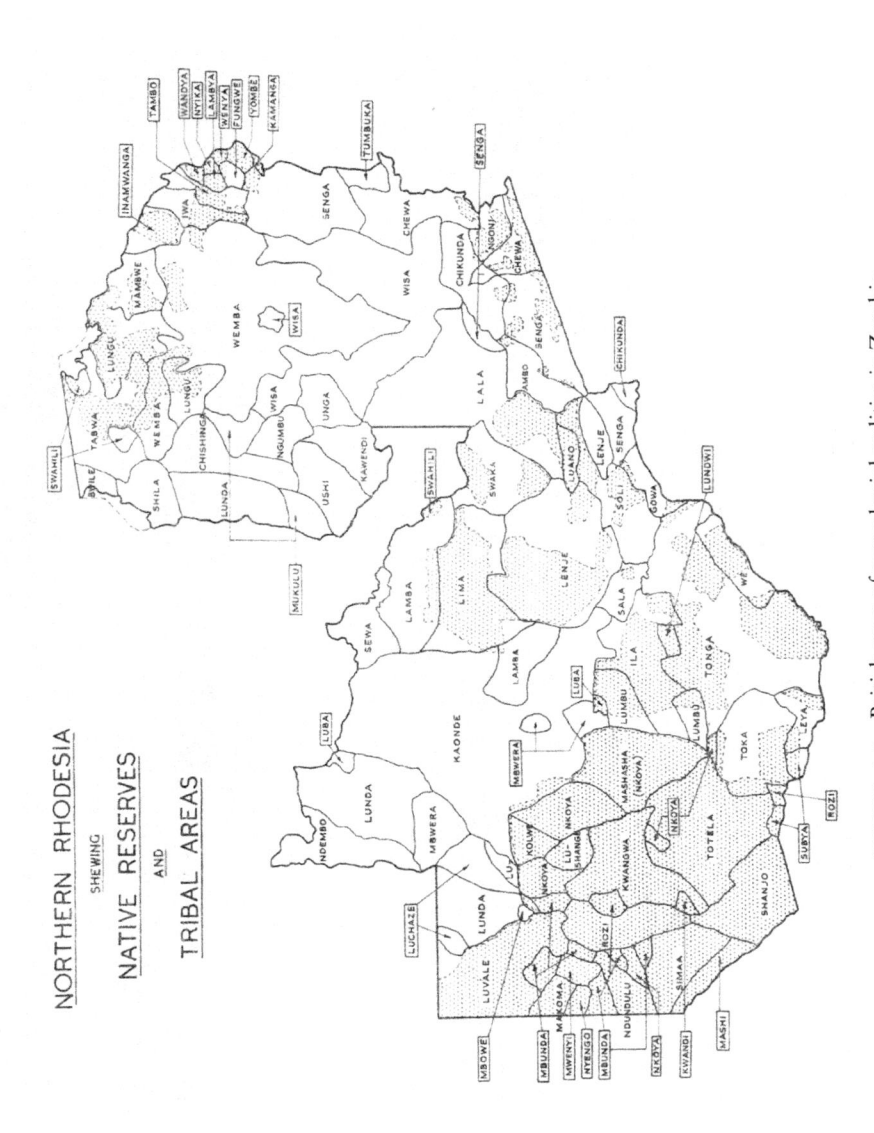

FIGURE 4.1. British map of precolonial polities in Zambia

Source: Northern Rhodesia, Survey Department, "Northern Rhodesia Shewing Native Reserves and Tribal Areas," 1938, London: His Majesty's Stationery Office. Available at: Princeton University Library Maps and Geospatial Data.

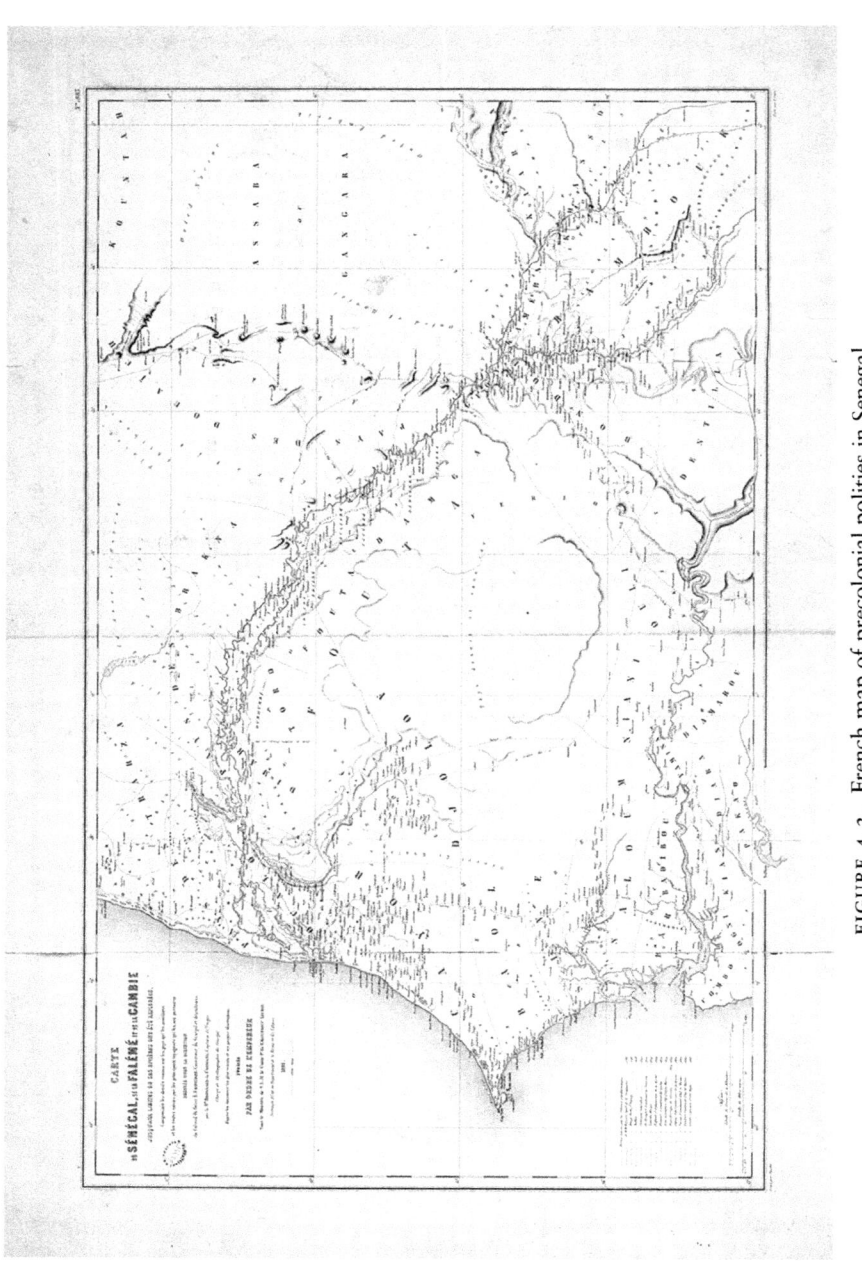

FIGURE 4.2. French map of precolonial polities in Senegal

Source: Charles-Paul Brossard de Corbigny and Léon Faidherbe, "Carte du Sénégal, de la Falémé et de la Gambie, jusqu'aux limites ou ces rivières ont été explorées," 1861, Paris: Dept. de la Marine et des Colonies. Available at Library of Congress.

populations, were from the Serer ethnic group.[15] In the east were smaller and newer states such as the ethnically mixed Boundou kingdom.[16]

Other areas of the territory featured decentralized, stateless precolonial institutions. Small federations of villages governed land in the east and southeast.[17] This included communities that practiced settled agriculture as well as Pulaar semi-nomadic herders. In the south, among the population now known as the Diola, individual "village kings" functioned autonomously.[18] These groups were not unified into a greater system of political authority prior to colonization, much like the Tonga example in Zambia. Thus, nineteenth-century Senegal featured polities with a mix of institutional structures, including smaller hierarchical kingdoms such as the Waalo, Gadiaga/Galam, N'Goy, Boundou, and Namandirou.[19] However, the six largest precolonial hierarchies were the Cayor, Sine, Saloum, Fouta Toro, Djoloff, and Baol. These six would withstand the French conquest and remain hierarchical into the colonial era, as discussed further in the following section.

Summary

The boundaries of contemporary Zambia and Senegal were imposed upon manifold precolonial political communities. Some of these were great conquest states with complex hierarchical structures; others were autonomous communities that regulated land access and exercised political power in the absence of authority above the village level. Both countries featured polities with both types of institutional structures. Beyond the effects of structural differences, these institutions impacted contemporary politics by establishing norms that are understood to be (or framed to be) endogenous to a group. Rules of resource access, for example, gain legitimacy from references to their historical origins. Further, these institutions generate identity narratives that unite community members, including mythologies of the origins of peoples and their rights. As Thomas Spear has so eloquently argued, the precolonial era created the raw materials for agents in the colonial and contemporary eras to draw upon: "Even genetically engineered plants derive genes from their predecessors and need fertile soil in which to succeed."[20] Further, he explains that "what gives tradition, custom and ethnicity their coherence

---

[15] Diagne 1967, 59.   [16] Gomez 1992; Tandjigora 2015.
[17] On the Gnokholo institutions in the southeast, see Camara 2015.
[18] Diouf 2001, 170–94.   [19] D. Diop 2006; Zuccarelli 1973.   [20] Spear 2003, 26.

and power is the fact that they lay deep in peoples' popular consciousness, informing them of who they are and how they should act."[21] Many books could be (and have been!) written about the ways in which the precolonial layer of institutional rules, norms, and processes are "raw materials" that impact many facets of contemporary politics.

However, for the focus of this book, the divergent structures of precolonial institutions are important because they endow institutions with relative differences in strength within each country. The following section explains what happened when the British and French established their colonial institutions on top of these existing systems of authority. It also maps the institutions with the strongest institutional endowments, the hierarchies that survived the colonial conquest (see Figures 4.3 and 4.4 in Section 4.2). The theoretical framework described in Chapter 3 predicts that the relative differences in strength of these institutions impacted their ability to shape the behavior of their members and, therefore, to retain their power over land. This is the first layer in the kaleidoscope of political authority over land in Zambia and Senegal.

4.2 COLONIAL INSTITUTIONS OF CUSTOMARY AUTHORITY AND LAND CONTROL

The next institutional layer that has long-term impacts on contemporary land politics are the British and French colonial institutions. French and British colonialism was fundamentally similar, as both powers entered foreign territories that had existing systems of sovereign authority and attempted to impose new colonial states. As Kwame Nkrumah explained of the comparison between the French and British, "their history of colonialist subjection differs from ours only in detail and degree, not in kind."[22] Both colonial powers employed violence to dominate and extract in the name of imperial ideologies. To justify their rule, both colonizers constructed narratives related to African systems of property rights. By repeating these claims, they created conceptualizations of customary land tenure that served their governance goals.

In Zambia and Senegal, the British and French built colonial political and economic institutions in response to a similar set of objectives and constraints. Like other colonial regimes in Africa, they had two central goals: to control the African populations within a vast foreign territory and to

---

[21] Ibid.   [22] Nkrumah 1963, xii.

extract the resources necessary to fund their administrations.[23] They both had limited bureaucratic capacity to directly govern a large and geographically dispersed population.[24] The question of how to engage with precolonial institutions and leaders to facilitate the colonial state's domination within new boundaries was consequently of central importance. Further, to achieve their second goal, both the French and the British identified the same solution: agriculture. Early in the colonial occupation of Zambia and Senegal, the framers of colonial policy regarded vast areas of agricultural land as one of the few options for funding their administrations. Senegal was always a primarily agricultural colony. However, even in Zambia, where copper mining revenues overtook agriculture in 1920, the colonial state continued to actively promote agricultural production of taxable cash crops.

Yet, despite the similarities among the two colonial regimes, they used land and customary authority policy in different ways to advance imperialist agendas. For the framers of French policies in Senegal, the precolonial authorities were at best an inconvenience they had to respond to, and at worst a threat that needed to be eliminated. Their colonial officers labeled the hierarchical institutions that withstood their conquest as a challenge to their administration. In Zambia, on the other hand, British officers described the precolonial hierarchies with admiration. The goal of the British policymakers was not to replace them but to rule through them. As a result, the British emphasized that their rights to give out land and to protect property rights were *granted* by existing authorities. By contrast, the French used treaties briefly to facilitate colonial occupation, but not as a basis for their authority in Senegal. They described their rights over land as a feature of the eminent domain of their state, which replaced all preexisting forms of land authority.

This section first describes differences in how the two European powers engaged with the leaders of precolonial institutions when they created the colonial states. Second, it explains how the colonial regimes established their land policies to conform to those divergent approaches to customary-state relations in the early colonial period. Third, it shows how each colonial administration incrementally adapted their policies over time. Fourth, I summarize the differences in the status of state authority over land, which resulted from the colonial institutions, on the eve of independence.

---

[23] van de Walle 2009.
[24] In Senegal, there were only 63 French administrators or 1 per 20,000 Africans in 1926 (Gellar 1976, 30). By 1937, the ratio of colonial officers to African populations had increased slightly to 1 per 14,800 in Senegal and 1 per 12,600 in Zambia (Richens 2009, 47).

Customary Authority and the Justification for Colonial Control of Land

The philosophies of colonial domination and governance advanced by each colonial power during the conquest and early colonial era became the foundations for the rest of their rule. As the European colonizers' governance strategies developed over time, they built upon their earlier colonial frameworks. In Senegal, French conquest began with trading posts along major rivers and seaside ports throughout the seventeenth and eighteenth centuries and accelerated through military expeditions in the middle of the nineteenth century. By the 1890s, the French had established a colonial administration and territorial control of Senegal.[25] British rule in Zambia began through expansion from their more established colonies to the south by missionaries and mineral prospectors. The colonial administration was initially under the auspices of Cecil Rhodes' British South Africa Company (BSAC); the British Colonial Office then consolidated its rule in 1924. Official colonial rule is generally dated as starting in 1895 in Senegal and 1889 in Zambia.

Both colonial powers focused on the problem of establishing control over land and African political authorities from the start of occupation. As a result, they began their conquest of the territories by amassing reports on the existing polities and sending agents of the metropole to negotiate treaties with anyone they could claim was a local leader. As their efforts to build colonial states ramped up at the end of the nineteenth century and into the twentieth century, their attempts to categorize and classify the systems of authority became increasingly systematic.[26] Both colonial powers used these early anthropological reports and treaties to construct their authority as colonial states. The European treaties themselves should be understood as "legal fictions" obtained in coercive and, at best, dubious circumstances.[27] However, the ways by which each regime employed treaties and engaged with existing political systems as instruments of colonial state power reveal distinct logics of controlling land and populations. This section explains British and French strategies in each colony, in turn.

---

[25] D. Diop 2006.

[26] For Senegal, see reports on individual ethnic groups in the colonial *Bulletin du Comité d'Études de l'AOF* and the *Journal Officiel de l'AOF*. See also Geismar, Administrateur en chef des Colonies, *Recuil des coutumes civiles des races du Senegal*, 1933, Senegal National Archives (henceforth ANS). On Zambia, see Northern Rhodesia, "Native Land Tenure," 1938, Box 2/324, Secretariat Series, National Archives of Zambia (henceforth NAZ) and British South Africa Company (BSAC), *District Notebooks* (1890–1924), NAZ.

[27] Ajala 1983, 180.

Zambia

The British relied on the narrative of rights delegated by precolonial leaders throughout their colonial regime. They began their occupation with an explicit interest in preserving preexisting systems of authority, in order to co-opt them to facilitate colonial rule. Their treaties with African leaders became a cornerstone for their legal justifications of control over land. The founding logic of their colonial governance required them to recognize the land claims and treaties of the existing authorities to assert that these chiefs had ceded rights to the colonial state for the areas of land that the state wanted. One African leader in particular was central to the British approach to establishing land claims: the head of the Lozi precolonial state, whose title was "the Lewanika." The Lewanika became a powerful official chief who controlled a large area of land and was, in many ways, treated as a symbol of these derived rights. For example, in 1902, he traveled to England to attend the coronation of King Edward VII. Treaties with the Lewanika were used to justify British land rights in Zambia throughout the entire colonial period.

Colonial Zambia was initially divided into North Western Rhodesia and North Eastern Rhodesia, then later unified into Northern Rhodesia in 1911. In North Western Rhodesia, the Lozi state, also known as Barotseland, was the only precolonial state; the rest of the territory was governed by nonhierarchical political institutions. The British primarily engaged with the Lewanika, who asserted that all other authorities in the vast territory were under his jurisdiction. The first treaty between the British and the Lewanika made the chief's realm a British protectorate in 1890. The treaty included British mining and commercial rights throughout the Lewanika's domain.[28] In exchange, the British promised the chief a yearly subsidy; a 4 percent royalty on minerals; and recognition of his authority in a treaty known as the Lochner Concession. The colonial authorities and the Lewanika then clarified and renegotiated the terms of the Lochner Concession in the following years.

The British wanted to obtain treaties to document their authority over as much land as possible. Therefore, their renegotiated treaties and documents explicitly defined the Lewanika's territory as including not only ethnic Lozi areas but all of his reported "subject tribes," extending his territory to cover southern and central Zambia.[29] Members of other

---

[28] The British also had to purchase an 1889 mineral concession (the Ware Concession) that the Lewanika had made with a private prospector.

[29] Official correspondence defined the Lewanika's territory as everything west of the Kafue River plus the territory of the Bashukolumbwe/Ila east of the Kafue River. In 1904 and 1906 letters, the Lewanika also clarified that settlers could move into designated areas and that the BSAC could profit from land grants in Batoka and Bashukolumbwe areas.

precolonial polities in North Western Rhodesia disputed the claim that they were subjects of the Lozi state, but this assertion served both the British and the chief. Thus, during the period between the earlier and later treaties, the Lewanika sent his Lozi officials to zones east and west of Barotseland to help support the claim that his precolonial empire covered most of North Western Rhodesia.[30] This interaction also provides an example of how the colonizers' emphasis on preserving customary authority to justify their rule created important opportunities for African elites to shape the process. These leaders provided the information that the British used in their attempts to codify and formalize African political institutions. Some, including the Lewanika, were able to use the colonial agenda to reinforce – or inflate – their personal power.

In these treaties, the Lewanika was able to dictate where the British had land rights, particularly for mineral prospecting and White settlement. He prohibited the British from accessing land in his direct zone of influence, Sesheke and the Barotse Valley, or "Barotseland proper," and approved British control of land in the rest of the vast area that comprised North Western Rhodesia.[31] In 1900, he sanctioned the route for the first railway within North Western Rhodesia on land occupied by communities in the nonhierarchical Tonga institutions. This facilitated the railway construction. Subsequently, the area became a designated zone of White agricultural settlement. This official recognition of the Lewanika's authority allowed him a direct channel for influencing the colonial state's control of land.

On the other side of the colony, in North Eastern Rhodesia, the British also relied on treaties with chiefs as the source of their authority, despite their lack of success in securing them. During the same era as the early treaties with the Lewanika, a different set of British agents searched for African leaders who would agree to protectorates with the British crown in North Eastern Rhodesia. Two representatives of the crown – a geologist and a lawyer fond of big game hunting – traveled around North Eastern Rhodesia to negotiate a set of treaties known as the Thomson–Sharpe treaties. They collected twenty protection treaties

---

See the "Lewanika to BSAC Administrators Correspondences, 1904 and 1906," Box 363/68, NAZ; 1900 and 1909 concessions with the Lewanika; Northern Rhodesia, "Report of the Commission Appointed to Enquire into the Financial and Economic Position of Northern Rhodesia (the Pim Report)," 49, 1938, The University of Zambia (UNZA) Special Collections.

[30] Roberts 1976, 166–67.
[31] Wilson H. Fox, "BSAC Memorandum: North Western Rhodesia: Proposed Land Law" 1903? Box 363/68, Shelf A3/21, BSAC2 NWR Collection, NAZ.

between 1890 and 1891.³² However, they failed in their negotiations with the two leaders they deemed most important, the heads of the Bemba and Ngoni precolonial states.³³ They also failed to enter treaties with their primary target in mineral-rich Katanga, which came under Belgian control soon after. Thus, even members of the British administration described the Thomson–Sharpe treaties as "absurd" and illegitimate, given that they did not include any of the chiefs that the British deemed powerful.³⁴ Nevertheless, the British needed to maintain the fiction of rights legally derived from African leaders and, therefore, the crown validated the Thomson–Sharpe treaties. In a 1900 order-in-council, they used these treaties to justify vesting the land in North Eastern Rhodesia to their commercial subsidiary, the BSAC.³⁵ This generated a chain of derived rights: from chiefs to the BSAC, and from the BSAC to the colonial government. Even when their own administrators acknowledged the treaties to be dubious, the British colonial architects were committed to using treaties with chiefs to support their assertions of territorial authority.

While the British colonizers established their claims in North Eastern Rhodesia through the Thomson–Sharpe treaties, they ultimately relied more heavily on the agreements with the Lewanika to justify their rule. The Lozi chief maintained the authenticity of the treaties and relied on them to reinforce his power. As a result, many British legal documents from the colonial era explicitly referenced the Lewanika and then made vague references to authority over land derived from treaties with unnamed chiefs in North Eastern Rhodesia. For example, each of the first colonial agricultural land titles named the Lewanika's treaty as the source of the colonial state's authority to grant titles.³⁶ Throughout the colonial era, the recurring preamble to land policies for all of Northern Rhodesia referred to "all such rights and interests in lands as [the BSAC] claimed to have acquired by virtue of the concessions granted by Lewanika" to justify that "the Crown should be completely free to administer" the land

---

[32] Northern Rhodesia, "Northern Rhodesia White Paper on British South Africa Company's Claims to Mineral Royalties (Concession Agreements; Succession of States)," 1964, as published in *International Legal Materials* 3 (6): 1133–70.

[33] The leaders of the Bemba and Ngoni hierarchies were known as Chitimukulu and Mpeseni, respectively, at the time. These are now the titles of their paramount chieftaincies. Although Chitimukulu and Mpeseni refused to sign agreements accepting the British flag or providing the BSAC with mineral rights, Gann (1969) reports that this set of treaties did include the Lunda leader known as Kazembe.

[34] Hanna 1960, 115.   [35] North Eastern Rhodesia, *Order in Council*, 1900, Article 16.

[36] BSAC, "Permit of Occupation" 1902?, Box 363/68, Shelf A3/21, BSAC2 NWR Collection, NAZ.

in the colony.[37] The repeated narrative was that British control over land was not by virtue of the colonial state replacing existing forms of sovereignty, but was delegated by precolonial authorities.

This logic of derived rights was constructed in coordination with their approach to governance through chiefs. The British attempted to capitalize on the precolonial political institutions as they began to establish dominance over not just land, but populations as well. Where they could not build their authority through protection treaties, they relied on military campaigns against the leaders of some of the strongest precolonial hierarchies. Yet their goal was to maintain the authority structures of these institutions through "pacification" campaigns, not to annihilate them. From the perspective of the British colonizers, "the essence of the system of government through native authorities as practiced is that it is founded on indigenous institutions adapted where necessary to modern needs and adaptable to suit varying conditions."[38] Thus, after pacification, the British attempted to reinforce existing institutional structures.

As a result, all four precolonial states in Zambia maintained their hierarchical structures into the colonial era. The strength of their internal organizations made them more valuable to the British, who then recognized their leaders with the title of paramount chief. This includes the Lewanika, as well as the heads of the Bemba, Chewa, and Ngoni institutions. The British colonial conquest also halted the expansion of these states by quelling wars of conquest between precolonial polities and fixing boundaries that had previously been fluid.[39] Figure 4.3 depicts the

---

[37] This preamble is used in The Northern Rhodesia (Native Trust Land) Order in Council 1945, The Northern Rhodesia (Crown Lands and Native Reserves) Order in Council 1928, The Zambia (State Lands and Reserves) Orders 1928–1964, among others. The full paragraph is: "The Company as from the 1st day of April, 1924, assigned and transferred to the Crown all such rights and interests in lands as it is claimed to have acquired by virtue of the concessions granted by Lewanika, upon which date the full and entire control of the lands throughout North-Western Rhodesia as well as elsewhere in Northern Rhodesia should be taken over by the Crown and thereupon (subject to certain provisions with regard to the rights of the Company to lands and minerals contained in the said Agreement) the Crown should be completely free to administer such lands in such manner as the Crown might in its discretion deem best in the interest of the native population and in the public interests generally."

[38] Government note, as quoted in Northern Rhodesia, "the Pim Report," 95.

[39] See, for example, the cession of conquests among the Ngoni and Chewa precolonial states in Zambia in Lukhero and Barnes 1999, 37.

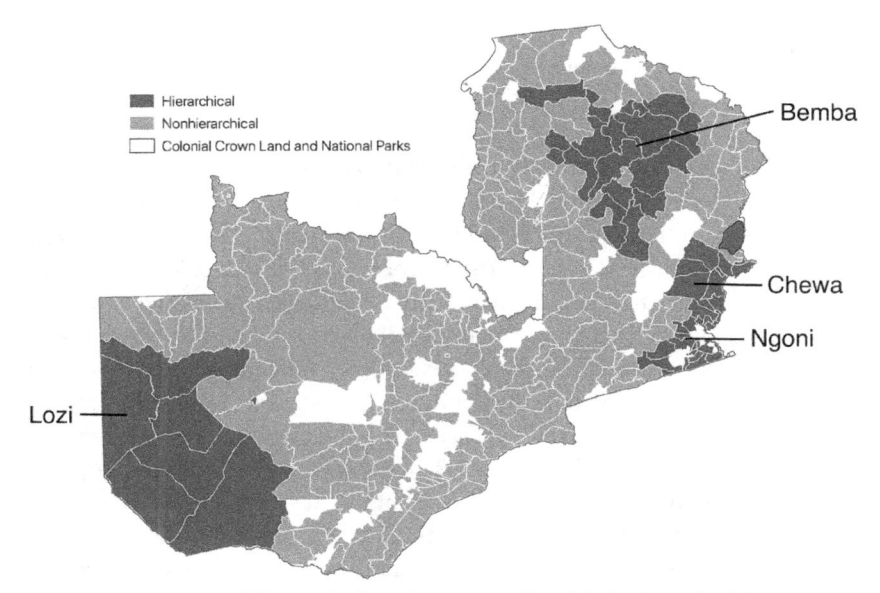

4.2 Colonial Institutions of Customary Authority

FIGURE 4.3. Hierarchical institutions in Zambia in the colonial era
Notes: State land (former Crown Land) was excluded from the original maps. The Lozi domain represents Lozi chiefdoms, not the largest extent of the Lewanika's sphere of influence during in the colonial era.
Source: Author's reproduction based on 1958 chiefdom maps by the government of Northern Rhodesia and the institutional affiliations of official chiefs codified by the House of Chiefs (2013).

locations of each these hierarchical institutions based on the chiefdom boundaries codified by the colonial authorities.[40]

In sum, the British placed an emphasis on recognizing sovereign precolonial leaders in the early colonial era and buttressing – not erasing – their institutions to justify and support colonial rule. They began formalizing the policy of governing through chiefs when the colony was still governed by the British South Africa Company. The 1916 Administration of Natives Proclamation recognized the authority of chiefs over local populations, established the chiefs' "subsides" (salaries) from the colonial regime and defined their duties to it, such as labor recruitment. This was a precursor to the expanded indirect rule framework of the later colonial

---

[40] The 1958 chiefdom boundaries map referred to here and in Chapter 5 is based on Republic of Zambia, "Map of Chiefs' Areas" for Copperbelt, Western, North-Western, Southern, Central, Eastern, Luapula, Northern Provinces, 1958, Lusaka: Northern Rhodesia Survey Department. This set of maps was created during colonial rule and maintained by the government of the Republic of Zambia.

period. The French would employ a very different strategy in creating the colonial state in the Senegal.

Senegal

The early French regime built its land authority through the claim to have replaced all existing political leaders and institutions. The French understood this as a right that resulted from territorial conquest and from gaining recognition as a state from other Europeans. Colonial officers provided evidence to justify French control of all land by writing extended reports, explaining that the African populations only had usage rights in the precolonial era because their "sovereigns" had complete rights over the land.[41] They argued that, by conquering these precolonial leaders, the chiefs' ownership of the land had been transferred directly to the French, regardless of whether the land was actively used by African populations.[42] The French strategy of establishing their "rights of the victor"[43] required two assertions. The first was that all precolonial leaders were sovereign authorities, or sometimes "feudal lords," who had equivalent rights, including ownership of all land in their domains, regardless of the structures and rules of their institutions. This was necessary to support the second claim, that the colonial state had acquired the rights of any and all precolonial authorities. These arguments allowed the French to deny that their administration violated African land rights when they expropriated or alienated any land in Senegal. This also provided the foundation for the colonial state to delegitimize any alternatives to their political authority. The French consequently considered their new control of land as a "complete property right," and any African rights as precarious rights of occupation.[44]

This strategy did not preclude the French colonizers in Senegal from amassing treaties with anyone they could count as African leaders prior to the Berlin Conference of 1884–85. The recognition of empire that the French gained from the conference and its subsequent negotiations halted their further pursuit of treaties, as they no longer needed to document to other Europeans that they had established a presence in West Africa. However, earlier in the eighteenth and nineteenth centuries, the French

---

[41] Gabriel Marie-Jacques, *Essai sur la Propriété Foncière Indigène au Sénégal*, 1895, Saint-Louis, Senegal: Government Printer; Roger Doublier, *La Propriété Foncière en AOF: Régime en Droit Privé*, 1952, Saint-Louis, Senegal: Government Printer, ANS.
[42] M. Arthur Girault, *Le Régime Des Terres Dans Les Colonies Françaises*, 1889, Brussels: l'Institut Colonial International.
[43] Verdier 1971. [44] Doublier, *La Propriété Foncière en AOF*.

registered hundreds of treaties with leaders, groups, and individual villages in Senegal. The terms of these treaties included freedom of movement and protection for French traders and officials. In return, the French offered tribute, promises to respect the leaders' authority, and recognition of specific lineages' authority. For example, among the nonhierarchical political communities in southern Senegal, the French signed forty different treaties between 1828 and 1894. Similarly, the French entered into forty-one treaties between 1785 and 1885 with representatives of the Fouta Toro precolonial state in northern Senegal.[45] Occasionally, these treaties included rights to small areas of land for official French posts. In the west and center-west, authorities representing the Cayor and Saloum precolonial hierarchies signed treaties ceding small areas of trading post land in 1765 and 1784, respectively. In the north, the French collected treaties with leaders in the Waalo precolonial state for land for agricultural experiments in 1819. These treaties facilitated their occupation of Senegal and established the basis for their claims in the global arena at a time when they were actively competing with the British and Portuguese for the territory. However, these treaties never became the basis of French rule or land rights and were rarely referenced in French colonial reports after the end of the nineteenth century, when the Europeans recognized French colonial statehood in Senegal.

The corollary of the initial French "rights of the victor" philosophy was a strategy grounded in attempts to eliminate African authorities, not to pacify and rule through them. As a result, the initial French conquest was more destructive to the precolonial political institutions than that of the British in Zambia. In the middle of the nineteenth century, prior to the Berlin Conference, French General Faidherbe declared war on several different precolonial states and leaders. The goal of these French military campaigns was to annihilate preexisting systems of authority. One colonial governor referred to this approach as a policy of "successively destroying" African sovereignty.[46]

The small Waalo kingdom is an example of the early French attempts at erasing – as opposed to co-opting – precolonial polities. In 1855, the French declared war, launched military campaigns, and completely dismantled the organization of the weak Waalo precolonial state. They

---

[45] Alexandre Sabatié, *Le Senegal: sa Conquête, son Organisation (1364–1925)*, 1925, Saint-Louis, Senegal: Government Printer, 232–34.
[46] Report by Camille Lucien Xavier, Senegal Colony Governor, to AOF Governor. June 1, 1907, Box 71, 13G, ANS.

burned down at least seventy-one Waalo villages, killed the regime's princes and hundreds of Waalo soldiers, and forced members of the ruling class into exile in other kingdoms. By December of the same year, the entire Waalo zone was declared a French territory.[47] This aggressive annexation reflected the underlying philosophy that guided French colonization of Senegal.

Their strategy was not always successful: The strongest precolonial states were able to withstand the French conquest. For example, the Cayor kingdom, just south of the colonial capital of Saint-Louis, mounted a prolonged resistance against the French. The French signed a treaty with the Cayor head of state,[48] named Lat Dior, for land to create a railroad in 1879. The treaty promised Lat Dior the right to travel on the railway for free with his entourage, twelve "beautiful Arab horses" per year, and other forms of support.[49] In exchange, Lat Dior agreed to provide labor (under specific conditions) and land access. However, within three years, he retracted his consent to cede the land, recognizing the danger of a French railway cutting through the heart of his territory.[50] In response, the French invaded his land and forced Lat Dior to flee to a neighboring kingdom; they abandoned any appearance of delegated rights and attempted to take it by force. For years, Lat Dior and his military launched a resistance campaign against the French, which ended with his death in battle in 1886. Despite French attempts to exile and control Cayor leadership, the institution's members remained powerful after colonization.[51] Through the beginning of the twentieth century, the colonial authorities considered the Cayor customary authorities as challengers to the colonial state. This history of successful resistance continues to be a powerful unifying narrative within communities that tie their institutional legacies to the Cayor precolonial state.

Consequently, the aggressive military campaigns of French conquest failed in some cases and succeeded in others.[52] In particular, the authority structures of the smallest and weakest states did not survive French conquest.[53] However, in addition to the Cayor, the Baol, Djoloff, Fouta

---

[47] Ba 1989.   [48] The title for a Cayor head of state is the "Damel."
[49] Sabatié, *Le Senegal*, 155.   [50] Pheffer 1975, 55.   [51] Ki-Zerbo 1972, chapter 9.
[52] This difference between the effects of French and British conquest on hierarchical legacies is consistent with patterns elsewhere on the continent. Müller-Crepon (2020) finds that in French colonies, 30 percent of ruling lines of succession for precolonial hierarchies survived throughout the colonial era, in contrast to 70 percent in British colonies.
[53] See Niane 1989 on the deterioration of the Gabou kingdom in the mid-nineteenth century and Barry (2012) on the Waalo state.

4.2 Colonial Institutions of Customary Authority 127

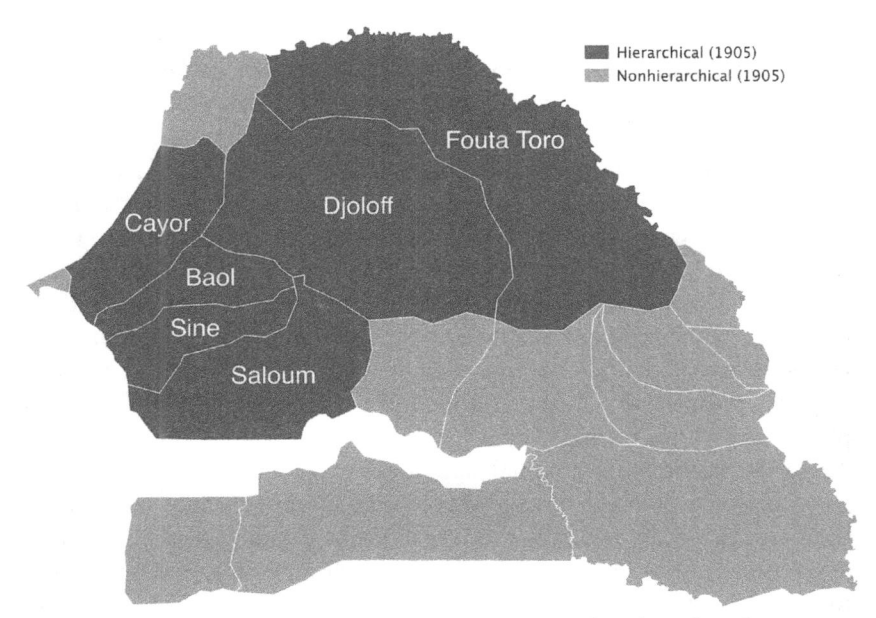

FIGURE 4.4. Hierarchical institutions in Senegal in the colonial era
Sources: Author's reproduction based on governmental Département d'Aménagement Territoriale (2000) map as cited in D. Diop 2006 and French colonial reports of hierarchies remaining in 1905.

Toro, Saloum, and Sine institutions retained their hierarchical structures at the start of colonialism. These six precolonial institutions had complex political organizations that made them a continuing challenge to the colonial state's monopoly of authority.[54] Elsewhere, precolonial institutions continued to shape aspects of citizens' lives, but they did so with distinctly weaker institutional endowments. Figure 4.4 maps the surviving hierarchical institutions, based on colonial reports on the status of kingdoms in 1905 and the government's map of precolonial political boundaries in 1854.[55]

---

[54] By 1905, colonial administrators identified these six precolonial states as the only ones that had survived the conquest and continued to function autonomously. Among other characteristics, they described these political institutions as having retained their legitimacy and as featuring leaders who were sustained by the tribute of their citizens. To the colonial governor these six were understood to "create an insurmountable barrier between the indigenous and the European administration." Report by Camille Lucien Xavier, Senegal Colony Governor, to AOF Governor. June 1, 1907, Box 71, 13G, ANS.
[55] These boundaries are also represented in Felix Brigaud, "Histoire Traditionnelle du Sénégal," 1962, Fascicule 9, Études Sénégalaises: Connaissance du Sénégal, Saint Louis:

The French regime began laying the legal framework that established the colonial state's eminent domain as the source of its land authority even before the end of the colonial conquest. In their Statutory Instrument of March 11, 1865, they formalized the claim that preexisting systems of property rights (customary land rights) had ceased to exist. The decree established that all untitled land belonged to the state. It asserted that the colonial state would only recognize land ownership that had been registered in their system of titles, for both African and European populations alike. This was an extension of a decree in 1862 that African populations did not have the right to sell any land. It alleged that, having inherited the rights of precolonial sovereigns, only the state had the right to alienate land to prospective buyers.[56] The policy made explicit the regime's philosophy of not recognizing any preexisting sources of land authority. These justifications for colonial state authority over land did not distinguish between different territorial zones, as the British had done within the Lewanika's domain. Instead, the French pronounced their right to administer land as universal and equally applicable throughout the territory, despite their own documented knowledge of the wide variation among precolonial polities. In areas where leaders governed through strong hierarchical institutions, as well as in those with no central organizations for hundreds of villages, the French claimed they had inherited the rights of all precolonial sovereigns, which they constructed as a complete right over land. In practice, the French colonial regime's interactions with different precolonial leaders and political communities varied. Yet the legal framework they created reflected a standardized logic of colonial land control: replacing all existing leaders and institutions. In doing so, the French colonial state tied its authority over land and property rights to its official policies related to chiefs. They could not assert that the state's authority came from replacing sovereigns while also recognizing their continuing authority.

CRDS. As with the chieftaincy maps in Zambia, these maps and boundary lines are a product of the colonial apparatus, designed to make dynamic precolonial polities legible to the state in order to facilitate colonial governance. These boundaries are the best available approximations of the real zone of territorial authority for these institutions. Gellar (1982) emphasizes the mobility of precolonial state capitals and boundaries in Senegal. Similarly, as Herbst (2000) has so effectively argued, for many precolonial institutions, control over people was a greater source of power than control over territory. Such boundaries among precolonial polities were soft and dynamic. See also the discussion of precolonial boundaries in Wilfahrt (2018).

[56] French Empire, Arrêté du 28 février 1862, Box 103, ANS.

4.2 Colonial Institutions of Customary Authority 129

This claim that French authority derived from replacing the rights of existing leaders undergirded their approach to colonial governance in Senegal, with African elites as auxiliaries of the regime. In 1887, the French established its *indigénat* policy in Senegal, which would last until 1946. This cornerstone of French colonial governance allowed administrators to impart harsh and arbitrary punishments on African populations, without any forms of judicial recourse.[57] To implement this policy and other elements of their colonial rule, the French incorporated Africans as agents of the administration. District officers (*commandants de cercle*) supervised these positions. They selected local elites to serve in the position of canton chief (*chef de canton*) and held them responsible for tasks such as compiling censuses, recruiting soldiers and labor, and collecting taxes.[58] These administrative chiefs were also expected to assist the district officer in implementing *indigénat* rulings, although the chiefs themselves were also subject to *indigénat*.[59] Accordingly, scholars have emphasized that, in the French colonial system, district officers held the real power in local governance.[60]

The selection of canton chiefs prioritized implementing the rules over reinforcing existing political institutions, in contrast to the British system in Zambia. This meant that, at times, district officers named representatives of precolonial institutions as canton chiefs, relying on their local legitimacy to help them administer the regime's directives. Yet they also selected chiefs based on education, French language skills, military service, and collaboration with the regime.[61] Hiring and replacing canton chiefs was at the discretion of the district officer, who could appoint any French-speaking local and then replace him for minor transgressions or noncooperation. African elites were incorporated into the colonial government as a subordinate level of the administration, without the power to govern independently.[62] As a result, robust systems of customary authority in Senegal remained outside of these official roles within the colonial state.

In 1904, the French officially divided the colony into two parts.[63] This bifurcated the colonial state, creating a separation between French citizens and subjects.[64] However, unlike the land–based British colonial bifurcation in Zambia described in the following section, this division

---

[57] Asiwaju 1978.   [58] Bruschi 2005, 505.
[59] Ajayi and Crowder 1974. See also G. Mann 2009.
[60] Gellar 2005, 36; Huillery 2009.   [61] Zuccarelli 1973.   [62] Crowder 1964.
[63] AOF, Décret du 13 février 1904.   [64] Owolabi 2017.

focused on political rights. African residents living within the four coastal cities of Gorée, Dakar, Rufisque, and Saint-Louis were formally French citizens. This small elite, known as the *originaires*, benefited from greater rights and political privileges.[65] Among them was Blaise Diagne, the first Black African deputy in the French National Assembly, elected in 1914. While the rest of the African population in the colony was subject to *indigénat* until 1946, the four communes were subject to French Metropolitan Law. This French bifurcation policy did not use land rights to separate citizen from subject. Instead, it was within zones of weaker political rights, *indigénat* rule, where the colonial state's land titles were adopted with the greatest frequency in the colonial period. Thus, in response to similar challenges and objectives of colonial domination, the British and French crafted different colonial institutions that reflect alternative narratives used to justify their authority, vis-à-vis precolonial polities and African leaders.

The Land Rights–Governance Nexus

These two distinct ways of exerting power in relation to customary authority shaped how the British and French organized the land in their colonies. As a result, land governance was markedly different in colonial Senegal and Zambia. The British implemented top–down land planning policies that divided the land in Zambia into areas controlled by customary authority and areas administered by the state. This formal division established that property rights protected by the colonial state (land titles) were accessible on state land but not on areas designated as "native land." Further, it empowered chiefs to govern within their own circumscribed domains. In Senegal, the colonial state used land policies to facilitate the slow dissolution of customary institutions. It treated canton chiefs as auxiliaries of the French colonial administration. When the French in Senegal engaged with popularly legitimate leaders who remained outside of the administration, they did so informally. The land policies that corresponded to the French approach to customary authority in Senegal thus looked dramatically different than the British policies in Zambia. The French regime permitted and promoted the statutory registration of African property rights in conjunction with a broader policy of ignoring alternatives to the colonial state's power. The legal foundations of

---

[65] Diouf 2000.

contemporary land policy in Zambia and Senegal reflect these early colonial state policies, which employed land rights in different ways to serve their political goals.

Zambia

The cornerstone of British land policy in Zambia was the native reserves. Starting in 1907, the British designed their land governance around the goals of strengthening chiefs and restricting the movement of African populations. The first native reserve was established on the eastern border of the colony, near the British fort that became the prominent town of Fort Jameson. The impetus for this first reserve was to clearly define where Africans (and Europeans) could farm. At that time, there were a total of twenty-six European farmers and ranchers in North Eastern Rhodesia.[66] Although these land divisions were initially implemented in areas where the British hoped to promote settler agriculture, native reserves were later created through the entire territory as a means for the British to bolster and circumscribe customary authority. Reserves quickly became a political tool, independent of actual or desired European interest in the land. The British used reserves to divide the land into bounded zones under the control of official "native authorities," ranging in size from 3,885 ha to over 2 million ha.[67] The reserves policy used territory to bifurcate the colony into crown and native land, the precursors to the contemporary categories of state and customary land, respectively.

The British land policy emphasized building the power of chiefs and creating a physically separate domain for state and customary authority. The colonial officers designed the reserves to overlap with existing political institutions whenever they deemed it was possible. They reported wanting to maintain the "tribal characteristic" of an area by making reserves ethnically homogenous and by preventing ethnic groups from migrating or mixing.[68] In line with this policy, they were conscious of keeping ancestral graves within the reserves,[69] which they hoped would

---

[66] BSAC, "Administrator's Report for the Two Years Ending 31st March 1905," 1905, A8/1/1, North Eastern Rhodesia Collection (BSAC1), NAZ.
[67] Northern Rhodesia, "Pim Report," appendix VIII.
[68] Northern Rhodesia, "Report of the Land Commission (Eccles' Report)," 1946, UNZA Special Collections; Northern Rhodesia, "Extract from Rhodesia-Nyasaland Royal Commission Report," March 1939, SEC 3/314, Secretariat Series, NAZ.
[69] Northern Rhodesia, "Pim Report," 40.

reinforce the spiritual power of chiefs. In practice, however, the reserves were more heterogeneous than the British intended.

The British colonial authorities were explicit about the political goals of their land policy. They described the mobility of African populations and the creation of new villages farther from the seat of a chief's power as "an evil which tended to break down all tribal authority."[70] In 1907, they banned the practice of shifting cultivation, known by the Bemba term *chitemene*. They feared this mobile agricultural system would weaken the chief's influence over local populations.[71] The colonial authorities enforced these bans against *chitemene* using violence and burning temporary camps (*mitanda*).[72] The authorities later acknowledged that these policies had contributed to famine.[73] In line with this approach, the British also "amalgamated" smaller villages into larger groups. For example, in the north, they forced 282 villages to merge into 74 villages, changing the average size from 95 to 200 per village.[74] The colonial regime designed these policies to strengthen the chief's ability to tax and govern local populations.

The British intended for their land policies to keep African populations reliant on and, therefore, under the control of their chiefs. Framers of this approach to governance acknowledged that they wanted to preserve "native institutions," which could help provide labor for the regime and serve as a local source of social cohesion and cooperation.[75] They believed that permitting African populations to access land titles or have individual land rights would undermine the chiefs' power.[76] This formalized a narrative in which African land tenure was solely collective and devoid of individual property rights. As Martin Chanock argued of this era:

> To imagine individual rights inside reserves creates the possibility of conceiving of such rights having existed outside them, and also the potential for Africans to demand legitimately and to establish such rights in European areas. Only if the indigenous system were different from the British one could the validity of segregated property rights be maintained ... That this was fundamentally in the interests of the existing African polities hardly needs emphasizing.[77]

The British in Zambia established the reserves policy to prevent African populations from securing their property rights through any authority

---

[70] Correspondence between BSAC Administrator to the High Commissioner for South Africa, January 6, 1915, HC/1/3/21 Northern Rhodesia Administrator Collections (BSA3), NAZ.
[71] Meebelo 1971, 105. [72] Musambachime 1992, 11.
[73] Northern Rhodesia, "Pim Report," 19. [74] Kay 1967, 10. [75] Meek 1946, 7.
[76] Ibid., 10. [77] Chanock 1991, 75.

other than their designated chief. Further, the early colonial government mandated that Africans could not adopt statutory land titles outside of the reserves or register individual rights within the reserves. These land divisions were designed to build the power of an official chief.

The British decided how to divide the land into reserves based on three key priorities: the economic goals of the colonial government; the interests of potential White settlers; and the consolidation of chiefs' authority. However, they also had limited resources and needed the cooperation of chiefs to govern. Thus, existing African settlement patterns were at times respected, even if they interfered with British interests. One documented debate over whether a prime plot of riverside land should be incorporated into a reserve or used for European wheat farming exemplifies this. The colonial administrators reported that they opted to include it in the reserve because they found it impossible "to face the natives to whom we have given the word of the Administration that they will not be further molested."[78] This is one of many reports designed to document "the Surrender of Native Rights."[79] Having acknowledged preexisting land rights, the British then created a paper trail to show that these rights had been ceded to the state. Thus, for the British reserve decisions, the difficulty of displacing communities due to their size, levels of resistance, or number of cattle also factored into these decisions, as costly inconveniences to be avoided.

Chiefs participated in the regional reserves commissions that determined the division and boundaries of the land. This created a forum for chiefs to shape and protest the colonizers' attempts to create "tribal" boundaries.[80] In addition, for the Lewanika, this division of land was an opportunity to establish a special status for the Lozi native reserve. The Lozi reserve was functionally equivalent to the other native reserve areas, yet colonial documents counted it separately from their tallies of native reserves and referred to it not as a native reserve but as Barotseland. This special designation implied greater sovereignty. Additionally, the Barotseland reserve was larger than all of the other reserves combined.[81]

---

[78] Mr. Tagart, BSAC Magistrate, as quoted in: "Proposed Mwembeshi Wheat Area: Summary of Mr. Tagart's Views," 1919, B1/45/4, Northern Rhodesia Administrator Collections (BSAC3), NAZ.
[79] Correspondence from A. W. Bonfield, Assistant Native Commissioner to The Native Commissioner. October 30, 1920. Box A3/6/2/7/3 808, NAZ.
[80] Meebelo 1971, 118.
[81] Total land for all native reserves was 14,047,772 ha in 1936, after all of the native reserves had been established. For Barotseland, the total was 14,900,202 ha. Northern

Colonial officers with no agricultural training or access to completed agricultural surveys selected the boundaries for Zambia's dual land tenure system. Prior to 1924, there was only one colonial officer with agricultural training.[82] As a result, the authorities dividing the land had limited ability to evaluate the agricultural impacts of their decisions. For some of the reserves, they determined the appropriate size by measuring local gardens and multiplying that by estimated population size. In others, they relied on an arbitrary estimate that .5 ha (1.25 acres) per person was sufficient for subsistence agriculture.[83] These calculations did not account for the impact of different soil types, agricultural practices, or animal husbandry needs.

They also had no information on the quality of the land and no resources to collect better information. It was not until 1938 that the colonial regime completed an ecological survey of Northern Rhodesia. Instead, the British relied on reports from district officers, who were responsible for a broad set of administrative tasks, including recording average rainfall, tax receipts, daily temperatures, and observations on "native culture" in their district notebooks. These district officers also occasionally noted the geographic features of their districts, such as reports of tsetse flies. Lacking any agricultural training or scientific knowledge, the British district officers could only provide rudimentary information on easily observable factors. At this time, trial and error was the primary option for identifying the suitability of land for agricultural production. By the time the land was surveyed in any systematic way, the British administrators had already formalized the boundaries of the dual tenure system. Consequently, political calculations had an important role in determining which land would be reserved for prospective European farmers as state land and where chiefs would reign. These native reserves and other British colonial land policies were devised to reinforce the regime's governance strategies.

Senegal
In contrast to British land policies intended to empower chiefs within bounded domains, French land planning in Senegal reinforced the claim

---

Rhodesia, "Ministry of Land Annual Reports," 1936, Shelf 16/Box 93A, Government Series, NAZ.
[82] Northern Rhodesia, "Pim Report," 132.
[83] Northern Rhodesia, "Report of the Land Commission on the North Charterland Concession Area," 1942, SEC 3/315, Secretariat Series, NAZ.

that the state had replaced all other forms of authority. The state owned all of the land. Therefore, they did not need to engineer specific zones of customary or state control. Nor were they concerned with using land policy to reinforce the power of chiefs. Instead, from the start of the colonial regime, the French designed land policies to weaken chiefs and to facilitate a direct relationship between the population and the state. They built their colonial land tenure regime upon policies that encouraged African land titling. When they observed that African farmers were not enthusiastically adopting papers recognizing property rights from an illegitimate colonial state, they created laws to make it easier to register individual land claims. A parallel system of customary institutions remained, but French land policies made it possible for their influence to dissolve over time, unlike the British regime in Zambia. As described earlier, colonial land policy in Senegal was grounded in the narrative that the state had replaced existing systems of customary rights; the colonial administration established itself as "the *inheritor* of the rights of the former masters of the land," according to Djibril Diop.[84] Thus, the foundational colonial land policies reflect the goal of erasing customary rights. Only later in the colonial era did the French slowly accept the resilience of customary land tenure and authority in the colony.

Land titling was an early preoccupation of the French colonial regime in Senegal. By 1832, they had a functioning land registry in their first colonial capital of Saint-Louis and, by 1861, they had opened a second registry office to serve the lower regions of the country on Gorée Island (later transferred to their second capital, Dakar). The architects of French colonial policy believed that creating a system of statutory titling was necessary to make the colony profitable; to generate greater property rights security; and as a foundation for agricultural producers to gain credit.[85] Like the British, their initial land policies reflected hopes of European agricultural settlement. At the same time, promoting individual titling also served the French colonial governance strategy. Their stated goal in opening these land registries was to create a system of property rights that would both replace the "traditional" system of land tenure and allow French settlers to develop land.[86]

Relatedly, the French had begun their rule in clear opposition to customary land tenure regimes. In 1837, one lieutenant reported that the potential breadbaskets of Senegal would never be realized under the

---

[84] D. Diop 2013, 73, emphasis added.   [85] Girault, *Le Régime des Terres*, 126.
[86] Verdier 1971, 92.

current "tyranny" of chiefs because their subjects lacked security of property rights.[87] To replace customary authority, the French instituted a single system of property rights for African and European populations alike, through the 1865 Statutory Instrument described earlier. The French then actively promoted land registration; they saw customary tenure as "incompatible" with modern life and believed private, alienable rights should replace it.[88] For example, in 1907, Georges François, a senior agent of the French colonial regime, argued that land registration is necessary for moral development because it ties a man to his land and allows him to reap the benefits of his labor.[89] The French approach to land policy in Senegal was, thus, fundamentally different than the British dual tenure system. Commenting on these differences, one British colonial officer in Kenya described the French as being "axiomatic" in their philosophy of promoting individual freehold for African farmers.[90] This comparison is particularly notable, as Kenya was the first British African colony to establish land titling and is often considered as an example of "direct rule" within the British colonial empire.[91]

The French colonial government made multiple attempts to increase rates of land registration by Africans. In 1906, the French colonial office reorganized the property rights regime across all of their French West Africa Federation territories, including Senegal.[92] The 1906 policy was intended to encourage titling by making the land registration process less onerous.[93] French colonial policymakers lauded this new land registration system as a vital means of accelerating the evolution of the African population from "captives" to independent producers, by making the use of land more efficient and clearly defining individual property rights.[94] Around the same time, the administration acknowledged collective rights to land for the first time. In 1904, they decreed that land collectively held

---

[87] Letter to the minister from a lieutenant in 1837, as cited in Georges Hardy, *La Mise en Valeur du Sénégal de 1817 À 1854*, 1921, Paris: Larose, 325.
[88] Doublier, *La Propriété Foncière en AOF*, 162.
[89] François, *L'Afrique Occidentale Française*, 188–89.   [90] Liversage 1945, 57.
[91] Ogot 1963.
[92] The French West Africa Federation (AOF) included contemporary Guinea, Côte d'Ivoire, Burkina Faso, Benin, Niger, Mali, Mauritania, and Senegal. Starting in 1902, its capital was in Dakar.
[93] AOF, Décret du 24 juillet 1906, portant organisation du régime de la propriété foncière dans les colonies et territoires relevant du gouvernement général de l'AOF.
[94] Georges Deherme, *L'Afrique Occidentale Française: Action Politique, Action Économique, Action Sociale*, 1908, Paris: Librairie Bloud, 520–21; Deherme describes the 1906 law as inspired by the Torrens model.

4.2 Colonial Institutions of Customary Authority

by communities or chiefs on behalf of communities could not be sold to individuals without the permission of the governor. This decree also replaced the earlier assertion that the colonial state was the owner of all land, with the state as the owner of all unused land *(terres vacantes et sans maître)*.[95] Although this is not quite parallel to a decentralization of power to chiefs in Zambia, it did represent a shift in the direction of the French colonial regime acknowledging the functionality and resilience of customary institutions. With these two policies, the French began to recognize the rights of customary land users, while still attempting to replace their tenure regimes with a system of statutory, individualized, and documented property rights.

The French framed their emphasis on land registration in connection to the regime's distrust of customary authorities. For example, in 1913, the colonial administration issued a memo stating that the colonized African population needed to be protected from chiefs and were "too ignorant" to understand the advantages of titling.[96] In a 1921 memo, the governor insisted that the administration could not recognize any ownership rights that were not based on titles and that it was their "duty to regulate" against customary ideas of land tenure by facilitating African access to title.[97] These comments highlight that the colonial authorities had designed their policies to weaken customary land tenure systems; however, they also reveal the regime's frustration with the slow expansion of land titling. Over time, it became clear that the French had failed to convince the African populations in Senegal to replace their customary property rights with titles. From the perspective of the French officers, this was due to both a lack of interest in registration and the resistance of chiefs to changing the existing land tenure system.[98]

The French approach to land planning in Senegal conformed not only to the regime's political goals but also to the colony's smallholder-based groundnut economy. In the nineteenth century, colonizers experimented with plantation crops such as tobacco and cotton in an attempt to attract European agricultural settlers.[99] However, they discovered early on that smallholder production of groundnuts had higher revenue potential for

---

[95] AOF, Décret du 23 octobre 1904 sur le domaine. Article 10.
[96] AOF, Circulaire 250 du 5 mars 1913 au sujet de notre politique agraire à l'égard des indigènes, 1O2, Colonial Senegal Collection, ANS.
[97] AOF, Circulaire 9 du 17 décembre 1921, 1O2, Colonial Senegal Collection, ANS.
[98] François, *L'Afrique Occidentale Française*, 213.
[99] Joseph Du Sorbiers de la Tourrasse, *De la Colonisation du Sénégal*, 1897, Paris: Arthur Savaète.

the colonial state. As early as 1854, the annual export of groundnuts was 4,820 metric tons; both the Saint-Louis and Gorée ports were profiting from it.[100] Production more than doubled between 1880 and 1898 alone, from 34,000 metric tons to 95,000 metric tons, with the development of the railway.[101] By 1913, annual groundnut exports had reached 240,000 tons and were the greatest source of revenue for the French colonial state.[102] In 1926, they opened a new land registration office to serve the major zone of groundnut production, Kaolack. This helped facilitate access to hundreds of new land titles per year for African farmers,[103] including some for marabouts who served as informal brokers within groundnut industry.[104] Encouraging individuals to obtain land titles on their land cohered with an economy based on African smallholder groundnut production.

Nevertheless, it would be a mistake to attribute this approach to land titling to the state's dependence on smallholder agriculture alone. British colonies in West Africa, such as the Gold Coast (Ghana) and Nigeria, also had economies based on smallholder agriculture, but they had land rights and customary authority policies that more closely resembled Zambia's colonial institutions. In these British colonies of West Africa, the colonial state encouraged smallholder cocoa and palm oil production while also refusing access to individual titles for African populations. As in Zambia, these British colonial regimes established chiefs as the authorities over the land farmed by smallholder producers.[105] Although the French emphasized that titling would promote African investments in their land,[106] their policy was also part of a broader philosophy of replacing customary authority with the state's authority. It was not merely a direct response to the burgeoning groundnut export industry. French land policies in Senegal reflected a clear political agenda, much like British land institutions in Zambia. All future governance strategies were then built upon the foundation of these early colonial approaches to land and customary authority.

---

[100] Hardy, La Mise en Valeur du Sénégal, 349.   [101] Moitt 1989, 27.
[102] Roubaud 1918.
[103] Calculations based on AOF, "Statistiques foncières: assiette de la propriété foncière consistance du domaine de l' État, livres foncières (1927–1935)," Box 2O9, Domaine et Enregistrement séries, ANS.
[104] See Appendix C on the role of marabouts in the colonial era. See also Copans 1980; Moitt 1989; Boone 1992 on marabouts as brokers within the groundnut industry.
[105] A. Phillips 1989.   [106] Deherme, L'Afrique Occidentale Française, 520.

Land Policies in the Late Colonial Era

The Europeans designed their land policies and governance strategies to be complementary within each colony. Their initial attitudes toward customary authority – whether they were seeking to replace them or to reinforce them – determined their approaches to land titling and land engineering. These policies reflected differences in the colonial philosophies of each colonial power.[107] However, the Europeans also responded to the local conditions in each colony. Consequently, both regimes gradually increased their recognition of and reliance upon customary authorities over time. This section describes the key changes and adaptations in colonial land institutions through the end of the colonial era.

Zambia

The British division of Zambia's land into native reserves began in 1907 and was completed in 1929. These boundaries were formalized and publicized through colonial orders-in-council. They assigned each reserve an ethnic or language group, as an explicit attempt to strengthen ties to customary institutions. The reserves policy established 38 percent of the territory as native land, amounting to 28.9 million ha for the African population of 1.4 million.[108] The remaining land was crown land, under

---

[107] Within the British and French empires, individual governors had the autonomy to establish policies for their colonies and could respond to local conditions in executing their agendas. As a result, the ideas emanating from the colonial offices in London and Paris were not universally and evenly applied within the colonies. In Senegal, there were two separate sets of laws: one that applied to all of the AOF and a second that applied to Senegal alone. The resulting legal framework reflected a mix of laws created by governors and those grounded in federal statutes. Furthermore, the implementation of federal statutes from Paris was subject to interpretation and adaptation by the governor. In Zambia, the offices of the governor and the BSAC colonial administrator could autonomously design policies for the colony. However, the pool of options they chose from was populated with examples of policies from within their metropole. For example, for their native reserve policy, Zambia's colonial government followed the policy of the BSAC administration in colonial Zimbabwe by dividing land into crown and native land. However, with fewer prospective settlers, they then modified it to allocate a higher percentage of land as native land and to remove racial restrictions on access to titles on crown land. Later, the Zambian administration copied colonial Malawi's native trust land policy. They also altered this policy in response to conditions in Zambia. Through similar policy adaptation processes, colonial administrators implemented policies specific to the conditions in Zambia and Senegal but did so within a metropolitan frame of reference.

[108] Calculations based on Northern Rhodesia, "Ministry of Land Annual Reports 1935–1946," Shelf 16/Box 93A, Government Series, NAZ.

the direct authority of the colonial administration. This included 2 million ha of forest and game reserves and 3.6 million ha of land titled or leased to Europeans. However, there were only 1,026 European farms on this 3.6 million ha of land by 1936.[109] The category of titled land included a handful of massive and mostly unexploited land titles from early exploration charters by companies such as the BSAC.[110] Instead, the majority of the 11,000 Europeans living in Zambia were engaged in mining and lived in the city of Ndola. The large remaining areas of untitled crown land were categorized as "unallocated crown land"; these 39 million ha were greater than the entire category of native land. Although African populations in Zambia gained the legal right to access land titles on crown land in 1924,[111] the administration continued to actively discourage individual landholdings by African farmers to keep them under a chief's control.[112]

The creation of native reserves designated the majority of Zambia's vast territory as crown land. This allowed the British to use this land as they wished, and, importantly, to forcibly move African communities living on crown land if there was any European or state demand for the land. However, the implementation of these formal land categories was uneven. After the colonial administration had established the boundaries of the native reserves, the decision to compel villages to move into the reserves was left to district officers. Many native reserves had no nearby settlers, given the limited European interest in agriculture in Zambia. As a result, colonial officers permitted communities to remain in some areas of crown land. For example, in the railway belt, the British categorized the entire area surrounding the railway between Livingstone and Broken Hill Mine (Kabwe) as crown land but allowed villages to stay on the otherwise unused land. For some groups, including the Bemba, Kaonde, and Ila, the

---

[109] Northern Rhodesia, "Ministry of Land Annual Reports," 1936, Shelf 16/Box 93A, Government Series, NAZ.

[110] Northern Rhodesia, "Native Affairs Annual Report for the Year 1934," 1934, Box 2/Shelf 8, African Affairs Annual Reports, Government Series, NAZ.

[111] Article 42 of the Northern Rhodesia Order in Council 1924 states that: "A native may acquire, hold, encumber, and dispose of land on the same conditions as a person who is not a native." The Northern Rhodesia policy diverged from Southern Rhodesia's explicit racial land categories, codified in its 1930 Land Apportionment Act.

[112] Northern Rhodesia, "Eccles' Report"; the barriers to titling were high and only crown land could be titled. As a colonial committee discussing indigenous land titling concluded in 1942, there was "no legal barrier to the acquisition of land by Africans on precisely the terms open to Europeans, but, in practice, few Africans have the financial qualifications demanded of European applicants" (Northern Rhodesia, "Report of the Native Land Tenure Sub-Committee of the Native Development Board," 1942).

colonial authorities acknowledged that the majority of their populations lived outside of native reserves.[113] Elsewhere, district officers did force communities into their designated reserves, removing African villages from crown land without demand for the land from European farmers. For example, in Mkushi, central Zambia, villages were displaced from their land when there were only three White settler farmers in the entire district.[114] Years later, British colonial officers would denounce and ridicule their predecessors for the: arbitrary boundaries of the reserves; lack of understanding of the differences in African agricultural methods; and unnecessary displacements.[115]

In coordination with the completion of their main land engineering policy, the British further systematized their policy of governing through chiefs in 1929.[116] Their new colonial administration created a system of native authority with chiefs as autonomous leaders of designated zones. Five years prior, the British colonial office took the reins from the BSAC, and Northern Rhodesia received its first colonial governor. Through a series of new laws, the colonial office clarified the official roles of chiefs and expanded their powers. Chiefs were responsible for all governance within their reserves and gained increased independent economic power within their domains, as the British formally designated them to be the recipients of all land rents, grazing fees, and forest royalties on reserves. The colonial government also implemented a native courts policy, putting chiefs in charge of conflict adjudication for the populations living within their bounded domains. The final stage in this empowerment of native authorities in Zambia was the 1936 policy that created native treasuries, modeled after those in Tanganyika (Tanzania) and Nyasaland (Malawi).[117] The architect of British indirect rule, Lord Lugard, argued that local populations needed to see their taxes going to their native authority. He proposed that chiefs should use the treasury for salaries and public goods within their bounded jurisdictions, after transmitting a portion of the taxes to the colonial state.[118] The colonial state thus designed these treasuries to build a fiscal social contract between chief

---

[113] "Memorandum: Native Reserve Fund, Note on Secretary of State's Despatch [sic] N. 380 of 17 August 1936" 1936?, SEC 3/315, Secretariat Series, NAZ.
[114] Northern Rhodesia, "Eccles' Report," chapter 2.
[115] Northern Rhodesia, "Pim Report."
[116] Northern Rhodesia. *Native Authority and Native Courts Ordinance*, 1929.
[117] The 1928 Northern Rhodesia (Native Reserves) Order in Council established Native Reserves Funds; Treasuries were established in the 1936 Native Authorities Ordinance.
[118] Lugard 1922, 201–8.

and population, strengthening the authority of chiefs in the lives of citizens.

In the later colonial period, the British increased their recognition of customary land rights in zones outside of the native reserves. Before 1947, 62 percent of Zambia's land – all land outside of reserves – was crown land. However, it became increasingly clear to the colonial authorities that European settlement would never be a major source of revenue in the colony and that there was no political or economic justification for such large areas of unused crown land. District officers had noted that their local reserves were too small to support the African populations even at the start of the reserves policy. Yet their reports on the injustices created by the partition of the land grew bolder in the later colonial period. For example, one British officer documented that: "Agriculture is a serious problem in Chief Shaiwila's area ... villages now line the Reserve side of the Mkushi River cheek by jowl, with hungry eyes at the unoccupied land opposite, behind them lies the commencement of a man-made desolation."[119]

Between 1938 and 1946, the British engaged in a second significant set of land engineering decisions to create the native trust land areas.[120] The new category of trust land was similar to native reserve land, with the notable exception that statutory leases were permitted. The policy transferred almost all of the crown's domain to native trust land, reducing the percentage of crown land in the territory from 62 to 8 percent.[121] The colonial administration approached the division of land into trust and crown land differently in the areas of the former North Eastern Rhodesia than in the former North Western Rhodesia. In the northeast, the default was to cede any crown land to native trust land unless it had been proven to be of value to the colonial regime. The underlying logic in the northwest was the inverse; they held on to the land unless it had been proven *not* to be of value to the crown. These differences in the debates over which areas should be crown or trust land reflected the continued British commitment to justifying their control over land as rights legitimately

---

[119] Northern Rhodesia, "Eccles' Report," 21.
[120] The trust land boundaries were formalized in the 1947 Northern Rhodesia (Native Trust Land) Order in Council.
[121] Calculations based on Northern Rhodesia, "Ministry of Land Annual Reports," 1935–1946, Shelf 16/Box 93A, Government Series, NAZ. An additional 2 percent of crown land shifted to native land before independence, such that in 1960, the percentage of crown land was 6 percent.

acquired from customary authorities and the colonial authorities' shift to focusing on mining as the foundation of the colonial economy.

In the northeast, the colonial authorities named all untitled land as trust land, even if it had not yet been surveyed for mineral resources. When the land commissions were adjourned to decide the new dual land tenure boundaries, there was not yet a comprehensive survey of mining resources (or the lack thereof) in the region. It was still uncertain where there were minerals, but the administration's default was to transfer crown land to native trust land; the Thomson–Sharpe treaties provided insufficient support to claim that the colonial state had derived its land authority from precolonial leaders in the area. Accordingly, one colonial officer explained that the entire northeast should be trust land because "it should be borne in mind in connection with North Eastern Rhodesia outside the concession areas that the natives have never resigned any rights in the land."[122] This was understood as a contrast to the land in the northwest, where the British used the Lewanika's treaties to assert that African populations had ceded their rights. Derived rights remained the bedrock of the British justification for state control over land even in the late colonial period.

Thus, in the northwest, colonial officers held longer debates on the division of land because the burden of proof was to show that the land was not of value to the crown before transferring it to trust land. They categorized land as trust land only if it had already been surveyed and found to be devoid of minerals, and if it was unlikely that any new railway would be built there. Conversely, land that had not been surveyed or could potentially accommodate a new railroad remained as crown land.[123] The first priority of the northwest's land committees was to retain zones with mining potential for the state. To this end, the administrators named all of the land in the four districts of the Copperbelt as crown land.[124] In their reports, they acknowledged both high demand from Africans for individual tenure in the zone and overcrowding of the existing native reserves, but made the decision that it would be

---

[122] Northern Rhodesia, "Pim Report," 45. That the chiefs in NER never gave up any land rights except for the Tanganyika concession is also discussed in Correspondence from Creech Jones, June 6, 1939, Box 3/314, Secretariat Series, NAZ.

[123] Trapnell, Ecologist for the Department of Agriculture, "Memorandum on the Suitability of Crown Land in North Western Rhodesia for European Settlement," September 18, 1935, SEC 3/283, Secretariat Series, NAZ.

[124] At the time of these decisions, the four Copperbelt Districts were: Luanshya, Kitwe, Mufulira, and Chingola.

"undesirable to permanently lock up land in the Copperbelt" for African use.[125] Their second priority was the interests of settler agriculture; to this effect, the stated goal was to retain the best agricultural land as crown land. The colonial officials discussed a few characteristics that made land unsuitable for European agriculture. Land that did not have proximity to the railway or other transportation for access to internal and international markets had low value to the crown. Similarly, undesirable land was heavily wooded, prone to tsetse flies, and had an unfavorable climate.[126] The information they used to evaluate land suitability in the northwest included ecological and agricultural survey reports, interviews with farmers and chiefs, and a few aerial surveys. The data available ranged by location. For example, for the land in the southern railway belt, a British ecologist carefully mapped the different soils.[127] By contrast, in Mkushi, which would later be a major center of commercial agriculture in Zambia, the local commission had no survey. Instead, they relied on the testimony of a missionary living there for information on soil quality.

The British continued to make land policies that upheld their narrative of rights derived from sovereign authorities four decades after the initial treaties with the Lewanika in the northwest and the failed attempts at signing treaties with powerful precolonial leaders in the northeast. They erred on the side of ceding crown land to customary tenure in the northeast and holding on to crown land in the northwest, where they maintained that agreements with the Lewanika had granted them "the full and entire control of the lands throughout North Western Rhodesia."[128] At the same time, the colonial state's desire to uphold the initial treaties to justify British land control also constrained its access to certain areas of high value land. The Lewanika's treaties had designated timber-rich land in the far west of Zambia as off-limits to the colonial administration. Even as colonial officers contemplated the economic value of different areas of land in Zambia during the trust land commissions, there was no debate over the land decisions enshrined in the early treaties with the Lewanika about the Lozi customary domain. Much like the previous colonial land policies, these dual land tenure boundaries reflected both political and economic considerations.

---

[125] Northern Rhodesia, "Eccles' Report," 13.   [126] Ibid.
[127] Trapnell, "Memorandum on the Suitability of Crown Land."
[128] Preamble to The Northern Rhodesia (Native Trust Land) Order in Council 1945. See footnote 37 for the full text.

Senegal

In the later colonial period, the French continued to encourage land registration while increasing their recognitions of customary institutions. In the period after World War I, it became apparent that the French had been unsuccessful in imposing their vision of land titling and direct rule on the population in Senegal. Instead, the French were forced to adapt their approaches to customary authority and land tenure, increasingly shifting to elements of indirect rule.

The French had failed to make land titling desirable or entirely accessible to the African population. Contrary to the expectations of colonial policymakers, farmers in Senegal did not flock to title their land. Instead, communities preserved their systems of complex group rights and resisted the regime's attempts to impose fully individualized tenure.[129] The French policies in this period reflected the continuing tension between the administration's desire to accelerate land registration and its growing appreciation of the durability of the customary land tenure regime. For example, in 1925, they issued a decree that both acknowledged the existence of customary land rights and established local land registries where individuals could gain certificates from the administration to codify these customary claims.[130] The French were recognizing that non-statutory rights existed while trying to make them individualized and legible to the state. They had justified their authority as freeing the African populations from inefficient customary land rights and feudal rulers.[131] Yet customary authorities retained their influence over property rights, even without being empowered as in Zambia.

Thus, in parallel with policies that conceded to the endurance of customary property rights, despite their best attempts to encourage land

---

[129] Faye 2008, 6.
[130] AOF, Décret du 8 octobre 1925 sur les droits fonciers des indigènes. See also N'gaide 2015, 81.
[131] They also continued to repeat the "rights of the victor" narrative to justify the colonial state's authority over land. For example, when the lieutenant governor of Senegal suggested in a 1923 letter that the members of the precolonial Lebou institution should be compensated for the land they lost when the port of Dakar was built, the head of the AOF reminded him of "the superior rights that are the claim of the state." He argued that it had been well established that there were no individual property rights among the indigenous populations prior to the colonial occupation. Instead land rights were "an attribute of the sovereignty belonging uniquely to chiefs ... [the chief] had eminent domain over the soil." He then reminded his lieutenant that the property rights of all precolonial sovereigns had transferred to the colonial state. Correspondence from M. Merlin, Governor General of AOF, to the Lieutenant Governor of Senegal. February 27, 1923. 1 R 050. ANS.

registration, the French also adapted their approach to chiefs in Senegal. In the 1930s, they incrementally increased their recognitions of customary authority rooted in institutions with popular legitimacy. Their 1935 decree on the reorganization of the African administration created a new policy in which local leaders had to provide verbal confirmation that the administration's choice of canton chiefs respected the customary system. Two years later, the regime implemented another policy, inviting customary authorities in the district to consult and vote for the new canton chief among a set of candidates selected by the administration.[132] These changes indicate that the French were slowly acknowledging their reliance on existing systems of authority, despite their initial philosophy of colonial conquest. Like the British, they needed African leaders to help them govern. Nevertheless, the canton chiefs continued to function as low-level agents in the regime who could be replaced. For example, both the British and the French relied on chiefs to collect taxes, but the French did not create native treasuries that gave chiefs discretion over the revenue. The French engaged with customary authorities without the intention of building an apparatus for their autonomous rule.

Resistance to and lack of interest in land registration continued until the end of French rule. On the eve of independence, the administration made a last-ditch effort to expand the system of land registration, this time by allowing registries to recognize collective land rights. Before this 1955 decree, statutory property rights were only for individuals. The new policy allowed a "land chief or other customary authority" to apply for a title for a collectively used piece of land.[133] To obtain a collective title, the chief was required to submit a written application with: the size of the land; information on the origins of the system of customary land rights; a list of families in the collective domain; and a map with the geographic features of the land. Then, a group of lineage heads and elites in the community or the general public would meet to evaluate the legitimacy of the request. The new law made it possible for a chief to apply for the colonial state to register his jurisdiction over a zone of collective rights, therefore authorizing small pockets of official customary authority over land. However, the process was burdensome and not widely adopted. Unlike in Zambia, collective land rights under the authority of an

---

[132] Zuccarelli 1973, 223.
[133] Republic of France, Décret 55-580 du 20 mai 1955. Its implementation was clarified in Republic of France, Décret 56-704 du 10 juillet 1956. These laws applied to both French West Africa (AOF) and French Equatorial Africa (AEF).

individual chief were not enforced from above. Instead, customary authorities retained their control of land informally. Chiefs continued to be the primary authorities governing property rights, adjudicating land conflicts, and allocating land for African populations within colonial Senegal. Yet they did so within institutions and domains that were recognized locally but not officially.

In early colonial rule, the French considered customary authorities from precolonial polities – those they termed chiefs or sovereigns – as challengers to the state that needed to be subdued. In the words of French colonial administrator (and historian) Hubert Deschamps, the French practiced "nonchalance" toward precolonial political institutions in sub-Saharan Africa; kingdoms and chiefdoms were "left to die," "abandoned to disrepair by our indifference."[134] Yet in the later colonial period, the colonial regime in Senegal implemented policies that increasingly embraced customary authority as a resource for their colonial projects. They granted small rights to customary authorities, such as consultation privileges in the choice of canton chiefs, and established informal ties with them. However, even when they relied on the de facto influence of customary institutions, they did not grant them the de jure power that the British did in Zambia. Similarly, unlike Zambia's coordinated, top-down dual land tenure institutions, the French policies recognizing customary property rights were incremental adaptations, given the failure of their attempts to replace existing authorities and property rights institutions with the state's.

Summary: The Status of State Authority over Land at Independence

This chapter has so far established the differences between the founding philosophies of the French and British in Senegal and Zambia, respectively, and how they used land policies to reinforce their approaches toward customary authorities. The European powers' policies were couched in two different paternalistic claims that fit within their broader colonial narratives and governance approaches. The British justified denying African populations access to land titling as a means of preventing them from becoming landless or indebted – they needed to be protected from markets. In addition, British discourses claimed that African populations could only understand local customs or "tradition," and this was why the colonial state needed to prevent the erosion of the preexisting

---

[134] Deschamps 1963, 303.

political institutions. The French also framed their policies with claims of helping the African populations. Instead of being protected from markets, however, they asserted that the Africans in Senegal needed to be protected from their chiefs. To the French, these systems of customary authority were akin to feudal exploitation. They believed individual rights were necessary for the population to invest in agricultural production.[135] Further, they hoped the customary system would atrophy if they ignored it and promoted titling.[136] In contrast to the British emphasis on conserving existing power structures, the French used the language of "evolution" and "progress" to describe their policies in Senegal.

Despite the differences in their land policies, the two countries had similar amounts of land under customary or state control at the end of colonial rule. In Senegal, scholars estimate that 95 percent of the land was customary at independence in 1960.[137] When Zambia became independent in 1964, 94 percent of the territory was customary land, according to government documents. However, beneath these similarities are meaningful differences in the characteristics of the 5–6 percent state land.

As the French made concessions to the customary tenure system, they retained their commitment to the philosophy of eminent domain and mass land titling. The colonial state had established its authority to access land through the 1904 policy, which deemed the state to be the owner of all unused land, and the underlying principle that the land ownership rights of all precolonial sovereigns had transferred to the state. This justification for the state's complete land authority did not require the French to create specific zones of customary or state land tenure as the British did in Zambia. The French designated a few zones as classified forests and created large land titles for specific commercial agricultural projects, but unlike British colonies, there were no major colonial resettlement or villagization schemes in Senegal. Much of the land under direct state control in Senegal had been individually registered through piecemeal titling, whereas in Zambia state land included massive areas that the colonial regime had designated as crown land for different purposes. French land planning was ad hoc relative to British land engineering and this generated differences in titling at the end of the colonial era.

The 6 percent of Zambia's land categorized as state land at independence included several very large agricultural titles and major areas of land

---

[135] Doublier, *La Propriété Foncière en AOF*.
[136] Georges François, *L'Afrique Occidentale Française*, 1907, Paris: Larose, 213.
[137] M. C. Diop 2013, 242.

reserved for the state. There were over 2 million ha of game reserves and forests and 2.5 million ha of titles granted to companies known as the "Big Concessions." Township areas were also designated as state land in Zambia's dual land tenure system, even if the land was untitled. In Senegal, state land included thousands of smaller land titles. Titles above 200 ha were rare, even on agricultural land.[138] In 1935, a year in which comparable data are available for both countries, Zambia had 671 freehold titles, 186 agricultural leases, 207 township leases, and 110 leases for mining and missions.[139] In the same year in Senegal, there were 9,272 titles in circulation, including township plots. This includes, for example, 2,385 titles in the greater Kaolack region on 23,857 ha of land and 1,420 titles in the greater Dakar area on 7,362 ha of land.[140] Although multiple French attempts to promote titling were ignored by the African populations who "continued to consider themselves as the real owners of the land of their ancestors, therefore having no need to change its status,"[141] there were still notable differences in the number of small-scale agricultural titles among the two colonies at independence, which reflected the two colonial powers' divergent approaches to land planning. These distinct land rights–governance nexuses created by British and French colonialism laid the legal groundwork for modern Zambia and Senegal. Just as the architects of the colonial layer responded to the precolonial institutions, independent governments in African countries had to build upon these colonial institutions.

4.3 CUSTOMARY AUTHORITY AND LAND CONTROL IN INDEPENDENT ZAMBIA AND SENEGAL

The institutions established by the colonial regimes related to land tenure and customary authorities have been remarkably resilient in the post-independence era. This is a result of their synchronicity. The colonial regimes designed policies for land governance and customary authority that were

---

[138] AOF, "Regime des Concessions," AOF R Series 1902–1946, 1R/00050, ANS; AOF, "Statistiques foncières: assiette de la propriété foncière consistance du domaine de l'État, livres foncières (1927–1935)," Box 2O9, Domaine et Enregistrement Séries, ANS.

[139] Northern Rhodesia, "Ministry of Land Annual Reports" 1935–1946, Shelf 16/Box 93A, Government Series, NAZ.

[140] Calculations based on AOF, "Statistiques foncières: assiette de la propriété foncière consistance du domaine de l'État, livres foncières (1927–1935)," Box 2O9, Domaine et Enregistrement Séries, ANS.

[141] D. Diop 2013, 74.

complementary, making them mutually reinforcing. However, this also made it harder to change them without calling into question the systems of property rights and local governance in Zambia and Senegal. As a result, the postindependence governments in each country have maintained these initial colonial institutions, with only incremental changes in land tenure regulations. The independent state institutions in Zambia have reinforced the colonial system of dual land tenure and official chiefs. By contrast, the state in Senegal has continued the policy of tolerating customary control of land while encouraging land titling. Despite several key laws in the independence era described in this section, the differences among British and French rule have had lasting impacts on land tenure in the two countries.

The postindependence leaders of African countries faced a common challenge of deciding how to engage with colonial era chiefs. In many African countries, including Senegal, independent governments nationalized land tenure and undermined the power of chiefs.[142] On the contrary, Zambia's government did not follow the trend of weakening chiefs' rights. Instead, the first Zambian constitution established the House of Chiefs, an assembly of chiefs tasked with advising the president and parliament on policy issues.[143] The government also retained the dual land tenure system, with official chiefs as the custodians of all land within established chiefdom boundaries. Barotseland, however, lost its special status relative to the other customary institutions in the new country. On the eve of independence, the reigning Lewanika signed an agreement with the first president of Zambia, Kenneth Kaunda, to be part of a unified Zambia with the same standing as other paramount chiefs.[144] With some incremental modifications, the Zambian government upheld the status quo of the colonial regime's customary land and customary authority policies.

The most important change in property rights institutions in independent Zambia occurred in 1975 under the one-party regime of Kaunda. Following his "watershed speech," the government transformed all freehold titles to ninety-nine-year leases.[145] Freehold titles were uncommon in British colonies after 1946 and not technically allowed in Northern Rhodesia,[146] so it was the freehold titles established earlier in the colonial era that were particularly affected by the 1975 land reform policy. The law expanded the state's control over land in relation to private

---

[142] D. Williams 1996; Diaw 2005; Ouedraogo 2011.
[143] Republic of Zambia, The Constitution of Zambia, 1964.
[144] Barotseland Agreement of 1964.
[145] Republic of Zambia, The Land (Conversion of Titles) Act, 1975.
[146] Meek 1946, 246.

4.3 Customary Authority and Land Control

individuals and noncitizens. It served to nationalize Zambia's land by switching from a freehold to leasehold model of titling. It did not, however, change the system of customary control over land.

Rather, it was a 1995 Lands Act that has gone the farthest in advancing the Zambian state's control of land in relation to chiefs.[147] The act clarified the procedure for converting customary land to statutory titles, in order to make titling more accessible. Previously, the process was outlined in an administrative circular from 1985, but was not well understood.[148] The Lands Act also declared that all land was vested in the president and established that all leasehold titles would be subject to ground rents (taxes). At the same time, the act empowered customary authorities by requiring the chief's approval for new titles on customary land. It, therefore, acknowledged customary tenure and customary land authority, while facilitating the expansion of state property rights.

In contrast to Zambia, legislation designed to weaken the powers of chiefs over land was a key policy priority for the government of newly independent Senegal. Its 1964 National Domain Law reversed the colonial state's (limited) recognitions of customary and collective rights. It established a unitary system of land registration and attempted to eradicate customary ownership rights, such as those based on lineage or inheritance, by designating all untitled land as part of the national domain. Therefore, any land that was not registered with state property rights was legally owned by the entire nation, not by its individual (or familial) users.[149] The law thus established that citizens can only have usage rights on the country's customary land. To own it, in the eyes of the state, they would need to title it.

The governance of customary land in Senegal was assigned to local elected councils starting in 1972.[150] These councils are under the authority of the sub-prefect level of administration. However, the councils had limited functionality until the 1996 Local Government Code reorganized the councils and provided them with greater resources and technical capacity to implement local governance, including overseeing the first stage of titling land in Senegal.[151] Despite the intent of the 1964 National Domain Law to undermine customary authorities' control over land by denying the existence of any lineage-based rights, the decentralized system, with councillors elected from within a community, has

---

[147] Republic of Zambia. Lands Act, 1995.
[148] Republic of Zambia. Procedure on Land Alienation. Land Circular No. 1, 1985.
[149] Republic of Senegal. Loi 64-46 du 17 juin 1964 relative au domaine national.
[150] Republic of Senegal. Loi 72-25 du 19 avril 1972 relative aux communautes rurales.
[151] Republic of Senegal. Loi 96-06 du 22 mars 1996 portant Code des Collectivités locales.

allowed for de facto customary control. The authority of Senegal's chiefs is not buttressed as a matter of official policy, but they still have opportunities to continue to exert influence over land (as described in Chapter 2). Thus, as Boone has argued of this law, placing the responsibility for land allocation in the hands of locally elected councils can "defend authority-based systems of control over land use rights."[152]

However, the Senegalese state has also used this decentralized land registration process to encourage land titling and extend its control over land. The contemporary legal framework permits any customary land to be converted to the state's property rights, at the behest of or with the permission of the current users and the councillors. This system is dissatisfying to many, yet challenging to change, given tensions between state and customary or local interests. As a result, land reform has been regularly debated in Senegal since the mid-1990s, and policymakers have circulated several draft land laws.[153] This includes the 2004 Framework for Agro-Sylvo-Pastoral Development (*loi d'orientation agro-sylvo-pastorale* or LOASP), which, as Ndiaye described, sparked "the scramble for land in Senegal" by promoting land markets and agricultural modernization.[154] The state's attempts to increase agricultural production at the start of the twenty-first century have further reinforced the spirit of the National Domain Law and contributed to the expansion of formal property rights. Chapter 6 begins at the advent of this rapid increase in demand for customary land in Senegal.

Both the 1996 Local Government Code in Senegal and the 1995 Lands Act in Zambia are part of a larger trend of governments facilitating the expansion of land titling. They reflect the doctrine that economic development through agricultural production requires formal, individual property rights. In this way, Zambia and Senegal represent similar responses to the interaction of precolonial and colonial land institutions, as well as the global push for land titling. In the postindependence era, both have permitted customary land to remain in place while also arranging for it to be replaced by land titles when demand arises. In doing so, they have both established processes of incremental state building.

4.4 CONCLUSION

This chapter has provided an overview of three key layers of political institutions in two countries on different sides of the African continent,

---

[152] Boone 1992, 108.   [153] Fall and Ngaïdo 2016.   [154] A. Ndiaye 2019, 152.

spanning 200 years. This is, consequently, the big picture, but not the complete picture. Nevertheless, all three layers contribute to the contemporary state of property rights regimes in the two countries that are the focus of the remainder of the book.

The colonial institutions received the greatest detail because these distinct colonial philosophies of customary authority and land governance generate the institutional context for contemporary state building in Zambia and Senegal. In Senegal, customary authorities have unofficial influence within society and over land. The French colonial administrators considered chiefs to be feudal lords, comparable to French feudalism, who undermined African economic development.[155] At the same time, they recognized the utility of collaborating with chiefs for assisting in local governance, maintaining stability, and facilitating the collection of taxes.[156] As a result, after the initial conquest, the French did little to disrupt customary systems of land management and, at times, tried to work with them. There was no massive reorganization of the territory or the customary domain. As it became clear to the French that customary land authority was enduring, they relaxed their efforts to replace it with state land registration. The French approach to customary property rights thus shifted over time from decreeing that anyone without titles had only "precarious occupation rights" in 1865,[157] to reducing the state's land ownership domain to only unused land (*terres vacantes et sans maître*) in 1904,[158] and finally to the 1955 accommodations for registering collective land tenure.[159] The French had created a regime where any land in the country could come under their direct authority through state titling, while simultaneously allowing chiefs and customary rules to determine access to the rest of the land. As a result, the continuing power of these rules and leaders depended on their influence over local populations and councils, with only informal ties to the state.

---

[155] For examples of this language, see Doublier, *La Propriété Foncière en AOF* and Geismar, Administrateur en chef des Colonies, *Recueil des coutumes civiles des races du Senegal*, 1933. ANS.

[156] On French administration's reliance on African authorities for tax collection, see Zuccarelli 1973, 237 on Senegal and Firmin-Sellers 2000b on colonial Côte d'Ivoire.

[157] French Empire, Arrêté du 11 mars 1865. In this text, Governor Faidherbe established that indigenous populations have the right to ask for titles and that in the future only land rights granted through titles will be recognized and protected (Doublier, *La Propriété Foncière en AOF*).

[158] AOF, Décret du 23 octobre 1904.

[159] Republic of France, Décret 55-580 du mai 20 1955 and Republic of France, Décret 56-704 du 10 juillet 1956.

While the French permitted customary control over land, the British enabled it. British colonial land policies and divisions of land supported this approach to customary authority. From the start of their occupation of Zambia, the British recognized existing political institutions and used them to justify their rule. Their early focus on identifying chiefs to legitimize their regime and facilitate African governance became an official policy of indirect rule. The partition of the land into native reserves directly supported this approach to colonial governance, by making a citizen's access to land contingent on ties with the chief and the ethnic group. This policy consolidated authority over the land of thousands of smallholders in the hands of individual chiefs. Today, the system of clearly defined boundaries between customary and state land remains. Each community residing on customary land officially derives its rights from one chief who the state treats as the custodian of that land. The institutions in which these official chiefs are embedded, and the networks of other customary authorities that influence their decisions, vary throughout the country.

The British colonial regime created the foundation for Zambia's system of state-recognized chiefs. An official role for chiefs provides them with opportunities to shape where the state accesses land, much like the Lewanika was able to do in the colonial era. Today, any new title on customary land must have the written permission of an official chief. Without it, the state's system of property rights cannot expand. However, while the Lewanika could set some terms, the British were also able to use their ties to him to justify the state's acquisition of land. Similarly, the official role for Zambia's chiefs means their authority depends, in part, on the state. This creates incentives for them to comply with the state's requests, drawing these influential social intermediaries closer to the state.

The rest of this book examines the contemporary role of customary institutions in the expansion of land titling. Customary authorities in the two countries function differently today as a result of the legal frameworks established by the two colonial regimes. They have different relationships with the state, and, therefore, with citizens, as a result. However, in each country their responses to land titling also reflect the institutions in which they are embedded. This, in turn, suggests parallels in how customary institutions retain power and shape patterns of national state building. Subsequent chapters thus explore the similar impacts of customary institutions within these very different countries. Chapter 5 examines the struggle to control land in Zambia.

5

The Unofficial Differences among Official Chiefs in Zambia

Vertical Accountability and Patterns of Land Titling

The problem is the government. They go straight to the chief, they discuss, and they ask for a big piece of land. They come with envelopes and all things are concluded privately. They have no consideration for the people. They should come to the people and discuss to address their concerns also. Not with chiefs only.
—citizen, northern Zambia[1]

It's mandatory actually, when a chief says no, even if the president comes to me and says "I want this land." The law tells me that I'm the authority.
—chief, southern Zambia[2]

A: The chief agrees any time.
B: That is true, as long as there is money.
C: As long as there is money, people can even sleep outside.
[What else?]
B: Just that.
C: Money.
—citizens, southern Zambia[3]

Despite rapid growth and significant urbanization, Zambia's capital city cannot extend east or south. Instead, it sprawls to the northwest. This is not a product of geography, uneven infrastructure, or demographics.

---

[1] Interview with smallholder farmers (FFG-539), northern Zambia, February 12, 2014.
[2] Interview with customary authority (CA-542), Lusaka, Zambia, October 29, 2013.
[3] Interview with smallholder farmers (FFG-543), southern Zambia, October 31, 2013.

There are plenty of people who would like to title land in the southeast. Some are middle-class Lusaka residents interested in acquiring land to set up small shops and weekend farms. Others are commercial agents, who would like to build strip malls and restaurants to serve the rapidly growing capital city. Demand is high for this land. However, it is not demand but supply that decides the geography of Lusaka's urban development. The growth of Lusaka is determined by the customary authorities whose lands border the city. The chief to the southeast refuses to allow titles in her land. Investors and local farmers alike face the same response in this zone – no titles. Anyone looking for land to title must look elsewhere.[4] Many turn instead to the chief on the northwest side of the city, who freely allows new titles in her domain. Records in the local council indicate that between 2007 and 2013, she consented to 2,900 new titles, or 26 percent of her customary land.[5] The city is rapidly growing in this direction.

This chapter and the next examine the power that chiefs wield over land titling outcomes and the impacts of customary institutions on their decisions. The example of the chiefs whose lands border Lusaka highlights the importance of customary authorities as a key set of agents in the state-building process. They can either prevent or facilitate land titling in their zones; their responses to land titling shape how the state expands its control over property rights. While these individual chiefs have an important role in land governance, they do not function independently – they are embedded in customary institutions. These institutions vary in their capacity to generate constraints on leaders' decisions. This, in turn, impacts how chiefs weigh the costs of land titling. This chapter considers these issues in Zambia, where customary authorities have legally recognized rights in relation to the state and to customary land.

One effect of an official system of customary authority is to pull chiefs closer to the state. In Zambia, chiefs require the state's recognition to access a variety of benefits. They draw salaries from the state for themselves and their assistants, known as *kapasus*.[6] They gain political power as the official representatives of thousands of citizens living in their

---

[4] Between 2007 and 2013, this chief consented to titles for just 95 ha, or .04 percent of her land.

[5] Calculations based on all applications for titles that had the documented consent of the chief between 2007 and 2013 from district council minutes. Total land for each chiefdom from the 1958 chiefdom boundaries map.

[6] Republic of Zambia, The Chiefs Act, 1965 establishes chiefs' governmental subsidies and the position of kapasus.

domains. Bureaucrats incorporate them into decision-making and refer to rural land and populations by the name of the local chief. The state empowers individual chiefs in this system with concentrated power over land titling decisions for large areas of land, weakening the relative influence of other rural elites or unofficial customary authorities. In this context, maintaining recognition from the state is an additional incentive for official chiefs to comply with state and investor requests.

The official role of chiefs in Zambia also empowers them with more direct channels for influencing the state. Chiefs must consent to any changes in the land's status.[7] They have real power over this decision. Chiefs have refused well-planned, developmentally oriented requests for titles without offering any justification. In other cases, they have exacted high conditions for their consent, even for land deals with strong governmental support. By refusing land titling requests, some chiefs in Zambia have protected citizens from large land deals that would displace them. Their recognition by the state draws them closer to it, but it also strengthens their ability to challenge it.

This chapter proceeds by describing the great rush to title Zambia's customary land during the primary study period, 2007–13. It then introduces the costs and benefits that chiefs weighed during their land negotiations, based on their own words and from the perspective of Zambian citizens. After establishing the complex nature of these land titling decisions, the chapter explores whether and how they are shaped by customary institutions. A comparison of the Bemba and Bisa institutions in northern Zambia illustrates how hierarchical institutions can generate ties of vertical accountability. Official chiefs may be similarly empowered by the state, but significant internal differences among their institutions remain. Statistical analyses of the relationship between customary institutions and patterns in land titling throughout Zambia suggest that strong, hierarchical customary institutions are better able to retain control over land. Finally, the chapter concludes by examining the implications of Zambia's official chieftaincy system for citizens.

5.1 LAND APPETITES IN ZAMBIA, 2007–2013

The Zambian government responded to the rising global interest in African land in the first two decades of the twenty-first century by

---

[7] Republic of Zambia. Lands Act, 1995.

welcoming and facilitating new land deals. The combination of state policy and booming land markets transformed the control of land and property rights on millions of hectares of customary land between 2007 and 2013. These changes in authority over land were the result of countless local negotiations and individual decisions to pursue land titles. The following is a description of how state control over land grew during this period.

The state's representatives identified the increased global interest in African agricultural land, starting in 2007, as an opportunity to diversify its economy from reliance on copper mining revenues. Politicians argued that Zambia needed to commercialize and modernize its agricultural sector to drive economic growth. They wooed investors with tax breaks and narratives of Zambia's plentiful land and water resources. To help make customary land available to commercial investors, the state established an investor relations agency, the Zambia Development Agency (ZDA), in 2007. The ZDA served international investors who needed guidance in navigating the customary land tenure system, while domestic agricultural investors generally approached chiefs to negotiate over land through their own networks. Between 2007 and 2012 alone, the ZDA helped establish 132 new commercial agricultural projects. The most frequent international investors in Zambia were their former colonial power, the British. This was followed by South Africa, China, United States, Greece, and Russia, respectively. The state justified their policy of encouraging such land deals through calculations that, collectively, this set of commercial farms would hire 19,000 workers and invest 1.2 billion USD in their projects.[8]

In addition to facilitating private investments, bureaucrats initiated new land deals on customary land for government projects during this era. The government designed a new program to create 100,000 ha farm blocks in every province of the country, which could then be leased to agricultural investors. The program required state agents to negotiate with chiefs for large areas of customary land to convert to state land titles. While some chiefs refused to participate, others agreed; by 2013, chiefs had consented to ceding 757,000 ha of customary land for the farm block program. State agents also expanded the stock of state land in the country through the government's land resettlement program, as described at the start of Chapter 1. Developing these planned agricultural

---

[8] Estimates from Zambia Development Agency database of agricultural investments, updated through 2012.

settlements for urban youths, retired civil servants, and refugees also required bureaucrats to identify chiefs willing to consent to permanently relinquish customary land. The state was able to access 490,000 ha of land for their resettlement program in this period. Finally, a third major source of demand for customary land from bureaucrats was the expansion of township boundaries. On customary land, the government did not have the authority to plan communities, markets, or land use, as a result of a law that significantly reinforced the autonomy of chiefs within their domains.[9] Instead, bureaucrats tasked with town planning duties had to negotiate with chiefs for customary land to be transferred to state land tenure in the form of new township land. After local governments acquired this customary land, they could lease it out as town plots. In three sampled provinces, townships contributed over 100,000 ha of additional land conversions.[10]

Global land markets were a catalyst for the expansion of land titling in this time period. Customary land in Zambia has no standard market value prior to titling, so negotiations with chiefs determine land prices.[11] Customary land was consequently perceived as both inexpensive and increasingly scarce in an era of visibly increasing large-scale land investments. Urban elites and middle classes observed the land rush and wanted to secure their own stakes. Politicians, including the president and the leader of the opposition, sought large areas of customary land as personal investments. Many land deals during this time were initiated by Zambians who saw acquiring land as a retirement strategy or investment for the future but did not have immediate plans to use the land. Land registration was particularly desirable for individuals who lived far from their new plots or were not intensively farming them. In this era, land deals initiated by private actors were even more numerous than those initiated by state actors, as described above. District council records in three of the nine provinces documented that chiefs had consented to private sector titling applications for 1,147,000 ha of customary land between 2007 and 2013.

---

[9] The Town and Country Planning Act of 1962 established that the government did not have planning authority on customary land. This was repealed in 2015 by the Urban and Regional Planning Act.

[10] When chiefs agree to cede customary land to expand the domain of the township, the land is then subdivided and planned by the district councils, who sell them as town plots for residences or businesses. In the sample of three provinces, 123,054 ha were converted for townships; calculations based on district council minutes.

[11] Any compensation is for displacement or the cost of improvements to the land, but not the land itself unless it is titled.

Some were titles for international investors, others were land titles for Zambian investors, elites, and middle classes.

If the local chief had agreed, this feverish expansion of land titling benefited the state. New titles generated revenue for the state from immediate application fees and long-term commitments to pay land taxes. They added to the stocks of state land by shifting authority from a chief to the state. The conversion of land was permanent, even if the actors named on the leasehold title lost interest in their agricultural projects. This was not an uncommon outcome in this era, as investors with limited experience in commercial farming realized that growing biofuels such as jatropha and palm oil were not quite as easy as they had imagined. When local populations were displaced by land deals or frustrated that they had not been consulted, the politicians could fault the chiefs. After all, a customary authority had consented to each new land title.

State actors encouraged and participated in this transformation in land tenure and property rights in Zambia in this era, yet they were reluctant to force a resistant chief to cede an area of land. They hesitated to use the state's power to impose land conversions on behalf of government programs or moneyed investors because they were wary of the chiefs' considerable influence over local populations. Instead, district council officers pleaded with chiefs "to surrender" land in order to extend their townships.[12] Bureaucrats reported that "the chiefs have the government on their knees begging for land."[13] Both state agents and private buyers recounted that if it was too difficult to obtain land from one chief, they sought out land governed by a more willing chief. Chiefs themselves were adamant that the government could not title their land without their permission.[14] As a result, the pattern of Lusaka's urban sprawl was

---

[12] For example, one council meeting in 2007 opened with the speech: "As Honorable Members are aware, the demand for land various development purposed [sic] in the district has more than trebled [sic] since the year 2000 ... I therefore wish to make an appeal to our traditional rulers who are the custodians of most land in the district to surrender part of their land to the council, to enable the council to re-plan it for various development activities required in the district." Three years later they lamented that "Although the government has already funded the council for the re-planning of the township, the exercise cannot be done until more land is secured for the expansion of the township." By the end of the study period in 2013, they still had not accessed land from chiefs for expanding the township. Such examples were common.

[13] Interview with bureaucrat (BUR-634), Lusaka, Zambia, October 22, 2013.

[14] For examples, "No, the government doesn't come to anyone to say 'convert these things to state land'" (interview with customary authority (CA-537), central Zambia, October 16, 2013); "When you don't want to convert land there is no offense, you don't want [to]" (interview with customary authority (CA-582); central Zambia, November 1,

repeated on land throughout the country. The locations of changes in the control over land reflected the decisions of chiefs.

5.2 CHIEFS' RESPONSES TO LAND TITLING

Chiefs in Zambia must consider a variety of competing issues in deciding on any new land titles. They are key decision makers in the transformation of customary land rights to the statutory system, yet they make these decisions in a low-information environment. They are not trained land technicians or agricultural officers. Some have a great depth of knowledge about the local populations and how they use the land. They may themselves be smallholder farmers. However, each official chief controls a large area of land – on average, 190,000 ha – without the resources or training to collect detailed and representative information.[15] Consequently, their evaluations of the potential political and economic ramifications of each land title have a large impact on their decisions.

The connection between retaining control over customary land and the institution's power is discussed openly among customary authorities in Zambia. For example, the constitution of Barotseland, the Lozi customary institution in Western Province, states: "Land, water, natural resources (animate and inanimate) within Barotseland, shall *forever* belong to the Nation and People of Barotseland."[16] Chiefs are aware that customary land is central to the institution's survival and continuing influence. Their authority to adjudicate conflicts, demand tribute, expropriate land, and reallocate it as they see fit is contingent on the untitled status of the land. Once it is titled, this source of power erodes.

The sentiment among chiefs that consenting to land titling reduces their influence was pervasive in my interviews with them. One flatly stated: "The more land I give away, the more power I give away."[17] Zambia's chiefs have also openly discouraged their peers from ceding customary land and campaigned to convince the public of their

---

2013); and "[if the chief says no to the council] It ends up there. We'll put a full stop. They will not have that land. It's law. It's mandatory actually when a chief says no, even if the President comes to me and says 'I want this land.' The law tells me that I'm the authority" (interview with customary authority (CA-542), Lusaka, Zambia, October 29, 2013).

[15] Calculations based on author's georeferenced 1958 chiefdom boundaries map, introduced in Chapter 4.
[16] Barotseland. *The Constitution of Barotseland*, Article 8.2, 2012. Accessed at www.barotseland.info/Constitution.html. Emphasis added.
[17] Interview with customary authority (CA-507), Lusaka, Zambia, July 18, 2012.

importance in effective land governance. They have warned each other to be careful about land conversions because titling "is a one-way traffic and so we find that one of the consequences is that we ourselves risk becoming landless."[18] Another chief cautioned his fellow chiefs that they needed to prevent "the evil manifestations of the powerful and merciless forces, both local and foreign, who are day and night scheming ways to alienate customary land and consignee [sic] the poorest of the poor to slavery far worse than death itself."[19] Echoing this sentiment that keeping land under customary authority is in the interest of the members of the institution more broadly, another chief told a reporter that: "We are worried because you can't be a chief without land. If the land goes in the hands of the President or the government, most of our people won't have an opportunity to have land. We are interested in helping those that can't manage to buy."[20]

The Zambian House of Chiefs (HoC), an advisory body composed of chiefs, has regularly discussed the topic of maintaining customary control of land. The HoC mobilized to block elements of the 2012 and 2014 draft constitutions that, in the words of its chair, "erode chiefs' powers over customary land by converting it into state land."[21] Chiefs from multiple customary institutions were quoted in the press speaking out against articles in the draft constitution that expanded the definition of state land to include surface rights for land where minerals are found and vested all land in the president.[22] Similarly, in 2018, they walked out of a meeting with the government over a land policy that they believed curtailed their powers.[23] Further, even the government's proposed land audit was understood by customary authorities to be part of the "battle between the government and the chief."[24] A land audit would make customary land more legible to the state and was therefore perceived as an infringement upon the sovereignty of chiefs.

---

[18] "Land in Zambia Will Soon Be in Foreign Hands, Warns Chief Mumena," *The Post*, June 18, 2012; "Puta Warns of Shocking Consequences over Land," *The Post*, March 11, 2014.

[19] Senior Chief Mwamba Kanyanta-Manga II (Henry Sosola), "A Paper Presented to the Participants at a Workshop on the Review of the Land Administration Circular No. 1 of 1985" (Chrismar Hotel, Livingstone, August 15, 2011).

[20] "Draft Land Article Annoys Nkomeshya," *The Post*, March 12, 2014.

[21] "Chiefs Call for Calm," *Times of Zambia*, March 14, 2014.

[22] "Chiefs Reject Draft Constitution," *The Post*, March 7, 2014.

[23] "House of Chiefs Reject Draft National Land Policy and Walk Out of Meeting," *Lusaka Times*, March 1, 2018.

[24] Interview with customary authority (CA-556), northern Zambia, January 14, 2014.

5.2 Chiefs' Responses to Land Titling

The theme of titling as collectively costly also appeared in chiefs' discussions of smallholder titling. Chiefs who opposed farmers adopting titles for their small plots of land emphasized the impact on the community. One chief reported that she refused smallholder title applications because she feared that her subjects would then quickly sell the titled land and become landless.[25] Another chief discouraged titling on the grounds that it would reduce community access to shared resources: "If anyone ever strays there to get mushrooms, caterpillars, or firewood, that is an offense and they can even be shot and killed and the chief would be answerable. So, in chiefdoms, we wouldn't punish the people like that by giving title deeds anywhere, anyhow. So, we don't give title deeds here."[26]

Underlying these justifications for refusing smallholder titling is an awareness of the long-term implications for the chiefdom and customary land tenure. This suggests that chiefs are as conscious of the power implications of smallholder titling as they are of large-scale land deals, despite the important differences in scale and visibility of the two processes. As one chief put it,

> We, as villagers, we depend on land, our living depends on land. So, if we get a title to every piece then we'll have problems. So, we are restricted, myself, in my chiefdom ... I'm strict on that one. Because I cannot allow anyone to get a title for a small piece of land. Why? That land can only be given to him, use it, if he fails, he fails, and then somebody else takes over.[27]

Another northern Zambian chief compared smallholder land titling to the experience of neighboring Tanzania, where *ujamaa* villagization schemes and land redistribution weakened historical customary institutions. He explained that if he allowed smallholders to title their land "everyone will jump at it and they'll just get 2 ha, 5 ha, and the whole place will just be titled and the chieftainship is as good as being killed ... I don't know if that's what development wants, to lead us to be like Tanzania where you have no chieftainships anywhere."[28] Chiefs revealed in interviews that when they evaluate prospective titles, they consider the loss of political power during their reigns, the erosion of the long-term power of the institution, and the implications of titling for community members more broadly.

---

[25] Interview with customary authority (CA-537), central Zambia, October 16, 2013.
[26] Interview with customary authority (CA-562), northern Zambia, January 29, 2014.
[27] Interview with customary authority (CA-546), northern Zambia, February 4, 2014.
[28] Interview with customary authority (CA-553), northern Zambia, February 10, 2014.

However, there are also individual benefits that motivate chiefs to agree to land titles, particularly for large land deals. Citizens on customary land were quick to report that chiefs receive material incentives for agreeing to land titles. In my focus groups, the greed of an individual chief was a common refrain. They compared chiefs who were "good" and refused land deals to those who were "bad" and readily agreed to titles on their customary land. Citizens from different chiefdoms reported: "As long as there is money, people can even sleep outside [be displaced]";[29] "The chief can convert the land because he loves money. So, if one of you has a lot of money, approach the chief to give you land and all of us here will be displaced";[30] and "We just hear that land has been sold and sometimes you see the chief driving a small car, exchanged for a very big piece of land where people have fields."[31] As community leaders, Zambia's chiefs negotiate compensation for the local population. The payments that chiefs receive are consequently described not as remuneration for land sales but as "customary tribute," with the implication that it will be shared. Elsewhere in Zambia, scholars have documented examples of customary tribute to chiefs including vehicles, "palaces" (chiefs' residences), and cash.[32] The individual economic benefits of agreeing to land titles are a powerful incentive for Zambia's chiefs, who often live in similar or only slightly better economic conditions than other members of their communities.

Chiefs weigh these material benefits and power considerations relative to their personal evaluations of the collective benefits of specific land deals and land titling more generally. When asked, chiefs most often cited "development" as the reason they agreed to large land deals. One reported ceding 100,000 ha to the state because "we were told that bridges would be built, roads will be improved, electricity will come over and there will be plenty of developments."[33] Other chiefs reported that they agreed to large-scale land deals due to potential job creation.[34] Agricultural investors were expected to bring jobs; the state was expected to bring roads. Chiefs (and citizens) often believe it is their role to attract

---

[29] Interview with smallholder farmers (FFG-543), southern Zambia, October 31, 2013.
[30] Interview with smallholder farmers (FFG-566), northern Zambia, February 17, 2014.
[31] Interview with smallholder farmers (FFG-565), northern Zambia, January 29, 2014.
[32] Brown 2005.
[33] Interview with customary authority (CA-586), central Zambia, October 18, 2013.
[34] Interviews customary authority (CA-644), northern Zambia, September 17, 2013; with customary authority (CA-562), northern Zambia, January 29, 2014; with customary authority (CA-520), southern Zambia, July 25, 2012.

development and negotiate with the state for resources in their areas.[35] However, chiefs have limited capacity to enforce the promises of the investors or the state after they have consented to the deal. Once land has been converted from customary to state title, the land and its users are no longer under the chief's control.

As described previously, chiefs have the agency to refuse land titling and negotiate for higher costs to access land in their domain. In addition, some chiefs in Zambia have developed their own "chief's titles" in order to prevent the loss of power through statutory land titling. This innovation addresses the demand from citizens for recognition of individual usage rights without the chief having to cede control over customary land to the state. These documents are unique to each chiefdom, developed by entrepreneurial chiefs. Examples collected during fieldwork included maps stamped by the chief, handwritten letters with descriptions of the land, color-printed certificates, and registry books to keep track of land usage. These often include spiritual symbols of the customary institutions, such as the elephant featured in the Lozi customary title[36] or the Bemba crocodile totem. Chiefs have taken the initiative to develop their own informal land papers in order to improve citizens' feelings of tenure security, without ceding authority over the land.[37] These are entirely outside of the statutory property rights regime and at the discretion of the customary authority. However, they further highlight how chiefs have attempted to slow the loss of customary land.

Chiefs are a core set of agents in the land titling process in Zambia. These two sections have established that chiefs in Zambia both publicly decried the titling of customary land and consented to the conversion of millions of hectares of land between 2007 and 2013. Beneath these two trends lies a vast range of responses by chiefs. As individual agents, they weigh multiple incentives in making highly consequential decisions about land titling in their zones. Their personal experiences, leadership styles, and visions for the community, among many other individual characteristics, shape their approaches to land titling. However, as the next sections will demonstrate, the institutions in which these individual authorities are embedded also shape how they weigh the costs of land titling. These customary institutions make it possible for chiefs to be

---

[35] Gould 2010. [36] Muyakwa, Munalula, and Mudenda 2003, 85.
[37] This type of institutional innovation in property rights has also been documented in West Africa and Madagascar. See Koné and Chauveau 1998; Lavigne Delville 2002; Jacoby and Minten 2007; Bellemare 2013; Honig 2022.

unconstrained in their land titling decisions or to be held accountable to group goals.

5.3 PRECOLONIAL HIERARCHY AND MODERN CHIEFTAINCY INSTITUTIONS

Chiefs in Zambia are embedded in customary institutions with diverse origins that impact their contemporary strength. As Chapter 4 described, Zambia was home to four precolonial states. Each of these hierarchical institutions – the Bemba, Chewa, Lozi, and Ngoni – survived the British conquest. The British colonial regime ruled through preexisting political structures wherever possible[38] and gave the four precolonial hierarchies the special designation of paramount chieftaincy systems. Even as the official powers of chiefs in Zambia waxed and waned under different independent governments, these hierarchies remained systematically stronger than other customary institutions in the country.

The remainder of the territory in precolonial Zambia was governed by nonhierarchical institutions. This includes a heterogeneous mix of political organizations that share one critical defining characteristic: They did not endogenously develop political centralization through processes of precolonial state building. However, the British colonial authorities sought to implement a coherent policy of indirect rule throughout the territory and attempted to create new hierarchies where such structures did not previously exist. They designated chiefs as "senior chiefs" or "tribal chiefs" who had authority over lower-level chiefs within the ethnic and linguistic groups that the British considered to be a "tribe." Some senior chieftaincies represented cohesive precolonial political institutions. For example, the nineteenth-century Luvale communities in northwestern Zambia were organized into chieftaincies that shared identity ties, rules of succession, and social norms. Yet, as one colonial-era anthropologist described, "Among the Luvale there was little in the earlier indigenous political structure that could be adapted to present-day requirements, since no overall political structure existed."[39] In the Tonga communities of southern Zambia, the British chose chiefs from among high status men in the area; they came to be known by their subjects as "government chiefs"[40] because their claims to leadership came from the state. Further, in addition to the senior chieftaincy systems, the British designated some

---

[38] Meebelo 1971, 101.   [39] White 1957, 73.   [40] Colson 1948.

5.3 Precolonial Hierarchy

zones with nonhierarchical precolonial institutions as independent chieftaincies. This was most common among smaller and more isolated ethnic groups.

Successive independent Zambian governments maintained the system established by the British. In 2012, each of Zambia's 286 chiefs held one of three official titles: paramount chief, senior chief, or chief.[41] Paramount chiefs are the leaders of the four hierarchical institutions; they oversee networks of subordinate official customary authorities with the titles senior chief or chief. However, the most common type of chieftaincy system in contemporary Zambia is the senior chieftaincy system, in which one senior chief has a higher official status than regular chiefs. Senior chieftaincies have nonhierarchical legacies, despite the colonial state's best attempts to mold them into hierarchical authority structures to facilitate their rule. Sixty-five percent of the chiefs in Zambia were part of a senior system in 2012. A further 43 of the 286 official chiefs were independent of senior or paramount systems. Table 5.1 provides an overview of the codified chieftaincy systems. It shows that the majority of the chiefs in Zambia were part of institutions without hierarchical legacies, while 20 percent of Zambia's chiefs were part of hierarchical (paramount) institutions.

TABLE 5.1. *Chieftaincy systems in Zambia*

Precolonial Structure (1850)	Status Defined by Colonial State (1951)[42]	Status Defined by Contemporary State (2012)	Number of Chiefs within System Type (2012)
Hierarchical: large states and kingdoms	Paramount	Paramount	56
Nonhierarchical: stateless language or ethnic groups; small, independent ethnic groups; decentralized chieftaincies	Tribal Chief	Senior	187
	Chief	Independent	43

---

[41] As noted earlier, the number of official chiefs increased to 288 after 2012.
[42] The colonial state published lists of chiefs and *indunas* (counselors) in 1930, 1940, 1951, 1954, and 1960.

Official recognition gives the state an additional source of leverage over chiefs, over and above the informal ties of patronage and dependence that shape customary-state relations more generally (see Chapter 2). For any of the 286 chiefdoms to gain state benefits from their status, they must be officially recognized or "gazetted." The state can remove this recognition and, on rare occasions, has done so. Fourteen of the 414 chiefs who held power at some point between 2003 and 2013 were degazetted.[43] Both the gazetting and degazetting of chiefs is publicized through a statutory instrument. The official justification for dethroning a chief is generally procedural, and the process is adjudicated in a state court or by the staff of the House of Chiefs. For example, a Karanga/Tonga chief was degazetted by the government in 2013 for not following the correct bloodline within the royal family, despite having ruled for more than fourteen years. In other cases, the state has refused to degazette sitting chiefs, effectively blocking popular attempts to dethrone them. This system of gazetting and degazetting chiefs generates an arena for the state to exert a role in adjudicating disputes among members of the customary institution, particularly related to succession. The state also gains leverage in an official system of customary authority through its control over other bureaucratic processes related to official recognition.[44] For example, state agents can delay the process of gazetting a chief or paying their stipends for political ends.[45] The state's ability to influence recognition is an added, though latent, threat for chiefs in an official system such as Zambia's.

The official chieftaincy system creates clear incentives for chiefs to comply with state demands for land, yet Zambian chiefs who are embedded in strong institutions have a competing set of incentives and constraints generated by the institution itself. As Chapter 3 described, one way that institutions impact land titling outcomes is by establishing ties of vertical accountability that reduce the autonomy of a chief's decisions. Institutional features that facilitate vertical accountability allow elites to monitor and punish even official chiefs through well-established hierarchies of authority. This includes institutional rules that give superior chiefs and their councils the authority to intercede if they disapprove of an

---

[43] Based on all statutory instruments from 2003 and 2013. There were 128 chiefs recognized by the government in this period, according to data collected from the offices of the Government Printer, Lusaka and the Zambia Legal Information Institute.
[44] van Binsbergen 1987.   [45] I am grateful to Kate Baldwin for this point.

individual chief's behavior or if a case is brought to them by local citizens. Such systems of vertical checks and balances gain the capacity to constrain from being perceived as legitimate by members of the institution. Zambia's hierarchical customary institutions differ from other institutions because of their long histories of institution building, which generated their precolonial states. As a result, they feature political processes, authority structures, and other rules that members recognize as having developed independently from the colonial regime. Regular interactions among elites within the institution; references to the narrative of precolonial statehood; and ceremonies celebrating the authority of the paramount chief reinforce the rules of the game, including those that generate internal forms of accountability. Examples of how one hierarchical institution facilitates processes of punishment and reward for chiefs are presented in the next section. Such hierarchical institutions can generate incentives for chiefs to conform to collective power prerogatives, countering the influence of the state.

By comparison, nonhierarchical institutions have a lower capacity to create constraints. Senior chieftaincies in Zambia provide an illuminating contrast to the hierarchical paramount chieftaincy institutions because the colonial state molded them into what could be considered a new or nominal hierarchy by establishing the position of senior chief. The state has reinforced these senior hierarchies to facilitate governance for nearly a century. For example, bureaucrats often consult with the senior chief on matters in all of the chieftaincies within the institution. Some senior chiefs are influential political actors or govern domains that are even larger than paramount chieftaincies, and could therefore be expected to have greater bargaining power. However, the senior chieftaincies differ from the paramount chieftaincies in their institutional endowments. Members cannot draw upon rules and processes of hierarchical authority, legitimized through a history of precolonial statehood, to constrain their chiefs. As a result, individual chiefs can more easily ignore internal procedures of accountability, when they exist. The residue of precolonial statehood strengthens contemporary hierarchical institutions relative to even the nominal hierarchies of senior chieftaincies. This, in turn, affects the constraints chiefs face in responding to land negotiations that impact a source of institutional power.

The following section illustrates how hierarchies generate accountability in Zambia today. There are real differences in the internal structures of Zambia's customary institutions that are a legacy of their different origins. These internal differences are informal and largely unwritten practices that determine how accountable a chief is to other elites in the institution. This close comparison of two neighboring institutions sheds light on internal dynamics that are otherwise difficult to discern.

5.4 ACCOUNTABILITY AND DECISION-MAKING AMONG NORTHERN CHIEFS

Two large customary institutions govern land in northern Zambia: the Bemba and the Bisa. Members of these two institutions hold much in common. They are neighbors, sharing the same ecological zone. Their land is accessible and desirable, and the railroad and highway from Lusaka to the nearest port, Dar es Salaam, traverses both Bemba and Bisa territory. Both have been targeted by agricultural investors as having unused fertile land.[46] Further, members of the Bemba and Bisa ethnic groups speak the same language and often act as an aligned political faction.[47]

Despite their similarities, historical legacies have endowed them with institutions that function differently. The Bisa institution was decentralized before colonization and has been designated as a senior chieftaincy system since the colonial era. It features a senior chief and chiefs who operate autonomously within the institution. By contrast, their neighbors, the Bemba, were historically hierarchical. The chiefs within the Bemba institution are accountable to a powerful royal council, headed by a paramount chief. They are more constrained in their behaviors than the Bisa chiefs. Examining these enduring institutional differences within one language group and ecological zone helps illustrate the real variation among customary institutions.

The contemporary Bemba institution is rooted in a powerful precolonial polity. At the start of colonization, the British described it as a state-like kingdom to be feared, the "one power that should be broken," and "the strongest in the northern part of the territory."[48] The colonial regime recognized the Bemba head of state, called Chitimukulu, as a paramount chief. They described him as a powerful force with unified chiefs.[49] Years

---

[46] Interview with investor (INV-603), Lusaka, Zambia, March 13, 2014.
[47] Posner 2003, 2005.
[48] BSAC, "Report from the Administrator, Major PW Forbes, on Affairs in Northern Rhodesia during 1896 in BSAC Reports 1896–1897" 1897, Shelf 8, Government Series, NAZ.
[49] Northern Rhodesia, "Native Affairs Annual Report for the Year 1935" 1935, Box 2/ Shelf 8, African Affairs Annual Reports, Government Series, NAZ.

5.4 Accountability and Decision-Making

of precolonial state building had constructed an institution that remained hierarchical into colonial rule. Under indirect rule, the leaders of the Bemba institution so efficiently governed its territory and collected taxes that the British acknowledged that it had "an almost sacerdotal hegemony."[50]

The Bisa had no such hierarchy or hegemony. The earliest notes from the British occupiers described the Bisa as an independent ethnic group.[51] Clear structures of authority above the village level did not exist within the organization. Instead, the Bisa institution fits a pattern of colonial attempts to create hierarchical structures where none existed in order to facilitate their rule. The British chose one Bisa leader to be at the top of the hierarchy, with the title of Senior Chief Kopa, despite objections from other Bisa chiefs.[52] The colonial authorities tried to foster cohesive institutions of stratified authority under the senior chief, such as that which existed among the Bemba. Yet the Bisa never developed the organizational capacity for administrative and financial autonomy under indirect rule. Stated delicately in a report by one colonial officer, "The efforts to unite the Bisa tribe under Chief Kopa have not proved entirely successful."[53] Accordingly, the British administration had difficulty collecting taxes in the Bisa zone, as in other areas with nonhierarchical customary institutions.[54] The colonial attempts to create hierarchical organization among the Bisa were unsuccessful.

The system and structures codified by the colonial state remained in place into the twenty-first century. The postindependence governments have continued to recognize the same formal boundaries of the two customary institutions, although many plots of customary land have transferred to state land as new titles since independence. Similarly, Senior Chief Kopa and Paramount Chief Chitimukulu have remained the seats of the superior Bisa and Bemba authorities, respectively. Figure 5.1 maps the boundaries of the neighboring customary institutions in northern Zambia, based on the 1958 chieftaincy maps. Table 5.2 summarizes their attributes.

---

[50] Northern Rhodesia, "Native Affairs Annual Report for the Year 1938" 1938, Box 2/ Shelf 8, African Affairs Annual Reports, Government Series, NAZ.
[51] BSAC, "Report from Mr. J. Thomson on His Expedition in BSAC Report 1889–1892: Presented to Shareholders at the Second Annual General Meeting, 29th November 1892" 1892, Shelf 8, Government Series, NAZ.
[52] Meebelo 1971, 203.   [53] Ibid., 205.   [54] Gann 1969, 104.

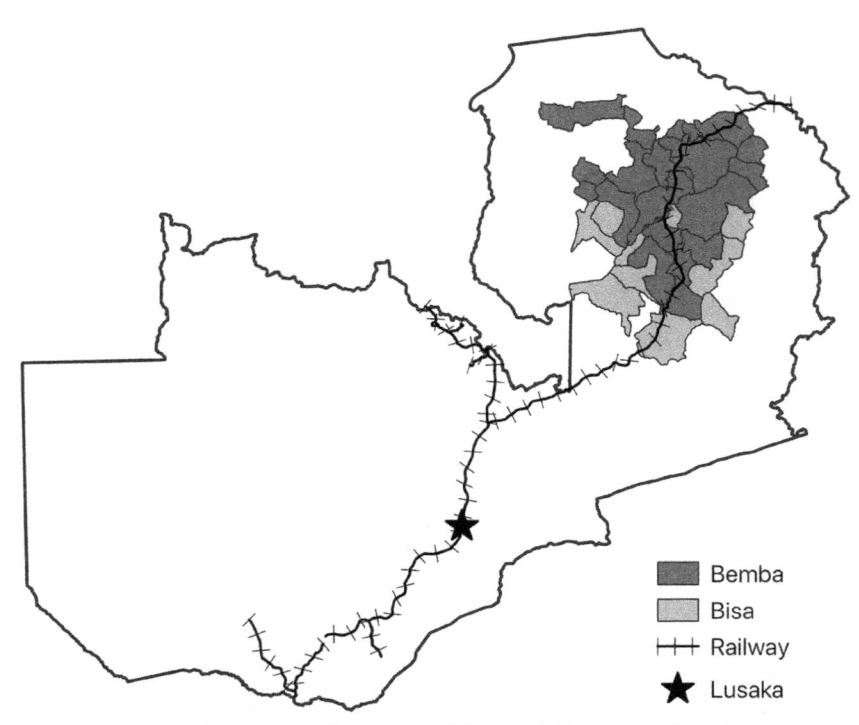

FIGURE 5.1. Locations of Bemba and Bisa chiefdoms, northern Zambia
Source: Author's reproduction based on 1958 chiefdom maps and the institutional affiliations of official chiefs codified by the House of Chiefs (2013).

TABLE 5.2. *Summary of attributes of Bemba and Bisa institutions in 2012*

	Bemba	Bisa
Total Population[55]	2,630,526	200,421
Number of Chiefdoms (2012)	18	10
Level of Official Hierarchy	Paramount	Senior
Precolonial Organization	Hierarchy	Nonhierachy
Selection of Chief	Bemba royal council for all chiefdoms	Family lineage within each chiefdom
Internal Process to Dethrone Chief	Well-established, via the Bemba royal council	Limited; "only death"
Customary Accountability Mechanisms	Punishment and reward by council, senior chiefs, and paramount chief	Limited

[55] Central Statistics Office, "2010 Census of Population and Housing."

Accountability in Bembaland

The contemporary Bemba customary institution generates is a strong hierarchical organization. During the study period, there were eighteen official chiefs within the institution who held the title of chief, senior chief, or paramount chief. These chiefs are consolidated into a hierarchical structure under the leadership of a council, known as the Bemba Royal Establishment or *bashilubemba*. The royal council is a seventy-two-person committee divided into smaller subcommittees, with lineage-based membership. It is headed by Paramount Chief Chitimukulu and headquartered near his palace. Although it is led by the paramount, its members are not selected by him. They hold their own customary titles, allowing them greater countervailing influence in relation to the paramount. As historian Andrew Roberts observed, the members of the bashilubemba are "no mere servants of the Chitimukulu,"[56] in contrast to the traditional councils elsewhere that effectively serve as deputies to their chiefs. The royal council chooses all eighteen of the Bemba chiefs, guided by internally shared succession rules. It also has the right to replace them. This authority is widely recognized by the institution's members, including chiefs. The council's right to appoint chiefs is popularly legitimate – more so than the state's policies.

The Bemba council also has the authority to punish any Bemba chief. They meet regularly to oversee governance within their institution, including monitoring each chief's behavior. If there are concerns, the council can open and investigate a case against any of the official chiefs. Punishments include suspension from power for a fixed period of time; complete "dethronement" or loss of power;[57] and preventing promotions to higher-level chiefdoms.[58] This is an established and well-understood process within the institution. Bemba chiefs acknowledged that they can be dethroned by this council for a wide variety of reasons, such as mistreating people, having a lack of integrity, committing adultery, being the subject of complaint from citizens to the royal council, going against tradition, insulting religious leaders, having a bad character, using vulgar language, exhibiting drunkenness, and misusing land.[59] These individual

---

[56] Roberts 1973, 15.
[57] Interview with smallholder farmers (FFG-539), northern Zambia, February 12, 2014.
[58] Interview with customary authority (CA-570), northern Zambia, January 17, 2014.
[59] Interviews with customary authority (CA-571), northern Zambia, January 10, 2014; with customary authority (CA-573), northern Zambia, January 10, 2014; with customary authority (CA-570), northern Zambia, January 17, 2014; with customary authority

chiefs rely on well-established accountability mechanisms within their institution to access and retain power.

The punishment and promotion of two Bemba chiefs further illustrate how this hierarchical institution functions. In the first case, a chief with profligate land conversions was suspended in 2012. Records from 2007 to 2013 reveal that the chief consented to the titling of 136,000 ha, which would have amounted to 88 percent of his land if all of the applications that he had approved were completed. This far surpassed the Bemba chiefdom average of approving applications for 10 percent of customary land in this time period.[60] The land in his domain had not previously had a large number of titles or major agricultural investments; the allocation of large plots of land was a new development during this chief's first four years in power. The large land deals to which he consented included plots of 30,000 ha and 88,000 ha to German biofuels investors in 2009 and 9,400 ha to an American sugar company. State agents reported that he agreed to give them an additional 28,000 ha in 2013 for a new resettlement scheme.[61] As a result of these deals, the chief developed a reputation for being very willing to cede vast areas of land. His subjects attributed land deals in their area to him as an individual, saying that "the present chief is selfish,"[62] and "if you have two cars and you give him one, saying 'give me this piece of land,' he would do it."[63] In contrast, "other chiefs before him did uphold the traditional norms and we were blessed in the land."[64]

In 2012, members of the bashilubemba traveled to his chiefdom to censure him. The traditional councillors suspended him from his position as chief and threatened future dethronement, which they justified as a consequence of adultery and mistreatment of his subjects.[65] The effect of their punishment was immediate and treated as law among members of the institution. The royal council and paramount chief were able to

---

(CA-564), northern Zambia, January 29, 2014; with smallholder farmers (FFG-565), northern Zambia, January 29, 2014; with customary authority (CA-553), northern Zambia, February 10, 2014.

[60] District council minutes.

[61] Interviews with bureaucrat (BUR-599), northern Zambia, April 28, 2014; with bureaucrat (BUR-609), northern Zambia, February 20, 2014. Note that this is not included in the figure of 136,000 ha, which counts the district council's data only.

[62] Interview with customary authority (CA-564), northern Zambia, January 29, 2014.

[63] Interview with smallholder farmers (FFG-565), northern Zambia, January 29, 2014.

[64] Ibid.

[65] Interviews with customary authority (CA-562), northern Zambia, January 29, 2014 and with smallholder farmers (FFG-565), northern Zambia, January 29, 2014.

reprimand him because his authority was derived from within the customary institution. However, the state also had a role. Some reported that the president of Zambia intervened to prevent the council from fully dethroning him.[66] Put differently, a chief who had repeatedly cooperated with the state's requests to cede land out of the Bemba customary domain was punished by the customary institution and protected by the government. Neither the interventions of the royal council nor of the state were explicitly named as a response to the chief's land conversions, yet the timing is notable. The case provides a clear example of how internal institutional processes can generate vertical accountability, even for chiefs with official status.

The next year, the Bemba elites rewarded a chief who had a reputation for making it difficult to title any land in his domain. In doing so, they challenged the state's attempt to influence a customary authority and won. The government had degazetted the chief by way of an executive order to remove his official recognition as chief.[67] They attributed this decision to his improper installation process, not to his vocal and public opposition to titling customary land. Despite the government's attempted interference, the royal council promoted him to the paramount chief of the Bemba. Although the chief's land surrounded the Northern Province capital, which should see high demand for land titles because it has relatively better transportation infrastructure, access to regional markets, and higher population density, this chief had refused most conversion attempts, consenting to less than 1 percent of his land (2,271 ha) to be titled between 2007 and 2013. He only agreed to titles for small plots, with just one large deal greater than 250 ha.[68] When the state repeatedly tried to extend the township boundaries for the regional capital into his land, he refused to consent to any loss of customary land, unless the state traded him the nearby classified forest. The state wanted to extend the township in order to plan the land and sell individual commercial and residential plots. Instead, the chief encouraged such forms of nonagricultural land usage on the customary land in his domain while refusing to

---

[66] Interviews with smallholder farmers (FFG-565), northern Zambia, January 29, 2014 and with customary authority (CA-564), northern Zambia, January 29, 2014.
[67] The statutory instrument justified degazetting him "based on the fact that the appointment was signed by the Vice President, contrary to the provisions of Section 3 of the Chiefs Act." Zambian National Assembly, "Report of the Committee on Delegated Legislation for the Third Session of the Eleventh National Assembly Appointed on 25th September 2013," 2013.
[68] District council minutes.

cede authority over it through titling. Further, in an unprecedented case, the chief had argued that an unused area of titled land should revert to customary land within his chiefdom. This extralegal request was partially granted. The land did not return to being customary land, but when the state expropriated the undeveloped land from the absentee investor, they granted the chief the right to allocate half of the plots as he saw fit.[69]

The royal council named this chief as their new paramount within two months of the government degazetting him. In their role overseeing both punishments and rewards of chiefs within their institution, they chose to promote this chief within the hierarchy. As an inferior-level chief, he had advanced the interests of the institution by reinforcing customary control of land. Even as the state attempted to wield its latent power over the uncooperative chief, the royal council responded by rewarding him. This became a public battle between the royal council and the administration of President Michael Sata,[70] which led to the resignation of a defense minister who considered himself to be a member of the customary institution and had visited the new paramount as a sign of respect. Ultimately the institution's choice of paramount prevailed, despite the state's challenge.

The influences of the state and the customary institution are clear in these two cases. While the interference of the Zambian state in customary affairs is relatively rare, it occurs. As a result, chiefs have reason to build rapport with the state. However, chiefs within the Bemba hierarchy also have clear incentives to uphold the interests of their customary institution. Members of the institution have reinforced processes of internal accountability between elites that generate constraints on individual chiefs. These cases provide examples of institutional features that can constrain chiefs. However, other customary institutions do not have such structures of accountability, leading to unconstrained chiefs. Lacking the Bemba's hierarchical institutional endowment, the Bisa institutions provide a counterexample.

---

[69] Interviews with bureaucrat (BUR-612), northern Zambia, January 14, 2014; with bureaucrat (BUR-611), northern Zambia, January 18, 2014; with bureaucrat (BUR-615), northern Zambia, January 18, 2014.
[70] President Sata, deceased in 2014, was ethnically Bisa. Some suspected that his attempted manipulation of the Bemba establishment was an effort to strengthen Bisa influence in northern Zambia. See Mukuka 2020, 120 for a description of this conflict over gazetting the paramount chief.

Autonomy in Bisaland

The Bisa institution differs internally from the Bemba, despite their shared language and ecological zone. As with the Bemba, multiple Bisa chiefs each have state-recognized power over a bounded area of land. They visit other Bisa chiefdoms when there are ceremonies or celebrations. Yet they also recognize each other's autonomy. Their hierarchical structure was created by the colonial state and does not generate strong accountability ties. The senior chief that the British named in the early colonial era continues to be the seat of the superior authority for the ten Bisa chiefdoms. However, the superior Bisa chief cannot select, monitor, or dethrone other chiefs. None of the interviewed Bisa customary authorities acknowledged internal institutional censures as a possibility.[71] Unlike the Bemba institution, the Bisa institution does not feature a strong set of rules and internal processes for chiefs to be monitored and sanctioned or rewarded by members.

Bisa chiefs gain and hold power independently of any larger institutional structure. This means that chiefs cannot easily be punished within the institution for bad behavior. As one group of Bisa citizens said, "only death can remove him. Whether good or bad ... you will just keep on complaining until death."[72] Each Bisa chiefdom governs its own succession, and there is no clear chain of authority that decides succession for all ten chiefs. Instead, Bisa chiefs come to power through a variety of different processes. Often the family of the incumbent chief – the royal family for that chiefdom – selects a new chief. Some customary authorities reported that nonroyal headmen also have a say in the succession decision. In one chiefdom, the previous chief selected the current chief before his death. The real authority of any larger institutional rules of succession is weak, as each separate chiefdom functions autonomously. Relative to chiefs embedded in the strong hierarchy of the Bemba, the Bisa chiefs have fewer institutionalized constraints in their decisions.

---

[71] Interviews with customary authority (CA-546), northern Zambia, February 4, 2014; with smallholder farmers (FFG-547), northern Zambia, February 4, 2014; with customary authority (CA-548), northern Zambia, February 4, 2014; with customary authority (CA-549, northern Zambia, February 4, 2014; with customary authority (CA-567), northern Zambia, February 10, 2014; with customary authority (CA-568), northern Zambia, February 17, 2014; with customary authority (CA-569), northern Zambia, February 6, 2014; with smallholder farmers (FFG-566), northern Zambia, February 17, 2014.

[72] Interview with smallholder farmers (FFG-547), northern Zambia, February 4, 2014.

This nonhierarchical system translates to more autonomous decision-making around land conversions. Individual Bisa chiefs are free to evaluate prospective land titles within their domains without risk of punishment (or opportunity for reward) from within the institution. They may consult with other elites on their decisions, but there is no entrenched system of accountability to constrain them. They have greater independence. In some cases, Bisa chiefs have refused investors seeking land because they were not personally satisfied with the terms of the project.[73] In other cases, they agreed to cede land because they personally concluded that it was for the broader good. For example, one chief described agreeing to a large-scale land deal for a hunting concession that faced high and explicit resistance from many members of the institution. He explained that he chose to accept the deal despite their concerns because "sometimes they will refuse because of ignorance, but the chief knows what it is to bring development."[74]

A major palm oil project in northern Zambia provides another example of such autonomy. Investors approached multiple Bemba and Bisa chiefdoms between 2005 and 2009, looking for 25,000 ha of land. Ultimately it was two Bisa chiefs who accepted the deal, and the company titled 20,000 ha of land. The state supported the deal and had facilitated the negotiations. The chiefs represented each of their chiefdoms as independent actors, not as a unified front. In one of the Bisa chiefdoms that accepted the land deal, traditional councillors reported not being part of the decision-making process. They had concerns about the collective implications of the loss of the large area of land, but sensed they could do nothing at the time because "it was just between the chief and the government."[75] These councillors had high status within the institution but were selected and replaced by the chief, weakening their abilities to challenge him.[76] Similarly, village heads did not feel that they could defy the chief, even if they disagreed about a land conversion. One explained that, as headman, "you are not above the chief. So if the chief says yes, who are you to say no? You just have to agree."[77] In the case of this palm oil project, the decision to cede a major portion of the customary land in the Bisa institution's domain was concentrated in the individual chief,

---

[73] Interview with customary authority (CA-546), northern Zambia, February 4, 2014.
[74] Interview with customary authority (CA-567), northern Zambia, February 10, 2014.
[75] Interview with customary authority (CA-548), northern Zambia, February 4, 2014.
[76] Interviews with customary authority (CA-546), northern Zambia, February 4, 2014; with smallholder farmers (FFG-547), northern Zambia, February 4, 2014.
[77] Interview with customary authority (CA-549), northern Zambia, February 4, 2014.

5.4 Accountability and Decision-Making

without strong checks from within his customary institution. He consented to the land deal after negotiating for a sum of money to compensate displaced smallholders, an ambulance for the community, and a vehicle for himself.

Comparing Customary Institutions

These two neighboring customary institutions differ as a result of their historical legacies. The Bemba independently developed a bureaucratic organization and clear lines of authority prior to colonization. Even as the Zambian and colonial states' policies changed, the customary institutions in the territory did not homogenize. Instead, the Bemba institution's historical endowment has been reproduced over time, allowing members of the contemporary institution greater opportunities to monitor individual customary authorities than members of nonhierarchical institutions. Chiefs in the Bemba institution are subject to constraints enforced by the paramount chief and bashilubemba. They can be deposed or punished. In interviews, the Bemba chiefs knew this was a possibility and could cite multiple examples. When the institution's representatives exercise this power, it reinforces the influence of their own rules and reminds chiefs that their authority derives from within. The Bisa customary authorities, by contrast, perceived themselves as autonomous from any larger hierarchy. Once in office, they can be relatively unconstrained in their decision-making, because there is no entrenched internal process for dethroning or sanctioning a chief. In this way, the differences among customary institutions establish variation in vertical accountability for chiefs.

Neither institution exhibited strong forms of downward or horizontal accountability in this research. Consider, for example, the potential role of village heads as customary authorities who could impact chiefs' decisions through more horizontal ties. Headmen and headwomen can help generate accountability by communicating the interests of members to their chiefs. However, there was limited evidence that they could constrain them to advance a collective goal. The comparison of the Bemba and Bisa revealed broad similarities in the weakness of village heads in relation to the official chiefs.[78] In both institutions, village heads oversee

---

[78] This section is compiled from a number of questions designed to probe for different sources of accountability with the institution. On the headman's role, the key questions were: "Who is eligible to be a headman?"; "Who chooses the headman?"; "Can the

governance and customary property rights in their communities. They considered themselves to be the "eyes of the chief"[79] who report on what is happening in the community. However, they oversee day-to-day community governance with relative autonomy. In both institutions, it is common for village residents to select the village head, from the village's royal lineage or, at times, "a commoner."[80] Yet the choice of headman or headwoman is ultimately at the chief's discretion; chiefs can veto the selection, name someone else, or replace the current leader. All of this weakens the village head's ability to function as a countervailing force to the chief.

In nearly every chiefdom sampled in Bembaland and Bisaland, numerous cases of village heads being dismissed by the chief in the past ten years were reported by citizens, chiefs, and village heads themselves. In the Bemba chiefdoms, village heads had been fired for poor governance violations, including adjudicating conflicts poorly, stealing, selling land, exhibiting drunkenness, fighting with or insulting community members, and being away from the village for too long. Bemba village heads also had been replaced for disloyalty to the chief – failing to follow his orders or to remit village tribute contributions – or on account of accusations of witchcraft or not having a legitimate right to the position (through family lineage). These same infractions were repeated in the Bisa communities, with additional examples of village heads being dismissed for "marrying off" a daughter at too young an age; for not coming when the chief called them to meetings; and for not keeping the village clean. In both Bemba and Bisa institutions, village heads were reported to be in a subordinate relationship with the chief.

Lastly, how do these differences in institutional structure impact citizens' perceptions of downward accountability? Citizens within the Bemba

community disagree with the chief's selection of headman?"; "Can the chief disagree with the community's selection of headman?"; "What is the role of the headman in [chiefdom name]?"; "What happens if a headman breaks a rule made by the chief?"; "Have any headmen been replaced in the past 10 years for breaking a rule in [chiefdom name]? Why and when?"

[79] This exact phrase to describe the role of the headman was used by chiefs, headmen, and citizens interviewed in southern, central, and northern Zambia. In northern Zambia alone, respondents used this phrase in interviews with smallholder farmers (FFG-566), northern Zambia, February 17, 2014; with customary authority (CA-553), northern Zambia, February 10, 2014; with customary authority (CA-563), northern Zambia, January 29, 2014; with smallholder farmers (FFG-547), northern Zambia, February 4, 2014; with smallholder farmers (FFG-565), northern Zambia, January 29, 2014.

[80] Interview with customary authority (CA-563), northern Zambia, January 29, 2014.

customary institution could clearly describe the vertical system of accountability for their chiefs. The potential for a chief to be reproached was not merely hypothetical to them. They understood that the Bemba elites deliberated on cases against chiefs, some of which had started with complaints from regular citizens within the community. But it was ultimately at the discretion of elites within the institution to decide which complaints to address. These internal ties of vertical accountability are no guarantee that citizens' grievances will be addressed. Consequently, community members expressed perceptions of limited direct accountability between chief and citizen, with some citizens in Bemba chiefdoms reporting feeling marginalized, stating, for example, "we do not have power over our chiefs."[81] In focus groups of Bisa citizens, similar expressions were frequent. This indicates that even if institutions facilitate collective action by reducing the loss of power over land, their forms of institutional recourse do not strongly empower citizens in everyday governance.

Individual chiefs have significant agency in land titling in Zambia. They hold a great deal of power in this state-building process through their decisions in local negotiations over land. As this chapter has illustrated so far, refusals to cede land are common, as are consents. A range of factors impact these decisions, including personal governance philosophies; the degree to which the chief prioritizes the power of the institution over concentrated benefits; and the details of each specific land conversion attempt. In some cases, Bemba chiefs have ceded large areas of land; in others, Bisa chiefs have refused deals. However, institutions matter. Strong customary institutions can generate constraints on their chiefs, even chiefs who are empowered by the state. Examining accountability within the Bemba and Bisa institutions helps illustrate this point. Nevertheless, these should be understood as specific examples of a broader pattern – each customary institution has its own practices.[82]

---

[81] Interview customary authority (CA-564), northern Zambia, January 29, 2014.
[82] In the Lozi hierarchy, for example, chiefs are subject to strong forms of internal accountability but do not move through the ranks of different chiefdoms like the Bemba. The Lozi council instead selects the paramount (or "Litunga") from among the sons of previous Litungas, known as "princes." Similarly, the Bisa example does not represent all of the variation within senior chieftaincy systems. Further, it is important to emphasize the distinction between a strong chief and a strong institution: Some senior chiefs, such as Senior Chieftainess Nkomeshya, are powerful as individual political actors within the state, despite (or because of) being members of weaker customary institutions.

The following section examines evidence of the continuing impacts of hierarchical legacies more broadly within Zambia.

5.5 NATIONAL PATTERNS OF LAND TITLING AND HIERARCHY IN ZAMBIA

Customary institutions derive power from control over land. The central argument of this book is that customary institutions impact land titling by shaping the responses of chiefs and citizens to potential titles. One way they can do this is by making it possible for members to hold chiefs accountable to collective goals, pushing them to resist or exact higher costs for their consent to titles. This section uses a quantitative, national-level data set to test an observable implication of this argument, that hierarchical institutions in Zambia make it harder to access customary land in their domain. If this is the case, attempts at land titling should be more likely to succeed where customary institutions were historically nonhierarchical, and thus are weaker and more fragmented today. By mapping historical institutions onto modern land titling outcomes, these analyses shed light on the long-term effects of hierarchy and broad patterns of state building in Zambia. Communities with stronger institutions – the result of hierarchical legacies in this context – should be better able to retain control over land.

Ideally, the national land tenure data set would measure both successful and unsuccessful land titling attempts; in reality we can only observe successes, so the outcome measure is truncated. Including multiple measures of the desirability of land as control variables helps to approximate some of the unobserved variation in demand for land titles. Yet fewer attempts to acquire customary land by the state or investors would be an alternative explanation to the mechanism of institutional accountability. Thus, in qualitative interviews and data collection related to specific land deals, I sought any evidence that actors were strategically selecting among types of customary institutions. I found that bureaucrats attempted to access customary land even in the domain of the Lozi hierarchy, an institution so strong its members periodically use it to justify secessionist claims. This includes, for example, bureaucrats venturing to Barotseland to repeatedly request 100,000 ha zones of customary land for the farm blocks program described earlier. Further, as the expansion of state control over land is a long-term process, if state and private actors were less likely to attempt to title land in hierarchies, it would likely reflect an indirect effect of the institution's ability to generate accountability to its power prerogatives. Nevertheless, the weakness of this analytical approach is that it cannot identify the mechanism or mechanisms connecting institutional strength to titling. However, these analyses can identify if customary institutions predict titling on land that is otherwise equal in quality and desirability, which provides strong evidence in favor of the effect of these institutions.

Dependent Variable

The Zambian state has established a clear one-way path for extending its control over land through titling. Each new land title on customary land transfers authority over property rights from chiefs to the state. To capture the expansion of state property rights, the dependent variable in the analyses that follow is the proportion of land per district that is titled. The measure of the total amount of titled land in each district is based on the Zambian government's national database of land titles, updated through 2012.[83] There were 26,681 unique titles, held by private individuals, state agencies, and businesses, among others. The median title size is 5.7 ha, the mean is 150 ha, and the largest in the data set is 183,632 ha. Calculating the combined size of these titles creates an aggregate measure of the total amount of land under state property rights in the district as of 2012. This is the numerator of the dependent variable. The denominator is the size of land that could potentially be titled in the district, calculated using the government's geospatial maps. This denominator therefore excludes areas where an applicant would be prohibited from titling land by the state, particularly in classified forests and national parks.[84] Further, these analyses include only districts with customary land and official chiefs. This omits Lusaka and some districts in the Copperbelt Province. Both the numerator and denominator of this measure reflect government data, so this variable represents the state's understanding of the reach of its formal property rights. Of the seventy-two districts that

---

[83] The year the title was created is not consistently recorded in this data set.
[84] It does not exclude Game Management Areas (GMA), which have a special status and are administered by the Zambia Wildlife Authority (ZAWA), and compose 23 percent of land in the country. GMAs are primarily on customary land, but land within GMAs can be converted to new titles. An audit of GMA areas in 2013 identified hundreds of titled plots on GMAs. By contrast, land titles in National Parks are illegal. In 2013, ZAWA had identified sixteen in existence.

existed in 2012, sixty-two have chiefs and customary land.[85] On average, 6.6 percent of the land in a district is under the direct control of state property rights in this data set. This ranges from 0 to 54 percent. Figure 5.2 illustrates these outcomes, highlighting the geographic unevenness of state property rights in Zambia.

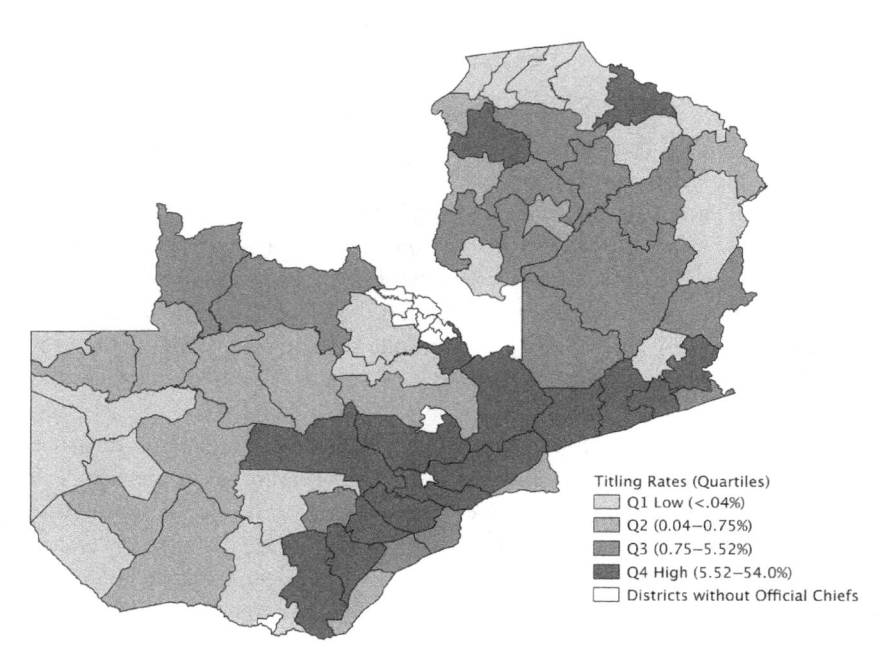

FIGURE 5.2. Map of the rates of land titling per district in Zambia through 2012
Notes: Map does not represent national parks and other areas of land that are ineligible for title and were deducted from the denominator of the dependent variable.

---

[85] My main specification uses the 2012 boundaries. However, the Zambian government has increased the number of local administrative units at semiregular intervals since independence, like other African countries (Grossman and Lewis 2014; Hassan 2016). The number of districts increased from 56 in 1996, to 72 in 2012, to 118 in 2018. This introduces a potential source of bias in the 2012 district boundaries: whether or not administrators retroactively updated the titles in their registries with new district names. This bias should underestimate titling in new districts and overestimate titling in the districts that were divided. As a result, I recalculated all measures with the 1996 boundaries to do parallel analyses of the 47 (of 56) with chiefs and customary land. The significant effect of the main independent variable is the same for both the 2012 and 1996 specifications. Results from the model using 1996 boundaries are reported in Table B.1.

Independent Variable

For this analysis of the relationship between customary institutions and state land titling, the main independent variable is whether the dominant customary institution in a district is hierarchical. Creating a measure of hierarchical or nonhierarchical institutions required a few steps. The first was to georeference the 286 chiefdom boundaries from the Ministry of Land's official maps, which were created in 1958 during the British colonial regime (see Chapter 4, Figure 4.2).[86] The next step was to confirm and update these locations with data from the Ministry of Chiefs and Traditional Affairs and the Zambia Wildlife Authority, the state agencies with the most in-depth spatial knowledge of rural areas. To assign a dominant customary institutional type to each district required overlaying the digital map of customary institutions onto modern administrative boundaries. This measure captures the institutional differences among the chiefs who govern land in Zambia. The dominant institutional type in fifteen of the sixty-two districts is hierarchy; their chiefdoms are embedded in paramount systems.[87] In the rest, the dominant institutional type is nonhierarchical; chiefs have greater autonomy as part of senior or independent chiefdoms.

An initial comparison of the proportions of district land with titles, or the "land titling rates," shows that the districts with hierarchical customary institutions have both lower overall titling rates and a more limited range of outcomes. This is consistent with the theory that chiefs in nonhierarchical customary institutions are unconstrained in their land titling decisions, leading to a wider set of possible outcomes. Some regularly refuse titles and some regularly comply with requests, but on average they have fewer institutional constraints than their peers who are embedded in hierarchies. While this distribution is not conclusive, as there are more districts with nonhierarchical institutions, the smaller range for the hierarchical category is what we would expect if such chiefdoms could censure members for ceding land out of customary control.

---

[86] The boundaries and statuses of chiefs established by the British are largely unchanged. The one significant change is the Lozi consolidation of their chiefdoms in Western Province from eighty-four to eleven.

[87] Most district and chieftaincy boundaries overlap in Zambia, as the colonial state designed the administrative boundaries to reinforce the power of chiefs. Among the sixty-two districts with customary land, three have less than 75 percent coverage of either hierarchical or nonhierarchical institutions: Luwingu, Mpika, and Mporokoso. Dropping these districts as a robustness check does not impact the findings.

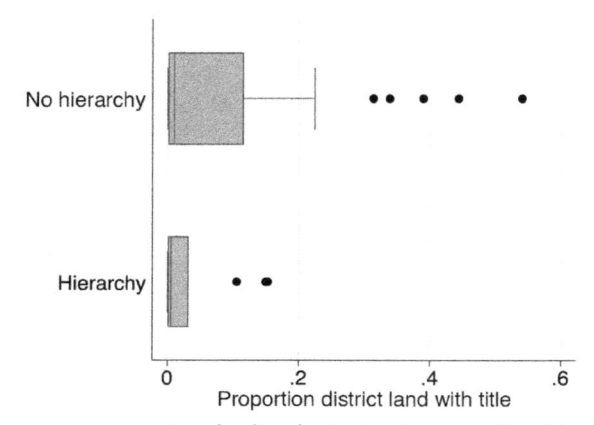

FIGURE 5.3. Land titling by institution type, Zambia
Notes: Figure depicts the key outcome variable in districts with and without hierarchical institutions.

Control Variables

Several control variables approximate land values, demand for land, geographic differences, and access to (or from) state administrative centers. Infrastructure is one of the most important determinants of land values in Zambia. Roads and railways generate access to markets for selling products and buying supplies. They increase access to social services, such as schools and health clinics. The road variable measures the density of road networks in the district: It is the proportion of the district's land within 10 km of a road. The rail variable is a dummy variable, measuring whether the railway passes through the district or not. Rails in Zambia also represent historical patterns of land titling. The colonial government reserved the area along the rail line for settlers as crown land. This is the initial heartland of titling in the country and we should expect the expansion of titling to be higher in areas where the government historically encouraged commercial agricultural and land titling. It is thus an important control variable in a model designed to identify any independent effect of customary institutions.

Distance from the capital serves in the following models as a proxy for land values and access to the state. In 2012, land titling was not functionally decentralized in Zambia and generally required travel to the capital city. Distance from the capital should therefore increase the costs of land titling. Proximity to the capital also approximates access to the largest market and to centralized infrastructure such as hospitals and universities, which also increases the desirability of land. In addition, the full model includes measures of soil type and rainfall to consider the possibility that particularly fertile geography is driving both land titling rates and hierarchy. Following this logic, population density is also a key control variable. See Table A.1 for summary statistics, measurement details, and sources for each variable.

Theories of state building predict a positive correlation between hierarchy and population densities. The logic is that increasing population densities lead to greater demand among residents for the hegemonic provision of justice and security from a nascent state. Similarly, an expanding state apparatus should attract populations who seek security and state-facilitated markets, thereby increasing population density. Bureaucracy and more complex governmental structures (hierarchy) should also develop through the growth of taxable populations. However, Osafo-Kwaako and Robinson empirically test this theory within Africa, finding that population densities are not associated with the development of hierarchical precolonial institutions.[88] Within Zambia, the relationship between population density and hierarchical customary institutions is positive, as expected, but weakly correlated ($r = 0.160$). This is nevertheless an indispensable variable in a model of land titling, as it is central to the theory of induced institutional change (IIC) in property rights detailed in Chapter 2. As competition over land increases, so should demand for land titling.

Analysis and Findings

Statistical analyses show a national pattern in which districts dominated by hierarchical institutions have lower rates of land titling in Zambia. The dependent variable approximates the proportion of customary land that has converted to titles. Given the nature of this outcome, I use a fractional logistic regression model with robust standard errors clustered at the provincial level. This is the preferred estimation strategy for continuous outcomes that are bounded between 0 and 1; these bounds are not observational, but are a function of the proportional outcome. Fractional logistic models generate predictions that remain within the unit interval, while also including the substantively meaningful zero values in these data.[89]

---

[88] Osafo-Kwaako and J. Robinson 2013. The authors find a significant relationship between population density and hierarchy globally, but provide evidence that state building in African polities was an exception to this pattern.

[89] Fractional logistic regression uses a generalized linear model with logit link function and binomial distribution. This estimation strategy follows Papke and Wooldridge 1996, 2008; Baum 2008, as well as similar investigations of proportional land tenure outcomes, such

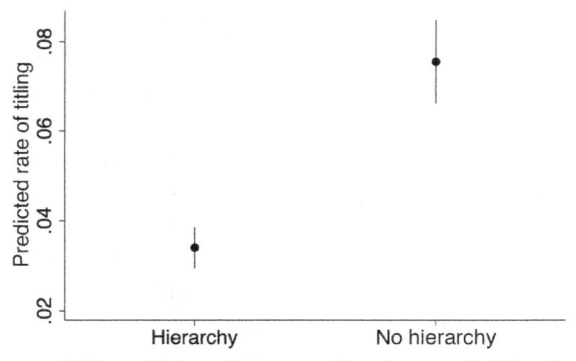

FIGURE 5.4. Effect of hierarchy on predicted rates of titling in Zambia
Notes: Figure presents the predicted proportion of titled land per district with 95 percent confidence intervals.

The statistical analyses reveal that hierarchy has a strong negative effect on land titling, even when accounting for the potentially confounding effects of a variety of indicators of land values and demand. I illustrate these findings graphically in Figure 5.4. The figure depicts the predicted land titling rates based on the baseline model that includes the full set of control variables (full results reported in Appendix Table B.1, Model 2). It shows that the predicted proportion of titled land increases from 3.4 percent (.034) in zones with hierarchical institutions to 7.5 percent (.075) on customary land governed by nonhierarchical institutions. While these rates of titling are low overall, they reveal a clear and significant pattern of differences between the two types of institutional contexts. These differences in land titling rates between areas dominated by hierarchical and nonhierarchical institutions are independent of soil type, district size, rainfall, transportation networks, and population density. These findings support the expectation that, among districts with the same land values and geography, titling replaces customary land more rapidly in the districts with nonhierarchical customary institutions.

Figure 5.5 investigates whether titling differs in zones with the two types of nonhierarchical institutions, senior and independent chieftaincies. Senior chiefdoms represent state attempts to establish hierarchies to facilitate indirect rule, but they lack the historical levels of precolonial organization of the paramount chiefdoms in Zambia. Thus, comparing

---

as Guirkinger and Platteau 2014. Ordinary least squares results are presented as a robustness check in the appendix.

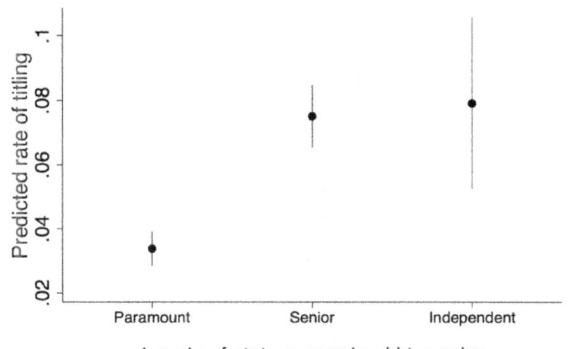

5.5 National Patterns of Land Titling

FIGURE 5.5. Comparing land titling among the three types of official chieftaincy systems in Zambia
Notes: Figure presents the predicted proportion of titled land per district with 95 percent confidence intervals.

paramount, senior, and independent chieftaincy institutions provides additional insight into the role of the internal organizational capacity that developed before the imposition of the colonial state. Figure 5.5 shows that zones of senior and independent institutions do not have significantly different rates of titling from each other. This is consistent with the theoretical expectation that hierarchy imposed by the colonial state does not generate strong ties of vertical accountability nor the ability to overcome real differences in historical institution-building processes. As Figure 5.3 illustrated, these unconstrained chiefs have a much wider range of responses to land conversion attempts than customary authorities within hierarchical institutions. The chiefs who are part of senior and independent chiefdoms are freer to make liberal or illiberal land titling decisions. Among the different incentives that may affect a chief's willingness to cede land, chiefs within hierarchical systems face additional constraints.

How robust are these findings? The relationship between customary institution types and rates of land titling withstands a number of alternative specifications and robustness checks. The significant and negative effect of hierarchy remains even in models that drop: influential observations; districts that include any portions of the colonial crown land along the railway;[90] and each of the four precolonial

---

[90] Colonial authorities reserved the land along the Southern Province railway as crown land for settler agriculture; this area was the earliest area of land titling in the country. Excluding the railway districts with colonial crown land does not impact the central finding on hierarchy; however, the exclusion does change the significant effect of railways

states.⁹¹ Further, the main results are unchanged in four alternative models reported in Table B.1 that: reduce the number of control variables; recode Lunda as a hierarchy;⁹² use ordinary least squares regression; and use the 1996 district boundaries.

It is also worth interrogating whether these findings reflect group size or electoral coalitions. Perhaps hierarchies do not have stronger institutions than nonhierarchies and it is, instead, increased bargaining power, resulting from control over larger populations, which drives the relationship between hierarchies and titling. Governing a larger identity group may provide chiefs with more freedom to resist requests for customary land by politicians. Or larger group size may lead to more interactions between chiefs and the politicians seeking to engage them as vote brokers. After all, political favor is one possible concentrated benefit of ceding land for customary authorities. This should be particularly salient if the identity group in question were a long-standing voting block for the ruling party or opposition.

One empirical approach to separate the effects of hierarchy and group size is to include measures of the three largest language groups in each district: Nyanja, Bemba, and Tonga. In the multiparty era, language group has been a politically salient identity group for Zambian citizens.⁹³ For example, in the 2011, 2015,⁹⁴ and 2016 presidential elections, the ruling Patriotic Front party had strongholds in the north and east among Bemba and Nyanja-speaking populations, while the opposition United Party for National Development received high support in the western half of the country, including the Tonga-speaking Southern Province. Adding measures of the degree to which citizens within the district share a group identity helps shed light on alternative mechanisms for the effect of hierarchy.

I find that that the significant relationship between hierarchy and titling remains even with controls for group size.⁹⁵ This is evidence of the

---

from the baseline models, indicating that the effect of proximity to railways on the rate of titling is largely a consequence of these colonial policies in Southern Province.

⁹¹ Provincial fixed effects constrain the model to three of the nine provinces that feature within-province variation. The findings are robust to this constraint.

⁹² See also footnote 4, Chapter 4.   ⁹³ Posner 2005.

⁹⁴ Special elections following the death of President Michael Sata.

⁹⁵ The effect of the customary institutional variable is also robust to two other measures of group size: ethnic group size and a historical measure of "tribe" size from the colonial era. This historical group size measure is derived from the first ethnic census in Zambia in 1955 and includes a larger number of ethnic groups. These ethnic identity groups were consolidated over time, informing the contemporary ethnic group size measure calculated

5.5 National Patterns of Land Titling

importance of institutional structure. Large identity groups have advantages in bargaining with outside actors (including the state); however, retaining customary land tenure requires that the groups have strong internal institutions that can constrain members. The Bemba and Bisa comparison, which are part of the same Bemba-language voting bloc, underscores this point. The Tonga and Lozi institutions in Zambia provide an additional example of the difference between group size and institutional strength. The Tonga are one of the largest ethno-linguistic groups in Zambia, comprising 14 percent of the population.[96] The British colonial regime organized them into a senior chieftaincy system, despite their history of nonhierarchical institutions. Yet each Tonga chief rules autonomously with weak institutional constraints among elites. By contrast, the Lozi ethno-linguistic group accounts for only 6 percent of the Zambian population, but their strong internal hierarchy shapes the decisions of chiefs and makes it harder to access titles in their domains. In these cases, the significant negative impact of a hierarchical legacy on titling is distinct from the size of the group.

Electoral politics and the desire to court political favor surely matter in chiefs' calculus, among other potential individual-level factors. For example, Baldwin found that personal connections between a member of parliament (MP) and a chief increase the likelihood that chiefs report having converted customary land in Zambia; yet whether the MP is part of the ruling party does not have any significant effect.[97] My results do not compete with explanations that emphasize the electoral role of chiefs. Instead, the results of analyses that include group size or control for linguistic voting blocs (qualitatively in the Bemba/Bisa case or quantitatively in this section) suggest that institutional strength has an independent effect on titling outcomes. They indicate that the core findings have not confounded partisan electoral cleavages or group size with institutional strength. Electoral politics still matter, but customary institutions create constraints that shape long-term patterns in the expansion of state power over land.

---

from the 2010 census. These groups are further aggregated in the language groups measure. None of the three forms of group size affect the strong inverse relationship between hierarchy and titling. For the colonial "tribe" size variable, see Northern Rhodesia, "African Affairs Annual Report for the Year 1955" 1955, Box 4/Shelf 8, African Affairs Annual Reports, Government Series, NAZ.

[96] Central Statistics Office, "2010 Census of Population and Housing."
[97] Baldwin 2016, 138.

The Effects of Land Values on Titling

This data set also illuminates the relationship between land values and land titling. Two key measures of demand for land, population density and road networks, consistently increase rates of land titling. Distance to the capital also has a stable inverse effect on the likelihood of titling: Land conversions from customary to state property rights decrease, the farther one is from the seat of state power. The more distant the land, the less likely it is to be titled in Zambia. This is consistent with arguments that the state's capacity weakens between core and periphery,[98] as well as the IIC theoretical expectation that increasing land values prompt shifts in property rights. Figure 5.6 graphically illustrates how customary institutions affect land titling when considering three different proxy measures of land values, based on calculations from the baseline model described earlier and reported in Appendix Table B.1, Model 2.

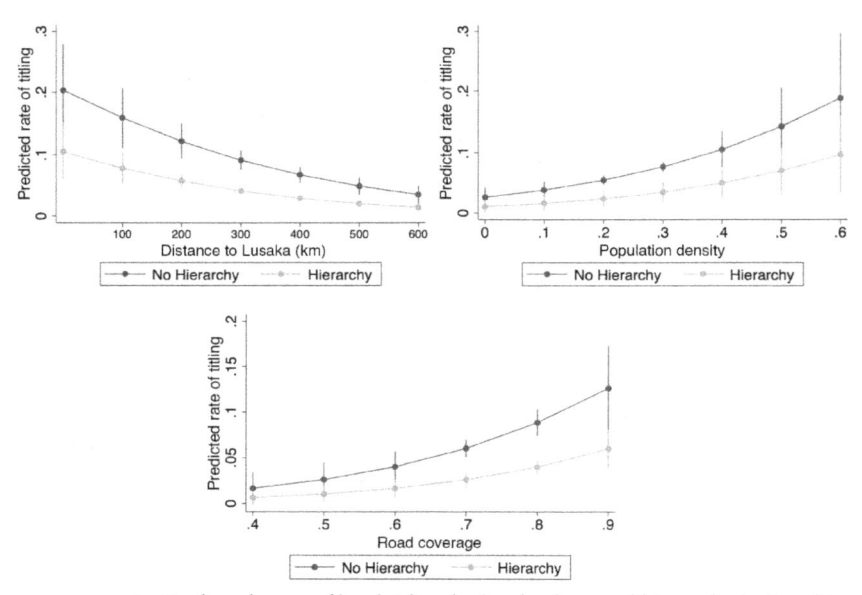

FIGURE 5.6. Predicted rates of land titling by land values and hierarchy in Zambia
Notes: Panels show the predicted proportion of land titled per district with 95 percent confidence intervals by three measures of land values.

---

[98] Herbst 2000.

5.5 National Patterns of Land Titling

The three plots in Figure 5.6 indicate that rates of titling increase along with population density and road coverage, while decreasing at higher distances from Lusaka. These results therefore suggest that less valuable and accessible land is more likely to remain under customary control. However, these plots also show why land values alone cannot sufficiently explain land tenure outcomes. Even as land value increases the likelihood of titling in this model, the impact of customary institutions remains. The model estimates consistently lower rates of titling in districts dominated by hierarchical customary institutions, when population density and infrastructure access is held constant. It indicates that there is something systematically different about districts dominated by historical hierarchies that make land titling less likely, which cannot be explained by observed measures of land values, population density, and distance to the state's economic and political capital. These analyses suggest that, even in areas with greater road access – which increases the value of land – customary institutions can reduce rates of land titling. Consider, for example, the effects of having a nonhierarchical customary institution and railway access. Among districts with no railways, the predicted rate of titling in the zones of nonhierarchical institutions is 4.6 percent, compared to 2 percent for districts with hierarchical institutions. In the more desirable districts with railway access, these rates double to 10.9 and 5.1 percent, respectively. Among districts with better or worse transportation networks, the pattern is the same – less land is titled in areas dominated by hierarchical institutions.

The national analysis of land tenure patterns in Zambia provides support for the argument that strong customary institutions can make it harder and costlier to title land in their zones. Hierarchical institutions generate extra checks on their chiefs' decisions, which help retain the institution's power over land. These findings suggest that when the state, an investor, or an individual attempt to access land to title in zones with hierarchical legacies, they are more likely to face refusals, indefinite delays, and high costs. This then pushes them to seek land elsewhere – on land that is easier to access due to customary politics. The result of this process is a spatial distribution of state property rights that is unanticipated by previous approaches to titling. Independent of land quality, land values, infrastructure access, and demography, customary institutions have a systematic impact on land titling.

5.6 HIERARCHY AND SMALLHOLDER TITLING IN ZAMBIA

So far, this analysis has examined the proportion of customary land that shifted to state property rights in a district, but it has not disaggregated titling by the amount of land at stake in each decision. It is possible that the theorized institutional effects primarily apply to negotiations over larger areas of land, which are included in the district titling data set. After all, a large land deal has more visible impacts on the community and should have higher collective costs than titling small plots of land for community members. Nevertheless, high rates of conversions for small plots of land also erode the institution's power base, so there is reason to anticipate that effects of heterogeneity among customary institutions would operate similarly for large and small land titles. The theory of customary constraints anticipates that chiefs embedded in hierarchical institutions will make it harder for smallholders to title land in their zones; therefore, citizens in these communities should be less likely to have land titles. This section tests this hypothesis, using an entirely different data set on land titling in Zambia. It replicates the same statistical patterns just presented, showing that titling is less common in hierarchical institutions, even for smallholder titling alone.

Chiefs can discourage or refuse smallholder titling in their domains through the formal or informal channels described in Chapter 2. Recall that in Zambia, the official chief must consent in writing to title applications before they can advance within the state bureaucracy. Further, customary authorities are a key source of information on land titling for rural citizens. This creates opportunities for them to influence titling in their domains through the information they share with the community. The chiefs I interviewed were not unified in their approaches to smallholder titling, within or across the two countries. As detailed elsewhere, customary authorities reported facilitating or refusing smallholder land titles in their domains according to: (1) the legitimacy of the land claim within the institution's rules; (2) the customary authority's personal evaluation of whether title would be beneficial for the individual smallholder farmer; and (3) the costs to the community of smallholder titling. The second and third claims were most common in Zambia.

To examine the relationship between hierarchy and smallholder titling, I rely on a survey of more than 7,000 farmers in Zambia.[99] Just as with

---

[99] RALS Zambia survey (2012). Survey details and sample characteristics are described in Chapter 7. The absence of a national survey for Senegal prevents me from doing a similar analysis in Chapter 6.

5.6 Hierarchy and Smallholder Titling in Zambia

my earlier analysis of the proportion of land converted in a district, many variables potentially impact the relationship between customary institutions and smallholder titling. Further, the data reveal that there are systematic differences between the farmers who reside in areas with hierarchical and nonhierarchical institutions, some of which are likely related to the structure of institutions. This presents a challenge to identifying the effects of the customary institution on the likelihood a smallholder has title. On average, chiefdoms in hierarchical institutions in Zambia have larger territorial sizes than those in nonhierarchical institutions. Further, the powerful precolonial states had conquered subject ethnic groups, so citizens embedded in institutions linked to them are, on average, less likely to report that they are "considered local." There are also significant differences in respondents' crops and modes of land access between hierarchical and nonhierarchical institutions. Households in hierarchical institutions are more likely to grow maize and cash crops, and less likely to grow cassava. While there is no difference across the groups in rates of purchasing land, households in hierarchical institutions are more likely to have inherited or been allocated land from the chief. Such systematic differences between the households in these institutions may influence their likelihood of titling. Whether a household is part of a hierarchical institution or not is, clearly, not randomly assigned. Further, testing for the impact of hierarchy is also complicated by the use of an existing survey sample that was not designed to be representative at the chieftaincy level. To mitigate these challenges, the statistical models presented in Table 5.3 adjust for the household's propensity to be embedded in a hierarchy.[100] This helps to improve our ability to compare these groups of smallholder farmers.

Models 1–3 show that households in hierarchical institutions are indeed significantly less likely to have titles. The first model is a comparison of all the households in the sample, divided into the two types of institutions (hierarchical and nonhierarchical).[101] The second and third

---

[100] Balance statistics are presented in Table B.2. They indicate improvement in the balance of nearly every variable in the model, with the exception of employment, cassava, groundnuts, and agricultural settlement. Importantly, the standardized differences are nearly zero and improved for the variables of particular concern: chiefdom size, migration, ethnicity, wealth, and kinship.

[101] The hierarchy measure for these analyses is calculated using the 1958 chiefdom boundaries, the institutional affiliation of each chiefdom, and the geolocation of the survey respondents. Households in nonhierarchical institutions are those residing in chiefdoms that are part of senior or independent chieftaincy systems. Households in hierarchical institutions reside in chiefdoms that are part of paramount systems.

TABLE 5.3. *Effects of hierarchy on smallholder land titling in Zambia*

	Title			Fallow		
	1	2	3	4	5	6
	Baseline	Restricted Sample	Alternative Hierarchy Measure	Baseline	Restricted Sample	Alternative Hierarchy Measure
Hierarchy (ATE)	-.019*	-.028**	-.024**	-.090**	-.110**	-.028
	(.009)	(.008)	(.008)	(.030)	(.023)	(.029)
No Hierarchy (POM)	.050**	.039**	.050**	.314**	.241**	.308**
	(.003)	(.007)	(.003)	(.008)	(.016)	(.008)
Hierarchy (POM)	.031**	.012**	.026**	.225**	.131**	.280**
	(.009)	(.004)	(.007)	(.029)	(.018)	(.028)
Observations	7,522	1,328	7,522	7,108	1,284	7,108
Sub-Sample	All	Only districts with both hierarchy and no hierarchy	All	Customary property rights (CPR) only	CPR only; districts with both hierarchy and no hierarchy	CPR only

Notes: Table presents average treatment effects (ATE) and potential outcome means (POM) with observations weighted by probability of living in the domain of a hierarchical institution. Outcomes are title (Models 1–3) and fallow (Models 4–6). Standard errors in parentheses. Models 3 and 6 categorize Lunda-Kazembe as a hierarchy as robustness checks. ** p ≤ 0.01, * p ≤ 0.05, + p ≤ 0.1.
Weight variables: chiefdom size, kinship with chief, population density, income, distance to infrastructure, distance to Lusaka, railroads, roads, education, employment, amount of land owned, wealth, migrant, local, youth-headed household, female-headed household, agricultural settlement, crops, modes of access.

5.6 Hierarchy and Smallholder Titling in Zambia

models present two alternative specifications as harder tests of the relationship. Given the important possibility of unobserved differences related to agriculture and environmental conditions, Model 2 limits the analysis to only districts with both types of institutions. This subsample follows the logic of the Bemba/Bisa case study, comparing neighboring institutions to control for as many unobserved land-related factors related to land as possible. Model 3 is an alternative coding of hierarchical institutions in Zambia as a robustness check.[102] All three models indicate that residing in a zone with hierarchical institutions has a significant negative average impact on land titling among smallholder farmers.

Examining differences in tenure security among farmers provides further insight into the roles of chiefs and customary institutions. One possible explanation for the correlation between hierarchy and titling is that smallholders in areas with hierarchical institutions might have lower demand for state titles because they feel that their customary property rights are more secure.[103] The security-enhancing effect of living in a community with stronger customary institutions and/or chiefs who have greater institutional constraints could be a second mechanism driving the hierarchy findings. To test this, Models 4–6 examine the relationship between hierarchy and the likelihood of fallowing. Fallowing, leaving land unused to regenerate its fertility, requires a high level of confidence in one's customary land rights. This is a particularly meaningful measure of tenure security in Zambia (and Senegal), where fallowing is common practice.

The models of fallowing reported in Table 5.3 do not support the second mechanism, that Zambia's hierarchies reduce smallholder land titling rates by increasing citizens' confidence in their customary property rights. The results suggest that tenure security is not, on average, stronger in hierarchical institutions. To the contrary, these models indicate that households in hierarchical institutions have lower rates of fallowing land than otherwise similar households in nonhierarchical institutions. The pattern remains even when the model is restricted to only districts with both types of institutions. This restricted sample is useful, given that fallowing practices vary regionally in Zambia.

---

[102] This Lunda as hierarchy recoding is also a robustness check in the district-level analysis. See also footnote 4, Chapter 4.
[103] Tenure security is a privilege an institution might provide citizens that would increase their desire to support the institution's power base and decrease their incentive to seek titles. This question will be fully explored with the other predictions of the customary privilege theory in Chapter 7.

Although the members of hierarchical institutions have retained more customary land in the face of global land markets than their peers in nonhierarchical institutions, these findings suggest that the institution's land governance does not generate more secure property rights. These analyses, therefore, reinforce the conclusion that hierarchical institutions in Zambia influence land titling by making it harder to access title, not by reducing demand for it. This is evidence that constrained chiefs are gatekeepers to title who prevent the loss of customary land, rather than security providers who slow demand by providing stronger customary property rights.

5.7 STATE RECOGNITION AND CITIZEN–STATE RELATIONS

This chapter has illustrated that chiefs in Zambia have an important role in determining where state property rights develop. It has also provided evidence that chiefs make land titling decisions with varying degrees of autonomy from their institutions. This final section returns to the broader context of state–customary relations by considering the implications of Zambia's official chieftaincy policy for citizens.

As described earlier, the system of chiefs as official land authorities draws them closer to the state and offers direct channels for them to impact land tenure outcomes. In a highly favorable view of this arrangement, the official chief is the representative of the community and advocates on its behalf. This serves state actors as well, by reducing the state's responsibility when smallholders are displaced in land conversions, because the chief can be blamed for the decision. In practice, this system of official chiefs in Zambia centralizes the negotiations over land in Zambia between chiefs and the state. This can create a chief–state alliance that excludes the citizens, who perceive that "the problem we are facing is that when government and the chief agree and plan something over land, there is nothing that the people can say which can be heard. Nothing at all."[104] The epigraph at the start of the chapter also reflects citizens' experiences of this dynamic.

Citizens often expressed feelings of powerlessness in relation to their chiefs and the state during my interviews. They reported that, when it comes to land governance, "we don't have the powers to decide."[105] Citizens in nonhierarchical chiefdoms explained in interviews that

---

[104] Interview with smallholder farmers (FFG-539), northern Zambia, February 12, 2014.
[105] Interview with smallholder farmers (FFG-547), northern Zambia, February 4, 2014.

"sometimes, you can be seated comfortably on that land, then later the same land will be given out to somebody else and they displace you" or "in other cases, many of you can be displaced and squeezed on a smaller land."[106] These are powerful expressions of insecurity, during an era when large-scale land deals were common in Zambia. These same groups of citizens explained that they had few opportunities to hold their chiefs accountable for protecting their interests. For example, when asked what happens if they disagree with a chief's decision, they reported that "even if we say something, nothing can be done," and "there is nothing we can do, so we just observe as slaves."[107]

The public struggle over land within one ethnic Goba chiefdom provides an example of the limits of citizen attempts to influence land decisions in the context of state recognition. In this nonhierarchical institution, the official chief had agreed to multiple large-scale land deals on the community's land. In addition, she had also ceded areas of prime riverside land to be titled for tourism projects. In response, the local residents have publicly attempted to dethrone their chief. They complained to the media about her poor land governance and willingness to sell their customary land. Other elites in the institution also tried to dethrone her. For example, one member of her royal family openly criticized her for evicting smallholder farmers and punishing her critics within the village, telling a newspaper reporter that "if it means dying we will die to protect this land for the future generation."[108]

When members went to state officials asking them to dethrone her, they were rebuked. The local member of parliament, who also serves as provincial minister, publicly declared that as a representative of the state, he could not get involved in disputes over customary land. Instead, he encouraged the community members to complain directly to her.[109] The chief herself acknowledged her liberty to cede any land within her chiefdom, saying in a public interview that "they cannot remove me. I have not done anything wrong unless they are trying to kill me [The only way I can be dethroned is death]. I haven't done any criminal act which can make me step down, I haven't killed anybody, I haven't done anything, I am not insane so why should they take me out?"[110] In this independent chiefdom,

---

[106] Interview with smallholder farmers (FFG-566), northern Zambia, February 17, 2014.
[107] Ibid.
[108] "Mwaliteta Implores Goba Royal Foundation to Resolve Chiawa Land Wrangles," *The Post*, November 7, 2013.
[109] "Mwaliteta Proposed Review of Customary Land Act," *The Post*, November 25, 2013.
[110] "Chieftainess Chiawa in Coup Threat," *Lusaka Voice*, October 20, 2013.

the customary authority's decisions are subject to limited ties of accountability among elites within the institution. Although it is possible for the state to censure an official chief, the state's representatives have limited motivation to stop a chief from ceding land to state property rights.

In contrast, vertical accountability mechanisms provide some recourse for citizens within a hierarchical institution: They have the option of appealing to superior customary authorities to punish subordinate chiefs. In the far east of Zambia, the Ngoni institution provides an example of elites within a hierarchical institution publicly punishing its chiefs. Much like the case of the Goba chief, citizens accused a Ngoni chief of giving away their land. Unlike the Goba chief, the Ngoni chief was subject to ties of hierarchy that allowed him to be censured from within the institution's processes by a superior chief.[111] The citizens appealed to the Ngoni paramount chief, who responded by punishing the chief for the misuse of customary land. In cases like these, where the state fails to represent citizens, there is potential for accountability processes within customary institutions to protect them. In Zambia, hierarchical customary institutions generate increased opportunities for members to monitor and sanction the decisions of official chiefs. Nevertheless, it is largely the elite members and other customary authorities within the institution that can exercise this power. Consequently, the accountability mechanisms described here are not downward accountability from chief to citizen, but upward, among different elites within the institution.

5.8 CONCLUSION

Zambia's system of official chiefs has facilitated state building by empowering actors who depend on the state for benefits with the authority to permanently cede large areas of customary land. In effect, the decision to convert the land occupied by thousands of smallholders is concentrated in relatively few individuals: 286 for a country larger than France. When the state or an investor seek a large area of land, they only need the consent of the chief instead of having to negotiate individually with farmers occupying the land. The internal consultation processes that chiefs do or do not undertake depend on each individual institution. Further, these official chiefs are beholden to the state, supported by the state's monthly salaries and continuing recognition. This is conducive to

---

[111] "Chief Mpezeni Suspends Chief Kapatamoyo for Illegal Land Allocation," *Lusaka Times*, May 21, 2013.

the expansion of state authority over customary land. It has also facilitated an increase in state and private agricultural investments in Zambia, some of which have been highlighted as examples of land grabbing by advocacy organizations and scholars.[112]

However, Zambia's customary authorities also have the power to determine where land titling occurs. They can resist the extension of state control over land and encourage applicants to seek out more willing chiefdoms. In this system, state bureaucrats and investors can access significant areas of land through negotiations with only one individual chief, but in certain areas, customary land is costlier or completely inaccessible. The price of accessing land is often unrelated to objective indicators of its value.

Examining the expansion of state authority through land titling in the context of official chiefs reveals that dependence on the state for recognition and salary has not extinguished the agency of customary authorities or the historical differences among customary institutions. As the example of two neighboring institutions demonstrates, institutional endowments have a persistent effect on the organization of customary institutions today. The hierarchical institutions that developed over years of precolonial state building retain greater ability to censure members, including their leaders, than other customary institutions. Chapter 6 explores the enduring legacies of hierarchical customary institutions in Senegal. Given the attempts of the French colonial regime and independent state to weaken customary control of land, how and why do historical institutions continue to impact land titling today in Senegal?

---

[112] See Chitonge 2019 and Land Matrix, "Land Matrix Database," 2015, http://landportal.info/landmatrix.

6

Holding Ground in Senegal

Horizontal Accountability, Institutional Legacies, and the Continuation of Customary Property Rights

> I'm 85 years old, so I know where my land is. Everyone knows exactly their land. The land belongs to the populations but the government wants to bring in investors – the landowners said "no, because it's our land." Now that's the situation. The government has its position and the landowners are on their side with their position, sticking to this system. There is no national domain ... customary rules are the rule here.
> —customary authority, northern Senegal[1]

> For them, a field that dates back 100 years, if it's the great-grandfather who cleared it, then it's their property. How can we make them understand that it doesn't belong to anyone? That is one of the most delicate questions that the state needs to regulate, as quickly as possible. That land does not belong in perpetuity to anyone. This is the fundamental problem with land in Senegal.
> —rural council bureaucrat, northern Senegal[2]

"The world shouts its emotion and expresses its condescension" began President Abdoulaye Wade's presentation to parliament of his plans to promote economic growth through commercial agriculture in Senegal. He explained that Africa needed to better exploit its "unused land" in order to be free of dependence on food aid, NGOs, and Western governments. With this, he introduced the *Grande Offensive Agricole pour la*

---

[1] Interview with customary authority (CA-153), northern Senegal, September 21, 2014.
[2] Interview with rural council member (RC-118), northern Senegal, September 16, 2014.

Nourriture et l'Abondance (GOANA)[3] in 2008. The initiative was ambitious. It proposed an investment of 815 million USD for production on 2.7 million ha of land, which would more than double the land under cereal crops in Senegal.[4] In the capital city of Dakar, agricultural technicians wrote GOANA plans with specific production goals for each district of Senegal, avoiding the question of who would facilitate the required changes in the use and control of land. Wade's government hoped that this would be the advent of a rural revolution, one that would transform the way the country's land was used and governed.

The "unused land" required for this agenda was part of the national domain, land legally defined by its lack of titles or registration (*terres non immatriculées*).[5] To the state – and the investors they sought to attract through the GOANA plan – such untitled land was an untapped resource. Officially, it was land without owners. Thus, one ministry of agriculture report classified only 1 percent (200,000 ha) of the country's arable land as "inhabited" and a further 76 percent of it as available for agricultural investment.[6] As the epigraph suggests, the state has been trying to make citizens understand that national domain land "doesn't belong to anyone" by replacing enduring but unwritten customary land claims with the state's laws. Formal institutions designed to erode customary control of land began with the colonial institutions described in Chapter 4, then continued with governmental policies that facilitated titling and defined national domain land as ownerless.

Yet outside of this formal institutional framework exist long-standing and dynamic systems of unofficial customary authority over land. As a result, rural citizens in Senegal have often experienced land deals not as an opportunity to capitalize on "unused land," but as an attempt by the state or investors to take away land that their ancestors had tilled. While customary land rights may be illegible to the state in Senegal, citizens in rural areas will tell you that all land has owners even if those rights are

---

[3] This roughly translates to The Great Agricultural Push for Food and Bounty.
[4] République du Sénégal Ministère de l'Agriculture, Programme Agricole 2008–2009: GOANA, "Évaluation des besoins du Programme GOANA 2008–2009," 2008. The Ministry of Agriculture recorded 1.12 million ha of cereal grain production for the 2006/2007 growing season, per data shared by the Direction de l'Analyse de la Prévision et des Statistiques (DAPS) – Ministère de l'Agriculture et de l'Équipement.
[5] Republic of Senegal. Loi 64-46 du 17 juin 1964 relative au domaine national.
[6] The other 23 percent of Senegal's arable land (*"terres aptes à l'agriculture au Senegal"*) is categorized as classified forest in Ministère de l'Agriculture et de la Pisciculture, "La Grande Offensive Agricole pour la Nourriture et l'Abondance. Programme Agricole 2009/2010 (GOANA an 2)," June 2009.

unwritten. They explain that untitled land is in use, even if the usage is low intensity, such as pasturing animals, seasonal use of flood zones, or leaving land fallow to regenerate. In zones with strong customary institutions, these property rights are often more legitimate to local populations than the state's land tenure laws.

This chapter examines the impacts of customary institutions and unofficial customary authorities on land titling in Senegal. It shows that, even in an era when facilitating commercial agriculture was a top priority for state politicians, the state's interests and investors' demand for prime land alone did not determine how state property rights developed. Customary institutions also influence land titling outcomes in Senegal. Yet, as in Zambia, there is significant variation among these institutions throughout the territory. Historical legacies shape their contemporary strength, which impacts members' ability to preserve customary control over land. Some communities are better at retaining the influence of the institution's property rights rules, which were (formally) erased by the National Domain Law. And some are better at slowing the expansion of state power over land through titling in their zones.

The qualitative case studies and quantitative analyses in this chapter focus on customary institutions with roots in the precolonial political institutions mapped in Chapter 4. A diverse set of elites gain their authority from these institutions. Those who fit the category of customary authorities or chiefs in this chapter include village chiefs with inherited power, lineage heads, rural "notables" or "masters of the village," and others with institutional roles overseeing specific issues, lineages, or resources.[7] Each institution has its own terminology and individual titles to reference different types of customary authority.[8] These customary institutions overlap with Senegal's Islamic brotherhood institutions, whose leaders are known as marabouts.[9] Marabouts were elites within some precolonial states; in the contemporary era, brotherhood

---

[7] As elsewhere in this book, "chief" is synonymous with customary authority, and does not exclusively refer to the title of village chief in Senegal.

[8] For example, citizens surveyed in 2014 in central and northern Senegal (Mbacké and Podor) reported that the customary authorities with active roles in their communities included the titles of Saltigue, Diagraf, Dialtabé, Farba, Laokhobe, Labo, and Gackou, among others. See Barry 1997 on the origins of a number of different terminologies and types of customary authority in Senegal.

[9] See Raison 1968; O'Brien 1971; Copans 1980; Moitt 1989; D. Robinson 1991; Boone 1992; Villalón 1995, 2000; Beck 2001; Guèye 2002; D. Diop 2006; M. Diouf 2013a, 2013b.

institutions and customary institutions rooted in precolonial polities often coexist within the same communities. However, I reserve exclusive discussion of the Islamic brotherhood institutions in Senegal for Appendix C.[10] Narrowing the scope of the analyses in this chapter allows me to explore a set of customary institutions that have received less scholarly attention in Senegal.

This chapter supports the argument that customary institutions shape the expansion of land titling – even in a context with unofficial chiefs – by linking the local dynamics of land negotiations to national trends in land authority. It begins with a description of the state-supported land markets that replaced customary control over land in 2007–2013, then continues with discussions of the enduring (but varied) influence of unofficial customary authorities over land governance outcomes and the significance of the institutions in which they are embedded. Next, a case study of negotiations over land in northern Senegal illustrates how strong institutions can influence land titling processes by creating horizontal accountability among chiefs. Following the case study, an analysis of an original data set of all new land titles in Senegal between 2007 and 2013 reveals patterns in the state's expansion of control over land: Zones with hierarchical institutions after the French conquest have stronger contemporary customary institutions and have lower rates of titling. By contrast, as in Zambia, the state's expansion of control over property rights has proceeded more rapidly in zones with weaker, nonhierarchical customary institutions. This provides further evidence that strong local institutions can slow the development of state property rights, contributing to long-term patterns of state building.

---

[10] One risk of narrowing the scope is that it may suggest a false dichotomy between customary institutions and brotherhood institutions. Instead, brotherhood institutions are integrated with the customary institutions that are rooted in precolonial polities. Within a community, village chiefs, lineage elders, and marabouts are often collaborators. Further, some marabouts function as customary authorities who exert political authority within local communities. This includes marabouts who are considered the "masters of the village" or are from a founding family, and govern land. However, the brotherhoods' authority over land grew in zones of precolonial hierarchy, as marabouts co-opted existing structures. The quantitative subnational analyses cannot separate the impact of strong maraboutic institutions and strong precolonial political institutions since they coexist in the same districts. Instead, popular affiliation with the strongest maraboutic hierarchy – the Mouride brotherhood – serves as a robustness check to ensure that this is not driving the statistical results in this chapter. Appendix C examines the relationships between marabouts, brotherhood institutions, and land titling.

6.1 LAND MARKETS AND STATE ATTEMPTS AT TRANSFORMATION, 2007–2013

The era of booming global markets for African land ushered in a period of increased land titling in Senegal, as in Zambia. State actors welcomed the heightened interest in the country's customary land and widely encouraged the expansion of land titling. They courted international investors with descriptions of inexpensive, plentiful, fertile land. They designed initiatives and policies, including GOANA, to attract global land markets. In 2008, Senegal's government offered a mix of subsidies and tax benefits for agribusinesses. They released investors from customs duties and offered a five-year exemption from taxes on agribusiness profits.[11] In doing so, the state signaled its willingness to forgo immediate taxes in hopes of transforming its land into a long-term source of revenue. To further these efforts to make land a profitable resource for the state and a driver of economic development, the state also established an investor support agency.[12] The agency was tasked with facilitating foreign agricultural investment, including assistance with negotiations over land with local communities. State actors actively facilitated large-scale land deals for private investors. The policies in this era paralleled state efforts in Zambia at the time.

Consequently, dozens of domestic, foreign, and multinational firms clamored to access land in Senegal in the period examined here, 2007–13. Investors poured in from Spain, Austria, the Netherlands, Morocco, the United Kingdom, Switzerland, Italy, China, Saudi Arabia, Libya, Romania, Norway, Cameroon, and Belgium, among others. Some had clear plans for one specific product. One set of French investors sought land to grow tomatoes for export. A Nigerian company proposed a sugar cane plantation. Other large-scale land deals were motivated by a general interest in owning land, with only vague agricultural plans. For example, one Indian firm proposed a grocery list of potential crops, including wheat, potato, onion, groundnuts, rice, and papaya on their 5,700 ha plot. Land deals for biofuel production, particularly jatropha, sugarcane for ethanol, and sunflower seeds, comprised nearly half of these

---

[11] Republic of Senegal. Loi 2008-45 du 3 septembre 2008 fixant le régime fiscal et douanier des activités effectuées dans le cadre de la Grande Offensive Agricole pour la Nourriture et l'Abondance, 2008.
[12] Agence pour la Promotion des Investissements et des Grands Travaux (APIX).

large-scale agricultural deals, the result of increased global interest in alternatives to fossils fuels.

Land deals initiated by private actors and facilitated by the state implicated hundreds of thousands of hectares of customary land in Senegal between 2007 and 2013 alone. My conservative estimate of 233,000 ha of land changing from customary to state property rights combines records of the land deals registered in the government's investor support agency and applications for titles that had reached the final stage of the titling process. The average smallholder in Senegal has less than 3 ha of land, so this is equivalent to the land used by more than 75,000 rural citizens. Less conservative estimates of the magnitude of land deals in Senegal during this time are even larger. Fieldwork by a Senegalese civil society organization identified twenty-nine large-scale agricultural land deals on 595,000 ha of land between 2008 and 2013. This compares to a total of four investments on 84,000 ha of land in the earlier period of 2000–7.[13] A radical shift in land markets in Senegal occurred in 2008, consistent with the timeline of the global land rush.[14]

Titles for state projects also expanded state control of land during this period. The government organized different programs for improving agricultural production that registered tracts of land previously used by communities for small scale agriculture.[15] The programs requiring communities to cede authority over customary land tenure included irrigated tracts for farmers unions and agricultural training sites for urban youths at high risk of emigration. These projects were designed in Dakar. Afterward, bureaucrats contacted communities throughout the country to acquire the customary land needed for the project. Such state land deals extended state property rights over an additional 3,800 ha of land. While that hectarage may pale in comparison to the private investments during this period, these remain an important source of changes in land tenure. They are part of the incremental process of shifting the way land is used

---

[13] Chérif Bocar Sy, El Hadji Thierno Cisse, Sidy Ba, Étude participative sur les acquisitions massives de terres agricoles en Afrique de l'ouest et leur impact sur l'agriculture familiale et la sécurité alimentaire des populations locales: État des lieux. Cas du Sénégal (Dakar: COPAGEN and REDTAC, January 2013). The Land Matrix data base, which relies on media reports, counted 262,229 ha of land deals between 2003 and 2014 (Land Matrix, "Land Matrix Database," 2015, http://landportal.info/landmatrix). See Dieng 2017 for a discussion of data issues and the production of knowledge around land deals.

[14] For additional discussion of large-scale land deals in Senegal in this era, see Buckley 2013; Gagné 2019; A. Ndiaye 2019.

[15] This includes Retour Vers l'Agriculture (REVA) and L'Agence Nationale d'Insertion et de Développement Agricole (ANIDA) programs.

and managed, transferring authority over property rights from customary institutions to the state.

6.2 THE DISJUNCTURE BETWEEN WRITTEN LAWS AND UNOFFICIAL CUSTOMARY LAND AUTHORITY

Chiefs have no legal authority in land governance in Senegal. Yet – as in many other countries with strong systems of unofficial land authority – customary authorities in Senegal retain a great deal of influence on the ground. This is due, in part, to the strategic choices of state actors. Politicians and bureaucrats have tolerated customary authority in Senegal because it is politically and socially advantageous, much like the French in the later colonial era. Long-standing systems of customary authority offer efficient local conflict resolution and social stability at a low cost to the state. Thus, state actors collaborate with or defer to chiefs to facilitate their governance, when it serves their interests. As elections have become more competitive, this has increasingly included attempts by state politicians to enlist customary authorities to broker votes.[16] These forms of informal engagement by state actors buttress customary institutions in Senegal, despite legislation designed to undermine their influence.

The 1964 National Domain Law is the legal foundation for Senegal's customary land tenure regime. The government enacted this policy as part of a wave of post-independence "land tenure nationalism" laws throughout the region that sought to disrupt customary property rights systems by declaring state ownership of all untitled land.[17] Similar laws were passed in other former French colonies, including Mali (1960), Côte d'Ivoire (1968), Cameroon (1974), and Burkina Faso (1984). This legislation laid the legal groundwork for land titling to be a smooth process of users registering their rights with the state, without chiefs as intermediaries. However, there is a significant gap between this law and the continued role of customary authorities as actors with the capacity to influence land titling outcomes. Consequently, the decree that the state owns all untitled land in Senegal is best understood as a nonfunctioning law or "*légalité inopérante*," in the apt words of one land expert.[18]

---

[16] Beck 2008; Koter 2016; Gottlieb 2017.   [17] Diaw 2005, 49.
[18] Interview with Senegalese land expert (EX-123), Dakar, Senegal, May 26, 2014. Name withheld due to interview confidentiality protocol.

The disjuncture between written laws and informal land practices contributes to an uneven distribution of authority over customary land within the country. Legally, elected rural councils govern the land. Each council oversees, on average, thirty-five villages and 50,000 ha of land.[19] The councils consult with village chiefs, among other elites they refer to as "notables" or "customary authorities," before deliberating on a land title request. However, Senegal's unofficial chiefs have no formal veto power over land conversions, unlike Zambia's official chiefs. Further, as described in Chapter 2, these councils are embedded in local politics and society. Councillors are often members of the nearby customary institutions; some elected councillors identify as representatives of customary authorities. As a result, many councils defer to local customary property rights systems.[20] The degree to which customary institutions impact these councils' decisions varies, in part, as a function of the strength of these institutions. The role of councils thus differs spatially within the country, along a continuum between being autonomous agents of state land authority and representatives of a customary institution.

Although the rural councils govern the first stage in land titling, customary authorities have multiple opportunities to exert agency in the process due to their political and social authority at the local level. Senegal's chiefs can persuade landowners who would otherwise consent to cede land. They can influence council members and politicians by expressing their dissatisfaction with proposals to title new areas of land. They can also mobilize smallholder farmers to resist land deals, giving state actors an added incentive to abide their recommendations. Senegal's customary authorities prevent land conversions or make them costlier through these informal channels. Their status in the community gives them a role in determining if land leaves the customary domain, even in the absence of official land authority.

Whether customary authorities resist land titling attempts or welcome them reflects a range of considerations, as we would anticipate based on the Zambia case. The types of land titles that customary authorities in central and northern Senegal described as costliest to the community were those that reduce their long-term stocks of land, that permanently title land in the name of "outsiders," and in doing so, challenge the legitimacy of the institution's tenure norms. Some customary authorities spoke explicitly about anyone titling land as a threat to the continuing influence

---

[19] Author's calculations based on Centre de Suivi Ecologique (CSE) Shapefiles, 2014.
[20] Traoré 1997, 96; Lavigne Delville 1999, 6.

of their institution. For example, one village chief described land registration as "innovations that people think are good but in reality the old system was a very good thing."[21] Another argued against titling, saying "the fact that the overwhelming majority don't have titles for their land is proof that people are not okay with land registration."[22] Yet others only described titling as costly when it was initiated by someone who did not have rightful land ownership rights. For example, one village elder (in a weak customary institution) reported that titling is "what's *de rigueur* right now, since the law says that people must search for papers for their land. If you don't have papers, it's like you don't have land."[23]

In discussing their attitudes toward smallholder titling specifically, a repeated narrative advanced by chiefs in Senegal concerned the legitimacy of the applicant's claim. Although land users have the legal right to title their land within the country's laws, only some users have legitimate ownership rights within the local customary institution. This was a key justification offered during interviews for hindering applications for title. One chief reported that the central question he considers is: "How can someone title land that he does not own?"[24] Customary authorities in both central and northern Senegal repeated the idea that, contrary to the state's law, usage is insufficient for the right to title the land.[25] In general, chiefs in Senegal explained customary land ownership as inherited rights to the land derived from being part of the lineage that cleared the land or from the inherited owner having given the land to a new owner.[26] For example, one village chief reported that only his family has "full rights. Those with other names, they don't have full rights."[27] The collective costs of titling articulated by chiefs thus vary among large land deals that significantly reduce the stocks of customary land; titles that challenge the continuation of the customary institution's rules of ownership relative to state law; and those that formalize existing customary property rights, which are far less costly to the customary institution.

---

[21] Interview with customary authority (CA-105), northern Senegal, September 21, 2014.
[22] Interview with customary authority (CA-149), northern Senegal, September 5, 2014.
[23] Interview with customary authority (CA-132), northern Senegal, September 9, 2014.
[24] Interview with customary authority (CA-121), northern Senegal, September 8, 2014.
[25] Interview with rural council member (RC-151), central Senegal, October 29, 2014.
[26] Interviews with rural council member (RC-124), central Senegal, October 30, 2014; with rural council member (RC-152), northern Senegal, September 25, 2014; with rural council member (RC-127), central Senegal, October 27, 2014; with rural council member (RC-151), central Senegal, October 29, 2014.
[27] Interview with customary authority (CA-138), central Senegal, October 18, 2014.

In this unofficial chieftaincy system, state actors have generally respected customary institutions, prioritizing peaceful interactions with local populations and the customary authorities who govern them. In the short term, they have little incentive to upset the status quo by replacing customary authority over land where there is no demand for titles from citizens, state programs, or investors. In interviews, bureaucrats reported permissive attitudes toward customary property rights, saying, for example, that the state "doesn't force people to regularize *right away* their legal situation on the land that they occupy. For the farmer currently cultivating his field, there's no problem."[28] State actors are similarly hesitant to force land deals on a resistant community, even when there is high demand for the land. For example, when the state initiated a new project to grow jatropha, they made requests for 321,000 ha of customary land – a plot in each rural council zone. However, they could only pursue the scheme on 3,000 ha because that was all they could obtain from local communities.[29] Elsewhere, the government offered communities irrigation and agricultural infrastructure on the condition that the land be titled to a state agency. When communities refused to allow land titles, state actors shifted the locations of the projects to more willing villages.[30] Even for state projects, new land titles reflect negotiations with those in power in local communities. Customary authorities themselves expressed a strong sense of agency in this process. In the words of a chief in the northern Dagana district, the rural council could not ignore his recommendation because "if the village chief refuses, it's all of the village that refuses."[31] With limited statutory power to prevent land from exiting the customary domain, these customary authorities instead rely on popular influence to thwart or facilitate land titling in their domains.

Even as high demand for large areas of agricultural land extends the state's control over property rights, local negotiations still determine which land shifts from customary to state authority. Individual customary authorities are agents in these negotiations, due to the country's decentralized council system and the continuing influence of customary institutions on the ground. Multinational investors and enterprising bureaucrats hoping to prompt an agricultural revolution must engage with them. As a result, the local politics of land titling mediate where this booming

---

[28] Interview with bureaucrat (BUR-116), Dakar, Senegal, June 11, 2014.
[29] Interview with bureaucrat (BUR-130), Dakar, Senegal, November 14, 2014.
[30] Interview with bureaucrat (BUR-113), Dakar, Senegal, November 10, 2014.
[31] Interview with customary authority (CA-168), northern Senegal, December 11, 2014.

demand is met with a supply of customary land. The following sections explore how variation among institutions in Senegal shapes the expansion of state property rights.

6.3 CONTEMPORARY CUSTOMARY INSTITUTIONS AND HISTORICAL LEGACIES

Many different historically rooted sets of shared norms, rules, and political processes govern land and communities in Senegal. In short – Senegal's constellation of customary institutions is complex and diverse. In the absence of an official system of customary authority like Zambia's, there is more fluidity in customary institutions and their leadership structures. Citizens in both countries opt in and out of customary rules and use them strategically. However, without official chiefs, citizens in Senegal have greater opportunities for institutional syncretism.[32] In addition, without official chiefs as land authorities, a broader group of community leaders who derive power from customary institutions may influence land governance. Yet, despite this diversity, customary institutions in Senegal share some commonalities. They govern aspects of community life and retain a source of legitimacy separate from the state. They provide processes and guidelines for conflict resolution among neighbors. Customary institutions in Senegal also establish the rules of legitimate access to and use of untitled land. Their leaders are often closer to local populations than representative of the state. Nevertheless, the role of customary authorities in citizens' lives in Senegal is not simply a result of the lack of strong state presence in rural areas; customary institutions also exert influence in areas with high state capacity.

The capital city provides a prime example of the continuing influence of customary institutions within the state's administrative core. In Dakar, the Lebou customary institution structures community life for many citizens by organizing labor for local public goods, adjudicating disputes, and managing property rights. The institution's influence is particularly prominent in several historical neighborhoods. Although many of its members are integrated in the state apparatus as state employees and politicians, they also share a set of collective interests. Much like other communities, the control of land is an institutional priority. Members of the Lebou institution have consistently challenged the state's authority

---

[32] For examples, see Galvan 2004.

over a large portion of valuable land in Dakar.³³ For example, in 2015, the community mounted increased pressure on the government to allow the institution to control the land surrounding the (now former) airport. They argued that they had a legitimate claim to the land that predated the state and wanted the right to allocate it to its members. Members of the institution organized protests and pressured politicians seeking reelection to advance the issue.³⁴ One of their stated goals was to block the state from issuing titles to new users who were outside of the authority of the Lebou institution. This urban customary institution has facilitated members' attempts to retain control over a resource, making it an illuminating example of a broader pattern. Even in the heart of the modern state, the struggle to control land is a window into the ability of customary institutions to advance collective priorities and maintain political power.

As Chapter 4 described, the colonial era is a key starting point for understanding the differences among contemporary customary institutions in Senegal. Its precolonial political institutions were not buttressed by the colonial state as they were in Zambia. Instead, the French attempted to dismantle the preexisting institutions, such that, by the start of colonial rule in 1895, six precolonial hierarchies remained. Other communities in the territory were governed by nonhierarchical institutions, either because they did not withstand conquest or because they already had nonhierarchical structures at the end of the nineteenth century. Although the colonial state did not attempt to preserve the precolonial institutions, they also did not succeed in homogenizing them. Instead, as the evidence presented in this chapter affirms, these historical institutional endowments have contributed to differences in the strength of customary institutions today.

The legacies of political institutions that reigned prior to and in parallel to the state have remained relevant in Senegal, even as the colonial and independent governments implemented state-building and nation-building policies. For example, citizens continue to reference the precolonial polities to describe zones within the country. As Diop explained, this symbolizes how precolonial institutions "remain deeply rooted in popular

---

³³ Betts 1971; Kaag, Gaye, and Kruis 2011.
³⁴ Makini Brice, "Senegal Airport Row Shows Land Right Tensions in West Africa," *Reuters*, July 16, 2015; Babacar Guèye Diop, "Yoff–Morcellement des Terres de l'Aéroport de Dakar Saltigué Mamadou Mbengue Interpelle Le Président Sall," *Le Quotidien*, December 22, 2017.

consciousness."³⁵ While zones in Zambia are described by their chiefdom names as a matter of state policy, in Senegal, this is the result of informal institutional persistence. Similarly, Leonardo Villalón has described how citizens have retained their sense of connection to the Sine kingdom in the Fatick Region, even though the institution has not had a functioning hierarchy since its last head of state (*Buur*) passed away in 1969.³⁶ Despite changes in the operations of hierarchical institutions from their precolonial predecessors, historically rooted differences in their institutional structures continue to affect a variety of political outcomes in Senegal.³⁷ As the following sections show, this heterogeneity among customary institutions also shapes the expansion of state authority over land.

How Customary Institutions Create Horizontal Accountability

Accountability is one key mechanism by which customary institutions impact land tenure outcomes, as described in the theoretical framework. Leaders in regimes without accountability "are free to act as they please," while those with accountability are constrained by different forms of institutional checks and balances.³⁸ The case of Bemba institutions in Zambia provided evidence that some customary institutions feature systems of vertical accountability, in which elites can punish other elites through clear ties of hierarchy. However, customary institutions can also facilitate a second form of accountability, among actors with relatively equal power: horizontal accountability. Three elements from Landry Signé and Koffi Korha's framework for assessing horizontal accountability in formal institutions are particularly helpful for understanding how customary institutions generate countervailing forces or increase the number of "veto points" on a leader's decisions.³⁹

Institutions create horizontal accountability by: (1) establishing rules (or laws) that empower agents with checks and balances functions; (2) facilitating the transparency of information; and (3) generating the ability to sanction.⁴⁰ One key example of rules that create checks and balances, the first element of this list, are consultation norms. A customary institution's consultation processes may be informal, but they can still be

---

³⁵ D. Diop 2006, 121.   ³⁶ Villalón 1995, 53.
³⁷ For additional examples within Senegal, see Boone 2003; Beck 2008; Gottlieb 2017; Wilfahrt 2018.
³⁸ Diamond, Plattner, and Schedler 1999, 1.   ³⁹ Signé and Korha 2016.
⁴⁰ Adapted from Signé and Korha 2016.

binding principles of appropriate decision-making behavior for chiefs. The second ingredient for horizontal accountability is information.[41] Customary institutions can increase the information shared among leaders by providing opportunities for frequent interactions, even if these are independent of consultation on a specific decision. For example, institutional expectations that customary authorities partake in ceremonial and social events also generate regular interactions, and therefore opportunities to establish and communicate shared goals.

The third way in which institutions generate horizontal accountability is through sanctioning. The institutional features that build transparency also increase members' awareness of violations of institutional processes or shared goals. This allows actors to monitor and sanction their peers. Similarly, by organizing forums for increased interactions among members, customary institutions create opportunities for sanctions to be enforced. If interactions among customary authorities are limited, social sanctions will have little effect as a punishment. These three means by which customary institutions can facilitate horizontal accountability should be reinforced by two other institutional elements: shared identities and privileges within the institution. By fostering a sense of group identity, institutions increase ties among members and heighten actors' sense of obligation to uphold the institution's rules. Thus, institutional elements such as narratives of precolonial empire and thick social ties can reinforce compliance with shared norms, including participating in consultation processes. Similarly, by conferring privilege, institutions can also increase actors' incentives to sanction others for defecting from institutional processes or goals. As a result, customary institutions can decrease the autonomy of chiefs and increase the likelihood they prioritize collective goals through vertical accountability.

The following section shows how customary institutions impact the autonomy or accountability of individual customary authorities in Senegal. It highlights the importance of the differences among the customary institutions in which chiefs are embedded, which shape the constraints they face on their decisions. In doing so, it illustrates what it looks like when customary institutions have a greater capacity to slow the adoption of new rules that weaken customary control over land and erode the institution's power.

---

[41] Schmitter 1999, 60.

6.4 CUSTOMARY CONSTRAINTS IN NORTHERN SENEGAL

The comparison of two neighboring districts in northern Senegal illuminates how strong customary institutions can facilitate horizontal accountability to collective goals, even in the presence of compelling individual incentives to agree to titles. This is the case in the Podor district, where customary authorities are embedded in customary institutions that trace their origins to the powerful Fouta Toro precolonial state. By contrast, in the neighboring Dagana district, customary authorities have greater autonomy from institutional constraints as the result of their nonhierarchical institutional endowment. Reconstructing a major land deal attempted in both zones sheds light on how local institutions affect land titling, while holding a variety of potentially confounding factors constant.

Prior to colonization, there were precolonial states in both of these districts. The Waalo kingdom reigned over what is now Dagana, in the Senegal River Valley. However, when the French selected nearby Saint-Louis for their first outpost (and later colonial capital), this small, ethnically Wolof kingdom was already undergoing an "irreversible process of disintegration."[42] Civil war and attacks from neighboring institutions had weakened the Waalo, so the kingdom of 11,000 people could not withstand the French invasion.[43] The French conquest did not merely "pacify" the Waalo to preserve the institutional structure and facilitate colonial rule, it annihilated the organization, forcing the Waalo elites to flee to other kingdoms.[44] By the start of colonial rule in 1895, the customary authorities in Dagana were independent of any hierarchical institutional structure. This institutional legacy in Dagana is a sharp contrast to its eastern neighbor, Podor.

Podor was home to the strong Fouta Toro state, one of the oldest states in precolonial West Africa. By the nineteenth century, the Fouta Toro had undergone nearly a millennium of state building. It governed an estimated 200,000 people.[45] The theocratic Islamic state consisted of provinces ruled by a powerful aristocracy; it reinforced its power with regular military campaigns against neighboring polities.[46] When the French

---

[42] Barry 2012, 131.   [43] Saint-Martin 1989, 62.   [44] Barry 2012, 226–31.
[45] Saint-Martin 1989, 62.
[46] Jean-Louis Boutillier and Jean Causse. *La Demographie du Fouta-Toro (Toucouleurs et Peulhs)*. Dakar: Mission Socio-économique de la Vallée du Fleuve Sénégal, 1959; AOF Colonial Government. "Mission d'Aménagement du Fleuve Sénégal. Les Hommes du Fouta-Toro." Dakar: Division Socio-Economique, 1960.

6.4 *Customary Constraints in Northern Senegal*

administrators declared war on the Fouta Toro in the early 1800s, it was a stable and internally peaceful state.[47] As a result, the Fouta Toro's consolidated political hierarchy remained intact even after French annexation in 1860[48] and throughout the colonial period.[49] Colonialism then fixed the customary institutional trajectories in these two districts. Podor was endowed with a unified, organized customary institution, while Dagana's ruling kingdom was extinguished, leaving behind fragmented, village-level customary institutions.

This initial institutional endowment put the customary institutions in the districts on two distinct paths. For example, Boone has described Podor's rural elites in the post-independence era as linked in a hierarchical network that allowed them to control deconcentrated benefits from the state.[50] Linda Beck's scholarship emphasized their ability to act as a unified electoral bloc, capable of effectively brokering elections at the end of the twentieth century.[51] In contrast, Dagana became host to increasing in-migration after independence. It gained a reputation as a zone where it was possible to access land, so new villages and communities were formed with little reference to the Waalo legacy. Its chiefs are largely autonomous today. However, contemporary customary authorities in Dagana and Podor have many of the same functions in the lives of citizens. Villages in both zones have leaders who derive the right to rule through lineage; oversee customary property rights; and govern their communities with reference to shared customary norms. Nevertheless, these diverse institutional endowments have contributed to long-term differences in the resilience of customary control of land in the two northern districts, depicted in Figure 6.1.

How do we know that the customary institutions in these two districts have different contemporary strengths? One indicator of institutional strength is the stability of norms of customary land ownership relative to the state's law. As described earlier, compliance with the National Domain Law has been uneven throughout Senegal.[52] The law transformed land rights on customary land to usage rights; in effect, a family cannot claim to own the land based on lineage while allowing someone else to use it temporarily. Put differently, whoever is using the land has the *only* legitimate claim to it, under the National Domain Law.

---

[47] Delaunay 1984, 26.   [48] D. Robinson 1975.   [49] Gellar 2005, 30.
[50] Boone 2003, 282–314.   [51] Beck 2008, chapter 4.
[52] See also Traoré 1997; M. C. Diop 2013, 244.

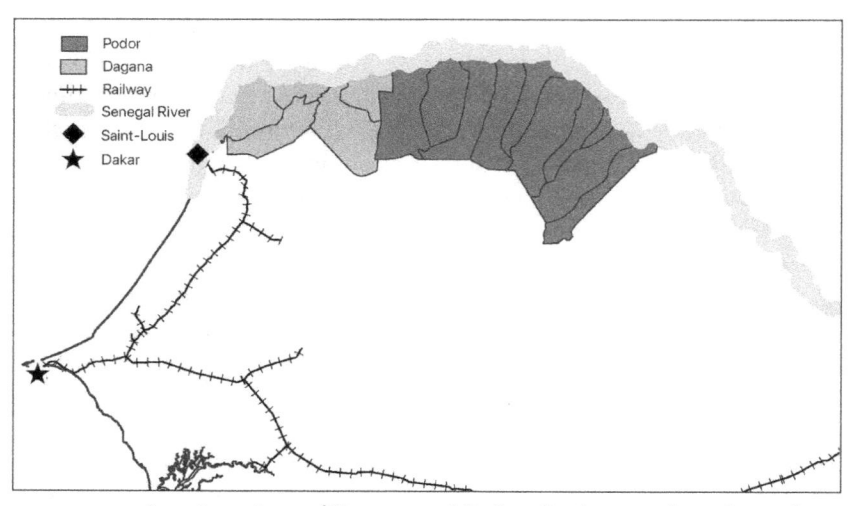

FIGURE 6.1. Locations of Dagana and Podor districts, northern Senegal

The rule of this state law has more successfully penetrated local understandings of customary property rights in Dagana than in Podor. As a result, elected councillors and chiefs in Dagana described customary property rights as an inherited or allocated right to *use* land. In interviews, village chiefs reported that the land "belongs to the nation" and is owned by whoever is using it.[53] Customary authorities in the former Waalo zone were also more likely to describe governing customary land ownership through the concept of usage rights, such that an owner can be anyone who lives in the village and pays residential taxes[54] or anyone who has the financial means to use the land.[55] The spirit of the National Domain Law was reflected in the discourses of customary authorities in Dagana.

By contrast, in Podor, customary property rights were treated as complete rights to the land, regardless of usage. Even the elected councillors responsible for administering the state's laws reported that the customary supersedes the legal. When asked who owns the land in Podor, councillors described how all of the land has established customary owners. At the same time, they acknowledged that, according to the law, customary land is owned by the nation. Some customary authorities

---

[53] Interview with customary authority (CA-106), northern Senegal, December 9, 2014.
[54] Interview with customary authority (CA-168), northern Senegal, December 11, 2014.
[55] Interview with customary authority (CA-164), northern Senegal, December 11, 2014.

6.4 Customary Constraints in Northern Senegal

who conceded to the existence of the National Domain Law indicated that they have actively resisted it in order to maintain their customary property institutions,[56] that the law was "just lies,"[57] or that the law represented a hidden government interest.[58] Others made no reference to the law and reported that the land belonged to individuals, families, or the descendants of the village founders. Members of the institution thus reinforce the strength of its rule by delegitimizing or refusing to acknowledge alternative logics of land rights. They reproduce the institution's power by repeating the narrative that customary property rights are an inalienable form of ownership, independent of usage.

The balance of power between council and customary authorities also mapped onto the differences in institutional strength in these cases. In Podor, the customary authorities had greater influence than the council; the opposite was true in Dagana. In both districts, council members stated that they consult with chiefs for advice in land governance. Yet, in Dagana, some council members reported that they can allocate land without the chief's approval, which is consistent with state law. By contrast, councillors are more dependent on customary authorities in Podor. They reported that they are "obliged, not for legality but for legitimacy"[59] to engage the chiefs. The stronger institution facilitates sanctions against council members that prevent them from advancing title applications without the consent of the chief. Illustrating this point, one customary authority joked, "if he did that, the women of the village would beat him to death!"[60] The contemporary strengths of these customary institutions differ, as do their institutional legacies.

This pair of districts are important cases for the argument in this book because they feature variation among customary institutions within a similar agricultural zone. This helps distinguish the role of institutions from the effects of geography, population density, and agricultural productivity. Podor and Dagana are neighbors within the Senegal River Valley of northern Senegal (see Figure 6.1). They both border the river and occupy the Sahelian climactic zone. In both locations, the rural populations are primarily engaged in subsistence agriculture of rice and cowpea

---

[56] Interview with customary authority (CA-153), northern Senegal, September 21, 2014.
[57] Interview with customary authority (CA-105), northern Senegal, September 21, 2014.
[58] Interview with customary authority (CA-149), northern Senegal, September 5, 2014.
[59] Interview with rural council member (RC-109), northern Senegal, September 23, 2014.
[60] Interview with customary authority (CA-110), northern Senegal, September 10, 2014.

production, with about a third of households owning cattle.[61] In Dagana, cash crops have a larger role.[62] The two districts share the highest usage of irrigated land in the country; the majority of smallholder farmers in both locations combine irrigated and rain-fed agriculture.[63] This is, in part, due to the presence of two state development agencies that have organized irrigation on thousands of hectares of land in both Podor and Dagana.[64] Both districts are consequently considered to be highly attractive agricultural zones. While Dagana has long been a priority area for agricultural projects,[65] Senegal's investment agency has also classified Podor as an "opportunity zone" for agricultural investors.

Key differences in agricultural practices and rural livelihoods in these two districts relate, in part, to their property rights institutions. While population density on rural land is only marginally lower in Dagana than in Podor,[66] there is a stark contrast in average plot size and production outcomes. In Dagana the average household farm is more than twice as large as in Podor, as are their crop outputs.[67] This has food security consequences: Podor is poorer, with higher rates of severe malnutrition

---

[61] Rice and cowpea are the first and second crops in both districts. In Podor, 32 percent of agricultural households had some cattle and 34 percent had cattle in Dagana, according to: Ministère de l'Agriculture/Food and Agriculture Organization (FAO), 1999, "Recensement National de L'agriculture 1998–1999," Dakar, Senegal. Government of the Republic of Senegal. Average cattle holding is seven for both Dagana and Podor, as described in O. Diop, Fofana, and Fall 2008, 28.

[62] In Dagana, 15 percent of land cultivated by smallholders is devoted to production of hibiscus and watermelon. Calculations based on the national agricultural census. Ministère de l'Agriculture/Food and Agriculture Organization (FAO), "Recensement National de L'agriculture."

[63] In Podor and Dagana, 67 and 71 percent of households practiced some irrigated farming, respectively. Ministère de l'Agriculture/Food and Agriculture Organization (FAO), "Recensement National de L'agriculture."

[64] These organizations are the Organisation pour la Mise en Valeur du Fleuve Sénégal (OMVS) and the Société d'Aménagement et d'Exploitation des Terres du Delta du Fleuve Sénégal (SAED). On SAED, see Adams 1977; van der Laan 1984; Boone 2003, 303–13.

[65] Until 1987, the delta region of the Senegal River Valley, including Dagana, was categorized as a "pioneer" zone, signaling that it was a high priority for agricultural projects. See Dahou and Ndiaye 2009.

[66] The rural population per hectare is 0.29 in Podor and 0.27 in Dagana. Agence Nationale de la Statistique et de la Démographie (ANSD), 2002, "Résultats Définitifs du Troisième Recensement Général de la Population et de l'Habitat," Dakar: Government of the Republic of Senegal.

[67] The 1999 agricultural census estimates average land cultivated as 2.02 ha in Dagana and 0.68 ha in Podor (Ministère de l'Agriculture/Food and Agriculture Organization (FAO), "Recensement National de L'agriculture"). More recent survey data confirms this pattern: The average size of cultivated land is 3.75 ha of a total 5.13 ha available to the

(17%) than Dagana (11%).[68] This difference in size of production partly reflects better access in Dagana to agricultural technology such as tractors and harvesters.[69] However, it is also a product of the more liberal access to land in Dagana that results from its customary institutions. For the analysis at hand, what is important to highlight is that the neighboring districts feature similar agricultural crops, soil, and proximity to the Senegal River, but land is easier to access in Dagana due to its nearly anarchic constellation of customary institutions.

Finally, to help isolate the impacts of customary institutions, this case selection also qualitatively controls for partisan electoral politics, as did the paired comparison in Zambia. We might anticipate, for example, that customary authorities in ruling party strongholds would be more willing to collaborate with the regime and facilitate state-sponsored land deals. State politicians may differ in how they engage with customary authorities in opposition or swing districts. However, partisan affiliations in the two districts are strikingly similar. In the 2000 elections that ushered in the first electoral turnover from Parti Socialiste (PS) domination, the ruling party gained 41 percent of votes nationally in the first round of elections.[70] However, in Dagana and Podor, 51 and 54 percent, respectively, voted for the longtime incumbent president Abdou Diouf. Similarly, in the 2007 presidential elections, 70 percent of voters in *both* districts voted for the incumbent president Abdoulaye Wade and his Parti Démocratique Sénégalais (PDS).[71] These similarities in partisanship, like the similarities in agricultural suitability of land, help focus our attention on the impacts of institutional differences.

Coordinating Collective Action: An Example

A close look at negotiations over one land deal in these two distinct institutional contexts sheds light on how customary institutions shape land titling outcomes through horizontal accountability mechanisms.

---

household in Dagana. In contrast, cultivated land is 0.98 ha in Podor of 3.02 ha available according to population size (O. Diop, Fofana, and Fall 2008, 25).

[68] Data from 2013, as presented in World Food Program, *Analyse Globale de La Vulnérabilité, de La Sécurité Alimentaire et de La Nutrition (AGVSAN)*: Senegal (Rome: World Food Program, July 2014).

[69] O. Diop, Fofana, and Fall 2008.

[70] See M. C. Diop, Diouf, and Diaw 2000; Koter 2013.

[71] In addition, 20 and 16 percent voted for the Parti socialiste (PS) in Dagana and Podor, respectively.

In 2011, investors from the Northern Agricultural Company (NAC)[72] sought a large area of land for rice production. Their goal was to obtain rights to between 2,000 and 4,500 ha of customary land. They targeted Podor, which looked like an ideal location on paper. Its proximity to the river permitted irrigated commercial production. The district had large areas of customary land populated by smallholder farmers and herders who used the land extensively. The investors expected the project to be an easy sell to local communities eager for economic development opportunities. Further, the NAC had the active support of the state and financing from an international financial institution to pursue their goals.[73] Their project aligned with the government's agenda to increase rice production. To ensure its success, the prime minister's office had created a committee to oversee the project.[74] However, the investors were surprised to find that despite their efforts, they were prevented from accessing land to title in Podor by actors who prioritized retaining customary control over land.

The company entered into negotiations with communities in the domains of three of Podor's rural councils between 2011 and 2013. In all three, they failed to access the land they had targeted. In the first rural council area, the NAC spent more than a year in negotiations with elected council members, village chiefs, lineage heads, and other elites. There, the company identified and requested 4,000 ha of land. They offered cash compensation for community members; financial assistance for the rural council; infrastructure development in the form of schools and health clinics; and promises to hire local labor. In individual meetings, some lineage heads and council members expressed support for the project. The negotiations were far enough along that the company had mapped and completed an environmental study of the land by the time the rural council met to vote whether the land could begin the process of titling. The NAC agents expected a "yes" vote based on their private discussions with individual councillors. However, when it came to the public forum, the deal was firmly rejected. The same customary authorities and councillors who had privately supported the project blocked the deal when they faced public scrutiny, given the political implications of ceding customary land. From the perspective of the investors, the negotiations failed due to

---

[72] Name changed to preserve confidentiality of sources.
[73] NAC Action Plan submitted to the Ministry of Environment and Sustainable Development, 2014.
[74] Interview with investor (INV-101), northern Senegal, December 8, 2014.

6.4 Customary Constraints in Northern Senegal

overwhelming resistance to the proposed transfer of control over community land.

The company then shifted its focus to two other areas within Podor, still in the zone of the Fouta Toro institutional legacy. There, they engaged in negotiations with two communities at once, hoping for greater leverage in the land deal. They also reduced the amount of land they were asking for to 2,500 ha, to help advance their cause. The benefits they offered for the conversion of land remained the same.

In the first new area, the deal failed when customary authorities and other community members coordinated to make demands that were untenable to the investors. The customary authorities in this zone met in advance of their meetings with the NAC. They presented a united front and insisted on strict conditions for the titling of customary land in their domain. They wanted 750 ha of the company's 2,500 ha to be irrigated and planned out for community use, in addition to the other infrastructural commitments and compensation. The NAC calculated that this type of land planning investment for the community would cost them millions of dollars.[75] Further, the chiefs demanded that the NAC provide this benefit immediately, *before* the NAC could start its own project. The company was invested in this process and continued trying to access land in this zone, despite this provision. They wrote up a draft of a memorandum of understanding to bring to the council with the amount of irrigated land for the community left blank. The company had decided that they could afford to irrigate up to 500 ha of land for the community, in addition to the other infrastructure commitments. However, the final meeting between the NAC, the council, and the local population ended in a heated disagreement over compensation. The NAC's attempts to access customary land in Podor once again failed.

The investors then switched focus to the third rural council zone in Podor. Customary authorities and other community members again coordinated to demand large areas of irrigated land in exchange for ceding any authority over their land. The size of this land was one sticking point in these negotiations. In addition, from the perspective of one council member, vocal customary authorities and community members seemed to share the perspective that the project should be refused on principle.[76]

---

[75] Interview with investor (INV-101), northern Senegal, December 8, 2014.
[76] Interview with rural council member (RC-104), northern Senegal, September 22, 2014.

The NAC made serious attempts at negotiating for the land in the domain of this strong customary institution. They had the financial resources to meet some of the high demands made by customary authorities. They had support from the government. Yet the NAC was unable to find customary land to title anywhere in the zone. Critically, the issue in these negotiations was not the *availability* of land but the conversion of that land out of the customary domain. The chiefs' concerns related to power and control over the land, not whether it was actively in use. After many failed negotiation attempts, the company accepted that it was too difficult to access land that could be titled in their preferred area.

After facing resistance in Podor, the investors shifted their attention to the weaker customary institution zone of neighboring Dagana, less than 100 miles west. There, the NAC organized public meetings about the project, attended by customary authorities, community members, and rural council members. As in Podor, the population expressed concerns about ceding land. Among other things, they worried about how the project would affect shared routes for cattle grazing and whether the company would comply with their promise to hire local labor. They expressed concerns that chiefs would not have a say in how the company was using the land as the project proceeded. However, there was no coordination of demands or group mobilization against the deal.

Due to the differences between the institutions in the two districts, the company's negotiations in Dagana were swift and successful. The non-hierarchical customary institutions in the former Waalo zone translated to weaker customary property rights and a stronger role for the rural councils in land governance. At the time of the company's negotiations, more lineage heads and customary landowners in Dagana had already started the process of registering their property rights with the rural council. The increased registration of land rights was both a sign and driver of the erosion of customary institutions' power over land. The company capitalized on this difference. It worked with the rural council to target families who had already taken this step to exit the customary system.

In Dagana, landowning families, village chiefs, and small farmers unions decided independently to cede land to the company. There, the NAC did not engage in long negotiations with groups of lineage heads and village chiefs to determine how they would be compensated. Instead, individuals who ceded land received a standardized per-hectare compensation, established by the company. Those who had registered their land with the council each submitted letters that ceded their rights to the NAC.

6.4 Customary Constraints in Northern Senegal 225

Over seventy-five families and fifteen small farmers unions in three villages in the zone accepted this deal. The company gave them 180,000 CFA ($360 USD) per hectare; the amounts each actor ceded ranged from 2 to 100 ha.[77] In a fourth village, the company negotiated directly with the village chief for 100 ha of land in exchange for an irrigated community space equivalent in cost to the per-hectare standardized price.[78] After spending two years in complicated negotiations in the zone of a strong customary institution, it took less than a year for the company to obtain the right to title over 2,000 ha of land in Dagana.

How did the customary institution in Podor impact this outcome? First, the chiefs convened to discuss the project prior to and in addition to their meetings with the company. Customary authorities from multiple villages presented a united front in the negotiations. They consulted with each other, to evaluate the costs and benefits of the land deal together. Institutional features, such as the voluntary practice among village chiefs within the institution to select a "chief of chiefs" from among their own ranks,[79] helped members to coordinate as a block. Their repeated interactions and meetings allowed them to formulate and communicate shared priorities in relation to the land deal.

One key narrative circulated in these meetings among customary authorities: that the deal was costly because of the permanency of land titling. They perceived the company's acquisition of a land title as "land grabbing" such that "they understood that once the land was given, the populations would become their slaves."[80] One village chief argued that they could never accept the permanent loss of land that rightfully belonged to members of the institution, which would occur if the company had papers for the land in its name. To metaphorically illustrate his point, he explained in an interview that allowing the land to be titled to the company would have been like putting another man's name on his marriage certificate to his wife. Customary authorities in another village suggested that they could participate if the land were registered in the name of the chief's family, not the NAC. They suggested that they could then lend out the land to the NAC for a limited fifteen-year contract with the stipulation that the company would be required to leave all of the

---

[77] NAC Action Plan, 2014.
[78] Interview with investor (INV-101), northern Senegal, December 8, 2014.
[79] Interview with rural council member (RC-103), northern Senegal, September 20, 2014.
[80] Interview with rural council member (RC-104), northern Senegal, September 22, 2014.

equipment they purchased behind.⁸¹ Behind the scenes, leaders within the institution coordinated their priorities, determining that land registration was the issue that would block the deal.⁸²

The institution's consultation norms and thick social ties among customary authorities also impacted this decision-making process. Individual chiefs did not make the decision to support or block the land deal autonomously. Some customary authorities saw the benefits of ceding land to the NAC; however, their responses were tempered by those who prioritized the collective costs. Social pressure and threats served as horizontal sanctions within the institution, which prevented individual customary authorities from freely ceding customary control of land. Within villages, lineage heads who seemed willing to cede the land were overpowered by strong refusals from others. They could not unilaterally cede land without fear of social consequences. Similarly, the NAC had identified customary authorities who were interested in accepting the agricultural investment, but found they were silenced when these views were subject to scrutiny from others within the institution.

Even members of the rural council, who have the legal authority to advance a state–supported agricultural land deal, were subject to institutional checks and balances. Councillors elected from the local community who supported the NAC project felt they had to tread carefully to avoid being subject to criticism, rumors, and threats.⁸³ A bureaucrat working with the rural council reported that he saw technical merit in the proposed development and supported the project, but sensed that as an "outsider" (*allochtone*) he did not have a say in this decision-making process.⁸⁴ The institution established who had the right to cede land, how these decisions should be made, and that deviations from institutional rules should be sanctioned. Customary authorities, as well as councillors and other elite members, were subject to institutional constraints on their decisions.

The customary institution in the Fouta Toro zone was able to mobilize collective action to prevent the loss of land, despite concentrated benefits that were attractive enough to lead to the rapid conversion of land in Dagana. Importantly, the land involved was not held by all members of the institution collectively or equally. Individual lineages owned the land,

---

⁸¹ Interview with rural council member (RC-103), northern Senegal, September 20, 2014.
⁸² Interview with customary authority (CA-105), northern Senegal, September 21, 2014.
⁸³ Interview with rural council member (RC-104), northern Senegal, September 22, 2014.
⁸⁴ Ibid.

often with a highly unequal distribution that reflected the castes within the institution. However, individual ownership was governed by the institution's system of customary property rights, and retaining control over property rights was a source of power for the institution. Consequently, the land deal was understood to be collectively costly to the institution; this triggered a coordinated response among its members. Individual customary authorities and landowners were constrained by the influence of their peers and encouraged to consider the impact of land titling on the institution as a whole. Without this strong customary institution, the outcome of these negotiations would likely have been quite different.

The comparison to Dagana helps illustrate how the negotiation process and the calculations of individual customary authorities differ in the absence of a strong customary institution. In this case, one set of actors in the negotiation remained constant in both customary institutional contexts: The NAC had the same financial and statutory resources to offer communities in both Dagana and Podor. However, the land was significantly costlier in Podor. One NAC employee involved in the negotiations posited that "the difference is that the populations of Podor are less accessible in terms of bargaining for the acquisition of land than in the zone of [Dagana]."[85] This accessibility in bargaining was a function of the customary institution's capacity to generate accountability to a collective goal of maintaining institutional power over land.

In Dagana, the very different institutional legacy translated to limited ties among customary authorities beyond the village level. There, village chiefs could function more independently than in Podor; ties across villages were personal, not institutional. This made it more difficult to sanction customary authorities and to coordinate group goals. There were limited expectations of cooperation among village chiefs, lineage heads, and other community elites in crafting their response to the potential land deal. Instead, individual decisions were atomized – not subject to constraints within a customary institution – and based primarily on their perceptions of individual benefits. They were determined within families or villages, not as part of a larger collective.

Further, these differences among customary institutions in neighboring districts were part of a dynamic process that shapes the collective costs of land titling. In both zones, customary authorities and citizens worried

---

[85] Interview with investor (INV-102), northern Senegal, December 8, 2014.

about the long-term loss of land for the community. As one chief in Dagana reported, "before giving land to someone, we should hold on to it for our future sons."[86] However, the collective costs to the continuing authority of customary property rights were not parallel in the two districts. Even if it is equally privately costly to an individual to cede land, members of a weak customary institution are less likely to perceive or prioritize the implications for the long-term power of the institution. Time horizons should be shorter in a weak institution relative to a strong institution. In Dagana, the monopoly of the authority of customary property rights had already significantly eroded. By contrast, the institution's members in Podor had more to lose if statutory land rights became the norm in their zone. This suggests that the long history of differences among institutions' abilities to sustain their control of land contributes to members' evaluations of the advantages of retaining customary property rights today. This further reinforces the heterogeneity between weak and strong customary institutions over time.

This NAC land deal is not an aberration but a reflection of a broader pattern between the two districts. The expansion of state control over land occurs more slowly in Podor than Dagana. For example, between 2007 and 2013, 1 percent of customary land was titled in Podor, compared to 11 percent in Dagana.[87] In that period, the state investor support agency actively encouraged investors to look for land in Podor; yet Podor hosted two agricultural investments while Dagana had thirty-two. Further, the same sequence as the NAC deal occurred in another state-sponsored agricultural project. In that case, the investors targeted an area of prime agricultural land in Podor (in a different rural council area than the ones featured in the NAC case). However, they faced strong resistance from local communities and were forced to seek land elsewhere. They moved on to Dagana, where they established their commercial farm on land that had previously been classified as a state forest. It has been reported that at least six villages were displaced from this land.[88] The comparison of the two districts thus helps illustrate how strong

---

[86] Interview with customary authority (CA-106), northern Senegal, December 9, 2014.
[87] Based on the national land tenure data set described in Section 6.5.
[88] Due to its large size, this ethanol land deal has been well documented by researchers and civil society. See Koopman 2012; Dieng 2017; Sy, Cisse, and Ba, "Étude participative sur les acquisitions massives de terres agricoles en Afrique de l'ouest"; CRAFS, GRAIN, and Re:Common, *Who Is Behind Senhuile-Senethanol?* (Barcelona: GRAIN, November 2013), www.grain.org.

6.4 Customary Constraints in Northern Senegal

hierarchical customary institutions can slow titling through coordinated resistance, pushing land deals to zones with weak customary institutions.

Insights into the Interaction of Customary Institutions, Land Values, and Geography

This paired comparison reveals why we cannot understand the expansion of state power over land without examining differences among the institutions that are replaced by titling. Piecemeal titling policies are designed to allow market forces and demand from state actors to determine where state property rights are adopted. Recall that the induced institutional change (IIC) model predicts that actors should first initiate the process of land titling where land is more desirable. This should be true of investors, state agents, and smallholder farmers alike. In the NAC case, land was, by all available measures, more valuable in Dagana and costlier in Podor. The land in Dagana was closer to key infrastructure, including the former colonial capital of Saint-Louis and the current capital of Dakar.[89] Another proxy for land values is the government's lists of prices for leases and indemnities in the two district townships. Although the rates for rural land in each district were equal, township land was more valuable in Dagana's principal town than in Podor's.[90] Consistent with the IIC land titling model, the NAC deal did result in a change in property rights on the more valuable land. However, this did not occur due to higher demand for titles on Dagana's land. Instead, the customary institution in Podor reduced the supply (or accessibility) of titling there, relative to Dagana.

State property rights developed on the more valuable land because the customary institutions there were weaker. Such institutional weakness is, in fact, consistent with the mechanisms of the IIC model: Actors should seek new property rights when the existing institution is no longer effective due to increasing competition for land. The NAC deal provides evidence in support of the argument that institutional weakness can increase the rate of change in property rights. However, it differs from the IIC model because it reveals that the weakness and strength of

---

[89] The townships in Dagana and Podor are 79 km apart. By road, Dagana to Dakar is 356 km. Podor to Dakar is 434 km.
[90] In 2010, list price per square meter in Dagana for township land was 6,000 CFA (12 USD) and in Podor 2,000 CFA (4 USD). For rural land in both districts it was 500 CFA (1 USD). Republic of Senegal. Décret 2010-439 du 6 avril 2010.

institutions may be exogenous to the factors that increase demand for land. In the case of the northern Senegal, historical institutional endowments led to the weakening of customary property rights and, consequently, more rapid shifts to state property rights.

This case also shows the limits of the state's agency in determining where customary institutions remain powerful. Despite state attempts to both weaken them and collaborate with them,[91] members of the Fouta Toro institution have retained autonomous power, beyond the state's designs. In the conquest years, the French tried to destroy the Fouta Toro institutions as they did to the Waalo; they failed. Similarly, when the French needed land, the colonial authorities sought first the more hinterland zone of the Fouta Toro. In their earliest colonial interventions of the nineteenth century, the French targeted land in Podor for colonial agricultural production. Yet opposition from the institution's leadership forced them to change their approach and seek land in the Waalo zone instead.[92] The colonial authorities, the state, and investors have repeatedly tried to access land in Podor.

In the era of GOANA and booming land markets, the NAC investors were backed by the state actors' vested interests in the success of their project. Facilitating such deals was a political priority. Nevertheless, communities in Podor were able to maintain customary control over land. Customary land tenure remained not because the land was undesirable or low priority for the state to facilitate titling; these non-statutory land rights were resilient because the hierarchical customary institution made it more challenging for the state's agenda and property rights to take root.

This case and the previous chapter have illustrated a common pattern across hierarchies thousands of miles apart in Africa: Strong institutions can advance collective agendas by constraining their leaders. The Bemba customary institution of Zambia and the Fouta Toro customary institution of Senegal use different mechanisms to generate accountability to group goals. Yet they both reveal that institutions can induce members to reinforce their own power and that the differences in institutional endowments are a source of heterogeneity that remains salient long after the formation of the modern state. Other customary institutions within the same state and geographic zone appear weaker relative to these strong institutions, as their leaders have greater autonomy from collective priorities and face lower constraints within the institution.

---

[91] See also Boone 2003; Beck 2008.
[92] Hardy 1921, 71; Delaunay 1984, 29; Barry 2012, 168.

The following section examines the role of institutional strength throughout Senegal, building on the insights gleaned from the comparison of Podor and Dagana. By the start of colonialism, the customary institutions in the two districts were on different institutional paths that sustained themselves over time. In Podor, a powerful precolonial empire laid the groundwork for the organizational rules and processes of a strong customary institution. The institution shapes leaders' decisions by facilitating ties of horizontal accountability, inducing them to prioritize the institution's power over land. Members opt-in to preventing the erosion of the institution's power by, for example, discounting the applicability of the National Domain Law in their zone. In contrast, the Dagana example illustrates the challenge of building strong customary institutions after the colonial state was imposed. There, a weak precolonial kingdom became a zone of fragmented customary institutions, with limited organization above the village level following French conquest. Weak institutions struggle to prevent defections and retain strong systems of customary land tenure; the state's rules of property rights more easily penetrate local understandings. As citizens and elites alike lose faith in customary property rights institutions, the benefits of maintaining the customary tenure regime become less appealing. This is a pathway through which historical institutional endowments shape local responses to the possibility of titling land, which aggregates into national-level differences in the state's expansion of power over land rights. It bears repeating that this is not an argument that institutions in Senegal are unchanged since colonialism, nor does institutional endowment determine all variation among contemporary institutions. However, customary institutions can reinforce their power over time. An endowment of hierarchy is a resource that allows members to replicate the institution's strength.

6.5 NATIONAL PATTERNS OF LAND TITLING AND HIERARCHY IN SENEGAL

Are stronger institutions better able to retain control over land throughout Senegal? This section examines the national-level implications of the argument. As in Zambia, historical institutional endowments have an important impact on the strength of customary institutions in Senegal. Analysis of a data set of all new land titles between 2007 and 2013 within Senegal sheds light on the relationship between the historical structures of customary institutions and contemporary systems of property rights.

Dependent Variable

The outcome of interest in the following models is the expansion of state property rights on customary land. This is measured as the proportion of land per district (*département*) that was registered as new land titles between 2007 and 2013: the rate of land titling. The total size of new land titles in this period is a combination of multiple sources of government data, which identify 1,798 unique land conversions on 236,724 ha during the six-year period. The first source is a record of all applications for new land titles on customary land from 2007 to 2013. This data is compiled from the minutes of the government's bimonthly National Land Commission (NLC) meetings. After gaining local-level approval, titling applications must receive national approval at the NLC. This is a necessary stage for land registration in Senegal, inclusive of land for government agencies and private actors. This process permanently shifts land out of the official category of national domain land by registering it, and the state then allocates the applicant a long-term lease, which can be canceled, extended, or sold. In addition, this measure includes land ceded by communities for new private, parastatal, and state farms in this period, using data from the government agencies charged with agriculture (ANIDA) and investor support (APIX). To be included in the data set, these land deals had to pass through a minimum stage of local consent for land conversion from customary land to state land. Duplicates among the data sources were removed.[93] Analyses exclude urban Dakar, Pikine, and Guédiawaye. The hectarage of these new titles generates the numerator of this measure of land titling. The denominator is the total amount of territory in a district available for conversion: the total land minus classified forests and parks. As Figure 6.2 illustrates, land titling does not occur at the same rates throughout the country. In the study period, the median district had a titling rate of 2 percent of land; the range of this variable is between 0 and 14 percent of the district's land.

Independent Variable

The key predictor of interest is a hierarchical institutional legacy in the district. To construct this variable, I georeferenced the government's map of the boundaries of the precolonial kingdoms and political communities,

---

[93] These data are measured at the district level. The NLC minutes do not consistently identify locations below the district.

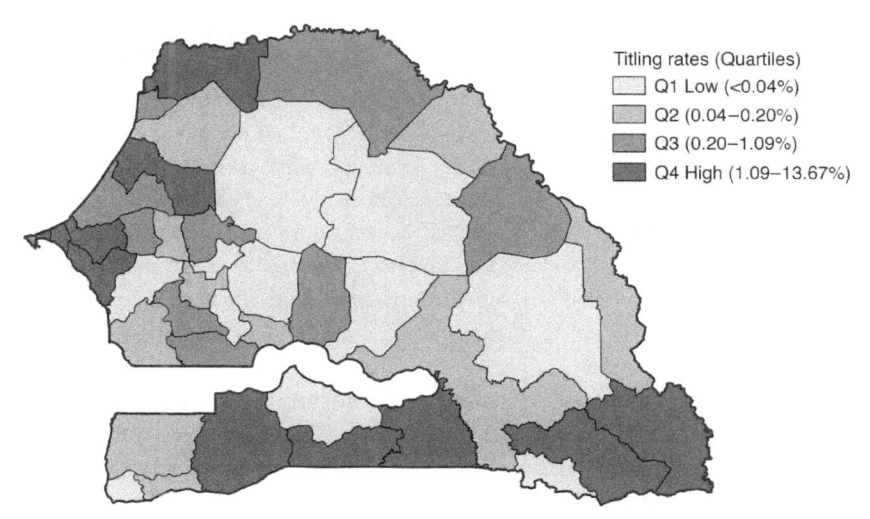

6.5 National Patterns of Land Titling and Hierarchy

FIGURE 6.2. Map of rates of land titling per district in Senegal, 2007–2013
Notes: Map does not represent national parks and other areas of land that are ineligible for title and were deducted from the denominator of the dependent variable.

depicted in Figure 4.4. As detailed in Chapter 4, French conquest razed some institutional structures in Senegal. Therefore, I used colonial reports and secondary sources to categorize institutional legacies as hierarchical or nonhierarchical after the start of colonial rule. I then overlaid the map of the hierarchies that survived the conquest, Figure 4.4, with the 2012 district boundaries, to create a measure of the dominant institutional legacy for each district.[94]

Control Variables

A range of measures captures the impact of land values and geography on land titling. Including them helps identify whether there is a relationship between customary institutions and land titling that is separate from the desirability of land. I approximate access to infrastructure and markets as the percentages of the district within 10 km of paved roads and with a dichotomous indicator of whether a railway passes through it. Distance to the capital is also a measure of land values given that resources, markets,

[94] This process identifies the customary institution that covered the largest percentage of territory in each district. Two have less than 75 percent coverage of either hierarchical or nonhierarchical institutions: Rufisque and Dagana. Dropping each district as a robustness check does not impact the findings.

jobs, and infrastructure are concentrated in Dakar. Population density represents demand for and competition over land.[95] It is also important given that higher populations historically led to hierarchical institutions elsewhere in the world. In contemporary Senegal, there is no observable relationship between hierarchical legacies and population density ($r = 0.066$). Two additional measures consider agricultural suitability and land desirability. First, a rainfall measure captures the annual variation between the district rainfall and the country average prior to the start of the study period, in the three-year period from 2005 to 2007. Second, an indicator of the dominant soil type in a district approximates agricultural suitability.

Each model also includes the size of the customary land in the district to account for any bias created by district size. In addition, to ensure that the differences in land titling rates between districts from 2007 to 2013 are not caused by earlier titling patterns, I collected data from regional land registries to generate an estimated measure of the number of prior titles. Descriptive statistics, data sources, and details of measurement are reported in Appendix Table A.2. This model specification parallels the approach to identifying the impacts of hierarchy in Zambia described in Chapter 5. To estimate the proportional outcome, bounded between 0 and 1, the following analyses use fractional logistic regression models.[96] Robust standard errors are clustered at the region.

Analysis and Findings

Statistical analyses identify a strong, systematic relationship between institutional legacies and contemporary titling rates. Titling is more common in districts with nonhierarchical institutions, independent of differences in population density, land values, infrastructure access, soil type, rainfall variation, and previous land conversions rates. Hierarchy has a strong negative effect on titling that is significant at a 99 percent confidence level. The fully specified baseline model and a reduced model are reported in Appendix Table B.3 (Models 1 and 2). Figure 6.3 graphically depicts the results of the baseline model. It shows that districts with nonhierarchical institutions have significantly higher rates of land titling.

---

[95] See footnote 88, Chapter 5 and the discussion of population density in Chapter 5.
[96] See the discussion of this estimation strategy in Chapter 5 and Papke and Wooldrige 1996, 2008; Baum 2008; Guirkinger and Platteau 2014. Ordinary Least Squares models are also reported in Table B.3.

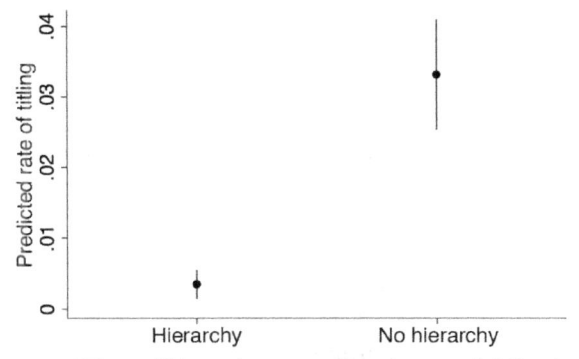

6.5 National Patterns of Land Titling and Hierarchy

FIGURE 6.3. Effect of hierarchy on predicted rates of titling in Senegal
Notes: Figure presents the predicted proportion of newly registered customary land per district between 2007 and 2013 with 95 percent confidence intervals.

The predicted rate of land titling from 2007 to 2013 in areas with nonhierarchical institutions is 3.33 percent (.033) compared to 0.35 percent (.003) in areas with hierarchical institutions. These findings suggest that, given two districts with the same density of road networks, population density, and soil type, titling would be less likely to occur in the district with a hierarchical institutional legacy.

A few additional analyses delve deeper into these patterns. Perhaps it is not institutional legacies that help some communities to slow the loss of customary land but the size of key identity groups. Shared ethnic ties have been shown to contribute to collective action in other circumstances.[97] Similarly, as described in Chapter 5, group size could be a source of bargaining power that increases chiefs' abilities to resist state-supported titling attempts. To explore any potential confounding effect of ethnicity, I included measures of the percentage of the district that identifies as part of the two largest ethno-linguistic groups in Senegal: Wolof and Pulaar (Appendix, Table B.3, Model 3). Importantly, the same ethno-linguistic group can correspond to different customary institutions, as there were multiple precolonial polities within each group. For example, both the Waalo and the Cayor kingdoms were ethnically Wolof. However, the results show that ethno-linguistic group size is not a significant predictor of land titling outcomes. Further, including them in the model does not interfere with the significant negative effect of hierarchy on land titling. This is unsurprising given the important variations within these groups

---

[97] For examples, see Miguel and Gugerty 2005; Habyarimana et al. 2009.

that result from their different customary institutions; the Pulaar communities in zones of nonhierarchical customary institutions in eastern Senegal should have lower capacity to coordinate to retain control of customary land than the Pulaar communities in the north, which draw on the institutional endowment of the Fouta Toro precolonial state.[98] Although ethnic ties are often related to and reinforce customary institutions, these results emphasize the importance of heterogeneity among customary institutions.

Further, this relationship between historical customary institutions and modern land titling outcomes in Senegal withstands a series of other robustness tests, including an alternative specification of the hierarchy variable[99] and a model that considers the influence of the Mouride brotherhood.[100] The findings cannot be attributed to influential control variables or observations,[101] and the results are unchanged when

---

[98] Notably, these ethnic categories reflect the state's construction of ethnic groups within its census. For example, Pulaar is the state's categorization; many Pulaar would categorize themselves as ethnically "Toucouleur," a term connected to the Fouta Toro customary institution.

[99] I also consider an alternative measure that does not take into account the effect of the colonial conquest. Instead, it divides the precolonial polities as they existed in 1854 into four categories: small diverse ethnic groups, unfederated chiefdoms, federated chiefdoms, and unified states. The full model with this alternative specification identifies a significant negative effect of increasing levels of precolonial organization on rates of titling. This suggests that the main results are not sensitive to categorization of hierarchy after conquest (measured in 1905) and provides additional support for the argument that the historical structures impact contemporary land titling (reported in Model 5, Table B.3). In addition, the Appendix reports ordinary least-squares estimation for the reduced and baseline models (Models 6 and 7, Table B.3).

[100] As described at the start of the chapter, brotherhood institutions often overlap with other customary institutions in Senegal. The Mouride brotherhood is a strong customary institution, and should also facilitate the coordination of collectively beneficial outcomes. However, the heartland of this customary institution is within the zone of the Baol hierarchical legacy, making it challenging to differentiate between the effects of overlapping institutions. Including a measure of the percentage of the district that identified as a member of the Mouride institutions allays concerns that the brotherhood could be driving the national institutional pattern. Instead, the hierarchy effect remains when accounting for the size of the Mouride community within the district (Model 4, Table B.3). See Appendix C for further discussion of the marabouts in Senegal.

[101] Of particular note is that the significant negative effect of hierarchy is present in models with and without the measure of prior titles. This variable is important because it protects against the possibility that land is titled more intensely during this period in some zones because rates of titling there had previously been low. However, including this measure introduces the possibility of a posttreatment bias, which results from including an outcome within the model. Thus, it is comforting that the significant negative effect of hierarchies remains when the previous conversions variable is excluded.

individual districts and predictors are excluded.[102] The main effect also remains when each hierarchical institution is sequentially dropped. This provides additional support for my argument that customary institutions impact the expansion of state property rights.

The Effects of Land Values on Titling

These analyses identify patterns in rates of land titling, and therefore in the growth of state authority over land. Land titling occurs at lower rates in zones with strong institutions – those with hierarchical legacies. However, these findings also shed light on structural factors that should influence land tenure outcomes. Figure 6.4 illustrates the effect of customary institutions on titling at different land values. In each of the three following graphs, the Y-axis reports the rate of land titling predicted by the fully specified model. The X-axes represent road coverage, distance to Dakar, and population density, respectively. Within each graph, the dark line represents the predicted rate of titling in areas dominated by non-hierarchical customary institutions, and the light line represents titling in districts with hierarchical customary institutions.

Consistent with the induced institutional change approach, these figures illustrate that land titling is more common at higher land values. Population density suggests greater demand for and competition over land; in Senegal, it increases the likelihood of titling. Similarly, these figures graphically illustrate that land with better infrastructure access, measured by road networks, is more likely to shift out of the customary domain. However, distance from Dakar does not have the anticipated effect on titling. Instead, land that is farther from the capital is more likely to be registered. There are a number of reasons why this may be the case. In particular, Dakar is not centrally located within the country, as Lusaka is in Zambia. As a result, smallholder and commercial farmers alike often turn to regional hubs such as Saint-Louis, Kaolack, Ziguinchor, and

---

[102] Adding regional fixed effects provides additional insight into this relationship, particularly within the 2 of 13 regions that feature variation in historical customary institutions (Senegal has 14 regions, but Dakar is excluded from these analyses). The effect of customary institutions is significant in reduced models with regional fixed effects and each control variable. This indicates that no individual control confounds the relationship within regions. However, the customary institutions variable loses significance under the burden of adding 13 regional dummies to the 9 variables in the full model; as the data set has only 40 observations, this creates significant concerns about degrees of freedom.

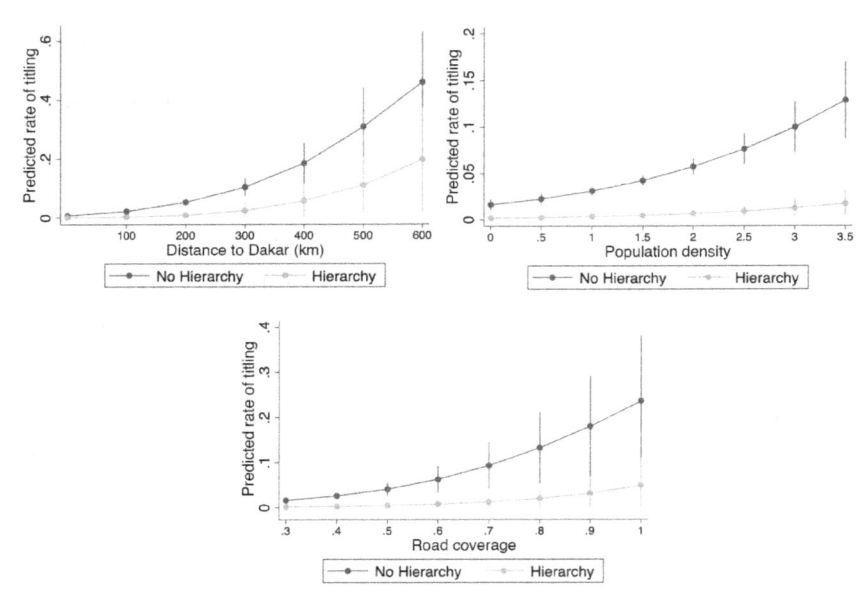

FIGURE 6.4. Predicted rates of land titling by land values and hierarchy in Senegal

Notes: Panels show the predicted proportion of newly registered customary land per district between 2007 and 2013 with 95 percent confidence intervals by three measures of land values.

Tambacounda instead of the capital city for state services, markets, and agricultural inputs. This makes the distance to the capital a weaker indicator of land values in the Senegal context. Instead, road access is a stronger test of the scholarly expectations that proximity to administrative centers decreases the state's cost of extending state power[103] and the transaction costs for titling applicants, while increasing the desirability of the land.[104]

Each graph also depicts the predicted effects of these land values measures in different institutional contexts. At both high and low land values, the rate of titling is systematically higher in zones without a legacy of strong, hierarchical institutions. Even as other factors increase the likelihood of titling, the institution effect remains. Taken together, these findings indicate that, while land values and population density do impact land titling, analyses of the state's expansion of control over property rights must also consider the role of customary institutions.

---

[103] Herbst 2000.
[104] Alston, Libecap, and Mueller 1999; Miceli, Sirmans, and Kieyah 2001.

6.6 REPLACING THE RIGHT OF THE AXE WITH THE RIGHT OF THE HOE

Land rental markets on customary land provide additional insight into the spatial variations in the strength of customary institutions. As described earlier, the state's legal framework establishes that all rights on customary land are usage rights. In other words, there are no owners outside of those who are currently using it. However, in the customary system, ownership is not exclusively defined by current usage. Rather, ownership reflects lineage, group membership, and social relations within the community. The National Domain Law thus supplants customary norms of property ownership. As Sylvie Fanchette has described, the law replaces the "right of the axe" with the "right of the hoe."[105] This is a shift from land rights derived from ancestral ties with those who first cleared the land (the axe) to those who are actively using the land (the hoe).

The state's success in replacing customary land ownership norms with usage rights has been highly uneven in Senegal. One common form of land dispute, described here by a rural council president, helps illustrate the difference between the right of the axe and the right of the hoe:

> [Man A] arrived long ago, in the period of abundant rain, when you only had to dig 5 meters to reach water for your well. Today, you must dig 20 to 30 meters. At that time [Man A] had a field and grew vegetables. When the period of drought came, he left ... After he left, [Man B] took over his field and began to farm on it. One day, [Man A] came back to reclaim his land. And, so, there was a dispute between the man who had previously used it and the current user ... Within the village, 12 people thought the new user was the owner and 24 believed it should be the previous user.[106]

Such differences in local understandings of customary land rights were also illustrated in the earlier comparison of Dagana and Podor. In Podor, the right of the axe is strong, and unused land can therefore be rented out by customary landowners to other residents. Nearly half of agricultural households in Podor stated in a government census that they access some land by way of rental. This contrasts with Dagana, where usage rights are paramount, and only 2 percent report accessing land through land rentals. Notably, in both districts, more than 90 percent of households

---

[105] Fanchette 2005.
[106] Interview with rural council member (RC-124), central Senegal, October 30, 2014.

reported accessing some land through "ownership."[107] This exemplifies how strong customary institutions can retain the influence of their rules, contrary to the state's assertion that all land rights on customary land derive from usage.[108]

Consequently, we can treat rental markets on customary land as an indicator of the strength of customary norms of land ownership. They provide evidence of the de facto influence of customary institutions. Legally, there can be no rentals on customary land because the land cannot have owners outside of individuals currently using it. Further, the state's law establishes that any individual using the land has the right to title it, because only users have any rights to the plot. Therefore, rentals of customary land require that citizens perceive the customary system of property rights to be stronger than the law of the state. If not, the customary landowners would be at high risk of losing their land if they agreed to let someone else use it as a rental.

In the following analyses, I explore the relationship between hierarchy and land rental markets in order to provide additional evidence that historical structure impacts contemporary institutional strength in Senegal, which, in turn, shapes land tenure outcomes. My measure of customary land rentals is compiled from the government's 1997–98 agricultural census, which surveyed 7,250 rural households throughout the country.[109] Among the thirty-seven districts sampled in the 1998 census, between 1 and 49 percent of agricultural households reported renting land. For example, in the eastern district of Goudiry, which features a nonhierarchical institutional legacy, only 1 percent reported land rentals. In Foundiougne, home to the Saloum hierarchy, 33 percent reported renting land. In the average (mean) district, 4.5 percent reported renting land.

The theory elaborated in this book suggests that the expansion of the state's regulations on customary land should be uneven within the country, and that the dominant customary institutions in an area should shape the state's ability to infiltrate local norms of customary tenure. Figure 6.5 presents bar graphs of the rates of land rentals between districts with and without hierarchical institutions. It reveals a wide gap between the two. Zones without hierarchical customary institutions have low rates of land

---

[107] Ministère de l'Agriculture/Food and Agriculture Organization (FAO), "Recensement National de L'agriculture 1998–1999."

[108] Policy stipulating that land belongs to (or should belong to) those who will productively use it is known as a "mise en valeur" approach in former French colonies.

[109] The agricultural census omits three districts in the Casamance that were subject to a low-level conflict at the time.

6.6 Replacing Right of Axe with Right of Hoe

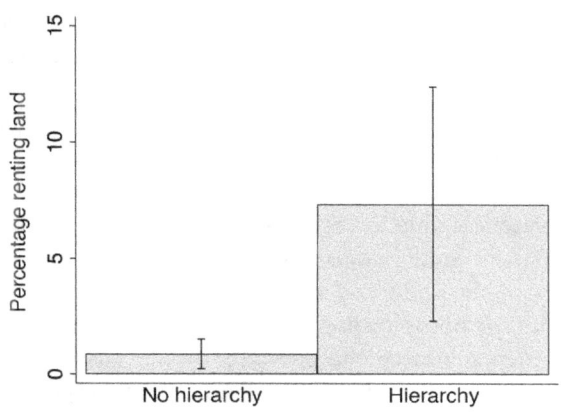

FIGURE 6.5. Evaluating the strength of customary property rights in districts with and without hierarchy in Senegal
Notes: Figure presents the percentage of agricultural survey respondents who reported land rentals, with 95 percent confidence intervals.
Source: Ministère de l'Agriculture/Food and Agriculture Organization (FAO), "Recensement National de L'agriculture 1998–1999."

rentals, consistent with ownership rights being tied to usage. In contrast, land rentals are far more common in districts with hierarchical institutions. This suggests that customary property rights for landowners are stronger today in areas with hierarchical legacies, where precolonial polities developed complex political institutions and withstood French conquest. Customary landlords can exist in such zones because compliance with the institution's property rights rules is greater than the state's land regulations.

Full models of the relationship between hierarchy and customary land rentals show that land rental rates are significantly higher in districts with hierarchical institutions, even when accounting for land values, population density, soil type, prior land conversions, and rainfall variation (Models 1 and 2, Appendix Table B.4). However, rental rates alone are not driving the land titling outcome presented earlier: Hierarchy continues to significantly reduce the likelihood of land titling even when including rental rates in the full model (Model 3, Appendix Table B.4).

It is particularly challenging to identify the continuing strength of historical hierarchies in countries with unofficial systems of customary authority. The boundaries of these institutions were not reinforced by the state as they have been in Zambia. Customary institutions that lose popular influence struggle to survive. However, this analysis of land rentals suggests that the legacy of hierarchy contributes to a greater institutional capacity to shape community norms of land ownership today. This supports the claim that hierarchy is an appropriate measure of contemporary institutional strength in Senegal. Using a different outcome measure and data set than the earlier analysis, these findings provide further evidence that strong customary institutions maintain their strength over time, relative to other customary institutions. The changes in national land policies and governments over the past century have not erased the differences among customary institutions in Senegal.

This analysis of land rentals also captures citizen-level engagement with the rules of the state and the customary institution in relation to land. When citizens opt to respect customary norms over the state's usage rights rules, they reinforce the strength of the customary institution. Unofficial customary authorities are reliant on the support of local communities to retain their power. The stability of the institution's influence on members' beliefs and behaviors, particularly related to land, is a significant indicator of strength and source of power for its leaders. Examining customary rental markets thus highlights the continuing relevance of customary authority and institutions, even in a context where the state has tried to weaken norms of lineage-based customary rights to land since 1964.

6.7 CONCLUSION

This chapter has illustrated how local communities can shape the state's ability to implement its agenda. The government designed its agricultural policies in 2007–13 to transform land tenure in Senegal. State actors invited large-scale land deals and facilitated the registration of customary land. Although the state has more power than local communities, and applicants for title often have more wealth, state and investor interests alone have not determined where the expansion of land titling occurs. Customary institutions facilitate coordinated resistance to land deals, as exemplified by the NAC land deal. Further, the broader land tenure patterns in Senegal indicate that communities with hierarchical institutional legacies slow the erosion of customary control of land relative to those with nonhierarchical institutions. This is consistent with the expectation that actors in weaker customary institutions can more easily respond to concentrated benefits of titling, with less concern for collective costs. Finally, the chapter has examined an additional indicator of the continuing strength of the hierarchical institutions: the perpetuation of customary norms of land ownership that challenge the state's National Domain Law, through land rental markets.

Senegal represents a most-different case from Zambia, yet a comparison of national patterns reveals important similarities. First, despite the divergence in official recognition, customary authorities in both countries have agency to resist or facilitate new land titles in their zones. Second, customary institutions shape the decisions they make. Customary authorities are not a homogenous set of actors because they are embedded in institutions that have very different capacities to constrain their decisions. Third, as the Podor/Dagana example in Senegal and the Bemba/Bisa comparison in Zambia illustrated, strong customary institutions generate mechanisms that hold leaders accountable to collective goals. Finally, in both countries, hierarchy predicts land titling. The expansion of the state's authority over land rights is slower in zones with stronger customary institutions, consistent with the argument that these institutions are better at constraining members' decisions during negotiations over land, generating higher costs to titling in their zones. By facilitating ties of accountability to preserve the institution's power base, hierarchical institutions impact the supply of land that can be titled.

However, as Chapter 3 described, customary institutions also shape demand for titles. The collective benefits of retaining customary power are not equally shared among members of a community. Customary institutions should, therefore, also influence citizens' perceptions of the attractiveness of state property rights. In doing so, they can impact the degree to which citizens engage with the customary institution or weaken it by titling their own land. Chapter 7 considers the role of customary institutions in citizens' evaluations of property rights regimes. The process of citizens adopting titles for their own small plots of land contributes to institutional pluralism in land rights, while also incrementally building the state's power. By influencing citizen demand for state rights, customary institutions mediate the relationship between state and citizen.

7

Exit or Engagement

How Status within Institutions Impacts Smallholder Titling

> Us landowners don't need title because it's our land.
> —smallholder farmer, Zambia[1]

> I don't feel the need to seek out this type of paper because the land already belongs to me. It's a way of calling into question my rights to ownership and usage.
> —smallholder farmer, Senegal[2]

> Even if you are poor, you should find the money to get the papers or you will be removed. Sometimes you are even afraid to develop the area for fear that you will be removed. So we would like the government to come to our rescue so we are safe.
> —smallholder farmer, Zambia[3]

Mrs. Sall's family had lived in Keur Gallo village for as long as anyone can remember. Her family was known as one of the families that helped found the village in Senegal. This made them a prominent lineage in the community. The village chief was from another of the first families in the village. When a neighbor's cattle ate Mrs. Sall's millet plants, her family and the neighbor's family went to the chief to discuss repayment. When her son decided to lend out a plot of the family's land while he spent a growing season at a temporary job in Dakar, she felt certain that the chief would

---

[1] Interview with smallholder farmers (FFG-543), southern Zambia, October 31, 2013.
[2] Respondent, author's Senegal smallholder survey, 2014.
[3] Interview with smallholder farmers (FFG-565), northern Zambia, January 29, 2014.

not forget that her family owned the land. The customary system worked well for Mrs. Sall's family. She had heard people in the community talking about going to the local council to get government papers for their plots of land. However, she did not have much confidence in the state system. Even if she had papers, would government agents really travel to a rural village to protect a subsistence farmer like her if there were a land dispute? She suspected they would be more likely to help someone who had been to a government school and could read in French. As a result, she felt no need to pay money and take time out of her day to travel to the council for such papers. She had limited incentive to replace the local institutions – which had overseen access to land for generations in her community – with the state's property rights documents.

These calculations were different for her neighbor, Mr. Cisse. He thought it was safer to get government papers for his land. He might still go to the chief to help resolve family disputes when it was convenient, but having papers for his land would mean that he wasn't entirely dependent on the chief's decisions when it came to his land rights. Mr. Cisse was born in the community but was not from one of the founding families. He knew that if he regularly planted crops on his land it would be very hard for anyone to take his land away, but he was concerned that if he wanted to leave it fallow for a season or two, someone could claim it as unused land. That would, after all, be consistent with state law. Further, he was not as invested in the continuing power of the chief and the customary rules. The chief's decisions often favored other families; for example, his family was not consulted when the decision was made to build a new water pump in the community, which was now noticeably far from his home. For Mr. Cisse, paying a fee and traveling to the local council to apply for papers was a worthwhile investment to ensure that his sons could inherit his land. He expected that the state's papers would make his land rights more secure. Even if it weakened the village's customary system, the gain in tenure security was more important to him.

The decision to title one's land is not the same for all smallholder farmers, even in the same community, as these stylized descriptions illustrate. Factors that vary across communities and over time impact individuals' calculations about securing property rights through the customary or statutory system. The material costs of titling surely influence the decision to adopt a title;[4] however, this chapter shows that citizens'

---

[4] Alston, Libecap, and Mueller 1999; Firmin-Sellers and Sellers 1999.

relationships with the customary institution and the state also impact whether they seek land titles.

Examining smallholder titling decisions in contexts with piecemeal titling policies, where individuals can choose to title their land or not, sheds light on the role of customary institutions in the everyday lives of citizens. The previous chapters explored how customary institutions shape the incentives of elites, creating constrained chiefs. However, these institutions also impact the decisions of regular citizens by generating different statuses, with corresponding levels of privilege within the customary system. This makes land titles more desirable to some citizens than to others.

The impact of customary institutions on citizens' demand for titles is important for two reasons. First, land titling initiated by individuals expands state control over land. While the amount of land that the average citizen titles may be small, the mass titling of thousands of small parcels aggregates into a major shift in authority over land. These titling decisions contribute to the commoditization of land, permanently registering it in the state's system of property rights and making individual plots taxable. Second, smallholder titling generates a new tie between citizen and state through the citizen's engagement with statutory property rights institutions. Each title is a contract between state and citizen over land rights, as the state promises to enforce the citizen's individual property rights in exchange for the citizen fulfilling certain (often financial) obligations. Titling in Zambia and Senegal makes this relationship between state and citizen legible. Further, with each new title on customary land, citizens opt out of exclusively relying on the customary institution for their land rights and opt in to the state's land institutions. Adopting a land title is thus a form of engagement with the state.

This chapter investigates the relationship between customary privilege and property rights outcomes for citizens titling their own land, drawing upon surveys of more than 900 farmers in Senegal and 8,000 farmers in Zambia. After introducing the characteristics of the households in the two surveys, I elaborate the argument that customary institutions impact demand for state property rights by establishing differences in customary privilege within a community; this demand drives variation in who titles their land and where the state's property rights develop first. Next, analyses of the surveys reveal that higher status members of customary institutions are consistently less likely to possess titles in both countries. I then examine the mechanisms that connect customary privilege to land tenure outcomes. The chapter concludes with a summary of the implications of the book's findings for classic models of land titling.

7.1 THE UNEVEN UPTAKE OF TITLES

Cases and Data Sets

Smallholder farmers in Senegal and Zambia have the option of titling their land. In both countries, the state has made it possible to individually register small agricultural plots but has not invested the resources required for a mass land titling campaign. Technocrats and bureaucrats speak enthusiastically about smallholder land titling as a long-term goal, but, in practice, smallholder titling is incremental and infrequent. Citizens bear the burden of initiating and completing the titling process. For small-scale farmers, it is far from certain that they will obtain economic benefits from titling or that the state will be able to enforce property rights more effectively than their local customary authorities. As a result, smallholder titling rates are low in both countries, hovering between 7 and 8 percent in the two samples examined here. Examining which smallholder farmers adopt titles helps illuminate how customary institutions and land rights function at the local level.

As described in Chapter 2, the process for accessing a land title is similar in the two countries, except for the official role of the chief. Citizens begin the application process at their local councils. In Senegal, village chiefs generally provide oral testimony to the council regarding the usage and ownership of the land but have no official veto rights. In Zambia, the application at the local council must include evidence that the chief has approved the new land title on customary land. Gaining a chief's consent for a smallholder title may involve visits to the chief's palace and gifts, such as chickens or cash payments. Consequently, citizens may be subject to titling fees from both within the chiefdom and the state administration. Following local council approvals, land titling applications must then advance through different stages in a centralized, bureaucratic process. In both countries, the titling process concludes with a plot of (previously) customary land being registered in the state's domain and the state issuing a long-term lease to the applicant. This chapter draws on the experiences of small-scale farmers in Senegal and Zambia to identify similarities in citizen patterns of land titling, across distinct national contexts and systems of customary authority.

In Zambia, I rely on a national survey to examine how customary institutions impact land titling. The national Rural Agricultural Livelihoods Survey (RALS) of smallholder farmers was conducted in 2012 by the Indaba Agricultural Policy Research Institute (IAPRI) in collaboration with the Zambian Central Statistics Office (CSO) and Michigan State University.[5] It was designed to be representative of agricultural households using under 20 ha of land at the provincial level.[6] My subsample of interest is households in areas with customary authorities, where respondents reported that their communities had chiefs and village heads. This smallholder farmer data is geocoded, allowing me to identify which chieftaincy the household was part of for the hierarchy analyses in Chapter 5 and whether the household was located on land categorized as state land in government maps. As a result of the Zambian and British policies of land engineering described in Chapter 4, some households that reported having customary authorities in their communities also sat on historical state land. This reflects unofficial chiefly power in Zambia as well as the gaps between lived experience and the state's maps. These differences in land tenure types were considered in the analyses that follow.

In Senegal, I designed and fielded an original survey with questions that paralleled key questions in the Zambia smallholder survey. My Senegal survey sample includes smallholder farmers in two diverse ecological and institutional zones, one in the north and one in the center-west. The sample was designed to be representative within the chosen districts, to identify any generalizable impacts of customary institutions on small-scale titling given the important differences between the two regions of the country.[7] The first district in the Senegal smallholder survey sample is Podor, in the northern Saint-Louis Region. This district features customary institutions rooted in the Fouta Toro institution discussed in Chapter 6. The second survey district is Mbacké, in the central Diourbel Region. Mbacké is also in a zone with a hierarchical institutional legacy (the Baol kingdom) and is the heartland of the Mouride brotherhood. However, some marabouts and respondents in the Mbacké sample were members of the Tidjane and Khadrya brotherhoods. In Podor, all of the

---

[5] Indaba Agricultural Policy Research Institute, Central Statistics Office, and Ministry of Agriculture and Livestock (IAPRI/CSO/MAL). 2012. *Rural Agricultural Livelihoods Survey (RALS)*. Lusaka, Zambia.

[6] Note that 1 percent of respondents in the Zambia sample (N = 99) and 5 percent of respondents in the Senegal sample (N = 46) reported possessing more than 20 ha of land. Excluding these observations does not significantly impact the model results presented in this chapter.

[7] I used a multistage sampling strategy within each district, clustered first by rural council area and second by village. Households were then sampled within villages using a random walk strategy.

sampled villages feature marabouts from the Tidjane brotherhood, consistent with broader patterns in the district. See Appendix C for further discussion of the role of marabouts in these communities.

In addition to these surveys, qualitative data provide further insight into the forces that shape land titling decisions in each country. I draw upon fifteen focus groups with smallholders in three provinces for additional information on citizens' experiences with land rights in Zambia. In Senegal, my survey featured open-ended questions that allowed respondents to provide more detailed information about their individual experience of accessing and securing land. Both sources of qualitative data inform the theory and analyses presented here.

Sample Characteristics

Community life for smallholder farmers on customary land in Zambia and Senegal shares some broad similarities. The vast majority of households in both samples reported they were considered "local" by others, a proxy for shared ethnicity that captures subjective understandings of group membership. The typical household had lived in the community for many years and described being headed by a man. While the head of the household may not have completed primary school, most households in both samples had a family member who had done so. The median household in the Zambia sample had a member who had attended secondary school. In Senegal, primary school was the highest level of formal education in the median household. This difference reflects the prevalence of informal Islamic schooling in Senegal, as the vast majority of the 33 percent of households with no formal education had attended a Quranic school.[8] By contrast, only 3 percent of households in the Zambia sample had no formal education.

---

[8] On the politics of Quranic schools in West Africa, see Bleck 2015. The Zambia survey specified "formal school" but did not differentiate between government schools, community-organized schools, private schools, and mission schools. However, in Zambia more than 80 percent of schools are government schools. (Government of the Republic of Zambia, Ministry of Education, Science, Vocational Training and Early Education (MESVTEE). "Education for All 2015 National Review Report: Zambia," 2015. Prepared for UNESCO and the World Education Forum.) The Senegal survey prompted for the type of school and the highest level, or number of years, completed. The formal education measures used in this chapter refer to government schools in Senegal and the respondent's interpretation of "formal" in Zambia.

The most common crop in both samples was also the staple of the country's national diet: maize in Zambia and millet in Senegal. In the Zambia sample, the second and third most common crops were cassava and groundnuts. In Senegal, they were cowpeas and groundnuts. In these two countries, groundnuts and maize are produced both for home consumption and agricultural markets. A smaller number of households produced non-staple crops that included tomatoes, melons, onions, okra, hibiscus, habanero peppers, cotton, soya, sunflowers, coffee, sugar, and paprika in the combined samples. These were aggregated into the category of cash crops in the analysis that follows, with the caveat that they may also be produced for home consumption. The broad trend within these two samples of farmers was that nearly everyone produced some staple crops for home consumption, even those who counted non-staples as one of their top three crops.

The vast majority of the households in these two samples relied on customary property rights, with no statutory documents to represent their land ownership.[9] They owned between 2 and 3 ha of land, a point of similarity across two very different countries that reflects the limits of non-mechanized, familial agricultural production. Most households in both samples accessed land through inheritance within their family lineage or an allocation from a customary authority, as Figure 7.1 illustrates. In Zambia, more households reported accessing land through allocations from customary authorities; while in Senegal, lineage-based inheritance was a more common mode of accessing land. A small number in both countries reported having paid for land. Purchasing land as a mode of access reflects the informal customary land markets that exist in both countries despite the official policy that customary land cannot be sold without it first being titled.[10]

The uptake of land titles among smallholders in these samples was uneven. Table 7.1 shows that households with land titles differ in some ways and not in others. The table reports the mean values for key characteristics of households with and without titles in Senegal and Zambia, and whether they are significantly different. This cross-section of the survey data identifies patterns in household characteristics, but not

---

[9] The rate within each sample is 7.51 percent in Zambia and 7.08 percent in Senegal. This encompasses any form of statutory property rights including titles, leases, and council registration papers.

[10] See Sitko 2010 on Zambia and Chimhowu and Woodhouse 2006 on vernacular land markets in Africa more generally.

7.1 The Uneven Uptake of Titles

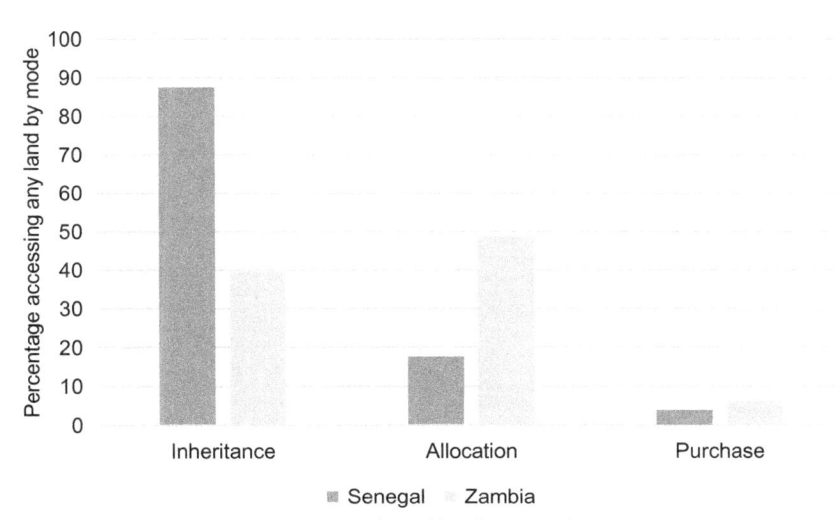

FIGURE 7.1. Modes of land access, by country
Sources: RALS Zambia survey (2012) and author Senegal smallholder survey (2014).

the direction of causal impacts. This is particularly important to note in regard to household characteristics such as wealth that could potentially be a consequence or a cause of land title.

Households with titles in these samples were closer to infrastructure, which is a characteristic of more desirable land. They were wealthier, more educated, and more likely to have a member with off-farm employment. These differences in land values and the financial ability to bear the costs of land titling are consistent with the expectation that the decision to title land reflects a calculation of the costs and benefits of exiting the customary system in favor of the state's property rights. Conditions that decrease the relative costs and increase the relative benefits of exit make seeking a title more appealing. Table 7.1 also reveals slight differences in the social characteristics of each group. Households without titles were younger. In Zambia, they were slightly more likely to have migrated in the past ten years and less likely to report that they are considered to be local. Among the households with titles in Zambia, 85 percent of households were local, compared to 89 percent of households without titles. This, albeit minor, pattern of dissimilarity among the groups, was reversed in Senegal, where 90 percent of households with state title and 87 percent of households without titles reported that they were local. The analyses that follow consider all of these characteristics as control variables. Full

TABLE 7.1. *Comparing households with and without titles*

	Zambia with Titles	Zambia without Titles	Senegal with Titles	Senegal without Titles
Household Wealth				
Wealth Index (Quintiles)	3.515	2.958*	3.373	2.971
	(1.443)	(1.404)	(1.241)	(1.423)
Total Land Owned	4.635	3.522*	3.499	5.696*
	(5.893)	(4.213)	(6.566)	(7.346)
Employment	.323	.184*	.618	.596
	(.468)	(.387)	(.490)	(.491)
Education	1.880	1.573*	1.088	.916
	(.661)	(.679)	(.824)	(.853)
Social Characteristics				
Local	.846	.892*	.897	.867
	(.361)	(.311)	(.306)	(.339)
Migrant (10 years)	.369	.257*	.059	.045
	(.483)	(.437)	(.237)	(.207)
Youth-Headed Household	.406	.453*	.279	.324
	(.491)	(.498)	(.452)	(.468)
Female-Headed Household	.195	.194	.176	.154
	(.396)	(.395)	(.384)	(.361)
Land Values				
Distance to Infrastructure (Quintiles)	2.499	3.033*	1.853	3.086*
	(1.329)	(1.413)	(1.330)	(1.383)

Notes: Mean reported and standard deviation in parentheses.
* indicates the difference in the means of each sample group is significant at $p \leq 0.05$.

descriptive statistics for each country sample are reported in Tables A.3 and A.4 in the Appendix.

7.2 CUSTOMARY PRIVILEGE AND SMALLHOLDER TITLING

Theoretical Expectations

Adopting a title for one's parcel of customary land is a form of exit, from exclusive reliance on the customary institution, in order to enter the state's property rights regime. How desirable this change is, for any given household, reflects the relative costs and benefits of titling land within a specific customary institution in a specific country context. Among potential benefits described in Chapter 3, expectations of tenure security are critical. The desirability of title thus reflects an individual's evaluations of both customary and statutory property rights institutions, particularly the degree to which they would protect his household's land claims. Customary institutions can impact these individual calculations in ways unexplored by existing models of small-scale titling.

Economic costs and benefits of land titling explain variation in the adoption of land titles in theories of induced institutional change (IIC) in property rights. The decision to title a small parcel of customary land for a smallholder farmer is costly. It requires time spent in administrative offices, away from one's field, and fees to have one's land ownership registered in the state's system of property rights. The farther the farmer lives from the state's offices, the higher the costs. Some smallholders bear these costs because titling provides them with written proof of individual land ownership that is recognized by state courts and by the banks that provide credit. The basic IIC framework predicts that the more competition there is for the individual's land due to active land markets and growing population density, the greater the incentive to seek state land titles.[11] Consequently, the wealth of the household, the value of its land, and the distance to the state's offices in the capital should all impact the likelihood a smallholder adopts land titles.[12]

The customary institution introduces additional political costs and benefits to these calculations through the allocation of status and, therefore, privilege among members. First, privilege within the customary institution increases the costs of exit, because these households benefit more from the continued power of the institution. Second, customary privilege decreases the relative benefits of title. All things being equal, households that derive privilege from the institution have less to gain and more to lose from titling than lower status households in the community.

The institutional costs of titling detailed in Chapter 3 are the foundation of the customary privilege effect. Recall that titling can weaken the customary institution by challenging the monopoly of its rules within the community and decreasing the stocks of land under its control. Customary land rights are a contract in which the institution's authorities and processes enforce property rights in exchange for obligations to chiefs and to the community. Continued access to land is contingent upon complying with the institution's norms and "the performance of

---

[11] Feder and Noronha 1987; Platteau 1996.   [12] See Alston, Libecap, and Mueller 1999.

reciprocal obligations in society," as described by Hastings Okoth-Ogendo.[13] By contrast, a title is a contract with the state. The citizen's land claim is supported by the state's system of property rights in a written document. Thus, when citizens gain titles, they are no longer exclusively dependent on the customary system for access to land. Having a title decreases their obligation to conform to the institution's rules to secure their land rights, for example, by respecting secondary land rights or abiding the chief's orders. This weakens the influence of the institution in their lives and removes a source of leverage for sanctioning within the institution. For example, customary authorities described this decrease in institutional obligations to Gear Kajoba during his research in Zambia, saying that a citizen with a title will "refuse to respect the headmen and participate in community work since they were now 'independent and answerable only to the President who grants title.'"[14]

Nevertheless, exiting the customary land tenure system through titling does not mean that citizens will fully disengage from obligations within the community. There may still be social benefits to being in good standing with one's neighbors and other members of the customary institution. However, titling weakens the link between compliance with institutional rules enforced by customary authorities and continued access to land. This makes it easier for citizens to choose to deviate from institutional processes if they please. The institution's power diminishes as citizens gain increased autonomy from its rules and norms of appropriate behavior.

Community members may experience the erosion of the institution's power over land as the weakening of rules that had previously structured community life. When members gain land titles, they can enclose their land and prevent others from accessing water or grazing lands. This change to institutional rules of secondary rights has led citizens in Zambia to express their dissatisfaction with new titles in their villages by cutting down newly raised fences.[15] Similarly, the customary dispute resolution mechanisms that many communities rely upon lose their efficacy if members with titles have greater autonomy to defy their judgements. More generally, the expansion of smallholder titling in a community may lead citizens to question the customary institution's monopoly of authority over property rights, thereby weakening it. As a result, land titling can impact the strength of the institution's rules within the community and its long-term power

---

[13] Okoth-Ogendo 1989, 12.   [14] Kajoba 2002, 51.   [15] Brown 2005, 96.

base, the control of land. However, institutional costs to titling are not evenly distributed within the community.

The citizens that benefit the most from the continuing power of the customary institution should face additional costs to land titling. By structuring political and social relations among members of the institution, the institution itself determines who is most invested in its continuing power. Customary institutions privilege some individuals with more important roles in community governance; better outcomes in property rights disputes; and more prominent places at village events. This function of generating different levels of privilege within the community is intrinsic to customary institutions, which, as described in Chapter 2, are types of political institutions. As Ann Swidler has argued, the chief's role in "storing" and distributing *status* is central to his influence within the community, including his ability to facilitate collective action.[16] Nevertheless, the characteristics that generate status and what privileges this brings vary widely across institutions. In different customary institutions, status could be related to attributes such as gender, age, caste, lineage, length of time in the village, and types of agriculture practiced (i.e., pastoralism or settled agriculture). Many of these status attributes are directly related to a local customary institution and would not be a source of privilege in another customary institution or the state. For example, the benefits of being from a noble lineage or clan are contingent on the continuing relevance and power of that customary institution. Consequently, those that benefit from customary privilege should be more invested in the survival and power of the institution.

Privilege within the customary institution may also increase citizens' expectations that it will provide them with secure land rights, thereby decreasing the relative benefits of a state land title. Those with high customary privilege should be more confident that their land ownership will be respected even in the event of a dispute, as their land claims are often treated as more legitimate. Extreme examples of low privilege in customary institutions and land tenure insecurity are seen in the land expulsions of non-coethnics in Côte d'Ivoire[17] or widows being dispossessed of their land following the death of a spouse in Zambia.[18] These politics of privilege within a customary institution also increase tenure security in more subtle ways; for example, Markus Goldstein and Christopher Udry argued that the advisors to customary authorities in

---

[16] Swidler 2013, 327.   [17] Babo 2010.   [18] Chapoto, Jayne, and Mason 2011.

Ghana had more productive plots because they had the tenure security to invest in them.[19] In Tanzania's urban settlements, Matthew Collin found that living near coethnics decreased reported expropriation risk and, correspondingly, demand for formal property rights.[20] Consequently, privilege may also impact individual decisions to seek a state land title by providing expectations of stronger customary property rights, therefore reducing the benefits of exiting the status quo.

For other citizens, it is a relief to be free of a customary property rights regime that generates systematic biases against those without privilege. While households with high status within the customary institution face additional political costs to titling, their lower status neighbors have no such constraint. As described in Chapter 3, land titling decisions often reflect trade-offs between collective costs and individual benefits. The reasons why titling is costly to the power of the institution are often the same reasons why some smallholders desire land titles: Citizens may seek titles because they want the right to build fences, and to be free of the obligation to participate in secondary land sharing systems or the institution's rules of conflict adjudication. Demand to exit the institution's regulations through land titling is thus intimately connected to how the benefits of its continued power are distributed. Smallholder titling decisions are consequently not solely a question of whether the household can afford the material costs of title, but are also a response to their status within their local customary institution. Those with low privilege within the customary institution have more to gain and less to lose by exiting from its system of property rights.

This framework, and the evidence that follows, is focused on the role of the customary institution. My argument is that customary institutions shape smallholder land titling by allocating privilege to citizens, which impacts the desirability of land titling. However, I have also explained that titling reflects confidence in the customary system *relative* to the state's property institutions, and vice versa. Therefore, citizens' expectations of the state also contribute to their calculations of the costs and benefits of seeking a title.

Citizens must evaluate whether the state is likely to protect their statutory property rights in order to assess the potential benefits of titling their land. Just as customary privilege increases the desirability of retaining customary rights, status within the state should also shape

---

[19] Goldstein and Udry 2008. [20] Collin 2020.

evaluations of state rights. For example, members of the ruling political party may have greater confidence in the security of land titles that would be enforced by state actors. Personal ties to politicians or government security forces should similarly increase the anticipated benefits of titling. The statistical analyses that follow shed light on a few characteristics that could impact citizens' expectations of the state. In particular, familiarity with the state might increase citizens' perceptions of its capacity and willingness to protect their land rights. Therefore, citizens who have regular, positive interactions with the state should find titles more desirable than citizens who have had limited or negative experiences with it. Spatial proximity to government services increases the likelihood of interacting with the state. In addition, education is an important form of citizen-state interaction. Beyond regularly meeting with state-employed teachers, those who speak and read the language of government business may feel more confident in their own abilities to advocate for themselves to the state. Similarly, bureaucrats may treat households differently based on characteristics such as education and wealth. There is every reason to anticipate that state privileges also impact titling, even if it is not the primary focus of this chapter. As Table 7.1 showed, households with customary property rights have, on average, lower formal education in both country samples. In addition, a measure of political knowledge in the Senegal sample reflects these differences in citizens' interactions with the state; among households with titles, 94 percent knew the current council president's name, compared to 87 percent of those with customary property rights. Yet, even among citizens with equally positive interactions with the state, the theory predicts that customary privilege will decrease the likelihood that individuals title their small plots of customary land.

Measuring Privilege: Kinship with Customary Authorities

Each customary institution has its own rules and norms that establish who has high or low privilege. In some, caste or lineage is a source of high status. In others, youth are disadvantaged relative to their elders. Likewise, the length of time in the village or the ethnicity of the household may impact rights within customary institutions.[21] This distinction is often represented by the politicized terms "stranger"/"native" in Anglophone countries and *"allochtone"/"autochtone"* in Francophone

---

[21] Brasselle, Gaspart, and Platteau 2002; Jacob and Le Meur 2010; Lentz 2013.

countries (henceforth "nonlocal"/"local"). Scholars have also focused on associations between gender and privilege within customary institutions, finding that women's land rights are often treated as secondary.[22] However, this too varies across institutions. For example, Tine and Sy described how women in Serer land institutions in Senegal "occupy privileged positions" relative to women in Pulaar and Wolof land institutions. They attributed these differences to institutional norms surrounding rice paddy cultivation and the matrilineal inheritance rules of the Serer institutions.[23] Men's levels of privilege also vary across customary institutions.[24] These sources of status are not consistent among all customary institutions, and the norms of customary land ownership differ between communities and over time.[25] This presents a challenge for measuring the effects of customary privilege among different customary institutions. As a result, this study relies on a relatively immutable measure of high customary status: kinship with the chief.

One commonality across the wide array of land tenure rules enshrined in customary institutions is that customary property rights are adjudicated by customary authorities. The role of customary authorities as the arbiters of institutional rules is a defining feature of customary land in Africa. Thus, the social proximity of the household to the institution's leadership is an important source of privilege. Kinship with the arbiters of customary rules captures the concept of customary privilege, yet is independent of the content of those rules, which vary greatly across customary institutions.[26] Further, while a household can opt in and out of other group characteristics that may affect privilege, by migrating, for example, there is no exit option for kinship. Kinship status is independent of different customary norms and free of the potential biases created by more mutable individual characteristics. It is a dichotomous indicator, which helps simplify a concept that is highly complex and theoretically a spectrum (i.e., levels of privilege), in order to advance our understandings of the roles of customary institutions.

Across a range of different customary institutions, the relatives of the authorities who interpret, protect, or create land rights for the community should have greater privilege than nonrelatives. This operationalization has an added advantage of identifying impacts of customary privilege that are independent of the strength and structure of the institution. As

---

[22] Hilhorst 2000; Kajoba 2002; Tripp 2004; Meinzen-Dick and Mwangi 2009.
[23] Tine and Sy 2003, 219.   [24] Matchaya 2009.   [25] Chanock 1985; Pottier 2005.
[26] On the procedural logic of customary tenure regimes, see Chauveau 1998.

7.2 Customary Privilege and Smallholder Titling

Chapter 5 showed, smallholder land titling is less common in hierarchies. However, customary privilege may covary with hierarchy: The privileges of high-status membership should be greater in stronger institutions. Further, institutions that endogenously developed centralized political authority are more likely to feature aristocracies or caste structures.[27] Hierarchical institutions should therefore have more rigid social divisions and more clearly defined elite roles, such as traditional councillors. By contrast, weaker customary institutions may have fewer or less durable social divisions that contribute to differences in privilege. However, kinship is a measure of privilege that is less likely to systematically vary between hierarchical and nonhierarchical institutions, which allows me to separate the effects of privilege within an institution from hierarchy, which is explored in other chapters.

The following analyses examine the impacts of a household member being related to the customary authority. In Zambia, this includes kinship with the chief or the chief's representatives in the village, the headman or headwoman. In Senegal, the primary measure is kinship with the village chief (see Appendix C for a discussion of kinship with a marabout). Both surveys used the word "related" (or its local language equivalent), allowing for the broadest interpretation of this term, inclusive of marriage or blood ties. Within the sample, 51 percent of the households in Zambia and 65 percent in Senegal reported kinship with the chief. These customary authorities are not distant authorities, but community members who influence the daily lives of village residents.

Results: Lower Rates of Exit among Households with Customary Privilege

Statistical analyses support the argument that households with and without customary privilege weigh different considerations in evaluating titling. The following models use logistic regression to estimate the impact of kinship with the chief on the probability of possessing a title, with fixed effects and clustered standard errors at the province and chiefdom levels (respectively) in Zambia and at the district level in Senegal.[28] This section

---

[27] Bates 1987.
[28] These standard errors are clustered at the institution level to account for nonindependence of observations *within* customary institutions. The chiefdom in Zambia and the district in Senegal approximate this.

TABLE 7.2. *Correlates of smallholder land titling in Zambia*

	1	2	3	4
	Reduced	Baseline	CL Only	Additional Controls
Kinship with Chief	−0.863**	−0.542**	−0.373*	−0.425**
	(0.158)	(0.140)	(0.174)	(0.136)
Population Density		0.025*	−0.083	0.029*
		(0.012)	(0.051)	(0.013)
Distance to Infrastructure		−0.028**	−0.044**	−0.030**
		(0.011)	(0.011)	(0.010)
Distance to Lusaka		−0.069	0.011	−0.011
		(0.114)	(0.094)	(0.111)
Railroads		−0.006**	−0.006**	−0.006**
		(0.002)	(0.002)	(0.002)
Roads		−0.009	0.000	−0.001
		(0.023)	(0.024)	(0.024)
Education		0.400**	0.335**	0.316**
		(0.084)	(0.096)	(0.087)
Employment		0.340*	0.408**	0.366**
		(0.133)	(0.137)	(0.129)
Total Land Owned		0.048**	0.046**	0.037**
		(0.011)	(0.012)	(0.011)
Wealth		0.163**	0.180**	0.130**
		(0.045)	(0.050)	(0.047)
Migrant (10 years)		0.202*	0.156	0.082
		(0.096)	(0.122)	(0.097)
Local		0.042	−0.035	0.101
		(0.171)	(0.196)	(0.183)
Youth-Headed Household		0.055	0.034	0.119
		(0.106)	(0.129)	(0.113)
Female-Headed Household		0.186	0.202	0.194
		(0.120)	(0.146)	(0.120)
Colonial State Land		1.694**		1.608**
		(0.403)		(0.398)
Agricultural Settlement		1.321**		1.122**
		(0.444)		(0.405)
Crops and Land Access Controls				Y
Constant	−3.001**	−4.712**	−4.248**	−4.658**
	(0.230)	(0.465)	(0.475)	(0.608)
Pseudo R^2	0.0667	0.1874	0.1293	0.2441
Observations	8,403	8,295	7,553	8,194

Notes: Logistic regression coefficients with province-level fixed effects and robust standard errors clustered at the chiefdom level presented in parentheses. Outcome is title. ** $p \leq 0.01$, * $p \leq 0.05$, + $p \leq 0.1$.

provides evidence that households with customary privilege were less likely to title their land in both Zambia and Senegal. It then considers two possible reasons for this finding. First, I explore whether households with privilege had lower demand for titles because their customary rights were more secure. Tenure security is, of course, an important benefit of privilege. Second, I investigate whether members responded to the loss of institutional power by examining resistant attitudes toward titling.

Zambia

The first set of models considers the relationship between kinship and titling in Zambia (Table 7.2). Model 1 shows a strong negative relationship between customary privilege and titling in a simple bivariate model. The second model includes a full set of controls for factors that might impact a household's likelihood of titling land. It considers several proxies for household wealth that could themselves be related to kinship: (1) combined income from crop sales, remittances, and wages; (2) whether anyone in the household is employed outside of family farming; (3) the household's highest level of formal education; and (4) the size of landholdings. As anticipated, all four measures of wealth increased the likelihood of titling. However, this model also reveals that, even among households with the same level of education or land wealth, the chiefs' kin were less likely to have titles than nonkin.

The baseline model also includes indicators of the value of the household's land. Because customary land in both countries has no formal market value, it is not possible to create monetary measures of land values. Instead, land value is, albeit imperfectly, approximated through access to infrastructure, roads, and railways. The infrastructure index is constructed as the average of the household's distance to schools, improved water sources, electricity, and health clinics. The measures of rails and roads capture the household's proximity to each. Proximity to key infrastructure increases the desirability of the land and facilitates the marketing of crops.[29] Finally, a measure of population density approximates local demand for land. Consistent with expectations, the results show that households were more likely to have titles on higher value land, particularly on land that was closer to key infrastructure and had higher population densities.

---

[29] Additional controls for soil type and annual rainfall do not impact these results.

It is plausible that other social attributes could be driving the relationship between kinship and title. For example, the strong impact of kinship may actually be capturing the difference between migrant and nonmigrant households. To address this important concern, the baseline model (Model 2) includes social control variables that may also be related to customary privilege in some institutions. These include the gender and age of the household head; whether the household was local or nonlocal; and whether the household migrated to the community within the last ten years. The effect of kinship remains statistically significant and negative, suggesting that even among households with the same local identities, customary privilege decreased the likelihood of adopting state property rights.

All of the households in this Zambia sample reported that their village had a chief and a headman or headwoman. However, some of these households were located on two types of state land, colonial crown land and agricultural settlement schemes, according government maps and the geocoded survey data. The customary authorities on such land may have unofficial influence within the community and weaker land authority in the eyes of the state. To consider the role of these differences in land status, the baseline model (Model 2) includes dummy variables that measure whether the geolocation of the household places it in an area mapped by the state as colonial crown land or an agricultural scheme. Model 3 excludes the households in these categories as a robustness check. This does not change the negative and significant impact of kinship on titling. In part, this consistent effect reflects how the status of land on government maps is often not representative of the reality on the ground, and therefore both agricultural settlement and colonial state land variables should be interpreted with caution.

Model 4 adds additional control variables to ensure that the customary privilege effect cannot be attributed to wealthy outsiders purchasing land in a community or the chiefs' relatives producing less commercialized crops, among potential alternative explanations related to agricultural practices and modes of accessing land. The model includes measures of the top three crops within the sample as well as an indicator of prominent cash crops.[30] Model 4 also considers

---

[30] The model includes maize, cassava, and groundnuts as separate dummy variables. The cash crops variable combines soya, cotton, sugar, paprika, coffee, sunflower seeds. Crop types also reflect differences in soil suitability, as well as access to markets, water, and inputs.

whether the household had obtained their land through inheritance, purchase, or allocation without payment (gifts). The significant negative association between kinship and land titling in Model 4 provides evidence that the consistent impact of customary privilege is independent of any observed differences in land inheritance, land purchasing, and the production of specific crops.

These results indicate that the household's relationship with the leader of the customary institution impacted its likelihood of having a land title. Kinship with the chief decreased the probability that a household had a title by 3.4 percentage points, which is a meaningful shift given that the overall probability of titling was only 7.6 percent. By comparison, the higher wealth and familiarity with bureaucratic processes that accompany off-farm employment only increased the probability of having a title by 2.7 percentage points. If land titles were equally desirable to all residents, independent of their status within the customary institution, the ability to pay should be the primary constraint on land titling. However, the impact of kinship was nearly the same as the shift from the lowest to the highest income categories (3.5 percentage points). The wealthiest households with customary privilege had the same likelihood of possessing a title as the poorest households without privilege (7.2%). This suggests that status within an institution – and the privileges that accompany status – is as important as wealth in shaping whether citizens adopt titles for their own land.

Figure 7.2 plots the predicted probability of title for households with and without kinship ties as income, education, and infrastructure vary. As we would anticipate, households with higher incomes, more advanced educational attainment, and greater access to infrastructure were all more likely to have titles. Yet, even accounting for the effects of these key factors, households with kinship ties were consistently less likely to have titles. The estimates in the previous paragraph and in these figures derive from the baseline model (Model 2, Table 7.2).

The results of these analyses also shed light on other attributes that could indicate customary privilege in Zambia. Although being local had no association with titling in any model, recent migrants were more likely to have titles in the baseline mode (Model 2). Whether the households were headed by women or youths also had no significant impact on the likelihood of titling. These attributes are important to examine given their prominence in scholarship on land tenure in Africa, yet these results suggest that while they may be highly salient determinants of privileges

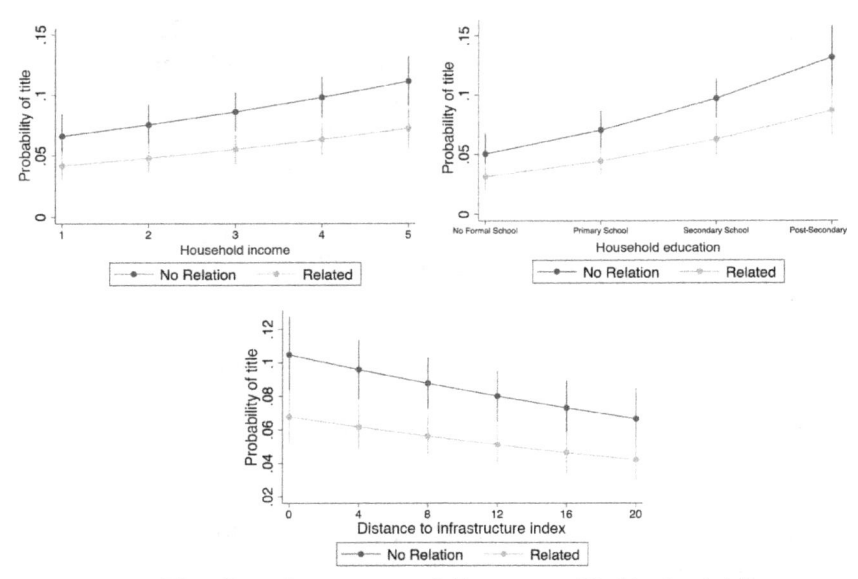

FIGURE 7.2. The effect of customary privilege on smallholder land titling at different levels of income, education, and land values in Zambia
Notes: Panels present the predicted probability of having a title. Infrastructure index is a measure of the distance (km) to electricity, an improved water source, a health clinic, and a primary school.

and land access in some communities, their impacts on land titling outcomes were not systematic within Zambia.

Senegal

Despite the many differences between Senegal and Zambia, analyses of the smallholder surveys show similar patterns. The results presented here indicate that, in both countries, privilege within the local customary institution decreased the likelihood that a household had titled its land. The bivariate Model 1 (Table 7.3) shows a strong negative association between titling and kinship with the village chief in Senegal. The second model includes measures of wealth,[31] infrastructure access, and social

---

[31] For the Senegal analyses, the wealth measure is an index of household building materials, cattle ownership, staple crop yields, and reported additional cash income. The infrastructure measure is an index of proximity to: a paved road, a dirt road, a market, an improved water source, a school, electricity, and a health clinic. These measurement strategies differ slightly from the Zambia analyses due to differences in the survey

TABLE 7.3. *Correlates of smallholder land titling in Senegal*

	1 Reduced	2 Baseline	3 Additional Controls
Kinship with Chief	−0.701**	−0.529**	−0.503**
	(0.165)	(0.015)	(0.008)
Distance to Infrastructure		−0.652	−0.558
		(0.482)	(0.430)
Education		0.019**	0.037
		(0.002)	(0.030)
Employment		−0.040	−0.032
		(0.193)	(0.208)
Total Land Owned		0.038**	0.046*
		(0.008)	(0.023)
Wealth		−0.044	−0.083
		(0.219)	(0.238)
Migrant (10 years)		−0.213	−0.340**
		(0.262)	(0.127)
Local		−0.450	−0.516
		(0.609)	(0.559)
Youth-Headed Household		0.299	0.334**
		(0.183)	(0.126)
Female-Headed Household		−0.027	0.028
		(0.281)	(0.309)
Crops and Land Access Controls			Y
Constant	−3.693**	−3.978**	−18.50**
	(0.0784)	(0.145)	(1.072)
Pseudo R^2	0.1136	0.1672	0.2052
N	961	908	908

Notes: Logistic regression coefficients with district-level fixed effects and robust standard errors clustered at the district level presented in parentheses. Outcome is title. ** $p \leq 0.01$, * $p \leq 0.05$, + $p \leq 0.1$.

characteristics. These results indicate that being related to the village chief significantly reduced land titling among smallholder farmers in Senegal, even when accounting for differences in the household's

instruments and samples. Whereas distance to a road is considered separately from infrastructure in the Zambia analyses, it is included within the Senegal infrastructure index to mitigate collinearity issues in the smaller and more geographically concentrated sample. See Tables A.3 and A.4 for variable descriptions and summary statistics.

resources, education, and land desirability. Further, the effect of kinship on land titling in Senegal was independent of other observed social characteristics, including whether the household migrated within the last ten years; whether it was considered local; and whether the household head was a woman or a youth.

These analyses provide evidence that customary privilege derived from kinship with a customary authority impacted land titling within two regions in Senegal that differ socially and geographically. The size of this customary privilege effect is substantively meaningful. Kinship with the chief decreased the predicted probability of having a title from 9.5 percent among nonkin to 6 percent among kin. Further, only kinship and infrastructure obtained standard levels of statistical significance in the baseline model. Thus, in addition to the systematic effects of customary privilege, this indicates that more valuable land was more likely to be titled in Senegal. As in Zambia, the model predicts that, given two households with the same level of education and income, the smallholder farmer who was not related to the customary authority was consistently more likely to have title.

Model 3 shows that the effect of kinship was independent of how citizens accessed their land and how they used it. This model considers the impact of the most important crops within the Senegal sample – groundnuts, millet, beans (*niébé*), and rice – as well as cash crops such as tomatoes and watermelons.[32] Growing cash crops increased the likelihood that a household had a title, consistent with expectation of the IIC approach that demand for formal land rights is higher on more valuable (or revenue-generating) land. The model also includes measures to control for modes of land access. As in the Zambia analyses, adding dummy variables for inheritance, purchase, and allocation of land ensures that the kinship results are not driven by an omitted variable related to modes of land access. The significant and negative coefficient on kinship in Model 3 remains when controlling for the different ways that respondents had accessed their land and the land use needs of different types of crops. The model predicts that among two households that had inherited their land, the household without kinship ties to the chief was more likely to have a land title.[33]

---

[32] Cash crops included in this sample are hibiscus leaves, citrus fruit, okra, melons, onion, watermelon, onion, scotch bonnet peppers (*piment*), tomatoes, and sweet potatoes. These may also be grown for home consumption.

[33] Subsample analyses confirm this point.

7.2 Customary Privilege and Smallholder Titling 267

This section has provided evidence of a pattern within many different types of customary institutions in Zambia and Senegal: Households with privileged status in the institution were more likely to retain exclusively customary property rights. Although these findings are consistent across the two countries, they may potentially underestimate the effect of privilege on demand for title. Kinship with the chief should also make it easier to access title, as closer ties to the customary authority may make the household's claims to the land stronger and decrease the costs of gaining the chief's consent. Nevertheless, even if households with customary privilege had lower barriers to accessing titles, they were still adopting titles at lower rates. The next section investigates the mechanisms that underlie the relationship between customary privilege and land titling outcomes.

Mechanisms: Why Does Customary Privilege Decrease Titling?

There are two interconnected reasons why privilege within a customary institution might decrease the likelihood that a household titles its land. First, privilege may decrease the relative benefits of land titling because the customary system works better for these households. In effect, customary privilege may reduce demand for a new form of property rights by increasing the security of a household's customary property rights. Second, the theory predicts that privilege increases the political costs of exit. Citizens that derive high status from the institution may be more invested in its continued power, beyond (or in addition to) their personal tenure security concerns. As a result, higher status households may be more resistant to changes in authority over land. This section considers the evidence that would support these two mechanisms.

Land Tenure Security

Property rights include a variety of different rights and protections, but a key indicator of whether a system of property rights is working well is whether it provides security of land tenure, defined here as the perceived ability that one can continuously use land without fear of encroachment or expropriation. There are several ways to measure tenure security. For example, the Senegal survey asked farmers to rank their tenure security. About a third (37%) reported that it was "probable" to "completely probable" that their land would be expropriated at some point. In a separate dichotomous question, 68 percent reported that their rights to continue using their land were completely secure. Most respondents indicated that the state was the most likely actor to expropriate their land (73%), followed by customary authorities (20%). Yet these self-reported measures of tenure security are prone to biases that could influence the findings. It is plausible that an individual with a closer relationship with the customary authority would hesitate to report anything negative about his or her land governance. Further, individuals may employ different understandings of tenure security, decreasing the reliability of this measure for comparing households.

An alternative strategy for measuring tenure security is to ask specific questions about one key type of property right: the ability to fallow. Land fallowing is the practice of leaving a field unplanted for one or more seasons to allow it to recover its fertility. The ability to fallow indicates more secure property rights because households that practice fallowing must believe that they can maintain their claim over an area of land without continuously using it. Insecure farmers cannot leave their land to fallow for fear that it will be expropriated.[34] The fallowing questions on the two surveys were slightly different. The Zambia survey asked respondents whether they had any land under fallow, and 30 percent reported that they did. In the Senegal survey, I asked whether the household believed that they *could* leave their land to fallow, with 53 percent reporting that they could.

Figure 7.3 illustrates the impact of customary privilege on the household's likelihood of fallowing, among households with customary property rights. In Zambia, households that were related to a customary authority were consistently more likely to report that they had land that was currently under fallow. As Figure 7.3 graphically illustrates, the probability that a household fallowed land increased from 26 percent among nonkin households to 33 percent for households that were related to the chief. Full logistic regression results are reported in Model 2, Table B.5 of the Appendix.

In Senegal, the kin of the village chief were significantly more likely to believe that they could fallow their land than otherwise similar households. As depicted in Figure 7.3, the probability that a household reported the ability to fallow land in Senegal increased from 54 percent

---

[34] Gray and Kevane 2001; Goldstein and Udry 2008.

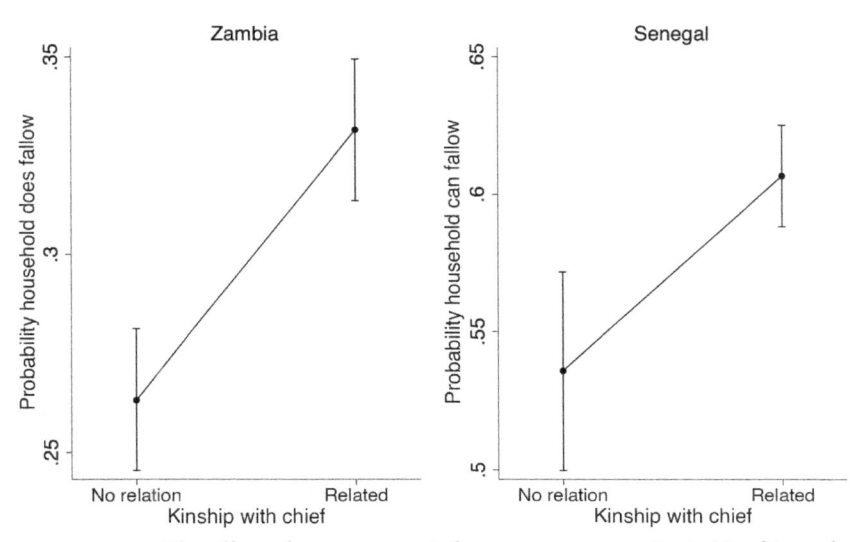

7.2 Customary Privilege and Smallholder Titling

FIGURE 7.3. The effect of customary privilege on tenure security in Zambia and Senegal
Notes: Panels present the predicted probability of having land in fallow (Zambia) and reporting that one could fallow (Senegal) with 95 percent confidence intervals.

for nonkin to 61 percent for kin. Figure 7.3 corresponds to a fully specified model of fallowing in Senegal, reported in the appendix (Model 2, Table B.6). For both countries, the fallowing models include control variables for different types of crops, as this impacts the strategic value of fallowing land. Fixed effects and clustered standard errors adjust for any regional differences in fallowing practices. These findings suggest that customary property rights function differently for those with and without customary privilege, which should have a systematic effect on the relative benefits of adopting new forms of property rights.

The fallowing results show that the customary property rights of households with higher status in the institution were more secure, in both country samples. Such households can more confidently leave their land unplanted without fear that it might be allocated to someone else. These findings support the argument that tenure security is one advantage that privileged members obtain from the continuing power of the institution, which should increase their incentive to invest in it. Further, these results suggest that customary privilege makes customary property rights more credible. These are the smallholders who can report that "us landowners don't need title because it's our land"[35] and trust that others will also respect this. Higher status households can have greater confidence that the institution's land rights norms will work for them. Lower status households (measured as nonkin) revealed through their fallowing behavior and their titling that they had lower confidence in their rights of continued access to land within the customary institution. The privilege generated by the customary institution shapes the benefits of an exit in favor of state rights.

Collective Political and Social Costs

Customary institutions also structure community relationships by providing social and political advantages to citizens, beyond secure property rights. Individuals that gain influence from the continued power of the institution should more acutely perceive the collective costs of titling, or the weakening of the material basis of the institution's power. Citizens experience the loss of institutional power that accompanies land titling within their communities in a variety of ways. In interviews, they expressed concerns about the enclosure of land, contributing to the loss of passageways and secondary rights to wild plants, and about changes from the social systems that have long organized community life. Such collective costs shape citizens' attitudes toward smallholder land titling. Yet these collective costs are not shared uniformly by members of an institution.

The loss of institutional power is more directly perceived by those whose personal power or status derive from the institution. This is one reason why chiefs discussed their open resistance to land titling in previous chapters. However, customary institutions feature far more complex social and political relationships than ruler and ruled (or chief and subject). Instead, my theory predicts that a broad tier of higher status members will also experience the loss of institutional power more acutely than others. For those with customary privilege, the loss of institutional power is an additional cost to consider in evaluating titling. Thus, a vested interest in retaining the influence of the institution within the community can prevent members from converting their customary claims to state land rights. Not titling land or being slower to adopt titles is an investment in the continuing power of the institution.

[35] Interview with smallholder farmers (FFG-543), southern Zambia, October 31, 2013.

Resistant attitudes toward titling in the Senegal survey provide evidence in support of this mechanism. If farmers reported that land titles were not available to them, we followed up with an open-ended question asking them why they believed this was the case. Many of the 257 households who said titles were inaccessible described the anticipated barriers to titling, such as a lack of resources and limited information on the process. One quarter of these respondents, however, provided a different type of explanation: Land registration was unwanted or inappropriate in their village. For the following analyses, responses such as "that's not our practice in this community" or "we don't need those; the land belongs to me" were coded as resistance to land titling. Kinship with the chief should predict such resistant attitudes toward titling if those with customary privilege hesitate to adopt titles because they perceive it as politically and socially costly.

The statistical results reveal that the chief's relatives were significantly more likely to state that titles are inappropriate or unwanted. The predicted probability that a household reported that titling is unavailable because it is inconsistent with local norms increases from 19 to 27 percent from nonkin to kin of the chief (Appendix Table B.6, Model 3). This represents a significant and substantively meaningful difference in perceptions of titling. Although this is not conclusive evidence that households with customary privilege were less likely to adopt titles because of the collective costs, it does suggest that higher status members consider the continuing influence of the customary institution in their evaluations of titling. The social and political trade-offs that result from the incremental expansion of land titling in the community were more salient to respondents with customary privilege.[36]

Two other predictors significantly increased the likelihood that households reported resistant attitudes toward titling: being local and having a higher level of formal education. Individuals that identified as local were more likely to report resistant attitudes than nonlocals. This

---

[36] The theory anticipates that customary privilege impacts evaluations of titling because of its costs to the institution's power base. An implication of this theory is that customary privilege effects should vary depending on members' time horizons for the institution's continuing land authority. This suggests that we should see different effects at different titling equilibria, such as a village where the majority have land titles, or where time horizons are short because of an impending mass land titling campaign.

is consistent with the theory, as local ethnicity can also be an indication of customary privilege relative to nonlocals within the community. Education also increased the probability that respondents expressed resistant attitudes toward titling, within the subsample of households who reported that titling is unavailable to them.[37] Higher education levels suggest increased information and familiarity with state bureaucracy. One interpretation of these results is that since educated households are not ignorant of the titling process, those who reported that titling was unavailable were more likely to have done so out of resistance to changes in land tenure. This is further evidence that citizens consider the political costs and benefits of titling in deciding to adopt titles or to retain customary property rights.

This chapter has examined how the status of smallholder farmers within a customary institution influences their decisions to bear the costs of transferring their property rights to the state's authority. Concern for the collective costs of titling is an additional constraint on citizens' land tenure decisions. Those with privilege may be less likely to title for political reasons, such as their desire to support an institution that provides identity ties and status, and because stronger customary property rights dampen their demand for exit. Customary institutions can, therefore, create constituencies invested in the continuation of customary control of land. In doing so, they change the costs and benefits of titling land, impacting citizens' decisions to engage with the state.

7.3 BROADER IMPLICATIONS

Implications for Classic Models of Land Titling

The findings of this chapter illustrate that the existing explanations for how property rights change are not incorrect, but incomplete. Demonstrating that customary institutions impact smallholder titling does not negate the classic IIC model of land titling, but, instead, reveals the importance of also accounting for heterogeneity in institutional strength (see Chapters 5 and 6) and customary privilege. Table 7.4

---

[37] By contrast, neither education nor local predicted the respondents' beliefs in the availability of titles for their land.

TABLE 7.4. *Evaluating support for alternative models of land titling*

Predictors of Titling	Theory and Mechanisms	Measures and Data Sets	Evaluation
Geography and Land Values	• The benefits of titling are higher for households with more desirable land, as greater competition over land makes informal rights less secure. • Increased contact between state and citizen that results from proximity to seats of state power, roads, and infrastructure decreases the costs of land titling by making titles easier to access.	Proximity to roads, railways, and other infrastructure *Smallholder and District Data Sets*	**Supportive** *Zambia Smallholders*: Proximity to infrastructure and railways predicted titling. Proximity to roads had no significant effect. *Zambia Districts*: Proximity to roads and the presence of railways predicted titling. *Senegal Smallholders*: Proximity to infrastructure did not significantly predict titling (but the coefficient of effects was in the expected direction). *Senegal Districts*: Proximity to roads predicted titling. Presence of rails had the inverse of the expected effect in a full model, but no effect in reduced models.
		Population density *Smallholder and District Data Sets*	**Supportive** *Zambia Smallholders*: Population density predicted titling. *Zambia Districts*: Population density predicted titling. *Senegal Smallholders*: Unable to test. *Senegal Districts*: Population density predicted titling.

(continued)

273

TABLE 7.4. (continued)

Predictors of Titling	Theory and Mechanisms	Measures and Data Sets	Evaluation
Geography and Land Values (continued)		Proximity to capital city *Smallholder and District Data Sets*	**Limited** *Zambia Smallholders*: No significant effect. *Zambia Districts*: Proximity to Lusaka predicted titling. *Senegal Smallholders*: Unable to test. *Senegal Districts*: Proximity to Dakar had the inverse of the expected effect in a full model, but no effect in reduced models.
Wealth	• Wealth decreases the relative material costs of titling.	Employment *Smallholder Data Sets*	**Mixed (Zambia Only)** *Zambia Smallholders*: Off-farm employment predicted titling. *Senegal Smallholders*: No significant effect.
		Total land owned *Smallholder Data Sets*	**Supportive** *Zambia Smallholders*: Size of land predicted titling. *Senegal Smallholders*: Size of land predicted titling.
		Income/wealth *Smallholder Data Sets*	**Mixed (Zambia Only)** *Zambia Smallholders*: Income predicted titling. *Senegal Smallholders*: No significant effect.
Education	• Education increases the household's status within the state's institutions and increases its familiarity with bureaucratic paperwork. This decreases the costs of seeking titles and increases the benefits by making it more likely that a household can advocate for the state to enforce its land rights.	Education level *Smallholder Data Sets*	**Supportive** *Zambia Smallholders*: Education level predicted titling. *Senegal Smallholders*: Education level predicted titling in the baseline model but the effect was inconsistent across models.

compares the results from this chapter to the conventional wisdom on the determinants of land titling, which emphasizes land values and material resources. Where possible, it also includes the findings from the data sets presented in Chapters 5 and 6 that use districts as the unit of analysis. Combined, the analyses of these four titling data sets show that population density and proximity to infrastructure do increase the likelihood of titling, as predicted by the theory that growing demand for land induces institutional change. Among the smallholder surveys, education and land size consistently predicted titling, but measures of wealth were only significant in the Zambia sample. Overall, the evidence in support of the basic IIC approach is stronger in the larger, nationally representative Zambia sample.

Land Titles, Customary Institutions, Citizens, and the State

As contracts between individuals and the government, land titles are one form of citizen–state engagement. They represent a shift from relying on the local community's processes to the nation's rules for securing property rights. By shaping whether individuals have land titles, customary institutions impact the role of the state in citizens' lives.

Customary institutions increase and decrease demand for the protections of the state through the privilege they distribute within the community. In Zambia and Senegal, households that derived greater benefits from the continuation of customary authority over land were less likely to exit the customary property rights regime. Further, the attributes that create privilege within customary institutions, such as lineage and kinship, may not be salient in the state's institutions. Therefore, for some community members, customary institutions offer status and accompanying benefits that the state does not.

However, those on the losing end of the institution's distribution of status within the community have more reason to engage with the state. These findings reveal that respondents who did not have an insider relationship with the chiefs who arbitrate customary property rights and resolve conflicts in the community were more likely to title their land. Even among households with inherited land rights and long-term residency, this indicator of lower status within the institution predicted the likelihood that members adopted the alternative: state land titles. This is evidence that customary institutions condition which citizens seek out the state's property rights and therefore how the state's authority is built within communities.

Further, customary institutions also impact citizens' engagement with the state because chiefs can make it more difficult to access titles in their domains. Chiefs are gatekeepers for small-scale titling; as Chapter 5 showed, smallholders were less likely to have titles in hierarchical institutions in Zambia. Even if there is high demand for state property rights, individual customary authorities have the ability to prevent the state's property rights from expanding into their zones and, therefore, into citizens' everyday lives. This helps maintain the institution's influence over populations and their land, while impeding the state's ability to monitor and tax its citizens.

Overall, these patterns of land titling illustrate the importance of customary institutions in citizens' lives in two very different African countries. Kinship with a customary authority contributed to meaningful differences in how survey respondents used and secured their land. The customary privilege effect reveals that customary institutions change citizens' behaviors, in relation to the state and to their economic livelihoods. The similarity of these findings across the dissimilar institutions within Senegal and Zambia demonstrates that customary institutions have meaningful impacts on community relations and state building, regardless of whether the state has recognized chiefs as land authorities.

7.4 CONCLUSION

Previous chapters examined the agency of customary authorities in the expansion of state power over land. This chapter speaks to the role of citizens. Citizens build the state's authority by opting to title their land. They reinforce the customary institution's power by exiting at lower rates. I have argued that such land titling decisions reflect individuals' statuses within customary institutions, and the degree to which they have a stake in the continuation of customary authority over land. The distributional impacts of customary privilege also help to extend the state's system of property rights, by generating increased demand for titles among those with lower status.

It is now clear that the resilience of customary land tenure is not a consequence of the lack of resources needed to access land titles alone. Households with the same financial means at their disposal make different decisions based on their positions within the customary institution. This highlights that customary property rights are not historical artifacts, destined to be replaced as incomes rise. Rather, demand for land titles reflects a more complex set of considerations related to the continuation of the customary norms of land ownership and the distribution of power within the community. The final chapter examines the implications of these findings for citizen–state relations, more generally, and our understandings of how property rights institutions change.

8

Conclusion

The Resilience of Customary Institutions and Property Rights, Beyond State Design

Policymakers and researchers have highlighted limited state capacity, or state weakness, as the root of many of the challenges that African countries face today.[1] Governments seek to build the state's administrative apparatuses in order to provide education, health care, and development programs to citizens. They emphasize how low state capacity makes it harder for them to promote peace and security within their territorial boundaries. Further, for governments attempting to build an internal tax base that is independent of minerals and foreign aid, increasing the state's ability to collect data on citizens and resources is a prerequisite. While state building has historically been a lower priority for the state in areas where customary authorities could fulfill some of the state's governance functions and provide rural stability, this calculus is changing. The convergence of increasing attention to state capacity and booming global land markets has created new opportunities for state building through the expansion of land titling.

Transforming or "modernizing"[2] land tenure has become a focal point for governments throughout Africa. Many state actors, including those in Senegal and Zambia, have courted international agricultural investors, arguing that land is their comparative advantage in the global economy. With the support of international institutions and donors, they have designed policies to encourage small- and large-scale land titling. In doing so, they have expanded their systems for collecting revenue from selling,

---

[1] Examples include Brautigam 1996; Englebert 2000b; Arriola 2009; Besley and Persson 2010; Bleck and Michelitch 2015.
[2] See Njoh 2017 on the linkages between land titling policies and modernization theory.

leasing, and taxing land. As they attempt to diversify the economy and respond to a range of governance challenges connected to state weakness, these governments have built formal systems that allow the state to control the resources and populations in its borders.

However, increasing the state's capacity in this domain transfers power over that function from another set of political actors. There are invariably trade-offs in this shift, particularly for the local authorities and communities that relinquish power to the state. Customary authorities see their power wane as the state's power grows. Examining the political implications of land titling for members of customary institutions reveals new reasons for the uneven expansion of state control over territory. These institutions remain influential, even if they are informal; some can slow the erosion of customary control over land – not in the absence of demand from the state and opportunities for titling – but in spite of it. This book has provided a new a set of theoretical tools for understanding why and how such institutions shape their members' responses to land titling. In doing so, it has also explained why customary institutions with hierarchical legacies have been able to retain their strength relative to others within the same countries. Historical differences among customary institutions in Zambia and Senegal have persisted.

In an era of pronounced focus on state capacity, my findings highlight the risk of treating state building as a neutral or technocratic development. I have argued and demonstrated in this book that state building outcomes hinge upon the institutions being replaced. In this concluding chapter, I explore the broader implications of these findings for the contemporary role of customary authorities as intermediaries between citizen and state; theoretical approaches to property rights; and land titling policies.

8.1 CUSTOMARY INSTITUTIONS IN CONTEMPORARY AFRICA

Customary institutions and their leaders remain relevant to citizens and the state because they function as an alternative to the state in some domains and as a partner to the state in others. Negotiations over land titling illustrate that customary institutions and chiefs retain autonomy from the state, despite a history of collaboration. Much has been written about the ways in which customary authority has been created and transformed by colonial and independent states.[3] As Chapter 4 described,

---

[3] For examples, see Ranger 1983; Chanock 1985; Geschiere 1993; Mamdani 1996; Boafo-Arthur 2001.

both colonial regimes designed their policies toward customary authority and land in concert, to serve the colonizer's need to dominate. Further, hybridity characterizes the relationship between customary and statutory authority in many contexts.[4] However, these findings reveal that, just because many chiefs derive power from the state, it does not follow that all chiefs are agents of the state or that they cannot challenge the state's agenda. Chiefs use the state to legitimize their power. They cooperate with state actors, such as by delivering votes to politicians or distributing government fertilizer subsidies to local populations. Yet, the control of land is central to the power of both customary institutions and the state. By preventing the transfer of authority over land, chiefs and other members of customary institutions pursue a separate set of interests that challenge the state's agenda. The struggle over land reveals that customary authorities who have been integrated within the state are not always the state's representatives. My findings highlight that one key source of differences among customary authorities is the institutions in which they are embedded.

These institutions can facilitate the advancement of a set of shared interests – including the survival of the institution – by shaping members' decisions. This book has explored how customary institutions generate ties of horizontal and vertical accountability that encourage leaders to prioritize the institution's power base. It has illustrated that customary institutions can facilitate sanctioning among elites, such that even powerful individual chiefs who benefit from state recognition may face internal veto points on their decisions. There is reason to expect that these mechanisms for promoting accountability to group interests apply beyond land issues. The challenge for rural farmers to collectively act is well established in the literature;[5] this book provides examples of how customary institutions facilitate collective action more generally. However, it has also highlighted that the internal processes within institutions do not equally empower members with the ability to constrain, such that institutions should most effectively resolve the tension between individual and group goals when the collective concerns have been embraced by the institution's elites. This suggests that the salience of the issue to higher status members and the strength of the institution should increase the likelihood of successful collective action.

---

[4] van Rouveroy van Nieuwaal 1999; Logan 2009; M. Williams 2010.
[5] Lipton 1977; Bates 1981.

8.1 Customary Institutions in Contemporary Africa

In showing that hierarchical institutions make it harder to access titles in their zones, this book has also emphasized the importance of the continuing differences among customary institutions. Customary authorities are a highly heterogeneous set of actors because they face different sets of constraints from within their institutions – or none at all. The broader lesson is that variation in the strength and internal organizations of customary institutions matter because they determine how members respond to challenges to the institution's power. For the cases of Zambia and Senegal, critical differences among contemporary customary institutions have historical roots. Hierarchical legacies endowed institutions with features, practices, and norms that increased their capacity to shape members' decisions and thus prevent their own elimination, part of a dynamic process of institutional resilience. Thus, even where the colonial state attempted to codify and homogenize the chieftaincy system, a historical institutional legacy remained beyond the state's control.

The comparison of former French and British colonies shows that institutional legacies matter regardless of each colonial state's policies. In Zambia, official chiefs were buttressed by and accountable to the colonial regime. The current system is a continuation of British colonial efforts to consolidate chiefs' powers in order to facilitate governance. One might anticipate that decades of British indirect rule would undermine chiefs' abilities to challenge the state. Or it would erase the differences among hierarchical structures created by the colonial regime and those that developed independently. However, the book has demonstrated that contemporary institutions with a legacy of precolonial hierarchy in Zambia remained systematically different than other institutions. Despite the state's attempts to pull customary institutions closer to its administration through official recognition and salaries, the state did not erase meaningful differences among historical institutions.

This is similarly true of customary institutions in Senegal, even though the French colonial state was less concerned with reinforcing customary authority than the British. As Chapter 4 described, the French sought to destroy existing political institutions and replace their authority in the conquest and early colonial era. They were successful in some cases, as the example of the Waalo kingdom illustrated. Further, even as the French gradually increased their recognitions of customary institutions and their representatives, chiefs were never empowered in Senegal as they were in Zambia. After independence, the government attempted to weaken customary land authority through the National Domain Law, in stark contrast to Zambia's policy of recognizing chiefs as the custodians of bounded domains of land. However, even in a country where the official policy was to ignore customary institutions and hope their influence would wither away, differences in the strength of customary institutions remained. In both the former French and British colonies, variations in historical processes of institution-building contributed to long-term, subnational differences among customary institutions.

The evidence that customary institutions can constrain their chiefs and advance a collective interest in retaining control over land suggests a broader lesson: Customary institutions have also endured because they are an alternative to the state's institutions. Citizens in Senegal and Zambia are embedded in both state and customary institutions. This book has explored citizens' roles and interests in relation to each institution, acknowledging that some may opt to engage with the customary institution and some may prefer the state's institutions. Land titling is just one domain of citizens' lives, but it is a revealing window because citizens' property rights, which are critical to their livelihoods, may be either statutory or customary in these countries. This duality offers an opportunity to see how citizens' engagement changes as a function of their status in customary institutions, given choices among plural institutions. Chapter 7 explained why citizens who are disadvantaged within the customary institution have greater demand for statutory rights. Those who gain power and privilege from a customary institution, on the other hand, are slower to participate in state titling. This suggests that customary institutions retain influence, in part, because the state has not provided a satisfactory alternative to the customary institution. Citizens remain engaged in the customary institution when they are dissatisfied with the state and the state gains power when citizens are dissatisfied with the customary institution. While other studies have emphasized collaboration between the statutory and customary authorities, these findings suggest that there may also be a substitution effect in their relationship.

This relationship between customary institutions, the state, and citizens applies beyond the domain of land rights. Afrobarometer's 2016 survey sheds light on the potential for a substitution effect between state and customary institutions. It shows that citizens' engagement with either type of authority is a function of their relationship with the other. As discussed in Chapter 2, the survey asked 40,000 citizens in twenty-six African countries with customary authorities whether they had contacted any authorities in the past year to report problems or express opinions. Many citizens did not engage with representatives of either institution

8.1 Customary Institutions in Contemporary Africa

(56%) or, at the opposite end of the spectrum, were very participatory, contacting multiple types of authorities to resolve problems (18%). A total of 11 percent had only contacted a state authority, which includes government officials, local councillors, and members of parliament. Finally, 15 percent reported that the only authority they had contacted was a customary authority ("traditional leader").

Studying these responses reveals that citizens who had high trust in customary authorities were less likely to engage with state actors. Similarly, those who were dissatisfied with the state were more likely to engage with chiefs. The following graphs illustrate this relationship. Figure 8.1 plots the likelihood that respondents reported contacting each type of authority as a function of their trust in customary authorities.[6] It shows that at high levels of trust in chiefs, citizens were far less likely to reach out to the state to express an opinion or resolve a problem. At the same time, high trust in customary authorities corresponds with an increase in the likelihood of engaging with them. These effects are independent of differences in urban and rural livelihoods, economic vulnerability, state trust, state performance, gender, education, and age. They show that, within the survey sample, citizens who were critical of customary authorities or expressed distrust in them behaved differently toward the state than citizens who trusted customary authorities.

Figure 8.2 provides additional evidence of a substitution effect between state and customary authorities. It shows that trust in the state also conditions the likelihood of contacting customary authorities.[7] While citizens with low trust in the state were more likely to engage with chiefs, the likelihood that they contacted customary authorities decreases as trust

---

[6] Figure 8.1 depicts the association between changes in trust in customary authorities and the probability the respondent reported only contacting the state or only a customary authority with a problem in the last year. Estimates based on multinomial logistic regression, with full results reported in Table B.7; coding details are in Appendix A.5. Respondents who reported neither or both were excluded. Model controls for trust in the state, evaluations of state performance, age, education, urban/rural location, economic insecurity, and gender, with country fixed effects. Countries included in the sample are Benin, Botswana, Burkina Faso, Burundi, Cameroon, Côte d'Ivoire, Eswatini, Ghana, Guinea, Kenya, Lesotho, Liberia, Madagascar, Malawi, Mali, Mozambique, Namibia, Niger, Nigeria, Senegal, Sierra Leone, South Africa, Togo, Uganda, Zambia, and Zimbabwe.

[7] Figure 8.2 depicts the predicted probability of contacting each authority at different values of state trust, based on the same regression model as Figure 8.1.

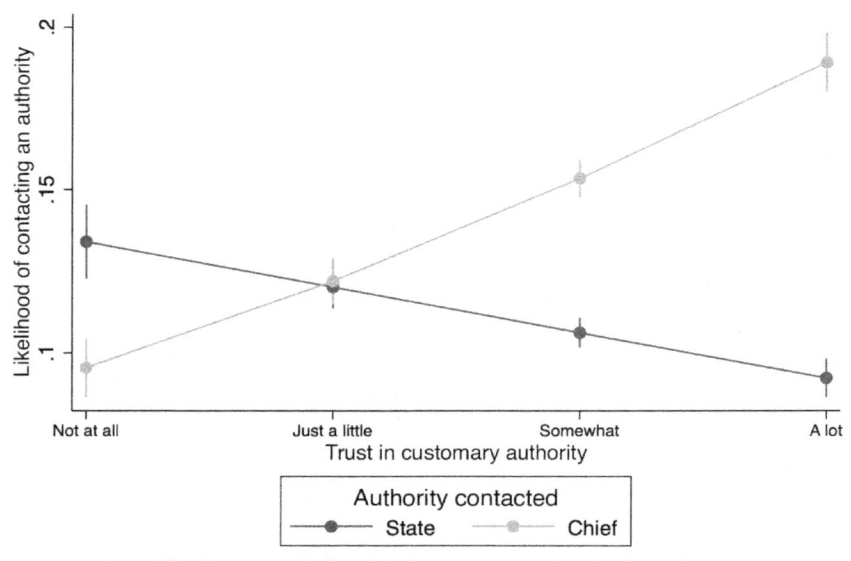

FIGURE 8.1. The inverse relationship between trust in chiefs and engagement with the state
Source: Afrobarometer 2016.

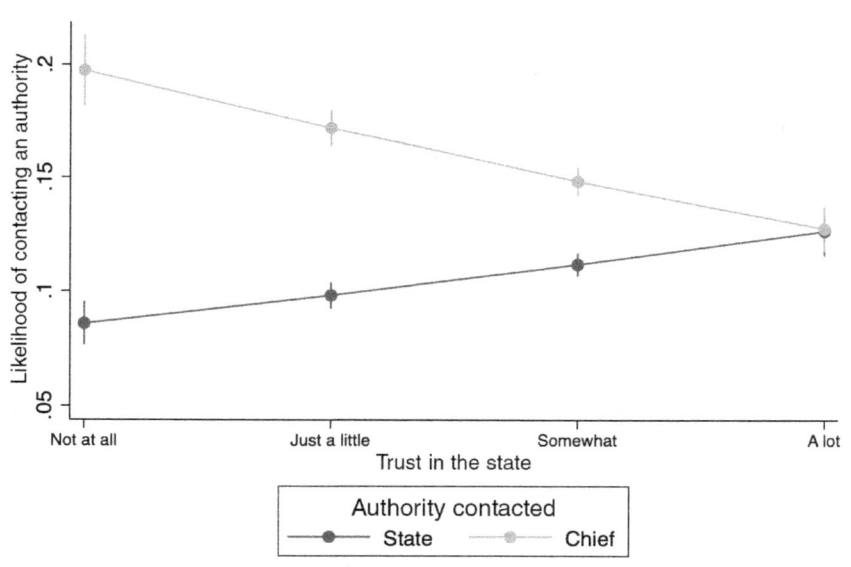

FIGURE 8.2. The inverse relationship between trust in the state and engagement with chiefs
Source: Afrobarometer 2016.

in the state increases. At the same time, low trust in the state corresponds with a decrease in the likelihood of engaging with state actors. These survey results suggest that citizens turn to the state when they are dissatisfied with customary authorities. They also support the hypothesis that when the customary institution's processes are satisfactory or provide opportunities the state does not, citizens should be less likely to engage with the state.

Citizen engagement with customary institutions as an alternative to the state is part of the reason customary institutions have remained relevant. However, this book has also described that chiefs can be corrupt and unaccountable to the citizens who rely on them. This is consistent with studies that find that customary authorities use their power to extract instead of promote development.[8] Further, chiefs have coercive power and may be feared by their communities.[9] In many cases, this contradiction between popular engagement with customary institutions and corrupt chiefs may reflect the foundational element of my approach to customary authorities: Chiefs and customary institutions are not one and the same. Citizens can be disappointed in the behavior of individual chiefs while still supporting the institution and the existence of customary authority more generally. This research suggests that customary institutions retain power because of their potential to provide recourse from the state. This is consistent with arguments advanced by Carolyn Logan and others that popular legitimacy, and not state weakness, is the reason for the resilience of customary institutions.[10]

The hope that customary institutions will advance a collective interest or bring social benefits is powerful. Customary authorities in Zambia and Senegal can protect citizens from state-supported land deals when they would otherwise have limited rights under state law. As in other countries, customary authorities can represent citizen interests to the state or outsiders.[11] They can bring developmental goods to their communities, and mobilize contributions for building schoolrooms and wells, where the state has neglected to do so.[12] Given the potential for positive impacts on citizens' lives, engaging with customary institutions can be a form of risk management. Participatory behaviors may reflect hope that the institution will function as an effective alternative to the state, even when individual leaders have not fulfilled this potential.

---

[8] Acemoglu, Reed, and J. Robinson 2014. [9] Ntsebeza 2005. [10] Logan 2013.
[11] Bado 2015; Dionne 2018. [12] Chiweza 2007; Swidler 2013; Baldwin 2019.

This indicates the need for greater attention to the grassroots sources of the continuing political power of customary institutions within the modern state. Substitution suggests that citizens participate in and, therefore, reinforce the power of a customary institution unless the state provides a better alternative. Likewise, Beatriz Magaloni, Alberto Díaz-Cayeros, and Alexander Ruiz Euler concluded that citizens in Mexico engage with customary institutions because they prefer them to local party operatives.[13] Customary institutions *may* offer different configurations of property rights, collective risk-sharing systems, social status, political power, and connections with alternative logics of justice. They *may* be more efficient and accessible than the state. As Chapter 7 emphasized, the value of these benefits to citizens varies greatly, depending on the individuals' statuses within the customary institution and within the state's institutions. As a result, customary institutions impact the relationship between citizen and state and vice versa: The state also impacts citizens' relationships with customary institutions. These findings predict that customary institutions will remain a central component of the modern state because citizens opt to engage and disengage with each of these forms of authority to fulfill different needs. In addition to the top-down policy choices of state governments to reinforce or undermine the power of customary authorities, local-level decisions contribute to the continuing influence of customary institutions.

8.2 THE POLITICAL DETERMINANTS OF PROPERTY RIGHTS INSTITUTIONS

A rich literature examines how different types of property rights shape a variety of economic, political, and social outcomes. Whether citizens rely on customary or statutory land tenure regimes impacts the nature and locus of conflicts.[14] Differences among property rights institutions can influence how citizens invest in their land and how they engage with the environment.[15] How individuals secure their land claims affects their ties to national or local communities. It can also impact their attitudes; for example, quasi-experimental evidence suggests that land titling changes citizens' beliefs about the economy and society.[16] However,

---

[13] Magaloni, Díaz-Cayeros, and Ruiz Euler 2019.   [14] Boone 2014.
[15] Besley 1995; Herring 2002.   [16] di Tella, Galiani, and Schargrodsky 2007.

understanding the consequences of different forms of property rights requires attention to the processes that created them. By contributing new theoretical frameworks and empirical analyses of the political determinants of changes in authority over land, the findings of this book also help us understand the effects of property rights institutions. The book illustrates how local politics impact who possesses different types of property rights; where new property rights develop; and why institutional pluralism is so prominent.

The cases of Senegal and Zambia reveal that customary institutions impact both the demand for and supply of land titles. As described previously, theories of induced institutional change (IIC) highlight the economic factors that create demand for new processes and rules.[17] Converting land from customary to state property rights is costly, but competition for land increases the benefits of a change. As a result, on land that is more valuable due to higher population densities, crop values, market access, or soil quality, actors should be more willing to bear the costs of institutional change. However, the findings of this book show that the informal land institutions in place – in this case, customary institutions – can moderate these structural factors to reduce demand for new forms of property rights. Citizens who benefit from social and political power within the old system have incentive to retain their customary property rights, even as land values and conflicts over land increase. In contrast, those who gain little from the continuing power of the customary institution, and those who are harmed by it, have greater demand for new forms of property rights. This logic is consistent with scholarship examining institutional change in domains ranging from economic reforms to democratic regimes, which has highlighted how politically or economically disenfranchised actors drive demand for new institutions.[18] In short, these results demonstrate that we must consider privilege within old and new institutions (in this case, customary and state) as a key factor that impacts desire for land titles.

In addition to shaping demand for new forms of property rights, these findings show that local power structures also impact the supply of these rights. This research has demonstrated that customary institutions

---

[17] Boserup 1965; Ahmad 1966; North and Thomas 1973; Ruttan and Hayami 1984; Platteau 2000b.
[18] Cammett 2007; Ansell and Samuels 2010.

influence the availability of titles, even when the land is equally desirable and the country's legal framework is held constant. Customary authorities, both the official and unofficial, can make it more difficult to access titles despite high demand from citizens or wealthy investors. Put differently, they can increase the costs of titling in their zones relative to other zones in the same country. They do so by directly refusing to give their consent; influencing local councils who would process titling applications; and discouraging land users who might apply for title. As a result, densely populated peri-urban land can have as few titles as peripheral low-value brushland, depending on the customary authorities and institutions overseeing the land. These findings from Zambia and Senegal, therefore, reflect Michael Lipton's observations of land politics in other contexts: Institutional change slows when the rural elites subvert land tenure reforms.[19]

By identifying the impacts of customary institutions on the supply of and demand for land titles, these findings counter the popular misunderstanding of informal property rights as a consequence of low land values and weak state capacity. My analysis of land politics in Senegal and Zambia shows that land without formal rights is not a vestige of state weakness to be replaced where fiscal benefits to the state and popular demand arise; rather, customary property rights may be actively maintained by local actors. Readers should take away from this book two key reasons why we should not envisage customary land as land that is waiting to be titled.

First, land users may anticipate that customary property rights provide more benefits than the alternative of state titles. Scholars have repeatedly argued and illustrated that informal property rights institutions can be more efficient at governing resources than state titles would be.[20] Thus land users may be opting not to seek formal property rights because they perceive that their local institutions are capable of enforcing property rights better than the state. Second, customary property rights may be actively maintained by local actors because land is a power resource. Even if the individual land users anticipate that a state title would be more secure than their customary property rights, members of local institutions – particularly elites – may prevent titling in their zones. Customary

---

[19] Lipton 2009, 151.
[20] For examples, see Ostrom 1990; Gibson, Lehoucq, and J. Williams 2002; Murtazashvili and Murtazashvili 2015.

property rights are a tie of dependence that leaders use to organize community governance, coordinate collective action, and extract resources. Hence, non-statutory land tenure regimes may remain in place because they are the domain of powerful authorities and communities. Such power dynamics may be present among brokers who organize property rights in informal settlements ("slums") in urban cities as well.[21]

In sum, this book has introduced a new approach to explaining the continuation of local, informal, and/or customary property rights institutions. Members of customary institutions have motivations to maintain control over land, both for its practical benefits to local populations and as a means of retaining political power. They are also able to mobilize toward this goal, pushing back against attempts to replace customary property rights. In the era of piecemeal land titling policies, customary institutions constrain the state's ability to convert land to a unitary system of state property rights. In doing so, they contribute to the persistence of institutional pluralism in land.[22] This suggests that, in the absence of mass titling campaigns, plural property rights regimes are likely to endure because customary institutions are deeply entrenched in society and can organize to maintain a key material basis of their power.

8.3 IMPLICATIONS FOR LAND TITLING POLICY

What do these findings mean for rural citizens in Africa, particularly for the millions of citizens living at subsistence level who depend on predictable access to fertile land? Given the politics of natural resource governance in Africa, how can policymakers design programs and laws that best serve these populations? What conclusions are generalizable from the very different cases of Senegal and Zambia?

One key conclusion of this research for land reform policy is that there is significant heterogeneity in demand for land titles within and across communities. Land titling contributes to improved tenure security for *some* farmers, but this is far from a universal outcome. The pro-titling orthodoxy assumes that land titling increases tenure security, which should increase citizens' abilities to invest and, ultimately, improve economic development. However, the evidence of anticipated benefits for

---

[21] See Paller 2019.
[22] Meinzen-Dick and Pradhan 2002; de Sousa Santos 2006; Benjamin 2008.

smallholder livelihoods or increased investments in their land has been fairly limited.[23] My findings highlight that the advantages of land titling must be evaluated in relation to the individual's specific customary institution and position within it. Further, the security of customary tenure is not the same for all citizens in a country or even a community. In particular, the case studies suggest that citizens in weak or eroded customary institutions may be more vulnerable to expropriations from large-scale land deals than members of stronger institutions. Further, the surveys indicate that individuals with lower status within customary institutions may have less secure land rights and higher demand for titles than those with high status. This highlights the need for further attention to the variation in demand for land titles, beyond land values and the citizen's ability to pay the fees associated with it. The narrative of land titling as the key to economic development may apply in some contexts, but not others.

In addition, this book has highlighted that land is a power resource and has emphasized that titling creates a documented record of ownership, backed by the state's legal system. Combined, this suggests a point of caution for land titling policies or interventions: Without explicit attention to equity concerns, titling can formalize power structures within families, communities, or the country. Elsewhere, scholars have described how titling can weaken the rights of certain community members; foment new conflicts; and be used to benefit the wealthy or well-connected.[24] In some cases, it can be "a tool for producing and reproducing intergroup inequality," as Franklin Obeng-Odoom described of land titling in South Africa.[25] This highlights the need for careful consideration of the *process* of formalizing land rights, even where there is high demand for title, lest it be co-opted by those with greater financial resources, connections with actors implementing land registration, or status within state institutions. Researchers and policymakers investigating land reform policies must take stock of the local and national power dynamics that could potentially impact the process of formalizing land rights in any given context. Policy recommendations that treat land titling as an

---

[23] Pinckney and Kimuyu 1994; Firmin-Sellers and Sellers 1999; Obeng-Odoom 2012.
[24] Shipton 1988, 107–8; Atwood 1990; Platteau 2000a, 2000b; Toulmin and Quan 2000b; Benjaminsen and Sjaastad 2002; Benjaminsen et al. 2009; Meinzen-Dick and Mwangi 2009; Ali, Deininger, and Goldstein 2014; Zuka 2019.
[25] Obeng-Odoom 2020, 103.

apolitical intervention will be, at best, incomplete, and, at worst, incorrect.

Given the evidence that statutory land titling is not a universal salve for citizens' tenurial troubles and that mass registration is often not feasible, scholars have advocated for increased attention to alternative approaches. Some have proposed customary land tenure reforms, in which policymakers build upon existing property rights institutions instead of attempting to replace them.[26] My findings and fieldwork generate a few such avenues for further exploration. They suggest that interventions that help customary authorities, committees, and institutional processes to become more inclusive and transparent may increase tenure security among land users who feel insecure. Support for community initiatives that facilitate downward accountability and internal checks on the power of individual chiefs could generate "constrained chiefs," while also ensuring that these accountability ties are not primarily among elites. Activities that help community members coordinate their expectations and mechanisms that promote transparency have the potential to strengthen the security of smallholders within customary land institutions. In some circumstances, governments might also mitigate insecurity on customary land by providing citizens with well-funded forms of institutional recourse. This might include, for example, increasing the accessibility of statutory land tribunals for customary land users to help protect them from unaccountable customary authorities. Similarly, laws that raise the requisite compensation for customary land users impacted by the expansion of commercial agriculture can ensure that non-elites benefit from the loss of customary land and reduce the number of displacements.

Ultimately, this book is about the political struggles that accompany shifts to new forms of property rights. It shows that the expansion of land titling is not an individual-level economic intervention alone; changes in land tenure regimes have political reverberations for the state and those who previously benefited from the control of land rights. Regardless of whether titling occurs through an incremental process as described in this book or through a top-down intervention, formalizing land rights transforms political authority over land. It impacts the citizen's relationship

---

[26] For example, John Bruce, Shem Migot-Adholla, and Joan Atherton concluded that land policy in relation to customary land tenure should shift from a "replacement paradigm" to an "adaptation paradigm" (Bruce, Migot-Adholla, and Atherton 1994, 261). See also Ensminger 1997; Platteau 2000b; Banda 2011.

with the state and the community. The evidence that customary institutions structure community responses to such changes indicates that these institutions are not only resilient when they serve the state's agenda, but also as a consequence of their own capacity to influence members' interests, power, and decisions. This raises the possibility that the prevalence of customary property rights and other forms of informality in the modern state reflects how they are maintained by powerful social actors and institutions, beyond the state's design.

APPENDIX A

Data Appendix

This appendix provides further information on the data sets, measures, and summary statistics for the analyses presented in Chapters 5–8. Sections A.1 and A.2 describe the two national level land titling data sets with districts as the unit of analysis. The main outcome from these two data sets is the proportion of land in the district that was registered in state property rights. These data sets were primarily constructed from the governments' own data on the territory, shared under the condition that they would only be published as analyses of aggregated land tenure patterns. The data sets in Sections A.1 and A.2 were designed for parallel analyses, when possible.

Sections A.3 and A.4 describe the smallholder land titling data sets in Zambia and Senegal. As explained in the text, the Zambia smallholder titling survey was designed and implemented by the Indaba Agricultural Policy Research Institute (IAPRI), Central Statistics Office, and Ministry of Agriculture and Livestock in 2012. IAPRI was my institutional host in Zambia in 2012 and 2013–14. Section A.4 describes the original Senegal smallholder data set that I designed and fielded to replicate key questions from the Zambia survey. See the main text for discussion of the differences in the samples. Finally, Section A.5 provides details on the variable coding for the Afrobarometer data analyzed in Chapter 8.

A.1 ZAMBIA LAND TITLES DATA SET

TABLE A.1. *Chapter 5: Zambia land titles data set: Summary statistics and variable descriptions*

Variable	Mean	SD	Min	Max	Description	Data Source
Land Titling Rate	0.07	0.12	0	0.54	Combined area of all land titles per district, divided by the district size variable.	Ministry of Lands. "Lands Information System (LIMS) Dataset." Lusaka, Zambia, 2013.
District Size	96.64	55.51	10.99	250.39	Size of land in district that could be titled, in 10,000 ha units; excludes national parks and state forests.	Zambia Wildlife Authority (ZAWA). 2014. Shapefiles.
Hierarchy	0.24	0.43	0	1	Hierarchy is the dominant customary institution in the district, by percentage of territory. Hierarchy is defined as precolonial hierarchies that survived colonial conquest: Bemba, Chewa, Ngoni, and Lozi institutions (paramount systems).	Republic of Zambia, "Map of Chiefs' Areas" for Central, Copperbelt, Eastern, Luapula, North Western, Northern, Southern, Western Provinces, 1958, Lusaka: Northern Rhodesia Survey Department. Henceforth: "1958 Chiefdom Boundaries Map." Additional data from the House of Chiefs.
Senior	0.63	0.49	0	1	Dominant customary institution in the district by percentage of territory is senior chieftaincy system.	Ibid.
Hierarchy with Lunda (Alt. Specification)	0.27	0.45	0	1	As above, with Lunda-Kazembe also coded as a hierarchy.	Ibid.
Distance to Lusaka	43.12	21.47	3.57	80.66	Distance from the centroid of the district to Lusaka in 10 km units.	ZAWA Shapefiles.

Population Density	0.21	0.16	0.04	0.85	Total population per ha of district land, excluding state parks and classified forests.	Central Statistics Office, "2010 Census of Population and Housing."
Soil	0.06	0.25	0	1	Majority of soil in the district is the soil class present in the district with highest land titling rate, Pu19/Lixisols.	ZAWA Shapefiles.
Rainfall	−0.07	.97	−1.71	1.87	Deviation from average annual rainfall within country from 1950 to 2000, in 100 mm units.	WorldClim. "Global Climate Data Version 1," 2016. http://worldclim.org.
Roads	0.68	0.16	0.27	0.96	Proportion of the district within 10 km of a road.	ZAWA Shapefiles.
Railroads	0.32	0.47	0	1	Railway passes through district.	ZAWA Shapefiles.
Group Size: Nyanja	12.52	26.76	0.01	83.92	Percentage of district population reporting: Nyanja is primary language.	Central Statistics Office, "2010 Census of Population and Housing."
Group Size: Bemba	29.57	36.67	0	84.78	Percentage of district population reporting: Bemba is primary language.	Ibid.
Group Size: Tonga	14.68	27.68	0	79.92	Percentage of district population reporting: Tonga is primary language.	Ibid.

Note: Summary statistics reflect 2012 district boundaries and districts with official chiefs.

A.2 SENEGAL LAND TITLES DATA SET

TABLE A.2. *Chapter 6: Senegal land titles data set: Summary statistics and variable descriptions*

Variable	Mean	SD	Min	Max	Description	Data Source
Land Titling Rate	0.02	0.03	0.00	0.14	Total land conversions from 2007 to 2013 per district, divided by the district size variable. Total land conversions is the sum of land registered in state property rights from three different governmental sources. Note: Districts denote *Départements* in Senegal's administrative system.	(1) Minutes from the *Commission de Contrôle des Operations Domaniales (CCOD)* (2) *Agence pour la Promotion des Investissements et des Grands Travaux (APIX)* (3) *Agence Nationale d'Insertion et de Développement Agricole (ANIDA)*
Land Rentals	0.05	0.09	0.00	0.49	Proportion of agricultural population per district that reported accessing any land through renting.	Ministère de l'Agriculture/Food and Agriculture Organization (FAO), "Recensement National de L'agriculture 1998–1999."
District Size	37.22	29.65	3.49	143.4	Size of land in district that could be titled, in 10,000 ha units; excludes national parks and state forests.	Centre de Suivi Ecologique (CSE). 2014. Shapefiles.
Hierarchy	0.55	0.50	0.00	1.00	Hierarchy is the dominant customary institution in the district, by percentage of territory.	Republic of Senegal, Département d'Aménagement Territoriale, Map of 1854 Political Boundaries. 2000, as reproduced in D. Diop 2006. Coding of institution's survival based

Distance to Dakar	27.69	15.53	2.81	63.88	Distance from the centroid of the district to Dakar in 10 km units.	CSE Shapefiles.
Population Density	1.05	1.41	0.04	7.79	Total population per ha of district land, excluding state parks and classified forests.	Agence Nationale de la Statistique et de la Démographie (ANSD), "Résultats Définitifs du Troisième Recensement Général de la Population et de l'Habitat–2002."
Soil	0.55	0.50	0.00	1.00	Majority of soil in the district is the soil class present in the district with highest land titling rate, Iron-Rich Tropical Soil.	CSE Shapefiles.
Rainfall Deviation from average annual rainfall within country from 2005 to 2007, in 100 mm units.	0.03 Food	1.02	1.69 and Agriculture Organization/ GeoSTAT raster files for 2005–7.	—	2.05	

Hierarchy is defined as precolonial hierarchies that survived colonial conquest: Baol, Cayor, Djoloff, Fouta Toro, Sine, and Saloum.

on: Report by Camille Lucien Xavier, Senegal Colony Governor, to AOF Governor. June 1, 1907, Box 71, 13G, ANS; secondary sources; and additional colonial archival materials.

(*continued*)

TABLE A.2. (continued)

Variable	Mean	SD	Min	Max	Description	Data Source
Roads	0.51	0.29	0.00	1.00	Proportion of the district within 10 km of a paved road.	CSE Shapefiles.
Railroads	.60	0.50	0	1	Railway passes through district.	USAID Shapefiles. 2014.
Prior Conversions	4.23	5.72	0.00	25.00	Estimated number of land titles 100 ha or above in district prior to 2007.	District and regional land registries.
1854 Hierarchy (Alt. Specification)	2.25	1.08	0	3	Ordinal measure of levels of centralization in 1854; based on the dominant customary institution in the district, by percentage of territory. The four categories of increasing centralization are: small diverse ethnic groups, small unfederated states, federated small states, and centralized states.	Categories for political organization in 1854 from Phillips 1981 and D. Diop 2006; cross-referenced with colonial reports on specific chiefdoms and treaties from the Senegal National Archives.
Group Size: Wolof	31.29	29.61	0.15	85.98	Percentage of district rural population reporting: ethnicity is Wolof.	Agence Nationale de la Statistique et de la Démographie (ANSD), "Résultats Définitifs du Troisième Recensement Général de la Population et de l'Habitat–2002."
Group Size: Pulaar	34.27	28.96	2.89	94.81	Percentage of district rural population reporting: ethnicity is Pulaar.	Ibid.
Group Size: Mouride	15.5	9.37	1.00	32.00	Percentage of district rural population reporting: religion is Mouride.	Ibid.

Note: Descriptive statistics for all districts included in statistical models. Excludes urban districts of Dakar and Pikine-Guédiawye.

TABLE A.3. *Chapters 5 and 7: Zambia smallholder data set: Summary statistics and variable descriptions*

Variable	Mean	SD	Min	Max	Description	Data Source
Land Title	.08	.26	0	1	Household has a title for any plot of land.	Indaba Agricultural Policy Research Institute, Central Statistics Office, and Ministry of Agriculture and Livestock (IAPRI/CSO/MAL). 2012. *Rural Agricultural Livelihoods Survey (RALS)*. Lusaka, Zambia.
Fallow	.30	.46	0	1	Household reports any land is under fallow.	Ibid.
Kinship	.51	.50	0	1	Household head or spouse is related to the chief or village head.	Ibid.
Population Density	.45	2.11	.04	40.56	Total population per ha of district land, excluding state parks and classified forests; full sample includes districts without official chiefs.	Central Statistics Office, "2010 Census of Population and Housing."
Distance to Lusaka	4.40	2.10	.10	8.33	Distance from household to Lusaka in 100 km units.	ZAWA Shapefiles.
Distance to Infrastructure	8.94	9.94	0	145	Index of reported distances to school, health clinic, electricity, and improved water source. Note: This measure divided into quintiles for interpretation in Table 7.1.	RALS.

(*continued*)

TABLE A.3. (*continued*)

Variable	Mean	SD	Min	Max	Description	Data Source
Railroads	139.4	105.0	.00	492.4	Distance in km from household to a railway.	ZAWA Shapefiles.
Roads	3.61	4.62	.00	53.48	Distance in km from household to a road of any surface.	ZAWA Shapefiles.
Education	1.60	.68	0	3	Highest level of formal education completed in household; categorized as primary, secondary, tertiary.	RALS.
Employment	.19	.40	0	1	Household member has employment outside of family agriculture.	Ibid.
Total Land Owned	3.61	4.37	0	50.00	Total *land owned* by the household in ha. (Median: 2.31).	Ibid.
Income	3.00	1.41	1	5	Quintiles of net household income from: agricultural and livestock production and sales; off-farm income.	Ibid.
Youth-Headed Household	.45	.50	0	1	Household head is 40 years or under.	Ibid.
Female-Headed Household	.19	.40	0	1	Household head is female.	Ibid.
Migrant (10 years)	.27	.44	0	1	Household arrived within the past 10 years.	Ibid.
Local	.89	.32	0	1	Household is considered local.	Ibid.
	.06	.24	0	1		1958 Chiefdom Boundaries Map.

Colonial State Land					Household is located within area designated as crown land.	
Agricultural Settlement	.03	.17	0	1	Household is located within area designated as an agriculture settlement scheme.	Ministry of Agriculture. 2014. Shapefiles. (Note: These boundaries are unofficial estimates).
Maize	.84	.37	0	1	Household produced maize in 2011/2012.	RALS.
Cassava	.33	.47	0	1	Household produced cassava in 2011/2012.	Ibid.
Groundnuts	.29	.46	0	1	Household produced groundnuts in 2011/2012.	Ibid.
Misc. Cash Crops	.26	.44	0	1	Household produced sunflower, soya, cotton, coffee, sugar, and/or paprika in 2011/2012.	Ibid.
Inheritance	.40	.49	0	1	Household has received land from within the family without payment.	Ibid.
Allocation	.49	.50	0	1	Household has received land without payment from someone outside of the family.	Ibid.
Purchase	.06	.24	0	1	Household has paid money for access to land.	Ibid.
Hierarchy	.28	.45	0	1	Household is located within a chiefdom that is part of a hierarchical customary institution.	1958 Chiefdom Boundaries Map.
Chiefdom Area	30.38	42.09	.20	250.9	Size of the chiefdom where household is located, in 10,000 ha units	Ibid.

A.4 SENEGAL SMALLHOLDER SURVEY DATA

TABLE A.4. *Chapter 7: Senegal smallholder data set: Summary statistics and variable descriptions*

Variable	Mean	SD	Min	Max	Description	Data Source
Land Title	.07	.25	0	1	Household has any form of statutory property rights (title, lease, or rural council extract of proceedings document) for any plot of land.	Senegal smallholder survey, 2014.
Kinship with Village Chief	.65	.48	0	1	Household member is related to the village chief.	Ibid.
Education	.93	.85	0	3	Highest level of formal education completed in household; categorized as primary, secondary, tertiary.	Ibid.
Employment	.60	.49	0	1	Household member has employment outside of family agriculture.	Ibid.
Wealth	3.00	1.41	1	5	PCA of building materials, cash income, staple crop yield 2013, number of cattle.	Ibid.
Total Land Owned	5.64	7.36	.01	48.15	Total land owned by the household in ha. (Median: 2.54).	Ibid.
Infrastructure Distance	−.02	1.58	−1.65	22.10	PCA of calculated distances to paved road and to dirt road; reported distances to market, improved water source, electricity, and health clinic with nurse. Note: This measure is divided into quintiles for interpretation in Table 7.1.	CSE Shapefiles; Senegal smallholder survey, 2014.
Youth-Headed Household	.32	.47	0	1	Household head is 40 years or under.	Senegal smallholder survey, 2014.

Variable					
Female-Headed Household	.16	.36	0	1	Household head is female.	Ibid.
Migrant (10 years)	.05	.21	0	1	Household arrived within the past 10 years.	Ibid.
Local	.87	.34	0	1	Household is considered local.	Ibid.
Fallow	.58	.42	0	1	Household reports that they can fallow any parcel of their land.	Ibid.
Resistance	.25	.43	0	1	Household expressed resistant attitudes toward titling in open-ended response to "why is title unavailable to you?"	Ibid.
Groundnuts	.43	.50	0	1	Household produced groundnuts in 2013.	Ibid.
Rice	.30	.46	0	1	Household produced rice in 2013.	Ibid.
Beans	.50	.50	0	1	Household produced beans (*niébé*) in 2013.	Ibid.
Millet	.58	.49	0	1	Household produced millet in 2013.	Ibid.
Misc. Cash Crops	.19	.39	0	1	Household produced hibiscus leaves, citrus fruit, okra, melons, onion, watermelon, onion, scotch bonnet peppers (*piment*), tomatoes, and/or sweet potatoes and listed it among top three crops in 2013.	Ibid.
Inheritance	.87	.33	0	1	Household has received land from within the family without payment.	Ibid.
Allocation	.18	.38	0	1	Household has received land without payment from someone outside of the family.	Ibid.
Purchase	.04	.19	0	1	Household has paid money for access to land.	Ibid.
Kinship with Marabout	.61	.49	0	1	Household member is related to the village marabout.	Ibid.
Mouride Marabout	.30	.46	0	1	Village marabout belongs to the Mouride Islamic brotherhood.	Ibid.
Marabout Land Involvement	.48	.50	0	1	Respondent reported that marabout has a role in land management in the village.	Ibid.

A.5 AFROBAROMETER SURVEY DATA

Figures 8.1 and 8.2 in Chapter 8 examine the relationship between trust in authorities and engagement, using Round 6 Afrobarometer survey data in all sub-Saharan countries with traditional leaders in the sample. The trust variables for this analysis are based on the Afrobarometer question: "How much do you trust each of the following?" The trust in customary authority variable is the respondent's reported trust in "Traditional Leaders." The distrust in state variable combines reported trust in the president, legislature, electoral commission, tax department, local government councillor, police, army, and courts. The variable coding inverts trust, to create a measure of distrust, for ease of interpretation. The state performance variable combines the respondent's reported dissatisfaction with the president and legislature.

The outcome variable measures whether the respondent reported contacting only state authorities, only customary authorities, both, or neither in the past year. It is based on the Afrobarometer question: "During the past year, how often have you contacted any of the following persons about some important problem or to give them your views?" Contact with the state includes contacting a member of parliament, local government councillor, and/or an official of a government agency. Reported contact with a traditional leader is coded as contact with a chief.

Control variables are coded as follows:

Age: dummy variable; respondent is above 35 years old.
Education: dummy variable; respondent has completed primary school.
Female: dummy variable; respondent is female.
Urban: dummy variable; respondent is in an urban area.
Economic Insecurity: mean reported frequency of "going without" basic needs (food, water, medical care, cooking fuel, cash income).

Full results of this model are presented in Appendix B, Table B.7.

APPENDIX B

Additional Tables and Analyses

TABLE B.1. *Chapter 5: Land titling and hierarchy with alternative specifications in Zambia*

	1 Reduced	2 Baseline	3 Senior	4 Ethno-linguistic Group Size	5 Alt. Hierarchy	6 1996 Boundaries	7 OLS Baseline
I. Customary Institutions							
Hierarchy	−2.078**	−0.973**	−1.044**	−1.118**		−1.287**	−0.103*
	(0.661)	(0.148)	(0.316)	(0.128)		(0.428)	(0.0434)
Hierarchy with Lunda (Alt. Specification) Senior System					−1.142**		
					(0.147)		
			−0.068				
			(0.243)				
Group Size: Nyanja				−0.003			
				(0.005)			
Group Size: Bemba				0.005			
				(0.008)			
Group Size: Tonga				−0.004			
				(0.006)			
II. Control Variables							
Distance to Lusaka		−0.039**	−0.039**	−0.038**	−0.037**	−0.038**	−0.002*
		(0.008)	(0.008)	(0.006)	(0.007)	(0.006)	(0.001)
District Size		0.005*	0.005**	0.004*	0.004*	0.010**	−0.000
		(0.002)	(0.002)	(0.002)	(0.002)	(0.004)	(0.000)
Population Density	5.615**	5.046**	5.072**	4.362**	5.078**	6.687**	0.308**
	(1.370)	(0.956)	(0.995)	(1.287)	(0.969)	(0.843)	(0.106)

Soil		1.092**	1.111**	1.128**	1.142**	0.670**	0.115+
		(0.159)	(0.199)	(0.197)	(0.150)	(0.218)	(0.058)
Rainfall		0.647**	0.657**	0.700**	0.662**	0.574**	0.011
		(0.173)	(0.186)	(0.217)	(0.163)	(0.084)	(0.025)
Roads		4.819**	4.822**	5.026**	4.943**	4.594**	0.229**
		(1.625)	(1.619)	(1.902)	(1.678)	(1.381)	(0.081)
Railroads		1.096**	1.107**	1.350**	1.045**	0.783**	0.074*
		(0.398)	(0.403)	(0.438)	(0.370)	(0.290)	(0.036)
Constant	−3.811**	−7.110**	−7.072**	−7.053**	−7.163**	−7.820**	−0.090
	(0.457)	(1.063)	(0.993)	(1.167)	(1.089)	(1.354)	(0.093)
AIC							0.651
R^2	.430	.518	.518	.516	.516	.597	
Observations	62	62	62	62	62	47	62

Notes: Fractional logistic regression coefficients with robust standard errors clustered by region presented in parentheses in Models 1–6; ordinary least-squares regression coefficients with regional fixed effects presented in Model 7. Outcome is proportion of land titled per district through 2012.

** $p \leq 0.01$, * $p \leq 0.05$, + $p \leq 0.1$.

TABLE B.2. *Chapter 5: Balance statistics for probability weighted analyses of hierarchy and smallholder land titling*

	Model 1				Model 2				Model 3			
	Standardized Diff.		Variance Ratio		Standardized Diff.		Variance Ratio		Standardized Diff.		Variance Ratio	
Covariate	Raw	Weighted	Raw	Weighted	Raw	Weighted	Raw	Weighted	Raw	Weighted	Raw	Weighted
Chiefdom Land Size	0.53	0.09	5.85	2.24	0.38	-0.02	5.47	2.41	0.46	0.12	5.33	2.37
Kinship with Chief	0.28	0.08	0.92	0.98	-0.09	0.05	1.07	0.96	0.21	0.07	0.95	0.99
Population Density	0.74	0.14	4.03	2.00	-0.31	-0.08	0.94	0.84	0.71	0.14	3.67	1.91
Infrastructure Dist.	0.14	0.01	1.31	1.03	0.28	0.05	1.75	1.12	0.03	0.03	1.24	1.87
Distance to Lusaka	0.81	0.51	0.19	0.14	0.80	0.00	0.37	0.54	0.91	0.58	0.18	0.14
Railroads	0.29	-0.03	0.87	0.87	-0.20	-0.04	2.66	1.82	0.44	0.12	0.89	1.07
Roads	0.24	-0.02	1.94	0.98	0.02	0.03	1.61	1.31	0.17	-0.02	1.85	1.13
Education	-0.10	-0.07	1.13	1.15	0.07	-0.09	0.91	1.05	-0.08	-0.07	1.13	1.10
Employment	0.01	0.03	1.01	1.04	-0.10	0.21	0.88	1.23	0.02	0.01	1.04	1.02
Total Land Owned	-0.04	-0.01	0.60	0.72	0.01	0.09	0.82	0.92	-0.09	-0.05	0.57	0.69
Wealth	-0.07	0.00	0.96	0.97	0.03	-0.01	0.94	0.94	-0.06	-0.03	0.95	0.95
Migrant (10 years)	-0.11	-0.01	0.87	0.99	0.11	0.01	1.13	1.01	-0.11	-0.01	0.88	0.99
Local	-0.09	0.02	1.24	0.95	0.15	-0.02	0.71	1.04	-0.06	0.03	1.17	0.92
Youth Headed	0.03	0.01	1.01	1.00	-0.15	-0.02	0.97	1.00	0.02	0.01	1.00	1.00
Female Headed	0.05	-0.02	1.08	0.97	-0.05	-0.07	0.92	0.89	0.03	0.00	1.05	0.99
Ag. Settlement	-0.05	-0.11	0.76	0.50	-0.12	-0.13	0.65	0.53	-0.07	-0.11	0.66	0.49
Maize	0.08	0.06	0.87	0.90	0.08	-0.03	0.84	1.07	-0.05	-0.02	1.09	1.04
Cassava	0.01	0.08	1.01	1.05	0.31	-0.08	1.38	0.91	0.15	0.17	1.09	1.07
Groundnuts	0.05	0.09	1.04	1.07	0.02	-0.02	1.01	0.99	0.06	0.08	1.06	1.06
Cash Crops	0.35	0.06	1.36	1.06	-0.15	0.18	0.96	1.01	0.26	0.00	1.27	1.00
N	7522.00	7522.00			1328.00	1328.00			7522.00	7522.00		
Treated	2058.00	3608.00			470.00	641.60			2274.00	3534.80		
Control	5464.00	3914.00			858.00	686.40			5248.00	3987.20		

	Model 4				Model 5				Model 6			
	Standardized Diff.		Variance Ratio		Standardized Diff.		Variance Ratio		Standardized Diff.		Variance Ratio	
Covariate	Raw	Weighted	Raw	Weighted	Raw	Weighted	Raw	Weighted	Raw	Weighted	Raw	Weighted
Chiefdom Land Size	0.52	0.08	5.48	2.05	0.38	-0.02	5.50	2.42	0.44	0.11	4.97	2.19
Kinship with Chief	0.29	0.05	0.91	0.99	-0.09	0.04	1.07	0.96	0.22	0.05	0.94	0.99
Population Density	0.76	0.11	3.99	1.96	-0.29	-0.07	0.94	0.84	0.73	0.12	3.62	1.88
Infrastructure Dist.	0.15	0.00	1.32	0.99	0.29	0.05	1.74	1.12	0.04	0.01	1.24	1.77
Distance to Lusaka	0.79	0.51	0.18	0.14	0.80	-0.01	0.38	0.54	0.89	0.58	0.18	0.14
Railroads	0.32	-0.05	0.86	0.86	-0.19	-0.04	2.64	1.83	0.47	0.11	0.88	1.08
Roads	0.25	-0.02	2.02	1.00	0.03	0.03	1.62	1.31	0.19	-0.02	1.92	1.15
Education	-0.11	-0.06	1.13	1.14	0.09	-0.09	0.92	1.06	-0.08	-0.05	1.13	1.11
Employment	0.01	0.04	1.02	1.07	-0.10	0.20	0.87	1.22	0.03	0.02	1.05	1.04
Total Land Owned	-0.02	-0.02	0.62	0.66	0.06	0.08	0.91	0.93	-0.07	-0.05	0.58	0.69
Wealth	-0.06	0.01	0.94	0.96	0.04	-0.01	0.94	0.94	-0.06	-0.02	0.93	0.95
Migrant (10 years)	-0.13	-0.02	0.85	0.98	0.09	0.00	1.12	1.00	-0.12	-0.01	0.86	0.99
Local	-0.06	0.03	1.16	0.93	0.16	-0.02	0.69	1.03	-0.03	0.03	1.09	0.93
Youth Headed	0.03	0.00	1.01	1.00	-0.15	-0.02	0.97	1.00	0.02	0.01	1.00	1.00
Female Headed	0.06	-0.02	1.09	0.97	-0.04	-0.06	0.94	0.90	0.04	0.00	1.06	1.00
Ag. Settlement	-0.05	-0.11	0.77	0.45	-0.11	-0.13	0.66	0.55	-0.07	-0.11	0.67	0.46
Maize	0.08	0.05	0.87	0.91	0.09	-0.03	0.84	1.07	-0.06	-0.02	1.10	1.04
Cassava	0.02	0.09	1.01	1.05	0.30	-0.08	1.35	0.91	0.17	0.16	1.10	1.07
Groundnuts	0.05	0.09	1.05	1.08	0.02	-0.03	1.02	0.98	0.07	0.08	1.07	1.06
Cash Crops	0.36	0.05	1.36	1.05	-0.14	0.17	0.96	1.01	0.26	-0.01	1.27	0.99
N	7108.00	7108.00			1284.00	1284.00			7108.00	7108.00		
Treated	1940.00	3455.50			460.00	618.10			2152.00	3370.90		
Control	5168.00	3652.50			824.00	665.90			4956.00	3737.10		

TABLE B.3. Chapter 6: Land titling and hierarchy with alternative specifications in Senegal

	1	2	3	4	5	6	7
	Reduced	Baseline	Ethno-linguistic Group Size	Mouride Group Size	Alt. Hierarchy	OLS Reduced	OLS Baseline
I. Customary Institutions							
Hierarchy	-2.069**	-2.353**	-2.257**	-1.877**		-0.027**	-0.036*
	(0.478)	(0.325)	(0.411)	(0.264)		(.010)	(0.013)
1854 Hierarchy (Alt. Specification)					-1.436**		
					(0.225)		
Group Size: Wolof			0.022+				
			(0.013)				
Group Size: Pulaar			0.005				
			(0.010)				
Group Size: Mouride				0.122**			
				(0.040)			
II. Control Variables							
Distance to Dakar		0.125**	0.138**	0.202**	0.149**		0.001*
		(0.027)	(0.029)	(0.045)	(0.030)		(0.002)
District Size		0.018*	0.025*	0.0237**	0.000		0.000
		(0.008)	(0.010)	(0.009)	(0.008)		(0.000)
Population Density	0.198**	0.690**	0.755**	0.810**	0.592**	.007*	0.012*
	(0.076)	(0.133)	(0.123)	(0.123)	(0.108)	(.003)	(0.005)
Soil		2.810**	2.822**	3.593**	1.682**		0.042**
		(0.352)	(0.338)	(0.504)	(0.304)		(0.013)
Rainfall		-0.505**	-0.200	-0.541**	-1.214**		-0.006
		(0.190)	(0.256)	(0.174)	(0.249)		(0.006)

	(1)	(2)	(3)	(4)	(5)	(6)	(7)
Roads		5.140**	5.734**	6.020**	3.913**		0.032
		(1.174)	(1.596)	(1.660)	(1.296)		(0.025)
Railroads		−1.971**	−2.208**	−2.819**	−0.355		−0.022+
		(0.728)	(0.713)	(0.795)	(0.702)		(0.011)
Prior Conversions		0.090**	0.114**	0.100**	0.134**		0.001
		(0.032)	(0.040)	(0.027)	(0.037)		(0.001)
Constant	−3.749**	−12.60**	−14.59**	−17.87**	−10.36**	.023**	−0.051
	(0.473)	(1.831)	(2.669)	(3.335)	(2.051)	(.008)	(0.033)
AIC	.267	.595	.694	.644	.595		
R^2						0.247	0.527
Observations	40	40	40	40	40	40	40

Notes: Models 1–5 report fractional logistic regression coefficients with robust standard errors clustered by region. Models 6 and 7 report ordinary least-squares regression coefficients. Outcome is proportion of land titled per district between 2007 and 2013. ** p ≤ 0.01, * p ≤ 0.05, + p ≤ 0.1.

TABLE B.4. *Chapter 6: Land rental markets, titling, and hierarchy in Senegal*

Outcome	Rent		Title
	1	2	3
I. Customary Institutions			
Hierarchy	3.425**	2.471*	−2.496**
	(0.739)	(1.173)	(0.350)
II. Control Variables			
Distance to Dakar	0.048+	−0.014	0.097**
	(0.029)	(0.038)	(0.015)
District Size	0.016	−0.000	0.015*
	(0.015)	(0.008)	(0.007)
Population Density	0.467+	0.202	0.549**
	(0.243)	(0.254)	(0.072)
Soil		−0.844	2.377**
		(0.660)	(0.157)
Rainfall		−0.213	−0.362*
		(0.473)	(0.166)
Roads		−0.784	4.798**
		(1.085)	(1.090)
Railroad		−1.793**	−2.170**
		(0.403)	(0.724)
Prior Conversions		0.066	0.095**
		(0.049)	(0.033)
Land Rentals			−0.770
			(1.864)
Constant	−8.167**	−3.397	−10.810**
	(1.342)	(2.463)	(1.405)
AIC	.527	.778	.695
Observations	37	37	37

Notes: Fractional logistic regression coefficients with robust standard errors clustered by region presented in parentheses. Outcomes are rent (proportion of district sample that reported land rentals in 1998) and title (proportion of land titled per district between 2007 and 2013). Robust standard errors in parentheses. ** $p \leq 0.01$, * $p \leq 0.05$, + $p \leq 0.1$.

TABLE B.5. *Chapter 7: Customary privilege and tenure security in Zambia*

	1	2
	Baseline	Additional Controls
Kinship with Chief	0.417**	0.395**
	(0.064)	(0.062)
Population Density	−0.289**	−0.282**
	(0.088)	(0.086)
Distance to Infrastructure	−0.002	−0.002
	(0.004)	(0.004)
Distance to Lusaka	0.024	0.030
	(0.055)	(0.052)
Railroads	−0.000	−0.000
	(0.001)	(0.001)
Roads	−0.002	−0.002
	(0.009)	(0.009)
Education	0.000	0.023
	(0.052)	(0.051)
Employment	0.244**	0.272**
	(0.087)	(0.087)
Total Land Owned	0.183**	0.181**
	(0.017)	(0.017)
Wealth	−0.167**	−0.170**
	(0.027)	(0.028)
Migrant (10 years)	−0.416**	−0.375**
	(0.074)	(0.074)
Local	0.188	0.151
	(0.118)	(0.119)
Youth-Headed Household	−0.111+	−0.135*
	(0.065)	(0.067)
Female-Headed Household	0.066	−0.046
	(0.079)	(0.078)
Agricultural Settlement	−0.201	−0.224
	(0.184)	(0.186)
Colonial State Land	0.152	0.145
	(0.189)	(0.191)
Maize		−0.158*
		(0.080)

(*continued*)

TABLE B.5. (continued)

	1	2
	Baseline	Additional Controls
Cassava		0.243*
		(0.109)
Groundnuts		−0.169*
		(0.067)
Cash Crops		0.160
		(0.100)
Purchase		0.198
		(0.183)
Inheritance		0.426**
		(0.113)
Allocation		0.266*
		(0.112)
Constant	−1.703**	−1.887**
	(0.224)	(0.241)
Pseudo R^2	0.1372	0.1391
Observations	7,667	7,566

Notes: Logistic regression coefficients with province-level fixed effects and robust standard errors clustered at the chiefdom level presented in parentheses. Outcome is fallow. ** $p \leq 0.01$, * $p \leq 0.05$, + $p \leq 0.1$.

TABLE B.6. *Chapter 7: Customary privilege, tenure security, and resistance in Senegal*

Outcome	Fallowing		Resistance
	1	2	3
Kinship with Chief	0.330*	0.305**	0.538*
	(0.147)	(0.114)	(0.275)
Distance to Infrastructure	0.011**	0.007	0.259
	(0.002)	(0.056)	(0.222)
Education	−0.060	−0.051	0.638**
	(0.115)	(0.134)	(0.192)
Employment	0.341**	0.325**	−1.443*
	(0.032)	(0.058)	(0.681)
Total Land Owned	0.045	0.044+	−0.084
	(0.027)	(0.026)	(0.159)
Wealth	−0.018	0.013	0.088
	(0.096)	(0.082)	(0.100)
Migrant (10 years)	−0.016	−0.029	0.311
	(0.103)	(0.046)	(0.578)
Local	−0.218	−0.358	1.816**
	(0.252)	(0.272)	(0.411)
Youth-Headed Household	0.142**	0.162**	−0.322
	(0.002)	(0.026)	(0.752)
Female-Headed Household	−0.180	−0.181	0.003
	(0.387)	(0.384)	(0.194)
Rice		−0.583**	
		(0.069)	
Beans		0.124	
		(0.503)	
Millet		0.176	
		(0.433)	
Groundnuts		−0.608**	
		(0.029)	
Cash Crops		−0.098	
		(0.333)	
Purchase		0.461	
		(0.758)	
Inheritance		0.535	
		(0.565)	
Allocation		0.170	
		(0.328)	
Constant	−0.232	−0.373	−3.241*
	(0.196)	(0.345)	(1.269)
Pseudo R^2	0.0239	0.0405	0.1882
Observations	810	810	234

Notes: Logistic regression coefficients with district-level fixed effects and robust standard errors clustered at the district level presented in parentheses. Outcomes are fallowing (Models 1 and 2) and resistant attitudes toward titling (Model 3). ** $p \leq 0.01$, * $p \leq 0.05$, + $p \leq 0.1$.

TABLE B.7. *Chapter 8: Analyses of the relationship between trust in chiefs and engagement with the state*

Outcome	Contact State Only	Contact Both	Contact Chief Only
	1	2	3
Distrust in State	−0.128**	−0.022	0.167**
	(0.035)	(0.034)	(0.033)
Trust in Customary Authority	−0.039	0.264**	0.340**
	(0.024)	(0.029)	(0.027)
State Performance	0.044	0.068*	−0.019
	(0.030)	(0.027)	(0.027)
Age	0.466**	0.687**	0.455**
	(0.042)	(0.038)	(0.042)
Education	0.563**	0.396**	0.053
	(0.067)	(0.061)	(0.052)
Urban	−0.003	−0.803**	−0.879**
	(0.061)	(0.082)	(0.073)
Economic Insecurity	0.072*	0.169**	0.209**
	(0.030)	(0.026)	(0.028)
Female	−0.497**	−0.780**	−0.457**
	(0.042)	(0.037)	(0.036)
Constant	−2.021**	−1.876**	−2.380**
	(0.249)	(0.210)	(0.229)
N	36,242	36,242	36,242

Notes: Multinomial logistic regression coefficients with country fixed effects. Standard errors in parentheses. Base outcome is Contact Neither. ** $p < 0.01$, * $p < 0.05$, + $p < 0.1$. Sample is twenty-six sub-Saharan African countries in Afrobarometer Round 6.

APPENDIX C

Marabouts and Land Titling in Senegal

Marabouts have important political and social roles in Senegal. This supplemental appendix provides a brief overview of this set of customary authorities and their influence over land. It situates them historically within Senegal and examines how the customary privilege theory applies to kinship relationships with marabouts in the contemporary era. Finally, it discusses how Senegal's marabouts offer an example of alternative strategies for retaining customary control of land through titling.

The marabouts discussed here are leaders from Sufi Islamic brotherhoods who have both "spiritual and temporal authority" over their followers.[1] These brotherhoods function as a type of customary institution in Senegal. Customary institutions are defined in the book's political science framework as institutions that derive their legitimacy from custom or tradition, which create communities bound together by shared expectations, norms, and practices. It is true that Senegal's brotherhoods also derive legitimacy from a global religion – Islam. However, these institutions govern a broader set of social and political relations with reference to historical norms and rules. As with customary institutions rooted in precolonial states, brotherhood institutions vary in their organizational structures, rules shaping privilege within the community, and processes for determining access to power. Note that the term marabout has multiple meanings in Senegal, and West Africa more generally; in some contexts, "marabout" may be used to refer to a Quranic teacher

---

[1] Villalón 2000, 475. See M. Diouf (2013a) for analysis of the political role of marabouts and brotherhood institutions in Senegal.

in a community or to someone with supernatural healing or divining powers.[2]

The vast majority of citizens in Senegal identify as members of one of four brotherhood institutions. The Tidjane brotherhood is the most numerous by population and is composed of multiple branches, most prominently the Niasse family branch in Kaolack and the Sy in Tivaouane.[3] In the 2002 census, 49 percent of the population reported affiliation with the Tidjane brotherhood. An additional 32 percent identified as members of the Mouride brotherhood, which is unified under a hierarchy based in its holy city of Touba. A further 9 percent reported membership in the Khadrya brotherhood and 1 percent were members of the Layenne brotherhood.[4] These brotherhood institutions coexist and overlap with other customary institutions that govern citizens' daily lives in contemporary Senegal.

C.1 MARABOUTS IN THE COLONIAL ERA

Marabouts were elites within many of Senegal's precolonial political institutions, but brotherhood institutions gained increasing prominence during the middle and late colonial era. In the Wolof kingdoms, including the Baol, Djoloff, and Cayor, marabouts were integrated into precolonial institutions as secretaries or advisers in the royal courts[5] and referred to as *sering*.[6] In the Fouta Toro precolonial state, marabouts were members of the aristocracy known by the title of *tyernoo*.[7] French conquest then produced economic, social, and political changes that created opportunities for brotherhood institutions founded by marabouts to emerge and gain influence.

Just as they did with other African leaders with popular legitimacy, the French colonial administration first approached marabouts as challengers to the state's authority. They created registries to track their social influence, financial circumstances, and family histories.[8] They attempted to weaken colonial era marabouts by imprisoning them and intervening in succession disputes. In 1895, the French exiled Cheikh Amadou Bamba, the founder of the Mouride brotherhood, fearing his ability to organize

---

[2] M. Ndiaye 2006.   [3] Villalón 1995.
[4] An additional 5 percent identified as "other Muslim" and 4 percent as Catholic. Agence Nationale de la Statistique et de la Démographie (ANSD), "Résultats Définitifs du Troisième Recensement Général de la Population et de l'Habitat–2002."
[5] D. Robinson 1991.   [6] Sow 2013, 50.   [7] Ibid.
[8] For colonial era examples, see the reports contained in *Politique musulmane, activité des marabouts* Box 67, 13G, ANS.

followers in resistance campaigns.[9] However, French attitudes toward the marabouts shifted as it became apparent that their influence was not weakening and that the leaders' abilities to mobilize labor made them effective economic and political brokers. Ultimately, marabouts became important intermediaries within the colonial state.[10]

Some marabouts in the colonial era parlayed their spiritual power into agricultural projects and control over land rights for villages of disciples. The Mouride brotherhood was particularly notable for their use of "the feudalism of the robe" to develop new areas for groundnut production.[11] They created religious training communities known as *daaras*, where disciples contributed agricultural labor. This model of agricultural production was a major source of revenue for the brotherhood.[12] Their colonial era *daaras* were concentrated in the center-west of Senegal, in the Cayor and Baol zones. Many scholars have described how the marabouts were able to develop new areas for groundnut production by co-opting the existing Wolof caste system.[13] In short, the historically aristocratic Wolof kingdoms featured large, mobile landless classes; these populations entered into patronage relationships with their spiritual leaders, as they had previously with nobles.

The marabouts established new communities of disciples in what is now known as the groundnut basin, but their customary land rights often lacked historical roots. Marabouts accessed land as gifts from followers, through purchasing or taking land used by semi-nomadic Pulaar populations, and by clearing unclaimed land. Unlike customary authorities who exerted power within established zones, the marabouts needed to create new territorial power. As a result of their weaker lineage-based land rights and their relationship with the colonial state, marabouts were some of the few customary authorities to take advantage of the opportunity for African titling in colonial Senegal. Senegal's land registries feature a handful of large titles issued to marabouts before 1960. These include four titles for Mouride marabouts of 400 to 500 ha each and three titles to marabouts from the Tidjane brotherhood, ranging from 100 ha to 140 ha. During this time, the Mourides also built their holy city of Touba on a 400 ha title.[14]

---

[9] Copans 1980 provides a review of the early literature on the Mouride brotherhood. See also Boone 1992; Guèye 2002; Beck 2008.
[10] Boone 1992.   [11] M. Diop 1972, 176.   [12] O'Brien 1971, 163–87.
[13] Raison 1968; Moitt 1989; D. Robinson 1991; Guèye 2002.
[14] The Mouride zone of influence around Touba was much larger than this 400 ha title. As discussed at the end of this appendix, they later gained a title for an additional 29,500 ha of land in Diourbel. See Ross 1995; Guèye 2002.

Consequently, marabouts were participants in the broader trend of land titling in the center-west of Senegal. By 1930, the land registration office in Kaolack, which serviced groundnut producers in the region, was processing between 100 and 300 applications for titles a year.[15] This zone had the highest concentration of new agricultural titles in the colony. For comparison, there were only 492 applications for land titles within all of Senegal in 1924. The marabouts are important to the history of colonial land tenure because the growth of land titles in the groundnut basin includes their practice of seeking land titles in their names for land cultivated by their followers. This practice continues today.

C.2 MARABOUTS IN THE CONTEMPORARY PERIOD: 2007–2013

Marabouts and Customary Privilege

Senegal's marabouts often function as customary authorities, in addition to being religious guides. As described in Chapter 2, customary authorities in African countries have three major roles: conflict resolution, organizing collective action for local public goods, and land allocation. Marabouts can also fulfill each of these functions.[16] However, the degree to which they do so varies among communities. The marabouts that most clearly operate as customary authorities are those considered to be the master (or owner) of the village, known in Wolof as *borom dek*. This often signifies the elder in the lineage of the village founder. The title of borom dek is synonymous with the village chief in some communities, but marabouts can also hold this title. This is particularly true of the marabouts who cleared land for their followers.[17] These villages are often described as maraboutic villages (*villages maraboutiques*). In many villages where a marabout is understood to be the owner of the village, the marabout's land authority is similar to that of the elder member of the founding lineage in other communities. Nevertheless, even in

---

[15] Calculations based on AOF, "Statistiques foncières: assiette de la propriété foncière consistance du domaine de l' État, livres foncières (1927–1935)," Box 2O9, Domaine et Enregistrement séries, ANS.

[16] Given their social embeddedness, popular legitimacy, and ties to the state, they can also serve as vote brokers much like chiefs elsewhere. This is particularly explicit within the Mouride institution, where the leader's *ndigal* or *ndiggël* (instruction) is understood as a call to vote for a certain candidate. See M. Diouf 2013b.

[17] Rocheteau 1975.

Appendix C: Marabouts and Land Titling Senegal

communities where a marabout is not considered to be "owner," one may be involved in village governance and serve as a customary authority.

The smallholder farmer survey presented in Chapter 7 sheds light on the role of marabouts and brotherhood institutions in land politics. The survey sampled two districts in Senegal: Podor and Mbacké. Podor is a prominently Tidjane brotherhood zone in northern Senegal and the home of the precolonial Fouta Toro state. Mbacké is in the center-west groundnut basin. It is the heartland of the Mouride brotherhood and includes the Mouride capital city, Touba. However, Mbacké is not exclusively a zone of Mouride influence. Randomly sampled villages in the district also featured Tidjane and Khadrya marabouts.[18] Within the two-district sample, 95 percent of households reported that there was a marabout in their village and 48 percent of households reported that the marabout had a role in land allocation.

The marabouts in the communities within the Senegal sample held social and political roles within local communities, beyond their positions as spiritual leaders embedded within brotherhood institutions. In all of these communities, the village chiefs and marabouts were collaborators. Some marabouts in the sample were related to the founders of the village or to the chief, while others were independent of these lineages. In all sampled villages in both districts, the village chief and marabout were members of the same brotherhood. Examining the impact of kinship with a marabout on the likelihood a household has a land title offers further evidence of a customary privilege effect on titling.

Table C.1 provides an overview of the differences among the communities within the sample by brotherhood. The sample was not designed to be representative of brotherhood institutions, so these descriptive statistics are not generalizable. This is particularly true of the one village where respondents reported that they were part of the Khadrya brotherhood. By contrast, fourteen communities were part of Tidjane institutions and nine identified as Mouride.

Of particular note in Table C.1 is the variation in whether community members reported that a marabout had a role in land allocation. In Mouride communities, 80 percent of respondents reported that marabouts were involved in land governance. In Tidjane communities, this percentage was far lower. Even within the Mbacké district alone, only 48 percent of respondents in Tidjane communities reported that the

---

[18] None of the sample villages in Mbacké were within the Touba land title.

TABLE C.1. *Differences among brotherhood communities in sample*

	Tidjane Marabout	Khadrya Marabout	Mouride Marabout
Marabout Involved in Land Allocation	Podor: 25% Mbacké: 48%	91%	80%
Kinship with Marabout	66%	94%	46%
Kinship with Chief	70%	91%	47%
Tribute *(to any customary authority)*	37%	79%	86%
Migrant *(10 years)*	5%	4%	5%
Local	94%	98%	69%
Accessed Land through Inheritance	93%	98%	73%
Have Title	Podor: 12% Mbacké: 1%	2%	2%
Fallow *(customary rights holders only)*	57%	65%	58%
Number of Respondents	577	46	279
Number of Communities	14	1	9
Sampled District Locations	Podor & Mbacké	Mbacké	Mbacké

marabout had a role in land allocation. The social differences among community members are also notable in this sample. While each of the three brotherhoods had similar rates of recent migration, the Mouride institutions had a lower number of members who reported that they were considered "local" and received their land through inheritance than in the other brotherhoods. This is consistent with the legacy of the Mouride daaras. On the other hand, these statistics show the risk of overemphasizing the uniqueness of Mouride villages: The majority of Mouride community members in this sample are locals (*autochtones*) and accessed their land through inheritance.

Table C.2 explores the customary privilege theory with kinship ties to marabouts as the measure of privilege. It reports the statistical effects of kinship with a village marabout on the likelihood a respondent had a title. Model 1 presents the findings of the baseline model. The negative and significant coefficient indicates that households that were related to a village marabout were significantly less likely to have titles for their land. This suggests that the status derived from social proximity to a village marabout is also a source of privilege within the community, similar to kinship with the village chiefs examined in Chapter 7. It supports the

TABLE C.2. *The impact of customary privilege in relation to Islamic marabouts in Senegal*

	1 Baseline	2 Brotherhood Type	3 Marabouts with Land Authority	4 Combined Chiefs and Marabout
Kinship with Marabout	−0.388*	−0.426**	−0.338**	−0.414
	(0.155)	(0.098)	(0.042)	(0.707)
Kinship with Chief				−0.780*
				(0.360)
Marabout Kinship * Chief Kinship				0.639
				(0.980)
Marabout Land Involvement			−0.910**	
			(0.006)	
Marabout Kinship * M Land Involvement			−0.460	
			(0.400)	
Mouride Marabout		−0.702**	−0.517**	
		(0.025)	(0.065)	
Infrastructure Controls	Y	Y	Y	Y
Wealth Control	Y	Y	Y	Y
Social Controls	Y	Y	Y	Y
Crop Controls	Y	Y	Y	Y
Land Access Controls	Y	Y	Y	Y
Constant	−18.57**	−18.16**	−16.13**	−17.20**
	(1.029)	(1.001)	(1.049)	(1.052)
Pseudo R^2	0.2005	0.2020	0.2192	0.2088
Observations	864	864	848	854

Notes: Logistic regression coefficients with district-level fixed effects and robust standard errors clustered at the district level presented in parentheses. Outcome is title. ** $p < 0.01$, * $p < 0.05$, + $p < 0.1$.

argument that, even among individuals with the same ethnicity, wealth, mode of land access, and education, customary privilege impacts the desirability of titling.

Model 2 considers the differences among brotherhoods. It compares households who reported that there was a Mouride marabout in their community to those who reported that the village marabout was Tidjane or Khadrya.[19] Relative to the Mourides, the Tidjane and Khadrya marabouts function with greater independence from their customary hierarchies and often come from lineages with longer roots in their specific villages. The statistical results indicate a negative and significant effect of having a Mouride marabout on the likelihood of title (Model 2). This suggests that the Mouride institution has a firmer grip on the land in its communities than other brotherhood institutions, even within the same district of the country. Nevertheless, kinship with a marabout remains a significant predictor of retaining exclusively customary land rights even when the brotherhood is considered in the model. The impact of kinship with a marabout is not limited to certain brotherhoods in the sample.

Model 3 examines the customary privilege effect in relation to marabouts with and without a direct role in land governance. It includes an interaction of the marabout's involvement in distributing land with the kinship variable, revealing that the effect of ties to the marabout was not contingent on his land authority. If kinship only reduced the likelihood of title when the marabout was involved in land governance, this would suggest that an individual's ability to influence (or expect preference from) a land authority was driving the customary privilege effect. Instead, these findings provide evidence that social proximity to a community leader shaped whether citizens adopted titles through more diffuse institutional privileges. It also highlights the importance of brotherhood institutions in communities, beyond their influence on land governance.

Finally, Model 4 reveals that kinship with the village chief had a more consistent negative impact on citizens' likelihoods of land titling than kinship with a marabout within these two districts in Senegal. The interaction of kinship with each authority is not significant, indicating that there was no additive effect of kinship with both chief and marabout on titling. The significant and negative coefficient for kinship with the chief in this model suggests that even among households with no relationship

---

[19] The sample includes only forty-seven households with a Khadyra marabout. The main effects remain the same when Tidjane and Khadrya are combined as a reference category and when Khadrya are excluded to make Tidjane alone the reference.

Appendix C: Marabouts and Land Titling Senegal 325

with the marabout, kinship with the chief significantly decreased the likelihood a household had title. However, the reverse was not true. Kinship with a marabout no longer had a significant effect when considering the village chief in the model. These findings reflect the wide variety of roles a marabout can have within a community and indicates that, on average, customary privilege in relation to a village chief was a stronger predictor of the property rights decisions of households in the sample. Overall, the results of Models 1–4 provide further support for the argument that customary privilege impacts how citizens weigh the costs and benefits of land titling. In addition, these findings highlight that marabouts are leaders embedded in customary institutions that have the power to structure community life and land relations.

C.3 MARABOUTS, TITLING, AND CUSTOMARY ADAPTATION

This book has demonstrated that fragmented state building through land titling generally moves in one direction, by converting customary property rights to state titles. It has also established that the control of land is a key resource for members of customary institutions. As strong institutions struggle to retain power over land, what alternative strategies are available to members of customary institutions to prevent defections from the institution's rules of control over land? This final section describes how the marabouts in Senegal provide an example of an adaptation strategy that is both exceptional and revealing: titling customary land in the name of a leader.

Titling a large area of land used by community members in the name of a customary authority formalizes the customary institution's control over a bounded domain. In doing so, customary authorities subvert the intention of the state's land policies, which is to issue titles to individual land users (and private commercial actors). This creates new challenges for the state. The case of the Mouride holy city of Touba is an important example of this practice. Touba is the second largest city in Senegal, with a population of over 500,000.[20] Touba is located on a land title that started as 400 ha in 1928 in the name of the Mouride leader, Serigne Mouhamadou Moustapha Mbacké.[21] In 2005 it was extended to 30,000 ha.[22] In addition to the city, there are also subsistence agricultural villages within the Touba land title.

---

[20] Guèye 2002.   [21] Ibid., 102.
[22] Abdoulaye Thiam, "Le Khalife Brandit le Titre Foncier de Touba: Statut Spécial de la Ville Sainte," *Sud Quotidien*, May 13, 2014. This has been reported elsewhere as between 29,500 and 33,000 ha.

Mouride marabouts have publicly argued that they should have complete authority over governance in the city because they hold title to it. For example, when the government insisted on gender parity in candidate lists for the 2014 local elections, the customary authorities in Touba refused and instead proposed a list of only men, claiming that they were outside of the state's jurisdiction *because of their land title*. After much debate, the state was ultimately unable to enforce its own law over the powerful customary institution.[23] Members of the institution treat the title as a recognition of sovereignty from the state as opposed to a recognition of a property right. While rare, the practice of titling land in the name of a customary authority for community use is an alternative form of resistance to the expansion of state control over land.

The Touba title is an important example of customary authorities subverting the state-building process to promote the institution's interest in land control. Chiefs creating their own property rights documents is a second example of such strategies. As discussed in Chapter 5, chiefs have invented new systems of written property rights, or "chiefs' titles," as an alternative to state titling in some parts of Zambia. These alternative forms of property rights are not supported or encouraged by the state; rather, the state's agents have promoted titling as the only secure form of land tenure. Both of these adaptation strategies are currently rare because they are extralegal and not sanctioned by the state. However, they reflect innovative ways in which members of customary institutions adapt to the expansion of statutory property rights, to retain elements of informality that allow them to continue to control access to land. Leaders of the strongest customary institutions – those that are most durable under pressure – are likely to keep exploring strategies for retaining customary land authority in the future and preventing defections from the institution's land allocation rules. This provides fruitful avenues for future research and suggests that even as global and local land markets grow, we can expect that customary institutions will continue to affect how state building occurs.

---

[23] Gifford 2016.

References

Acemoglu, Daron, Camilo García-Jimeno, and James A. Robinson. 2015. "State Capacity and Economic Development: A Network Approach." *American Economic Review* 105 (8): 2364–409.

Acemoglu, Daron, Simon Johnson, and James Robinson. 2003. "An African Success Story: Botswana." In *In Search of Prosperity: Analytical Narratives on Economic Growth*, edited by Dani Rodrik, 80–122. Princeton, NJ: Princeton University Press.

Acemoglu, Daron, James A. Robinson, and Rafael J. Santos. 2013. "The Monopoly of Violence: Evidence from Colombia." *Journal of the European Economic Association* 11 (S1): 5–44.

Acemoglu, Daron, Tristan Reed, and James A. Robinson. 2014. "Chiefs: Economic Development and Elite Control of Civil Society in Sierra Leone." *Journal of Political Economy* 122 (2): 319–68.

Adams, Adrian. 1977. "The Senegal River Valley: What Kind of Change?" *Review of African Political Economy* 4 (10): 33–59.

Afrobarometer. 2008. "Merged Round 4 Data." www.afrobarometer.org.

——2016. "Merged Round 6 Data." www.afrobarometer.org.

Ahmad, Syed. 1966. "On the Theory of Induced Invention." *The Economic Journal* 76 (302): 344–57.

Aiyedun, Adenike, and Ada Ordor. 2016. "Integrating the Traditional with the Contemporary in Dispute Resolution in Africa." *Law, Democracy & Development* 20 (1): 154–73.

Ajala, Adekunle. 1983. "The Nature of African Boundaries." *Africa Spectrum* 18 (2): 177–89.

Ajayi, Jacob F. A. 1968. "The Continuity of African Institutions under Colonialism." In *Emerging Themes of African History: Proceedings of the International Congress of African Historians Held at University College, Dar Es Salaam, October 1965*, edited by Terence O. Ranger, 189–200. Nairobi: East African Publishing House.

Ajayi, Jacob F. A., and Michael Crowder. 1974. "West Africa, 1919–1939: The Colonial Situation." In *History of West Africa*, Vol. 2, edited by Jacob F. A. Ajayi and Michael Crowder, 514–41. London: Longman.

Akinola, Shittu R. 2008. "Coping with Social Deprivation through Self-Governing Institutions in Oil Communities of Nigeria." *Africa Today* 55 (1): 89–107.

Albertus, Michael. 2015. *Autocracy and Redistribution: The Politics of Land Reform*. New York: Cambridge University Press.

Albrecht, Peter. 2017. "The Hybrid Authority of Sierra Leone's Chiefs." *African Studies Review* 60 (3): 159–80.

Alden Wily, Liz. 2012. "Enclosure Revisited: Putting the Global Land Rush in Historical Perspective." In *Handbook of Land and Water Grabs in Africa*, edited by Tony Allan, Martin Keulertz, Suvi Sojamo, and Jeroen Warner, 11–23. New York: Routledge.

———2015. Estimating National Percentages of Indigenous and Community Lands: Methods and Findings for Africa. Data file from *LandMark: The Global Platform of Indigenous and Community Land*.

Ali, Daniel Ayalew, Klaus Deininger, and Markus Goldstein. 2014. "Environmental and Gender Impacts of Land Tenure Regularization in Africa: Pilot Evidence from Rwanda." *Journal of Development Economics* 110: 262–75.

Ali, Merima, Odd-Helge Fjeldstad, and Abdulaziz B. Shifa. 2020. "European Colonization and the Corruption of Local Elites: The Case of Chiefs in Africa." *Journal of Economic Behavior & Organization* 179: 80–100.

Alissoutin, Rosnert Ludovic. 2008. *Les Défis du Développement Local au Sénégal*. Dakar: CODESRIA

Alsan, Marcella. 2015. "The Effect of the TseTse Fly on African Development." *American Economic Review* 105 (1): 382–410.

Alston, Lee J., Gary D. Libecap, and Bernardo Mueller. 1999. *Titles, Conflict, and Land Use: The Development of Property Rights and Land Reform on the Brazilian Amazon Frontier*. Ann Arbor: University of Michigan Press.

Anderson, Terry L., and Peter J. Hill. 1975. "The Evolution of Property Rights: A Study of the American West." *The Journal of Law and Economics* 18 (1): 163–79.

Andersson, Krister P. 2004. "Who Talks with Whom? The Role of Repeated Interactions in Decentralized Forest Governance." *World Development* 32 (2): 233–49.

André, Catherine, and Jean-Philippe Platteau. 1998. "Land Relations under Unbearable Stress: Rwanda Caught in the Malthusian Trap." *Journal of Economic Behavior & Organization* 34 (1): 1–47.

Andrews, Matt, Lant Pritchett, and Michael J. V. Woolcock. 2017. *Building State Capability: Evidence, Analysis, Action*. New York: Oxford University Press.

Ansell, Ben, and David Samuels. 2010. "Inequality and Democratization: A Contractarian Approach." *Comparative Political Studies* 43 (12): 1543–74.

Ansoms, An, and Thea Hilhorst. 2014. *Losing Your Land: Dispossession in the Great Lakes*. Suffolk: Boydell & Brewer Ltd.

Archibong, Belinda. 2019. "Explaining Divergence in the Long-Term Effects of Precolonial Centralization on Access to Public Infrastructure Services in Nigeria." *World Development* 121: 123–40.
Arriola, Leonardo R. 2009. "Patronage and Political Stability in Africa." *Comparative Political Studies* 42 (10): 1339–362.
Asiwaju, Anthony I. 1978. "Control through Coercion: A Study of the Indigenat Regime in French West African Administration, 1887–1946." *Journal of the Historical Society of Nigeria* 9 (3): 91–124.
Asombang, Raymond N. 1999. "Sacred Centers and Urbanization in West Central Africa." In *Beyond Chiefdoms: Pathways to Complexity in Africa*, edited by Susan Keech McIntosh, 80–87. Cambridge: Cambridge University Press.
Atwood, David A. 1990. "Land Registration in Africa: The Impact on Agricultural Production." *World Development* 18 (5): 659–71.
Autesserre, Séverine. 2010. *The Trouble with the Congo: Local Violence and the Failure of International Peacebuilding*. New York: Cambridge University Press.
Ayittey, George. 1991. *Indigenous African Institutions*. Leiden: Brill.
—2010. "Traditional Institutions and the State of Accountability in Africa." *Social Research: An International Quarterly* 77 (4): 1183–210.
Ba, Oumar. 1989. *L'Histoire du Sénégal au Jour le Jour: Période de la Conquête Coloniale, 1855–1856*. Dakar: Presses de l'Imprimerie Saint-Paul.
Babo, Alfred. 2010. "Conflits Fonciers, Ethnicité Politique et Guerre en Côte d'Ivoire." *Alternatives Sud* 17 (2): 95–118.
—2013. "The Crisis of Public Policies in Côte d'Ivoire: Land Law and the Nationality Trap in Tabou's Rural Communities." *Africa* 83 (1): 100–19.
Bado, Arsène Brice. 2015. "La Démocratie au Burkina Faso aux Prises avec les Systèmes Traditionnels de Gouvernance." *Études* 4: 19–30.
Baland, Jean-Marie, and Jean-Philippe Platteau. 1996. *Halting Degradation of Natural Resources: Is There a Role for Rural Communities?* New York: Food & Agriculture Organization of the United Nations.
—1999. "The Ambiguous Impact of Inequality on Local Resource Management." *World Development* 27 (5): 773–88.
Baldwin, Kate. 2014. "When Politicians Cede Control of Resources: Land, Chiefs, and Coalition-Building in Africa." *Comparative Politics* 46 (3): 253–71.
—2016. *The Paradox of Traditional Chiefs in Democratic Africa*. New York: Cambridge University Press.
—2019. "Elected MPs, Traditional Chiefs, and Local Public Goods: Evidence on the Role of Leaders in Co-Production from Rural Zambia." *Comparative Political Studies* 52 (12): 1925–56.
Baldwin, Kate, and Katharina Holzinger. 2019. "Traditional Political Institutions and Democracy: Reassessing Their Compatibility and Accountability." *Comparative Political Studies* 52 (12): 1747–74.
Banda, Janet L. 2011. "Romancing Customary Tenure: Challenges and Prospects for the Neo-liberal Suitor." In *The Future of African Customary Law*, edited

by Jeanmarie Fenrich, Paolo Galizzi, and Tracy E. Higgins, 312–35. New York: Cambridge University Press.
Bandyopadhyay, Sanghamitra, and Elliott Green. 2016. "Precolonial Political Centralization and Contemporary Development in Uganda." *Economic Development and Cultural Change* 64 (3): 471–508.
Barry, Boubacar. 1997. *Senegambia and the Atlantic Slave Trade*. New York: Cambridge University Press.
—2012. *The Kingdom of Waalo: Senegal before the Conquest*. New York: Diasporic Africa Press.
Bates, Robert H. 1981. *Markets and States in Tropical Africa: The Political Basis of Agricultural Policies*. Berkeley: University of California Press.
—1987. *Essays on the Political Economy of Rural Africa*. Berkeley: University of California Press.
—1989. *Beyond the Miracle of the Market: The Political Economy of Agrarian Development in Kenya*. Cambridge: Cambridge University Press.
Bauer, Gretchen. 2016. "'What Is Wrong with a Woman Being Chief?' Women Chiefs and Symbolic and Substantive Representation in Botswana." *Journal of Asian and African Studies* 51 (2): 222–37.
Baum, Christopher F. 2008. "Stata Tip 63: Modeling Proportions." *Stata Journal* 8 (2): 299–303.
Bayart, Jean-François. 1989. *L'État en Afrique. La Politique du Ventre*. Paris: Fayard.
Beall, Jo, and Mduduzi Ngonyama. 2009. "Indigenous Institutions, Traditional Leaders and Elite Coalitions for Development." (No. 55.2). Crisis States Research Centre Working Paper.
Beck, Linda J. 2001. "Reining in the Marabouts? Democratization and Local Governance in Senegal." *African Affairs* 100 (401): 601–21.
—2008. *Brokering Democracy in Africa: The Rise of Clientelist Democracy in Senegal*. New York: Palgrave Macmillan.
Bellemare, Marc F. 2013. "The Productivity Impacts of Formal and Informal Land Rights: Evidence from Madagascar." *Land Economics* 89 (2): 272–90.
Benjamin, Charles E. 2008. "Legal Pluralism and Decentralization: Natural Resource Management in Mali." *World Development* 36 (11): 2255–76.
Benjaminsen, Tor A., and Espen Sjaastad. 2002. "Race for the Prize: Land Transactions and Rent Appropriation in the Malian Cotton Zone." *The European Journal of Development Research* 14 (2): 129–52.
Benjaminsen, Tor A., Stein Holden, Christian Lund, and Espen Sjaastad. 2009. "Formalisation of Land Rights: Some Empirical Evidence from Mali, Niger and South Africa." *Land Use Policy* 26 (1): 28–35.
Bennett, Tom, Eva Brems, Giselle Corradi, Lia Nijzink, and Martien Schotsmans. 2012. *African Perspectives on Tradition and Justice*. Cambridge: Intersentia.
Berry, Sara. 1992. "Hegemony on a Shoestring: Indirect Rule and Access to Agricultural Land." *Africa* 62 (3): 327–55.
Besley, Timothy. 1995. "Property Rights and Investment Incentives: Theory and Evidence from Ghana." *Journal of Political Economy* 103 (5): 903–37.

Besley, Timothy, and Torsten Persson. 2010. "State Capacity, Conflict, and Development." *Econometrica* 78 (1): 1–34.
Betts, Raymond F. 1971. "The Establishment of the Medina in Dakar, Senegal, 1914." *Africa* 41 (2): 143–52.
Bianco, William T., and Robert H. Bates. 1990. "Cooperation by Design: Leadership, Structure, and Collective Dilemmas." *American Political Science Review* 84 (1): 133–47.
Bierschenk, Thomas, and Jean-Pierre Olivier de Sardan. 1997. "Local Powers and a Distant State in Rural Central African Republic." *The Journal of Modern African Studies* 35 (3): 441–68.
—2003. "Powers in the Village: Rural Benin between Democratisation and Decentralisation." *Africa* 73 (2): 145–73.
Bigagaza, Jean, Carolyne Abong, and Cecile Mukarubuga. 2002. "Land Scarcity, Distribution and Conflict in Rwanda." In *Scarcity and Surfeit: The Ecology of Africa's Conflicts*, edited by Jeremy Lind and Kathryn Sturman, 50–82. Pretoria: Institute for Security Studies.
Billaud, Anthony. 2009. "Négociation et Reconfiguration Des Pouvoirs Locaux. Le Cas de La Ville de Yoff Au Sénégal." *Afrique Contemporaine* 2 (30): 167–85.
Bleck, Jaimie. 2015. *Education and Empowered Citizenship in Mali*. Baltimore, MD: Johns Hopkins University Press.
Bleck, Jaimie, and Kristin Michelitch. 2015. "The 2012 Crisis in Mali: Ongoing Empirical State Failure." *African Affairs* 114 (457): 598–623.
Blundo, Giorgio. 1996. "Gérer les Conflits Fonciers au Sénégal: Le Rôle de l'Administration Locale dans le Sud-Est du Bassin Arachidier." *Cahiers Africains*, 23–24: 101–19.
Boafo-Arthur, Kwame. 2001. "Chieftaincy and Politics in Ghana since 1982." *West Africa Review* 3 (1): 140–57.
Boege, Volker. 2006. *Traditional Approaches to Conflict Transformation: Potentials and Limits*. Berlin: Berghof Research Center for Constructive Conflict Management.
Boone, Catherine. 1992. *Merchant Capital and the Roots of State Power in Senegal: 1930–1985*. New York: Cambridge University Press.
—2003. *Political Topographies of the African State: Territorial Authority and Institutional Choice*. New York: Cambridge University Press.
—2007. "Property and Constitutional Order: Land Tenure Reform and the Future of the African State." *African Affairs* 106 (425): 557–86.
—2014. *Property and Political Order in Africa: Land Rights and the Structure of Politics*. New York: Cambridge University Press.
Boserup, Ester. 1965. *The Condition of Agricultural Growth: The Economics of Agrarian Change under Population Pressure*. London: George Allen & Unwin LTD.
Brambor, Thomas, Agustín Goenaga, Johannes Lindvall, and Jan Teorell. 2020. "The Lay of the Land: Information Capacity and the Modern State." *Comparative Political Studies* 53 (2): 175–213.
Brasselle, Anne-Sophie, Frédéric Gaspart, and Jean-Philippe Platteau. 2002. "Land Tenure Security and Investment Incentives: Puzzling Evidence from Burkina Faso." *Journal of Development Economics* 67 (2): 373–418.

Brautigam, Deborah. 1996. "State Capacity and Effective Governance." In *Agenda for Africa's Economic Renewal*, edited by Benno J. Ndulu and Nicolas van de Walle, 81–108. Piscataway, NJ: Transaction Publishers, Inc.

Bromley, Daniel W. 1989. "Property Relations and Economic Development: The Other Land Reform." *World Development* 17 (6): 867–77.

—2009. "Formalising Property Relations in the Developing World: The Wrong Prescription for the Wrong Malady." *Land Use Policy* 26 (1): 20–27.

Brown, Taylor. 2005. "Contestation, Confusion and Corruption: Market-Based Land Reform in Zambia." In *Competing Jurisdictions: Settling Land Claims in Africa*, edited by Sandra Evers, Marja Spierenburg, and Harry Wels, 79–102. Leiden: Brill.

Bruce, John W. 1993. "Do Indigenous Tenure Systems Constrain Agricultural Development?" In *Land in African Agrarian Systems*, edited by Thomas J. Bassett and Donald Crummey, 35–56. Madison: University of Wisconsin Press.

—1998. "Country Profiles of Land Tenure: Africa 1996." LTC Research Paper 130. Land Tenure Center, University of Wisconsin–Madison.

Bruce, John W., Shem E. Migot-Adholla, and Joan Atherton. 1994. "The Findings and Their Policy Implications: Institutional Adaptation or Replacement." In *Searching for Land Tenure Security in Africa*, edited by John W. Bruce and Shem E. Migot-Adholla, 251–65. Dubuque, IA: Kendall/Hunt.

Bruschi, Francesca. 2005. "Politique Indigène et Administration au Sénégal (1890–1920)." *Il Politico* 70 (3): 501–22.

Buckley, Lila. 2013. "Chinese Land-Based Interventions in Senegal." *Development and Change* 44 (2): 429–50.

Buur, Lars, and Helene Maria Kyed. 2005. *State Recognition of Traditional Authority in Mozambique: The Nexus of Community Representation and State Assistance*. Discussion Paper 28, Uppsala: Nordic Africa Institute.

Byamugisha, Frank F. K. 2013. Securing Africa's Land for Shared Prosperity: A Program to Scale Up Reforms and Investments. *Africa Development Forum series*. Washington, DC: World Bank.

Camara, Sadio. 2015. *Le Gnokholo Traditionnel: Géographie-Histoire-Culture-Économie: Monographie d'une Ancienne Province du Sénégal*. Dakar: CODESRIA.

Cammett, Melani Claire. 2007. *Globalization and Business Politics in Arab North Africa: A Comparative Perspective*. New York: Cambridge University Press.

Carneiro, Robert L. 1970. "A Theory of the Origin of the State: Traditional Theories of State Origins Are Considered and Rejected in Favor of a New Ecological Hypothesis." *Science* 169 (3947): 733–38.

Centeno, Miguel A. 2002. *Blood and Debt: War and the Nation-State in Latin America*. University Park, PA: Penn State Press.

Centeno, Miguel A., Atul Kohli, and Deborah J. Yashar. 2017. "Chapter 1: Unpacking States in the Developing World: Capacity, Performance, and Politics." In *States in the Developing World*, edited by Miguel A. Centeno, Atul Kohli, and Deborah J. Yashar, 1–32. Cambridge: Cambridge University Press.

Chanock, Martin. 1985. *Law, Custom, and Social Order: The Colonial Experience in Malawi and Zambia*. Cambridge: Cambridge University Press.
—1991. "Paradigms, Policies, and Property: A Review of the Customary Law of Land Tenure." In *Law in Colonial Africa*, edited by Richard Roberts and Kristin Mann, 61–84. Portsmouth, NH: Heinemann.
Chapoto, Antony, T. S. Jayne, and Nicole M. Mason. 2011. "Widows' Land Security in the Era of HIV/AIDS: Panel Survey Evidence from Zambia." *Economic Development and Cultural Change* 59 (3): 511–47.
Chauveau, Jean-Pierre. 1998. "La Logique des Systèmes Coutumiers." In *Quelles Politiques Foncières en Afrique Rurale?*, edited by Philip Lavigne Delville, 66–75. Paris: Editions Karthala.
—2000. "Question Foncière et Construction Nationale en Côte d'Ivoire." *Politique Africaine* 2 (78): 94–125.
Chikulo, Bornwell. 2009. "Local Governance Reforms in Zambia: A Review." *Commonwealth Journal of Local Governance* (2): 98–106.
Chimhowu, Admos, and Phil Woodhouse. 2006. "Customary vs Private Property Rights? Dynamics and Trajectories of Vernacular Land Markets in Sub-Saharan Africa." *Journal of Agrarian Change* 6 (3): 346–71.
Chitonge, Horman. 2019. "Customary Land in Zambia: The New Scramble and the Evolving Socio-political Relations." In *Reclaiming Africa: Scramble and Resistance in the 21st Century*, edited by Sam Moyo, Praveen Jha, and Paris Yeros, 203–23. Singapore: Springer.
Chitonge, Horman, Orleans Mfune, Bridget B. Umar, Gear M. Kajoba, Diana Banda, and Lungisile Ntsebeza. 2017. "Silent Privatisation of Customary Land in Zambia: Opportunities for a Few, Challenges for Many." *Social Dynamics* 43 (1): 82–102.
Chiweza, Asiyati Lorraine. 2007. "The Ambivalent Role of Chiefs: Rural Decentralization Initiatives in Malawi." In *State Recognition and Democratization in Sub-Saharan Africa: A New Dawn for Traditional Authorities?*, edited by Lars Buur and Helene Maria Kyed, 53–78. New York: Palgrave Macmillan.
Coldham, Simon. 2000. "Land Reform and Customary Rights: The Case of Uganda." *Journal of African Law* 44 (1): 65–77.
Colin, Jean-Philippe, Pierre-Yves Le Meur, and Eric Léonard. 2009. "Introduction: Identifier les Droits et Dicter le Droit: La Politique des Programmes de Formalisation des Droits Fonciers." In *Les Politiques d'Enregistrement des Droits Fonciers: Du Cadre Légal aux Pratiques Locales*, edited by Jean-Philippe Colin, Pierre-Yves Le Meur, and Eric Léonard, 5–67. Paris: Editions Karthala.
Colin, Jean-Philippe, and Philip Woodhouse. 2010. "Introduction: Interpreting Land Markets in Africa." *Africa* 80 (1): 1–13.
Collier, Paul, and Anthony J. Venables. 2012. "Land Deals in Africa: Pioneers and Speculators." *Journal of Globalization and Development* 3 (1): 1–20.
Collin, Matthew. 2020. "Tribe or Title? The Effect of Coethnic Neighbors on the Demand for Formal Property Rights in a Tanzanian Slum." *Economic Development and Cultural Change* 68 (3): 899–945.

Colson, Elizabeth. 1948. "Modern Political Organization of the Plateau Tonga." *African Studies* 7 (2–3): 85–98.

—1949. *Life among the Cattle-Owning Plateau Tonga: The Material Culture of a Northern Rhodesia Native Tribe*. Vol. 6. Livingstone: Rhodes-Livingstone Museum.

—1966. "Land Law and Land Holdings among Valley Tonga of Zambia." *Southwestern Journal of Anthropological Research* 22 (1): 261–68.

Copans, Jean. 1980. *Les Marabouts de l'Arachide: La Confrérie Mouride et les Paysans du Sénégal*. Paris: Editions L'Harmattan.

Crowder, Michael. 1964. "Indirect Rule – French and British Style." *Africa* 34 (3): 197–205.

Daannaa, H. S. 1994. "The Acephalous Society and the Indirect Rule System in Africa: British Colonial Administrative Policy in Retrospect." *Journal of Legal Pluralism and Unofficial Law* 26 (34): 61–85.

Dahou, Tarik, and Abdourahmane Ndiaye. 2009. "Les Enjeux d'une Réforme Foncière." In *Libéralisation et Politique Agricole Au Sénégal*, edited by Tarik Dahou, 49–69. Paris: Editions Karthala.

D'Arcy, Michelle, and Marina Nistotskaya. 2017. "State First, Then Democracy: Using Cadastral Records to Explain Governmental Performance in Public Goods Provision." *Governance* 30 (2): 193–209.

de Juan, Alexander. 2017. "'Traditional' Resolution of Land Conflicts: The Survival of Precolonial Dispute Settlement in Burundi." *Comparative Political Studies* 50 (13): 1835–68.

de Kadt, Daniel, and Horacio A. Larreguy. 2018. "Agents of the Regime? Traditional Leaders and Electoral Politics in South Africa." *The Journal of Politics* 80 (2): 382–99.

de Soto, Hernando. 2000. *The Mystery of Capital: Why Capitalism Triumphs in the West and Fails Everywhere Else*. New York: Basic Books.

de Sousa Santos, Boaventura. 2006. "The Heterogeneous State and Legal Pluralism in Mozambique." *Law & Society Review* 40 (1): 39–76.

Deininger, Klaus, and Hans Binswanger. 1999. "The Evolution of the World Bank's Land Policy: Principles, Experience, and Future Challenges." *The World Bank Research Observer* 14 (2): 247–76.

Deininger, Klaus, and Derek Byerlee. 2011. *Rising Global Interest in Farmland: Can It Yield Sustainable and Equitable Benefits?* Washington, DC: World Bank Publications.

Deininger, Klaus, and Gershon Feder. 2001. "Land Institutions and Land Markets." In *Handbook of Agricultural Economics*, Vol. 1, edited by Bruce L. Gardner and Gordon C. Rausser, 287–331. Amsterdam: Elsevier Science.

Delaunay, Daniel. 1984. *De la Captivité à l'Exil: Histoire et Démographie des Migrations Paysannes dans la Moyenne Vallée du Fleuve Sénégal*. Travaux et Documents de L'ORSTOM 174. Paris: ORSTOM.

di Tella, Rafael, Sebastian Galiani, and Ernesto Schargrodsky. 2007. "The Formation of Beliefs: Evidence from the Allocation of Land Titles to Squatters." *The Quarterly Journal of Economics* 122 (1): 209–41.

Dia, Mamadou. 1996. *Africa's Management in the 1990s and Beyond: Reconciling Indigenous and Transplanted Institutions*. Washington, DC: The World Bank.
Diagne, Pathé. 1967. *Pouvoir Politique Traditionnel et Afrique Occidentale: Essaies sur les Institutions Politiques Précoloniales*. Paris: Présence Africaine.
Diamond, Larry J. 2008. *The Spirit of Democracy: The Struggle to Build Free Societies throughout the World*. New York: Macmillan Publishers.
Diamond, Larry J., Marc F. Plattner, and Andreas Schedler. 1999. "Introduction." In *The Self-Restraining State: Power and Accountability in New Democracies*, edited by Andreas Schedler, Larry J. Diamond, and Marc. F Plattner, 1–10. Boulder, CO: Lynne Rienner Publishers.
Diaw, Mariteuw Chimère. 2005. "Modern Economic Theory and the Challenge of Embedded Tenure Institutions: African Attempts to Reform Local Forest Policies." In *Institutions, Sustainability, and Natural Resources: Institutions for Sustainable Forest Management*, edited by Shashi Kant and R. Albert Berry, 43–81. Dordrecht: Springer.
Dickerman, Carol W., Grenville Barnes, John W. Bruce, et al. 1989. "Security of Tenure and Land Registration in Africa: Literature Review and Synthesis." Madison: University of Wisconsin–Madison, Land Tenure Center.
Dieng, Rama Salla. 2017. "'Land Grabbing' and the Politics of Evidence: The Case of Senegal." *Africa Insight* 46 (4): 25–40.
Dionne, Kim Yi. 2018. *Doomed Interventions: The Failure of Global Responses to AIDS in Africa*. Cambridge: Cambridge University Press.
Diop, Abdoulaye-Bara. 1981. *La Société Wolof: Tradition et Changement: les Systèmes d'Inégalité et de Domination*. Paris: Editions Karthala.
Diop, Cheikh Anta. 1960. *L'Afrique Noire Pré-Coloniale*. Paris: Présence Africaine.
Diop, Djibril. 2006. *Décentralisation et Gouvernance Locale au Sénégal: Quelle Pertinence pour le Développement Local?* Paris: Editions L'Harmattan.
—2013. "La Problématique de l'Accès au Foncier à Dakar." In *Repenser les Moyens d'une Sécurisation Foncière Urbaine: Le Cas de l'Afrique Francophone*, edited by Michel Max Raynaud, Djibril Diop, and Claire Simonneau, 69–91. Montréal: Éditions Trames.
Diop, Majhemout. 1972. *Histoire des Classes Sociales dans l'Afrique de l'Ouest*, Vol. 2. Paris: François Maspéro.
Diop, Momar Coumba. 2013. *Sénégal, 2000–2012: Les Institutions et Politiques Publiques à l'Épreuve d'une Gouvernance Libérale*. Paris: Editions Karthala.
Diop, Momar Coumba, Mamadou Diouf, and Aminata Diaw. 2000. "Le Baobab a été Déraciné. L'Alternance au Sénégal." *Politique Africaine* 2 (78): 157–79.
Diop, Oumar, Moussa Bocar Fofana, and Amadou Abdoulaye Fall. 2008. "Caractérisation et Typologie des Exploitations Agricoles Familiales du Sénégal. Tome 1. Vallée du Fleuve Sénégal." *Institut Sénégalais de Recherches Agricoles* 8 (1): 1–38.
Diouf, Mamadou. 2000. "Assimilation Coloniale et Identités Religieuses de la Civilité des Originaires des Quatre Communes (Sénégal)." *Canadian Journal of African Studies/La Revue Canadienne Des Études Africaines* 34 (3): 565–87.

—2001. *Histoire du Sénégal: Le Modèle Islamo-Wolof et Ses Périphéries*. Paris: Maisonneuve & Larose.
—ed. 2013a. *Tolerance, Democracy, and Sufis in Senegal*. New York: Columbia University Press.
—2013b. "Introduction: The Public Role of 'Good Islam': Sufi Islam and the Administration of Pluralism." In *Tolerance, Democracy, and Sufis in Senegal*, edited by Mamadou Diouf, 1–35. New York: Columbia University Press.
Djiré, Moussa. 2007. Land Registration in Mali-No Land Ownership for Farmers? Observations from Peri-Urban Bamako. *Drylands Issue Paper 144*. London: International Institute for Environment and Development (IIED).
Dubertret, Fabrice, and Liz Alden Wily. 2015. "Percent of Indigenous and Community Lands." Data file from *LandMark: The Global Platform of Indigenous and Community Lands*.
du Plessis, Jean. 2005. "The Growing Problem of Forced Evictions and the Crucial Importance of Community-Based, Locally Appropriate Alternatives." *Environment and Urbanization* 17 (1): 123–34.
Englebert, Pierre. 2000a. "Pre-colonial Institutions, Post-colonial States, and Economic Development of Tropical Africa." *Political Research Quarterly* 53 (1): 7–36.
—2000b. *State Legitimacy and Development in Africa*. Boulder, CO: Lynne Rienner Publishers.
—2002. "Patterns and Theories of Traditional Resurgence in Tropical Africa." *Mondes en Développement* 2 (118): 51–64.
Ensminger, Jean. 1990. "Co-opting the Elders: The Political Economy of State Incorporation in Africa." *American Anthropologist* 92 (3): 662–75.
—1992. *Making a Market: The Institutional Transformation of an African Society*. Cambridge: Cambridge University Press.
—1997. "Changing Property Rights: Reconciling Formal and Informal Rights to Land in Africa." In *The Frontiers of the New Institutional Economics*, edited by John N. Drobak and John V. C. Nye, 165–96. San Diego: Academic Press.
Evans, Peter. 1997. "The Eclipse of the State? Reflections on Stateness in an Era of Globalization." *World Politics* 50 (1): 62–87.
Fall, Mamadou, and Moustapha Ngaïdo. 2016. *Land Investments, Accountability and the Law: Lessons from Senegal. Land, Investment and Rights Series*. London: International Institute for Environment and Development (IIED).
Fanchette, Sylvie. 2005. "Patrimoines Locaux et Législations Foncières à l'Heure de la Décentralisation en Haute-Casamance (Sénégal)." In *Patrimoines Naturels au Sud: Territoires, Identités et Stratégies Locales*, edited by Marie-Christine Cormier-Salem, Dominique Juhé-Beaulaton, Jean Boutrais, and Bernard Roussel, 97–134. Marseille: IRD Editions.
Fanthorpe, Richard. 2006. "On the Limits of Liberal Peace: Chiefs and Democratic Decentralization in Post-war Sierra Leone." *African Affairs* 105 (418): 27–49.
Faye, Jacques. 2008. *Foncier et Décentralisation: l'Expérience du Sénégal. Dossier des Zones Arides Series 149*. London: International Institute for Environment and Development (IIED).

Feder, Gershon, and Raymond Noronha. 1987. "Land Rights Systems and Agricultural Development in Sub-Saharan Africa." *The World Bank Research Observer* 2 (2): 143–69.
Fergusson, Leopoldo, Horacio Larreguy, and Juan Felipe Riaño. 2018. "Political Competition and State Capacity: Evidence from a Land Allocation Program in Mexico." No. 0011. LACEA Working Paper Series. Latin American and The Caribbean Economic Association.
Firmin-Sellers, Kathryn. 2000a. "Custom, Capitalism, and the State: The Origins of Insecure Land Tenure in West Africa." *Journal of Institutional and Theoretical Economics (JITE)* 156 (3): 513–30.
—2000b. "Institutions, Context, and Outcomes: Explaining French and British Rule in West Africa." *Comparative Politics* 32 (3): 253–72.
Firmin-Sellers, Kathryn, and Patrick Sellers. 1999. "Expected Failures and Unexpected Successes of Land Titling in Africa." *World Development* 27 (7): 1115–28.
Fisiy, Cyprian F. 1992. *Power and Privilege in the Administration of Law: Land Law Reforms and Social Differentiation in Cameroon.* Research Reports 48. Leiden: African Studies Centre.
—1995. "Chieftaincy in the Modern State: An Institution at the Crossroads of Democratic Change." *Paideuma* 41: 49–62.
Fokwang, Jude. 2009. *Mediating Legitimacy: Chieftaincy and Democratisation in Two African Chiefdoms.* Oxford: African Books Collective.
Fortes, Meyer, and Edward Evan Evans-Pritchard. 1940. *African Political Systems.* London: Oxford University Press.
Gagné, Marie. 2019. "Resistance against Land Grabs in Senegal: Factors of Success and Partial Failure of an Emergent Social Movement." In *The Politics of Land (Research in Political Sociology, Vol. 26)*, edited by Tim Bartley, 173–203. Bingley: Emerald Publishing Limited.
Galvan, Dennis Charles. 2004. *The State Must Be Our Master of Fire: How Peasants Craft Culturally Sustainable Development in Senegal.* Berkeley: University of California Press.
Gann, Lewis H. 1969. *A History of Northern Rhodesia: Early Days to 1953.* New York: Humanities Press.
Gardini, Marco. 2013. "Oracles, Chieftaincies, and Witchcraft Accusations in South-Western Togo." *The Journal of Legal Pluralism and Unofficial Law* 45 (2): 249–65.
Geddes, Barbara. 1994. *Politician's Dilemma: Building State Capacity in Latin America.* Berkeley: University of California Press.
Gellar, Sheldon. 1976. *Structural Changes and Colonial Dependency: Senegal, 1885–1945.* Beverly Hills, CA: Sage Publications.
—1982. *Senegal: An African Nation between Islam and the West.* Boulder, CO: Westview Press, Inc.
—2005. *Democracy in Senegal: Tocquevillian Analytics in Africa.* New York: Palgrave Macmillan.
Gennaioli, Nicola, and Ilia Rainer. 2007. "The Modern Impact of Precolonial Centralization in Africa." *Journal of Economic Growth* 12 (3): 185–234.

Geschiere, Peter. 1993. "Chiefs and Colonial Rule in Cameroon: Inventing Chieftaincy, French and British Style." *Africa* 63 (2): 151–75.

Ghebru, Hosaena, Bethlehem Koru, and Alemayehu Seyoum Taffesse. 2016. "Household Perception and Demand for Better Protection of Land Rights in Ethiopia." Working Paper 83, International Food Policy Research Institute.

Gibson, Clark C. 1999. *Politicians and Poachers: The Political Economy of Wildlife Policy in Africa*. New York: Cambridge University Press.

Gibson, Clark C., Margaret A. McKean, and Elinor Ostrom. 2000. *People and Forests: Communities, Institutions, and Governance*. Cambridge, MA: MIT Press.

Gibson, Clark C., Fabrice E. Lehoucq, and John T. Williams. 2002. "Does Privatization Protect Natural Resources? Property Rights and Forests in Guatemala." *Social Science Quarterly* 83 (1): 206–25.

Gifford, Paul. 2016. "Religion and Politics in Contemporary Senegal." *African Affairs* 115 (461): 688–709.

Gochberg, William. 2021. "The Social Costs of Titling Land: Evidence from Uganda." *World Development* 142: 105376.

Goist, Mitchell, and Florian G. Kern. 2018. "Traditional Institutions and Social Cooperation: Experimental Evidence from the Buganda Kingdom." *Research and Politics* 5 (1): 1–9.

Goldstein, Markus, and Christopher Udry. 2008. "The Profits of Power: Land Rights and Agricultural Investment in Ghana." *Journal of Political Economy* 116 (6): 981–1022.

Gomez, Michael A. 2002. *Pragmatism in the Age of Jihad: The Precolonial State of Bundu*. Cambridge: Cambridge University Press.

Goodfellow, Tom, and Stefan Lindemann. 2013. "The Clash of Institutions: Traditional Authority, Conflict and the Failure of 'Hybridity' in Buganda." *Commonwealth & Comparative Politics* 51 (1): 3–26.

Gordon, David. 2001. "Owners of the Land and Lunda Lords: Colonial Chiefs in the Borderlands of Northern Rhodesia and the Belgian Congo." *The International Journal of African Historical Studies* 34 (2): 315–38.

Gottlieb, Jessica. 2016. "Greater Expectations: A Field Experiment to Improve Accountability in Mali." *American Journal of Political Science* 60 (1): 143–57.

—2017. "Explaining Variation in Broker Strategies: A Lab-in-the-Field Experiment in Senegal." *Comparative Political Studies* 50 (11): 1556–92.

Gould, Jeremy. 2010. *Left Behind: Rural Zambia in the Third Republic*. Lusaka: Lembani Trust.

Goundiam, Ousmane. 1965. "Aspects du Régime Foncier Sénégalais." *Civilisations* 15 (1): 82–90.

Grabowski, Richard. 1988. "The Theory of Induced Institutional Innovation: A Critique." *World Development* 16 (3): 385–94.

Gray, Leslie C., and Michael Kevane. 1999. "Diminished Access, Diverted Exclusion: Women and Land Tenure in Sub-Saharan Africa." *African Studies Review* 42 (2): 15–39.

—2001. "Evolving Tenure Rights and Agricultural Intensification in Southwestern Burkina Faso." *World Development* 29 (4): 573–87.

Greif, Avner. 1994. "Cultural Beliefs and the Organization of Society: A Historical and Theoretical Reflection on Collectivist and Individualist Societies." *Journal of Political Economy* 102 (5): 912–50.

—2006. *Institutions and the Path to the Modern Economy: Lessons from Medieval Trade.* New York: Cambridge University Press.

Grossman, Guy, and Janet I. Lewis. 2014. "Administrative Unit Proliferation." *American Political Science Review* 108 (1): 196–217.

Guèye, Cheikh. 2002. *Touba: La Capitale des Mourides.* Paris: Editions Karthala.

Guirkinger, Catherine, and Jean-Philippe Platteau. 2014. "The Effect of Land Scarcity on Farm Structure: Empirical Evidence from Mali." *Economic Development and Cultural Change* 62 (2): 195–238.

Habyarimana, James, Macartan Humphreys, Daniel N. Posner, and Jeremy M. Weinstein. 2009. *Coethnicity: Diversity and the Dilemmas of Collective Action.* New York: Russell Sage Foundation.

Hanna, Alexander John. 1960. *The Story of the Rhodesias and Nyasaland.* London: Faber.

Hardin, Garrett. 1968. "The Tragedy of the Commons." *Science* 162 (3859): 1243–48.

Hardy, Georges. 1921. *La Mise en Valeur du Sénégal de 1817 à 1854.* Paris: Larose.

Harris, Adam, and Lauren Honig. 2022. "Mutual Dependence and Collective Action." *Journal of Politics,* forthcoming.

Hassan, Mai. 2016. "A State of Change: District Creation in Kenya after the Beginning of Multi-party Elections." *Political Research Quarterly* 69 (3): 510–21.

Helmke, Gretchen, and Steven Levitsky. 2004. "Informal Institutions and Comparative Politics: A Research Agenda." *Perspectives on Politics* 2 (4): 725–40.

Hendricks, Fred, and Lungisile Ntsebeza. 1999. "Chiefs and Rural Local Government in Post-apartheid South Africa." *African Journal of Political Science/Revue Africaine de Science Politique* 4 (1): 99–126.

Henn, Soeren J. 2020. "Compliments or Substitutes? How Institutional Arrangements Bind Chiefs and the State in Africa." Working Paper, University of Chicago.

Herbst, Jeffrey. 2000. *States and Power in Africa: Comparative Lessons in Authority and Control.* Princeton, NJ: Princeton University Press.

Herring, Ronald J. 2002. "State Property Rights in Nature (with Special Reference to India)." In *Land, Property, and the Environment,* edited by John Richards, 263–97. Oakland, CA: Institute for Contemporary Studies.

Hesseling, Gerti, and John Eichelsheim. 2009. "Tenure Security in the Periphery of Ziguinchor: The Impact of Politics and Social Relations." In *Legalising Land Rights: Local Practices, State Responses and Tenure Security in Africa, Asia and Latin America,* edited by Janine M. Ubink, André J. Hoekema, and Willem J. Assies, 271–92. Leiden: Leiden University Press.

Higgins, Daniel, Tim Balint, Harold Liversage, and Paul Winters. 2018. "Investigating the Impacts of Increased Rural Land Tenure Security: A Systematic Review of the Evidence." *Journal of Rural Studies* 61: 34–62.

Hilhorst, Thea. 2000. "Women's Land Rights: Current Developments in Sub-Saharan Africa." In *Evolving Land Rights, Policy and Tenure in Africa*, edited by Camilla Toulmin and Julian Quan, 181–96. London: DFID/IIED/NRI.

Hintze, Otto. 1975. "The Formation of States and Constitutional Development: A Study in History and Politics." In *The Historical Essays of Otto Hintze*, edited by Felix Gilbert, 157–77. New York: Oxford University Press

Hjort, Jonas. 2010. "Pre-colonial Culture, Post-colonial Economic Success? The Tswana and the African Economic Miracle." *The Economic History Review* 63 (3): 688–709.

Holland, Alisha C. 2017. *Forbearance as Redistribution: The Politics of Informal Welfare in Latin America*. New York: Cambridge University Press.

Holzinger, Katharina, Roos Haer, Axel Bayer, Daniela M. Behr, and Clara Neupert-Wentz. 2019. "The Constitutionalization of Indigenous Group Rights, Traditional Political Institutions, and Customary Law." *Comparative Political Studies* 52 (12): 1775–809.

Holzinger, Katharina, Florian G. Kern, and Daniela Kromrey. 2016. "The Dualism of Contemporary Traditional Governance and the State Institutional Setups and Political Consequences." *Political Research Quarterly* 69 (3): 469–81.

Honig, Lauren. 2022. "The Power of the Pen: Informal Property Rights Documents in Zambia." *African Affairs*, forthcoming.

Huillery, Elise. 2009. "History Matters: The Long-Term Impact of Colonial Public Investments in French West Africa." *American Economic Journal: Applied Economics* 1 (2): 176–215.

Hydén, Göran. 1980. *Beyond Ujamaa in Tanzania: Underdevelopment and an Uncaptured Peasantry*. Berkeley: University of California Press.

Ikenberry, G. John. 1994. "History's Heavy Hand: Institutions and the Politics of the State." University of Pennsylvania. Unpublished Manuscript.

Jacob, Jean-Pierre, and Pierre-Yves Le Meur. 2010. *Politique de la Terre et de l'Appartenance: Droits Fonciers et Citoyenneté Locale dans les Sociétés du Sud*. Paris: Editions Karthala.

Jacoby, Hanan G., and Bart Minten. 2007. "Is Land Titling in Sub-Saharan Africa Cost-Effective? Evidence from Madagascar." *The World Bank Economic Review* 21 (3): 461–85.

Joireman, Sandra Fullerton. 2011. *Where There Is No Government: Enforcing Property Rights in Common Law Africa*. New York: Oxford University Press.

Kaag, Mayke, Yaram Gaye, and Marieke Kruis. 2011. "Land Conflicts in Senegal Revisited: Continuities and Emerging Dynamics." In *Land, Law and Politics in Africa: Mediating Conflict and Reshaping the State*, edited by Jan Abbink, and Mirjam de Bruijn, 141–61. African Dynamics Series. Leiden: Brill.

Kajoba, Gear M. 2002. "Women and Land in Zambia: A Case Study of Small-Scale Farmers in Chenena Village, Chibombo District, Central Zambia." *Eastern Africa Social Science Research Review* 18 (1): 35–61.

Kane, Oumar. 2004. *La Première Hégémonie Peule: le Fuuta Tooro de Koli Tenella à Almaami Abdul*. Paris: Editions Karthala.

Kanyinga, Karuti. 1998. "Politics and Struggles for Access to Land: 'Grants from Above' and 'Squatters' in Coastal Kenya." *European Journal of Development Research* 10 (2): 50–69.

Kay, George. 1967. *Social Aspects of Village Regrouping in Zambia*. Institute for Social Research, University of Zambia.

Kenyatta, Jomo. 1938. *Facing Mount Kenya: The Traditional Life of the Gikuyu*. Nairobi: East African Educational Publishers.

Kevane, Michael, and Leslie C. Gray. 1999. "A Woman's Field Is Made at Night: Gendered Land Rights and Norms in Burkina Faso." *Feminist Economics* 5 (3): 1–26.

Ki-Zerbo, Joseph. 1972. *Histoire de l'Afrique Noire, d'Hier à Demain*. Paris: Hatier.

Klaus, Kathleen, and Matthew I. Mitchell. 2015. "Land Grievances and the Mobilization of Electoral Violence Evidence from Côte d'Ivoire and Kenya." *Journal of Peace Research* 52 (5): 622–35.

Klopp, Jacqueline M. 2000. "Pilfering the Public: The Problem of Land Grabbing in Contemporary Kenya." *Africa Today* 47 (1): 7–26.

Kobusingye, Doreen Nancy, Mathijs van Leeuwen, and Han van Dijk. 2016. "Where Do I Report My Land Dispute? The Impact of Institutional Proliferation on Land Governance in Post-conflict Northern Uganda." *The Journal of Legal Pluralism and Unofficial Law* 48 (2): 238–55.

Koné, Mariatou, and Jean-Pierre Chauveau. 1998. "Décentralisation de la Gestion Foncière et 'Petits Reçus': Pluralisme des Règles, Pratiques Locales et Régulation Politique dans le Centre-Ouest-Ivoirien." *Bulletin de l'APAD* 16: 1–24.

Koopman, Jeanne. 2012. "Land Grabs, Government, Peasant and Civil Society Activism in the Senegal River Valley." *Review of African Political Economy* 39 (124): 655–64.

Koopmans, Ruud, and Susanne Rebers. 2009. "Collective Action in Culturally Similar and Dissimilar Groups: An Experiment on Parochialism, Conditional Cooperation, and Their Linkages." *Evolution and Human Behavior* 30 (3): 201–11.

Koter, Dominika. 2013. "Urban and Rural Voting Patterns in Senegal: The Spatial Aspects of Incumbency, c. 1978–2012." *Journal of Modern African Studies* 51 (4): 653–79.

—2016. *Beyond Ethnic Politics in Africa*. New York: Cambridge University Press.

Kouassigan, Guy-Adjété. 1966. *L'Homme et la Terre : Droits Fonciers Coutumiers et Droit de Propriété*. Paris: O.R.S.T.O.M.

Kranton, Rachel E. 1996. "The Formation of Cooperative Relationships." *The Journal of Law, Economics, and Organization* 12 (1): 214–33.

Kuba, Richard, and Carola Lentz. 2006. *Land and the Politics of Belonging in West Africa*. Leiden: Brill.

Kyed, Helene Maria, and Lars Buur. 2007. "Introduction: Traditional Authority and Democratization in Africa." In *State Recognition and Democratization in Sub-Saharan Africa*, edited by Lars Buur and Helene Maria Kyed, 1–28. New York: Springer.

Lal, Priya. 2015. *African Socialism in Postcolonial Tanzania: Between the Village and the World*. New York: Cambridge University Press.

Langworthy, Harry W. 1971. "Conflict among Rulers in the History of Undi's Chewa Kingdom." *Transafrican Journal of History* 1 (1): 1–23.

Lavigne Delville, Philippe. 1999. *Comment Articuler Législation Nationale et Droits Fonciers Locaux: Expériences en Afrique de l'Ouest Francophone. Dossier des Zones Arides Series 86*. London: International Institute for Environment and Development (IIED).

—2000. "Harmonizing Formal Law and Customary Land Rights in French-Speaking West Africa." In *Evolving Land Rights, Policy and Tenure in Africa*, edited by Camilla Toulmin and Julian Quan, 97–122. London: DFID/IIED/NRI.

—2002. "When Farmers Use 'Pieces of Paper' to Record Their Land Transactions in Francophone Rural Africa: Insights into the Dynamics of Institutional Innovation." *The European Journal of Development Research* 14 (2): 89–108.

Lee, Melissa M., and Nan Zhang. 2017. "Legibility and the Informational Foundations of State Capacity." *The Journal of Politics* 79 (1): 118–32.

Lentz, Carola. 2013. *Land, Mobility, and Belonging in West Africa: Natives and Strangers*. Bloomington: Indiana University Press.

Levitsky, Steven, and María Victoria Murillo. 2009. "Variation in Institutional Strength." *Annual Review of Political Science* 12: 115–33.

Libecap, Gary D. 1989. *Contracting for Property Rights*. Cambridge: Cambridge University Press.

Lieberman, Evan S. 2002. "Taxation Data as Indicators of State-Society Relations: Possibilities and Pitfalls in Cross-National Research." *Studies in Comparative International Development* 36 (4): 89–115.

Lipton, Michael. 1977. *Why Poor People Stay Poor: Urban Bias in World Development*. Cambridge, MA: Harvard University Press.

—2009. *Land Reform in Developing Countries: Property Rights and Property Wrongs*. London: Routledge.

Liversage, Vincent. 1945. *Land Tenure in the Colonies*. Cambridge: Cambridge University Press.

Logan, Carolyn. 2009. "Selected Chiefs, Elected Councillors and Hybrid Democrats: Popular Perspectives on the Co-existence of Democracy and Traditional Authority." *The Journal of Modern African Studies* 47 (1): 101–28.

—2013. "The Roots of Resilience: Exploring Popular Support for African Traditional Authorities." *African Affairs* 112 (448): 353–76.

Lugard, Lord. 1922. *The Dual Mandate in British Tropical Africa*. 5th ed. London: F. Cass & Co.

Lukhero, Matshakaza Blackson, and John Barnes. 1999. "Chieftainship, Tradition and Change in Ngoni Society." *Cambridge Journal of Anthropology* 21 (2): 17–40.

Lund, Christian. 2001. "Questioning Some Assumptions about Land Tenure." In *Politics, Property and Production in the West African Sahel: Understanding Natural Resources Management*, edited by Tor Arve Benjaminsen and Christian Lund, 144–62. Uppsala: Scandinavian Institute of African Studies.
—2008. *Local Politics and the Dynamics of Property in Africa*. New York: Cambridge University Press.
—2011. "Property and Citizenship: Conceptually Connecting Land Rights and Belonging in Africa." *Africa Spectrum* 46 (3): 71–75.
Magaloni, Beatriz, Alberto Díaz-Cayeros, and Alexander Ruiz Euler. 2019. "Public Good Provision and Traditional Governance in Indigenous Communities in Oaxaca, Mexico." *Comparative Political Studies* 52 (12): 1841–80.
Mahoney, James. 2010. *Colonialism and Postcolonial Development: Spanish America in Comparative Perspective*. New York: Cambridge University Press.
Mahoney, James, and Kathleen Thelen. 2009. "A Theory of Gradual Institutional Change." In *Explaining Institutional Change: Ambiguity, Agency, and Power*, edited by James Mahoney and Kathleen Thelen, 1–39. New York: Cambridge University Press.
Mainga, Mutumba. 1973. *Bulozi under the Luyana Kings: Political Evolution and State Formation in Pre-colonial Zambia*. London: Longman.
Mamdani, Mahmood. 1996. *Citizen and Subject: Contemporary Africa and the Legacy of Late Colonialism*. Princeton, NJ: Princeton University Press.
Manji, Ambreena S. 2006. *The Politics of Land Reform in Africa: From Communal Tenure to Free Markets*. London: Zed Books.
Mann, Gregory. 2009. "What Was the 'Indigénat'? The 'Empire of Law' in French West Africa." *The Journal of African History* 50 (3): 331–53.
Mann, Michael. 1984. "The Autonomous Power of the State: Its Origins, Mechanisms and Results." *European Journal of Sociology* 25 (2): 185–213.
Matchaya, Greenwell. 2009. "Land Ownership Security in Malawi." *African Journal of Agricultural Research* 4 (1): 001–013.
Mbow, Penda. 2000. "Démocratie, Droits Humains et Castes au Sénégal." *Journal des Africanistes* 70 (1–2): 71–91.
Médard, Claire, and Valérie Golaz. 2013. "Creating Dependency: Land and Gift-Giving Practices in Uganda." *Journal of Eastern African Studies* 7 (3): 549–68.
Meebelo, Henry S. 1971. *Reaction to Colonialism: A Prelude to the Politics of Independence in Northern Zambia 1893–1939*. Manchester: Manchester University Press.
Meek, Charles Kingsley. 1946. *Land Law and Custom in the Colonies*. Oxford: Oxford University Press.
Meinzen-Dick, Ruth, and Esther Mwangi. 2009. "Cutting the Web of Interests: Pitfalls of Formalizing Property Rights." *Land Use Policy* 26 (1): 36–43.
Meinzen-Dick, Ruth, and Rajendra Pradhan. 2002. "Legal Pluralism and Dynamic Property Rights," (no. 22) CAPRi Working Paper, Washington, DC: IFPRI.

Miceli, Thomas J., C. F. Sirmans, and Joseph Kieyah. 2001. "The Demand for Land Title Registration: Theory with Evidence from Kenya." *American Law and Economics Review* 3 (2): 275–87.

Michalopoulos, Stelios, and Elias Papaioannou. 2013. "Pre-colonial Ethnic Institutions and Contemporary African Development." *Econometrica* 81 (1): 113–52.

Migdal, Joel S. 1988. *Strong Societies and Weak States: State-Society Relations and State Capabilities in the Third World*. Princeton, NJ: Princeton University Press.

Miguel, Edward, and Mary Kay Gugerty. 2005. "Ethnic Diversity, Social Sanctions, and Public Goods in Kenya." *Journal of Public Economics* 89 (11–12): 2325–68.

Moitt, Bernard. 1989. "Slavery and Emancipation in Senegal's Peanut Basin: The Nineteenth and Twentieth Centuries." *The International Journal of African Historical Studies* 22 (1): 27–50.

Moore, Sally Falk. 1978. *Law as Process: An Anthropological Approach*. London: Routledge.

—1986. *Social Facts and Fabrications "Customary" Law on Kilimanjaro, 1880–1980*. New York: Cambridge University Press.

Moyo, Sam, Praveen Jha, and Paris Yeros. 2019. "The Scramble for Land and Natural Resources in Africa." In *Reclaiming Africa: Scramble and Resistance in the 21st Century*, edited by Sam Moyo, Praveen Jha, and Paris Yeros, 3–30. Singapore: Springer.

Mukuka, Richard. 2020. *Ababemba no Bubemba: Understanding the Bemba Cultural World*. Kasama: Kalebalika AVS.

Müller-Crepon, Carl. 2020. "Continuity or Change? (In)direct Rule in British and French Colonial Africa." *International Organization* 74 (4): 707–41.

Müller-Crepon, Carl, Philipp Hunziker, and Lars-Erik Cederman. 2021. "Roads to Rule, Roads to Rebel: Relational State Capacity and Conflict in Africa." *Journal to Conflict Resolution* 65 (2–3): 563–90.

Muriaas, Ragnhild Louise. 2009. "Local Perspectives on the 'Neutrality' of Traditional Authorities in Malawi, South Africa and Uganda." *Commonwealth & Comparative Politics* 47 (1): 28–51.

Murtazashvili, Ilia, and Jennifer Murtazashvili. 2015. "Anarchy, Self-Governance, and Legal Titling." *Public Choice* 162 (3/4): 287–305.

Musambachime, Mwelwa C. 1992. "Colonialism and the Environment in Zambia, 1890–1964." In *Guardians in Their Time: Experiences of Zambians under Colonial Rule, 1890–1964*, edited by Samuel N. Chipungu, 8–29. London: Macmillan Press.

Musembi, Celestine Nyamu. 2007. "De Soto and Land Relations in Rural Africa: Breathing Life into Dead Theories about Property Rights." *Third World Quarterly* 28 (8): 1457–78.

Muyakwa, Stephen L., Mulela Margaret Munalula, and Fredrick S. Mudenda. 2003. *Impact of the Land Act 1995 on the Livelihoods of the Poor and Peasants in Zambia*. Lusaka: Catholic Commission for Justice and Peace (CCJDP).

Nabudere, Dani W. 2004. "Traditional and Modern Political Systems in Contemporary Governance in Africa." *Journal of African Elections* 3 (1): 13–41.

Nathan, Noah L. 2019. "Electoral Consequences of Colonial Invention: Brokers, Chiefs, and Distribution in Northern Ghana." *World Politics* 71 (3): 417–56.

Ndiaye, Abdourahmane. 2019. "The Scramble for Agricultural Land in Senegal: Land Privatisation and Inclusion?" In *Reclaiming Africa: Scramble and Resistance in the 21st Century*, edited by Sam Moyo, Praveen Jha, and Paris Yeros, 143–62. Singapore: Springer.

Ndiaye, Modou. 2006. "Le Champ Sémantique du Mot *Marabout* en Français du Sénégal." In *Mots, Termes et Contexte: Actes des Septièmes Journées Scientifiques du Réseau de Chercheurs Lexicologie Terminologie Traduction*, edited by Daniel Blampain, Philippe Thoiron, and Marc van Campenhoudt, 337–46. Paris: Éditions des Archives Contemporaines.

N'gaide, Abderrahmane. 2015. "Logiques d'Heritages et Superposition de Droits: Conflits de Pratiques dans l'Afrique Contemporaine le 'Légitime' Contre le 'Légal.'" In *Land in the Struggles for Citizenship in Africa*, edited by Sam Moyo, Dzodzi Tsikata, and Yakham Diop, 69–98. Dakar: CODESRIA.

Ngwenya, Barbara Ntombi, and Donald Letsholo Kgathi. 2011. "Traditional Public Assembly (Kgotla) and Natural Resources Management in Ngamiland, Botswana." In *Rural Livelihoods, Risk and Political Economy of Access to Natural Resources in the Okavango Delta, Botswana*, edited by Donald Letsholo Kgathi, Barbara Ntombi Ngwenya, and Michael B. Darkoh, 231–48. Environmental Research Advances series. Hauppauge, NY: Nova Science Publishers.

Ng'ombe, Austine and Ramin Keivani. 2013. "Customary Land Reform to Facilitate Private Investment in Zambia: Achievements, Potential and Limitations." *Urban Forum* 24 (1): 33–48.

Ng'ong'ola, Clement. 1982. "The Design and Implementation of Customary Land Reforms in Central Malawi." *Journal of African Law* 26 (2): 115–32.

Niane, Djibril Tamsir. 1989. *Histoire des Mandingues de l'Ouest: Le Royaume du Gabou*. Paris: Editions Karthala.

Njoh, Ambe J. 2017. *Planning in Contemporary Africa: The State, Town Planning and Society in Cameroon*. London: Routledge.

Nkrumah, Kwame. 1963. *Africa Must Unite*. New York: Frederick A. Praeger.

Nkurunziza, Emmanuel. 2015. "Implementing and Sustaining Land Tenure Regularization in Rwanda." In *How Innovations in Land Administration Reform Improve on Doing Business: Cases from Lithuania, the Republic of Korea, Rwanda and the United Kingdom*, edited by Thea Hilhorst and Frederic Meunier, 10–20. Washington, DC: World Bank.

Nolte, Kerstin. 2013. "Large-Scale Agricultural Investments under Poor Land Governance Systems: Actors and Institutions in the Case of Zambia." Giga Working Papers No. 221.

North, Douglass C. 1990. *Institutions, Institutional Change and Economic Performance*. New York: Cambridge University Press.

North, Douglass C., and Robert P. Thomas. 1973. *The Rise of the Western World: A New Economic History*. New York: Cambridge University Press.

Ntsebeza, Lungisile. 2005. *Democracy Compromised: Chiefs and the Politics of the Land in South Africa*. Leiden: Brill.

Nuesiri, Emmanuel O. 2014. "The Re-emergence of Customary Authority and Its Relation with Local Democratic Government." (No. 6) RFGI Working Paper, Responsive Forest Governance Initiative, Dakar: CODESRIA.

Nyamnjoh, Francis B. 2014. "'Our Traditions Are Modern, Our Modernities Traditional': Chieftaincy and Democracy in Contemporary Cameroon and Botswana." *Modern Africa: Politics, History and Society* 2 (2): 13–62.

Oba, Abdulmumini A. 2011. "The Future of Customary Law in Africa." In *The Future of African Customary Law*, edited by Jeanmarie Fenrich, Paolo Galizzi, and Tracy E. Higgins, 58–80. New York: Cambridge University Press.

Obeng-Odoom, Franklin. 2012. "Land Reforms in Africa: Theory, Practice, and Outcome." *Habitat International* 36 (1): 161–70.

—2020. *Property, Institutions, and Social Stratification in Africa*. New York: Cambridge University Press.

Obeng-Odoom, Franklin, and Frank Stilwell. 2013. "Security of Tenure in International Development Discourse." *International Development Planning Review* 35 (4): 315–33.

O'Brien, Donal B. Cruise. 1971. *The Mourides of Senegal: The Political and Economic Organization of an Islamic Brotherhood*. Oxford: Clarendon Press.

Ocheje, Paul D. 2007. "'In the Public Interest': Forced Evictions, Land Rights and Human Development in Africa." *Journal of African Law* 51 (2): 173–214.

O'Donnell, Guillermo A. 1998. "Horizontal Accountability in New Democracies." *Journal of Democracy* 9 (3): 112–26.

Ogot, Bethwell A. 1963. "British Administration in the Central Nyanza District of Kenya, 1900–60." *The Journal of African History* 4 (2): 249–73.

Okoth-Ogendo, Hastings. 1989. "Some Issues of Theory in the Study of Tenure Relations in African Agriculture." *Africa* 59 (1): 6–17.

Olson, Mancur. 1965. *The Logic of Collective Action: Public Goods and the Theory of Groups*. Cambridge, MA: Harvard University Press.

Onoma, Ato Kwamena. 2009. *The Politics of Property Rights Institutions in Africa*. New York: Cambridge University Press.

Osafo-Kwaako, Philip, and James A. Robinson. 2013. "Political Centralization in Pre-colonial Africa." *Journal of Comparative Economics* 41 (1): 6–21.

Ostrom, Elinor. 1990. *Governing the Commons: The Evolution of Institutions for Collective Action*. New York: Cambridge University Press.

Ouedraogo, Hubert M. G. 2011. "De la Connaissance à la Reconnaissance des Droits Fonciers Africains Endogènes." *Études Rurales* 187: 79–93.

Owolabi, Olukunle Patrick. 2017. "The Developmental Legacies of the Bifurcated Colonial State: Statistical Evidence from Sixty-Seven British, French, and Portuguese Colonies." Working Paper no. 419. Helen Kellogg Institute for International Studies, University of Notre Dame.

Paller, Jeffrey W. 2019. *Democracy in Ghana: Everyday Politics in Urban Africa*. New York: Cambridge University Press.

Palmer, Robin. 2000. "Land Tenure Insecurity on the Zambian Copperbelt, 1998: Anyone Going Back to the Land?" *Social Dynamics: A Journal of African Studies* 26 (2): 154–70.

Papke, Leslie E., and Jeffrey M. Wooldridge. 1996. "Econometric Methods for Fractional Response Variables with an Application to 401(k) Plan Participation Rates." *Journal of Applied Econometrics* 11 (6): 619–32.

—2008. "Panel Data Methods for Fractional Response Variables with an Application to Test Pass Rates." *Journal of Econometrics* 145 (1): 121–33.

Peters, Pauline E. 2004. "Inequality and Social Conflict over Land in Africa." *Journal of Agrarian Change* 4 (3): 269–314.

Pheffer, Paul Edward. 1975. "Railroads and Aspects of Social Change in Senegal, 1878–1933." Doctoral Dissertation, University of Pennsylvania.

Phillips, Anne. 1989. *The Enigma of Colonialism: An Interpretation of British Policy in West Africa*. Bloomington: Indiana University Press.

Phillips, Lucie Colvin. 1981. *Historical Dictionary of Senegal*. Metuchen, NJ: Scarecrow Press.

Phiri, Kings M. 1988. "Pre-colonial States of Central Malawi: Towards a Reconstruction of Their History." *The Society of Malawi Journal* 41 (1): 1–29.

Pierson, Paul. 2000. "Increasing Returns, Path Dependence, and the Study of Politics." *American Political Science Review* 94 (2): 251–67.

Pinckney, Thomas C., and Peter K. Kimuyu. 1994. "Land Tenure Reform in East Africa: Good, Bad or Unimportant?" *Journal of African Economies* 3 (1): 1–28.

Pitcher, M. Anne. 2002. *Transforming Mozambique: The Politics of Privatization, 1975–2000*. New York: Cambridge University Press.

Place, Frank, and Keijiro Otsuka. 2002. "Land Tenure Systems and Their Impacts on Agricultural Investments and Productivity in Uganda." *Journal of Development Studies* 38 (6): 105–28.

Place, Frank, Michael Roth, and Peter Hazell. 1994. "Land Tenure Security and Agricultural Performance in Africa: Overview of Research Methodology." In *Searching for Land Tenure Security in Africa*, edited by John W. Bruce and Shem E. Migot-Adholla, 15–39. Dubuque, IA: Kendall/Hunt.

Plançon, Caroline. 2009. "Droit, Foncier et Développement: Les Enjeux de la Notion de Propriété: Étude de Cas au Sénégal." *Revue Tiers Monde* 50 (200): 837–51.

Platteau, Jean-Philippe. 1996. "The Evolutionary Theory of Land Rights as Applied to Sub-Saharan Africa: A Critical Assessment." *Development and Change* 27 (1): 29–86.

—2000a. "Does Africa Need Land Reform?" In *Evolving Land Rights, Policy, and Tenure in Africa*, edited by Camilla Toulmin and Julian Quan, 51–74. London: DFID/IIED/NRI.

—2000b. *Institutions, Social Norms, and Economic Development*. Amsterdam: Harwood Academic Publishers.

Posner, Daniel N. 2003. "The Colonial Origins of Ethnic Cleavages: The Case of Linguistic Divisions in Zambia." *Comparative Politics* 35 (2): 127–46.

—2005. *Institutions and Ethnic Politics in Africa.* New York: Cambridge University Press.

Pottier, Johan. 2005. "'Customary Land Tenure' in Sub-Saharan Africa Today: Meanings and Contexts." In *From the Ground Up: Land Rights, Conflict and Peace in Sub-Saharan Africa,* edited by Christopher David Huggins and Jenny Clover, 53–75. Pretoria: ACTS Press/Institute for Security Studies.

Prunier, Gérard. 1995. *The Rwanda Crisis: History of a Genocide.* New York: Columbia University Press.

Quan, Julian. 2000. "Land Tenure, Economic Growth and Poverty in Sub-Saharan Africa." In *Evolving Land Rights, Policy, and Tenure in Africa,* edited by Camilla Toulmin and Julian Quan, 31–50. London: International Institute for Environment and Development (IIED).

Raison, Jean-Pierre. 1968. "La Colonisation des Terres Neuves Intertropicales." *Études Rurales* (31): 5–112.

Ranger, Terence. 1983. "The Invention of Tradition in Colonial Africa." In *The Invention of Tradition,* edited by Eric J. Hobsbawm and Terence Ranger, 211–62. Cambridge: Cambridge University Press.

Ribot, Jesse C. 1998. "Theorizing Access: Forest Profits along Senegal's Charcoal Commodity Chain." *Development and Change* 29 (2): 307–41.

—1999. "Decentralisation, Participation and Accountability in Sahelian Forestry: Legal Instruments of Political-Administrative Control." *Africa* 69 (1): 23–65.

Ribot, Jesse C., and Nancy Lee Peluso. 2003. "A Theory of Access." *Rural Sociology* 68 (2): 153–81.

Richens, Peter. 2009. "The Economic Legacies of the 'Thin White Line': Indirect Rule and the Comparative Development of Sub-Saharan Africa." *African Economic History* 37: 33–102.

Roberts, Andrew. 1973. *A History of the Bemba: Political Growth and Change in North-Eastern Zambia before 1900.* London: Longman.

—1976. *A History of Zambia.* London: Heinemann.

Robinson, David. 1975. *Chiefs and Clerics: Abdul Bokar Kan and Futa Toro, 1853–1891.* Oxford: Clarendon Press.

—1991. "Beyond Resistance and Collaboration: Amadu Bamba and the Murids of Senegal." *Journal of Religion in Africa* 21 (2): 149–71.

Robinson, James A. 2002. "States and Power in Africa by Jeffrey I. Herbst: A Review Essay." *Journal of Economic Literature* 40 (2): 510–19.

Rocheteau, Guy. 1975. "Pionniers Mourides au Sénégal: Colonisation des Neuves et Transformations d'une Économie Paysanne." *Cahiers ORSTOM* 12 (1): 19–53.

Ross, Eric. 1995. "Touba: A Spiritual Metropolis in the Modern World." *Canadian Journal of African Studies/La Revue Canadienne Des Études Africaines* 29 (2): 222–59.

Roubaud, Émile. 1918. "L'État Actuel et l'Avenir du Commerce des Arachides au Sénégal." *Annales de Géographie* 148–49: 357–71.

Runge, Carlisle Ford. 1986. "Common Property and Collective Action in Economic Development." *World Development* 14 (5): 623–35.

Ruttan, Vernon W., and Yujiro Hayami. 1984. "Toward a Theory of Induced Institutional Innovation." *The Journal of Development Studies* 20 (4): 203–23.

Saint-Martin, Yves-Jean. 1989. *Le Sénégal sous le Second Empire: Naissance d'un Empire Colonial (1850–1871)*. Paris: Editions Karthala.

Samatar, Abdi I. 2005. "National Institutions for Development. The Case of Botswana." In *Towards a New Map of Africa*, edited by Ben Wisner, Camilla Toulmin, and Rutendo Chitiga, 229–64. Abingdon: Routledge.

Sandefur, Justin, and Bilal Siddiqi. 2013. "Delivering Justice to the Poor: Theory and Experimental Evidence from Liberia." In *World Bank Workshop on African Political Economy*, Washington, DC.

Schmidt, Stephan, and Edmund Zakayo. 2018. "Land Formalization and Local Leadership in Moshi, Tanzania." *Habitat International* 74: 18–26.

Schmitter, Phillippe C. 1999. "The Limits of Horizontal Accountability." In *The Self-Restraining State: Power and Accountability in New Democracies*, edited by Andreas Schedler, Larry Diamond, and Marc. F. Plattner, 59–62. Boulder, CO: Lynne Rienner Publishers.

Scott, James C. 1998. *Seeing Like a State: How Certain Schemes to Improve the Human Condition Have Failed*. New Haven, CT: Yale University Press.

Shipton, Parker. 1988. "The Kenyan Land Tenure Reform: Misunderstandings in the Public Creation of Property." In *Land and Society in Contemporary Africa*, edited by R. E. Downs and Stephen P. Reyna, 91–135. Lebanon, NH: University Press of New England.

Signé, Landry, and Koffi Korha. 2016. "Horizontal Accountability and the Challenges for Democratic Consolidation in Africa: Evidence from Liberia." *Democratization* 23 (7): 1254–71.

Sikor, Thomas, and Christian Lund. 2009. "Access and Property: A Question of Power and Authority." *Development and Change* 40 (1): 1–22.

Sikor, Thomas, and Daniel Müller. 2009. "The Limits of State-Led Land Reform: An Introduction." *World Development* 37 (8): 1307–16.

Simbizi, Marie Christine Rohan Dushimyimana, Mark Bennett, and Jaap Zevenbergen. 2014. "Land Tenure Security: Revisiting and Refining the Concept for Sub-Saharan Africa's Rural Poor." *Land Use Policy* 36: 231–38.

Sitko, Nicholas J. 2010. "Fractured Governance and Local Frictions: The Exclusionary Nature of a Clandestine Land Market in Southern Zambia." Special issue, *Africa* 80 (1): 36–55.

Sjaastad, Espen, and Daniel W. Bromley. 1997. "Indigenous Land Rights in Sub-Saharan Africa: Appropriation, Security and Investment Demand." *World Development* 25 (4): 549–62.

Slater, Dan. 2008. "Can Leviathan Be Democratic? Competitive Elections, Robust Mass Politics, and State Infrastructural Power." *Studies in Comparative International Development* 43 (3–4): 252–72.

Smith, Robert E. 2003. "Land Tenure Reform in Africa: A Shift to the Defensive." *Progress in Development Studies* 3 (3): 210–22.

Snyder, Francis G. 1981. "Colonialism and Legal Form: The Creation of 'Customary Law' in Senegal." *The Journal of Legal Pluralism and Unofficial Law* 13 (19): 49–90.

Soifer, Hillel. 2008. "State Infrastructural Power: Approaches to Conceptualization and Measurement." *Studies in Comparative International Development* 43 (3–4): 231–51.

Sow, Ibrahima. 2013. *Le Maraboutage au Sénégal*. Dakar: Institut Fondamental d'Afrique Noire Cheikh Anta Diop.

Spear, Thomas. 2003. "Neo-traditionalism and the Limits of Invention in British Colonial Africa." *The Journal of African History* 44: 3–27.

Spruyt, Hendrik. 2002. "The Origins, Development, and Possible Decline of the Modern State." *Annual Review of Political Science* 5 (1): 127–49.

Straus, Scott. 2013. *The Order of Genocide: Race, Power, and War in Rwanda*. Ithaca, NY: Cornell University Press.

Swidler, Ann. 2013. "Cultural Sources of Institutional Resilience: Lessons from Chieftaincy in Rural Malawi." In *Social Resilience in the Neoliberal Era*, edited by Peter A. Hall and Michèle Lamont, 319–45. New York: Cambridge University Press.

Swidler, Ann, and Susan Cotts Watkins. 2017. *A Fraught Embrace: The Romance and Reality of AIDS Altruism in Africa*. Princeton, NJ: Princeton University Press.

Tandjigora, Abdou Karim. 2015. *Colonisation et Inégalités de Développement au Sénégal : Le Boundou et le Gadiaga: 1885–1980*. Paris: Harmattan.

Taylor, Brian D., and Roxana Botea. 2008. "Tilly Tally: War-Making and State-Making in the Contemporary Third World." *International Studies Review* 10 (1): 27–56.

Thaler, Gregory M. 2013. "Land Grabbing: Issues and Implications." In *The Oxford Handbook of Food, Politics, and Society*, edited by Ronald J. Herring. New York: Oxford University Press.

Thies, Cameron G. 2004. "State Building, Interstate and Intrastate Rivalry: A Study of Post-colonial Developing Country Extractive Efforts, 1975–2000." *International Studies Quarterly* 48 (1): 53–72.

—2009. "National Design and State Building in Sub-Saharan Africa." *World Politics* 61 (4): 623–69.

Tilly, Charles. 1990. *Coercion, Capital and European States: AD 990–1992*. Cambridge: Blackwell.

Tine, Ngone Diop, and Mouhamadou Sy. 2003. "Women and Land in Africa: A Case Study from Senegal." In *Women and Land in Africa: Culture, Religion, and Realizing Women's Rights*, edited by Lynne Muthoni Wanyeki, 207–31. London: ZED Books/David Philip Publishers.

Toulmin, Camilla, and Julian Quan. 2000a. "Evolving Land Rights, Tenure and Policy in Sub-Saharan Africa." In *Evolving Land Rights, Policy, and Tenure in Africa*, edited by Camilla Toulmin and Julian Quan, 1–30. London: International Institute for Environment and Development (IIED).

—2000b. "Registering Customary Land Rights." In *Evolving Land Rights, Policy, and Tenure in Africa*, edited by Camilla Toulmin and Julian Quan, 207–28. London: International Institute for Environment and Development (IIED).

Traoré, Samba. 1997. "Les Législations et les Pratiques Locales en Matière de Foncier et de Gestion des Ressources Naturelles au Sénégal." In

Développement Durable au Sahel, edited by Philippe Tersiguel and Charles Becker, 89–102. Paris: Editions Karthala.
Tripp, Aili Mari. 2004. "Women's Movements, Customary Law, and Land Rights in Africa: The Case of Uganda." *African Studies Quarterly* 7 (4): 1–19.
Tsai, Lily L. 2007. *Accountability without Democracy: Solidary Groups and Public Goods Provision in Rural China*. New York: Cambridge University Press.
Ubink, Janine. 2007. "Traditional Authority Revisited: Popular Perceptions of Chiefs and Chieftaincy in Peri-Urban Kumasi, Ghana." *The Journal of Legal Pluralism and Unofficial Law* 39 (55): 123–61.
Unruh, Jon D. 2008. "Carbon Sequestration in Africa: The Land Tenure Problem." *Global Environmental Change* 18 (4): 700–7.
Valsecchi, Pierluigi. 2003. "Kingship, Chieftaincy and Politics: A View from Nzema (Ghana)." In *Le Retour des Rois: Les Autorités Traditionnelles et l'État en Afrique Contemporaine*, edited by Claude-Helene Perrot and François-Xavier Fauvelle-Aymar, 63–81. Paris: Editions Karthala.
van Binsbergen, Wim M. J. 1987. "Chiefs and the State in Independent Zambia: Exploring the Zambian National Press." *Journal of Legal Pluralism and Unofficial Law* 19 (25–27): 139–201.
van der Laan, Ellen. 1984. "Factors Contributing to the Rapid Development of Small-Scale Irrigation Schemes along the Senegal River." *Organising the Distribution and Use of Irrigation Water* 17 (4): 203–13.
van de Walle, Nicholas. 2007. "Meet the New Boss, Same as the Old Boss? The Evolution of Political Clientelism in Africa." In *Patrons, Clients and Policies: Patterns of Democratic Accountability and Political Competition*, edited by Herbert Kitschelt and Steven I. Wilkinson, 50–67. New York: Cambridge University Press.
—2009. "The Institutional Origins of Inequality in Sub-Saharan Africa." *Annual Review of Political Science* 12 (1): 307–27.
van Gelder, Jean-Louis. 2010. "What Tenure Security? The Case for a Tripartite View." *Land Use Policy* 27 (2): 449–56.
van Rouveroy van Nieuwaal, E. Adriaan B. 1996. "States and Chiefs: Are Chiefs Mere Puppets?" *Journal of Legal Pluralism and Unofficial Law* 28 (37–38): 39–78.
—1999. "Chieftaincy in Africa: Three Facets of a Hybrid Role." In *African Chieftaincy in a New Socio-political Landscape*, edited by E. Adriaan B. van Rouveroy van Nieuwaal and Rijk van Dijk, 21–47. Hamburg: LIT Verlag.
Verdier, Raymond. 1971. "Évolution et Réformes Foncières de l'Afrique Noire Francophone." *Journal of African Law* 15 (1): 85–101.
Villalón, Leonardo Alfonso. 1995. *Islamic Society and State Power in Senegal: Disciples and Citizens in Fatick*. New York: Cambridge University Press
—2000. "The Moustarchidine of Senegal: The Family Politics of a Contemporary Tijan Movement." In *La Tijâniyya: Une Confrérie Musulmane à la Conquête de l'Afrique*, edited by J.-L. Triaud and David Robinson, 469–97. Paris: Editions Karthala.

Viola, Lynne. 1996. *Peasant Rebels under Stalin: Collectivization and the Culture of Peasant Resistance*. New York: Oxford University Press.
Wane, Yaya. 1966. *Les Toucoleurs du Fouta Tooro (Sénégal): Stratification Sociale et Structure Familiale*. Dakar: Centre National de la Recherche/Scientifique/Institut Fondamental d'Afrique Noire (CNRS/IFAN).
Watson, William. 1958. *Tribal Cohesion in a Money Economy: A Study of the Mambwe People of Zambia*. Manchester: Manchester University Press.
—1976. "British Colonial Policy and Tribal Political Organization." In *A Century of Change in Eastern Africa*, edited by William Arens, 169–82. Berlin: De Gruyter Mouton.
Weber, Eugen. 1976. *Peasants into Frenchmen: The Modernization of Rural France, 1870–1914*. Redwood City, CA: Stanford University Press.
White, Charles Matthew Newton. 1957. "Clan, Chieftainship, and Slavery in Luvale Political Organization." *Africa* 27 (1): 59–75.
Wilfahrt, Martha. 2018. "Precolonial Legacies and Institutional Congruence in Public Goods Delivery: Evidence from Decentralized West Africa." *World Politics* 70 (2): 239–74.
Williams, Donald C. 1996. "Reconsidering State and Society in Africa: The Institutional Dimension in Land Reform Policies." *Comparative Politics* 28 (2): 207–24.
Williams, J. Michael. 2010. *Chieftaincy, the State, and Democracy: Political Legitimacy in Post-apartheid South Africa*. Bloomington: Indiana University Press.
Willis, Justin. 2013. "Chieftaincy." In *The Oxford Handbook of Modern African History*, edited by John Parker and Richard Reid. New York: Oxford University Press.
Xu, Yiqing, and Yang Yao. 2015. "Informal Institutions, Collective Action, and Public Investment in Rural China." *American Political Science Review* 109 (2): 371–91.
Yaro, Joseph A. 2013. "Neoliberal Globalisation and Evolving Local Traditional Institutions: Implications for Access to Resources in Rural Northern Ghana." *Review of African Political Economy* 40 (137): 410–27.
Young, Oran R. 2002. "Institutional Interplay: The Environmental Consequences of Cross-Scale Interactions." In *The Drama of the Commons*, edited by Elinor Ostrom, Thomas Dietz, Nives Dolšak, Paul C. Stern, Susan Stonich, and Elke U. Weber, 263–91. Washington, DC: National Academies Press.
Zimmermann, Robert C. 1994. "The Common Property Forests of Canton Ticino, Southern Switzerland: Relations between Traditional Institutions and the Modern State 1802–2003." University of Indiana. Unpublished manuscript.
Zuccarelli, François. 1973. "De la Chefferie Traditionnelle au Canton: Évolution du Canton Colonial au Sénégal, 1855–1960 (Evolution of the Colonial 'Canton' (County) in Senegal, 1885–1960)." *Cahiers d'Études Africaines* 13 (50): 213–38.
Zuka, Sane Pashane. 2019. "Customary Land Titling and Inter-generational Wealth Transfer in Malawi: Will Secondary Land Rights Holders Maintain Their Land Rights?" *Land Use Policy* 81: 680–88.

Index

accountability, 13, 95–99, 104, 185, 281, 291
  Bemba, Bisa, compared, 170, 172, 179–82, 243
  Bemba and, 172–76, 214, 230
  Bisa and, 177–79
  citizens on, in Zambia, 180–81
  in hierarchical institutions, 168–76, 179–83, 214, 230, 243
  in nonhierarchical institutions, Zambia, 169
  in northern Senegal, 216–31, 243
  state and customary, in Zambia, 98, 174–76
accountability, downward, 179–81, 291
accountability, horizontal, 13, 96–98, 214–15, 226
  sanctioning in, 215, 226, 280
  in Senegal, 36, 216, 226, 231
  in Zambia, 98, 179–81
accountability, vertical, 13, 96–97, 280
  in Zambia, 35–36, 168–69, 174–75, 179–81, 188–89, 214
Afghanistan, 76
Africa, customary institutions in contemporary, 40–47, 279–86
Africa, customary land in, 50–56
Afrobarometer survey data, 43–44, 61, 63–64, 282–84, 302–16
agriculture
  in British colonies, 116–17, 132, 138
  population practicing, in Sub-Saharan Africa, 6

agriculture, Senegal, 29–30
  agricultural census, 1997–1998, 218, 240
  colonial, 116–17, 137–38
  in Dagana district, 219–21
  GOANA and promoting, 202–3
  groundnut economy, 137–38
  in Podor district, 219–21
  smallholder farmers in colonial, 137–38
  state and, 202–3, 205–6, 211–12, 220, 242
  state control, of land, and, 2007–13, 211–12, 242
  state development agencies, 220
agriculture, Zambia, 29–30, 138
  chitemene, 132
  colonial, 116–17, 132, 134, 142–44
allochtone (nonlocal), 257–58. *See also* locals, land titling and
arable land, Senegal, 203
Arrêté du 11 mars 1865. *See* Statutory Instrument of 1865
asymmetrical benefits, in customary institutions, 99–101, 289–90
autochtone (local), 257–58. *See also* locals, land titling and

Barotseland. *See* customary institutions, Zambia; Lozi
Bashilubemba. *See* Bemba; customary institutions, Zambia
Bates, Robert, 16
Bayart, Jean-François, 101–2
Bemba, 170–72, 295, 306. *See also* customary institutions, Zambia

Bemba (cont.)
  Bashilubemba, 170, 172–76, 179
  customary institutions of, 121, 157, 170–76, 179–82, 214, 230, 243
  language, 190–91
  Paramount Chief Chitimuluku, 120–21, 170–71, 173–74
  precolonial state, 121, 170–71, 179
biofuels, 7, 160, 174, 206–7. See also land markets
Bisa, 176. See also customary institutions, Zambia
  customary institutions of, 157, 170–72, 177–82, 243
  Senior Chief Kopa, 171
Boafo-Arthur, Kwame, 26
Boone, Catherine, 18, 75–76, 149, 217
Boserup, Ester, 79
Botswana, 18, 97
British colonialism, 118–24
  agriculture under, 116–17, 132, 138
  control, of land, under, 129–31
  customary authorities under, 117
  French compared with, 34–35, 47–48, 109–10, 116–17, 129–31, 135–36, 138–49, 281–82
  hierarchical institutions surviving under, 126
  land policy under, French compared with, 129–31, 135–36, 138–49
  Lozi and, 119–22, 133, 143–44, 149–50
  smallholder farmers under, 138
  in West Africa, 138
British colonies, former, 101–2
  customary land in, 50–51
  French compared with, 109–10, 281–82
  institutional pluralism in, 59–65
  official customary authorities in, 48
British South Africa Company (BSAC), 118–22
Burkina Faso, 60–61

canton chief (*chef de canton*), 129, 145–46
capital, distance from
  in Senegal, 229, 233–34, 237–38, 273, 297, 312
  in Zambia, 186–87, 192–93, 260, 273, 294, 299, 306–9, 313
case selection, 29, 31–32
Cayor, 126, 235–36. See also customary institutions, Senegal

Chanock, Martin, 132
chef de canton (canton chief), 129, 145–46
Chewa, 111, 122–23, 166. See also customary institutions, Zambia
chiefs. See customary authorities
chief's titles, in Zambia, 165, 326
chitemene, 132
citizens, 3–5, 12–13, 28
  agency of, 33–34
  costs, benefits for, from land titling, 87–89, 91
  customary land rights protests of, 83–84
  institutional syncretism and, 27–28, 282–86
  state, smallholder land titling, and, 246, 272–73, 276
  state privileging, differences in, 257
citizens, customary authorities and, 10, 12–13, 49, 155, 198–99
  citizen evaluation of customary authorities, 45–47
  land access and, 53
  Zambian state and, 198–200
citizens, customary institutions and, 10, 12–13
  impact of customary institutions, 36, 243, 275–76
  preferences shaped by, 13–14
  state and, 43–44, 98, 275–76, 282–86, 291–92, 316
citizens, in Senegal
  customary authorities and, 49
  rental markets and, 242
  state and, 242, 246
citizens, in Zambia
  on accountability, 180–81
  customary authorities and, 49, 155, 198–200
  hierarchical institutions and, 200
  nonhierarchical institutions and, 199–200
  state and, 198–200, 246
citizenship. See state, citizens and
collective action models
  asymmetrical benefits, 99–100
  customary institutions and, 94–96, 102–3, 280
  land titling and, 12, 84–94
colonial control, of land, 129–31
  justification for, customary authorities and, 118
  in Senegal, 124–30, 139, 145
  in Zambia, 119–24, 129–34, 139

colonial era, 109–10, 116–17
  colonial governors, autonomy of, 139
  colonial states, customary institutions and, 26–27
  customary authorities in, 26–27, 42, 117–18, 139–47
  customary land tenure under, 116
  land policies in late, 139–47
  land rights, governance and, 130–38
  precolonial institutions in, 116
  property rights in, 116, 128, 135–36
colonial era, Senegal, 118, 124, 139, 213–14. *See also* French colonialism
  agriculture in, 116–17, 137–38
  customary authorities in, 117, 130–31, 134–35, 137–48, 153
  customary land in, 135–38
  hierarchical institutions in, 101–2, 109–10, 124–30, 232–33
  land policy in, 130–31, 134–49, 153, 171
  land rights, governance and, 130–31, 134–38
  marabouts, Islamic in, 317–20
  precolonial institutions in, 112–15, 125–27, 216–17, 230, 281–82
  smallholder farmers in, 137–38
colonial era, Zambia, 118, 129–30, 139, 281. *See also* British colonialism
  agriculture in, 116–17, 132, 134, 142–44
  crown land in, 139–44, 189–90
  customary authorities in, 117, 119–24, 130–34, 138–47, 154, 166–67
  customary authorities in, rights derived from, 144
  land policy in, 130–34, 139–44, 147–49, 154
  land rights, governance and, 130–34
  railway in, 120, 140–41, 143–44, 189–90
colonial legacy
  British and French, compared, 109–10, 281–82
  customary authorities, state, and, 42, 47–48
  customary institutions and, 29, 34–35, 42, 47–48, 101–2, 281
  in Senegal, contemporary, 213–14, 216–18, 223
  of Senegal and Zambia, compared, 34–35, 47–48

competing explanations. *See also* capital, distance from; infrastructure; land titling rates; land titling rates, Senegal; land titling rates, Zambia; land values; population density; railway; wealth, of smallholder farmers
  geography, land titling prediction and, 74–75, 229, 273
  induced institutional change (IIC), 33–34, 78–81, 229–30, 253, 272–75, 287
  land markets and land values, 78–81
  state capacity and interests, 72–77, 230
compulsory and systematic registration, 8, 50
conflicts, land, 5–6
copper mining, Zambia, 29–30, 119, 142–44, 158
costs, of land titling
  accountability and collective, 104–7
  collective, 86, 89–93, 99–100, 104–7, 227–28, 256–75
  customary authorities, Senegal, on, 225–28
  customary authorities, Zambia, on, 156–57, 161–63, 194
  customary authorities and, 91, 94, 104–7, 156–57, 161–63, 194, 225–28
  customary institutions and collective, 89–93
  customary privilege and, 267, 270–72
  land values and, 201
  for smallholder farmers, 253–54
  transaction costs, 79–80
crops
  Senegal, 250, 266, 303, 315
  Zambia, 250, 260, 262–63, 301, 308–9, 313
cross-national extent, of customary land, 50–56
crown land, Zambia, 139–44, 189–90
customary authorities. *See also* customary institutions; hierarchical institutions
  agency of, in land titling, 68–71, 86
  benefits for, from land titling, 11, 86–87, 89
  under British and French colonialism, compared, 117, 281
  citizen engagement with state and, 282–86, 316
  citizen evaluation of, 45–47, 155, 198–99

customary authorities. (cont.)
  in colonial era, 26–27, 42, 117–18, 139–47
  constrained, unconstrained, 95–99, 104
  costs for, of land titling, 91, 94, 104–7, 156–57, 161–63, 194, 225–28
  in customary institutions, 10, 12–13, 41–42, 279–80
  definition of, 9–11, 40–41
  hybrid authority of, 27–28, 279–80
  land governance by, 53, 56, 58
  official, unofficial, 29, 48–49, 98
  power, increased, of, 42–43, 46
  roles of, 9–11, 44–45
  state and, 25–26, 42–44, 47–48, 72–77, 98, 275–76, 279–80, 282–86, 291–92
  substitution effect between state and, 282–86
  trust in, 45–47, 304, 316
customary authorities, Senegal. *See also* customary institutions, Senegal; hierarchical institutions, Senegal
  in colonial era, 117, 130–31, 134–35, 137–48, 153
  conflict resolution under, 44
  in Dagana district, 216–19, 221, 224–25, 227–29, 231, 233, 243
  electoral politics and, 221
  after independence, 149, 151–52
  kinship with, 259, 264–69, 271, 302–3, 322–25
  on land titling, 209–10, 225–28, 325–26
  marabouts as, 48–49, 205, 320–25
  National Domain Law resisted by, 202, 218–19
  in Podor district, 216–19, 221–28, 230–31, 243
  terminology for, 52–53, 204–5
  unofficial influence of, 29–30, 47–49, 69–71, 107–8, 153, 203–5, 208–12, 247
  Zambia compared with, 49, 145–47, 243
customary authorities, Zambia, 3. *See also* customary institutions, Zambia; hierarchical institutions, Zambia
  benefits, of land titling, and, 164–65
  chief's titles of, 165, 326
  in colonial era, 117, 119–24, 130–34, 138–47, 154, 166–67
  conflict resolution under, 44

  costs, of land titling, and, 156–57, 161–63, 194
  customary institutions and, 156–57, 165–70, 243
  gazetting, degazetting of, 167–68, 175–76
  headmen and headwomen, 179–80
  after independence, 149–51, 167, 171, 185
  kinship with, 259–63, 267–69, 299, 302, 308–9
  land deals, 2007–13, 158–61, 174
  to land titling, responses of, 161–66
  Lusaka, expansion of, and, 155–56
  as official, 29–30, 35–36, 47–49, 69, 87, 98, 107–8, 154, 156–57, 166–70, 174–76, 181–82, 198–201, 281–82
  Senegal compared with, 49, 145–47, 243
  state and, 98, 156–57, 168–69, 174–76, 181–82, 198–201
  state building and, 156, 181–82, 200–1
  trust in, 316
customary institutions, 3–5, 9–10, 35, 81, 154
  in Africa, contemporary, 40–47, 279–86
  as alternative, to state, 282, 285
  asymmetrical benefits, in customary institutions, 99–101, 289–90
  citizens, customary authorities in, 10, 12–13, 41–42, 279–80
  citizens, state, and, 43–44, 98, 275–76, 282–86, 291–92, 316
  on citizens, impact of, 13–14, 36, 243, 275–76
  collective action framework and, 12, 86–94, 99–100, 102–3
  colonial legacy and, 29, 34–35, 42, 47–48, 101–2, 281
  in comparative case studies, 31–32
  definition of, 9–10
  historical legacies and, 14–19, 34, 101–3
  land titling and power of, 11–14, 86–94
  property rights and, 11, 49, 287–88
  smallholder farmers impacted by, 36, 194–98, 252–57, 276
  state building and, 9
  strength of, 14–15, 85, 101–3, 106–7, 272–77, 279, 281
  Tswana, Botswana, 18

customary institutions, Senegal. *See also* customary authorities, Senegal; hierarchical institutions, Senegal
  Baol, 236, 318–19
  Cayor, 126, 235–36, 319
    Lat Dior, 126
  in Dagana district, 216–19, 221, 224–25, 227–29, 231, 233, 243
  Djoloff, 112–15, 318
  Fouta Toro, 112–15, 318
    French war on, 216–17, 230
    legacy of, 216, 223, 226–27, 230, 235–36
  heterogeneity of, 212–14, 227–28
  historical legacies of, 36, 204, 213–14, 231–37
  Islamic brotherhood institutions and, 204–5, 236–37, 317–18, 320–23
  Lebou, 145, 212–13
  marabouts and, 48–49, 204–5, 317–18, 320–25
  NAC land deal negotiations and, 221–30, 242
  in Podor district, 216–19, 221–28, 230–31, 243
  precolonial structures, 112–15
  Pulaar, 235–36, 258, 297–98
  Saloum, 112–15
  Serer, 258
  Sine, 112–15, 213–14
  state and, 204, 230, 242
  Waalo, 112–15, 125–26, 230, 235–36, 281–82
    French war on, 216
customary institutions, Zambia, 156, 165–70. *See also* customary authorities, Zambia; hierarchical institutions, Zambia
  Bemba, 170–72, 295, 306
    Bashilubemba, 170, 172–76, 179
    customary institutions of, 121, 157, 170–76, 179–82, 214, 230, 243
    language, 190–91
    Paramount Chief Chitimuluku, 120–21, 170–71, 173–74
    precolonial state, 121, 170–71, 179
  Bisa, 176
    customary institutions of, 157, 170–72, 177–82, 243
    Senior Chief Kopa, 171
  Chewa, 111, 122–23, 166

Goba, 199–200
heterogeneity of, 166–70
Ila, 111–12
independent chieftaincy systems among, 166–67, 188–89, 194–95, 199–200
Lozi, 111, 119, 181, 185, 190–91
  British agreements with, 119–22, 143–44, 149–50
  constitution of, 160–61
  Lewanika, 119
  Lewanika, territory of, 119–20
  Lochner Concession with, 119
  native reserve for, 133
Lunda, 111, 121, 189–90
Lungu, 111–12
Luvale, 166–67
Mambwe, 111–12
Ngoni, 121, 200
paramount chieftaincy systems among, 121, 167, 170–73, 175–76, 179, 181, 188–89, 194–95, 281, 294
senior chieftaincy systems among, 166–67, 170, 181, 188–89, 194–95, 281, 295
smallholder farmers and, 163, 253–54, 259–60, 262, 276, 301, 308–9
Tonga, 111–12, 190–91
customary land, 56–57
  across Africa, 50–56
  in British colonies, former, 50–51
  colonial institutions and, 116
  customary authority-as-owner in, 53–55
  definition of, 49–51
  lineage rights on, 52–53
  terminology for, 50–52, 110–23
customary land, Senegal, 110–23
  under French colonialism, 135–38
  national domain land, 50–52, 151–52, 202–3
  titling of, 2007–13, 206–8
  Zambia compared with, 52–58
customary land, Zambia
  cost of, 159–60
  Senegal compared with, 52–58
  state planning and, 158–59
  titling of, 2007–13, 157–61
  ZDA and, 158
customary land rights. *See* property rights, customary
customary privilege, 100–1, 105–6, 246, 252–57, 267–72, 275, 287–90

customary privilege (cont.)
  costs, of land titling, and, 267, 270–72
  gender and, 257–58
  kinship and, 258–71, 313, 322–24
  marabouts and, 320–25
  measuring, 257–59
  smallholder farmers, Senegal, and, 259–61, 264–69, 271
  smallholder farmers, Zambia, and, 259–64, 267–69
  tenure security and, 255–56, 261–71, 313, 315
customary property rights. *See* property rights, customary

Dagana district, Senegal, 218–21
  agriculture in, 219–21
  customary authorities in, 216, 219, 227–29, 231, 243
  customary property rights in, Podor compared with, 221, 239–40
  land values in, 229
  NAC land deal negotiations in, 224–25, 227–30, 242
  National Domain Law in, 217–19
  nonhierarchical institutions in, 216–17, 224–25, 227, 231, 242
  partisan electoral politics in, 221
  usage rights in, 218, 239–40
Dakar, Senegal
  distance from, 229, 233–34, 237–38, 273, 297, 312
  Lebou customary institution in, 212–13
data sources. *See also* case selection
  land titling rates (district level) data sets, 31, 182–84, 231–32, 293–98
  paired comparisons, 17–18, 31–32, 169–70, 219–20
  surveys
    Afrobarometer survey data, 43–44, 61, 63–64, 282–84, 302–16
    on land titling, 31–32, 194–95, 293, 299–302
    qualitative data collection, 32–33
    on rental markets, 239–41
    Rural Agricultural Livelihoods Survey, Zambia (RALS), 247–48
data sets, on land titling rates, 293–98
decentralized despotism, 26–27
degazetting. *See* gazetting, degazetting, in Zambia

demand, for property rights, 287–90
de Soto, Hernando, 66
Diagne, Blaise, 129–30
Diop, Cheikh Anta, 16
Diop, Djibril, 134–35, 213–14
Diouf, Abdou, 221
district size
  in Senegal, 234, 296–98, 312
  in Zambia, 294, 306–7
distrust. *See* trust
Djiré, Moussa, 90
Djoloff, 112–15
downward accountability, 179–81, 291
dual land tenure, 60. *See also* customary land; customary land, Senegal; customary land, Zambia; property rights, customary; property rights, statutory

education, 256–57, 271–72
  in Senegal, 249, 252, 257, 265, 273, 302, 315
  in Zambia, 249, 252, 260, 263–64, 273, 300, 308–9, 313, 316
electoral politics
  Senegal, 221
  Zambia, 190–91
enforcement, of property rights, 56–59
Englebert, Pierre, 18
ethnic census, Zambia, 190–91
ethnic identity groups
  Senegal, 235–36
  Zambia, 190–91

fallowing, 269–70
  in Senegal, 268–69, 303, 315, 322
  in Zambia, 196–97, 268–69, 299
Fanchette, Sylvie, 239
fiscal capacity, state, 23–24
formal recognition, of customary authorities. *See* customary authorities
formalization, of property rights. *See* land titling process, Zambia and Senegal
Fouta Toro, 112–15, 318. *See also* customary institutions, Senegal
  French war on, 216–17, 230
  legacy of, 216, 223, 226–27, 230, 235–36
freehold titles, 68, 150–51
French colonialism, 117, 135–38
  British compared with, 34–35, 47–48, 109–10, 116–17, 126, 129–31, 135–36, 138–49, 281–82

indigénat policy, 129–31
land policies, 135–36, 138–48
relations with customary authorities, 125–27, 129, 147–49, 216–17, 230, 281–82
Statutory Instrument of 1865, 128, 135–36
statutory property rights under, 128, 135–36, 149
French colonies, former, 101–2
British compared with, 109–10, 281–82
institutional pluralism in, 60–63
land tenure nationalism laws in, 208
national domain land in, 50–51, 203

Game Management Areas, Zambia (GMAs), 183
gazetting, degazetting, in Zambia, 167–68, 175–76
GDP per capita, Senegal and Zambia, 30
Ghana, 26, 42–43, 64–65, 97
global investors. *See* land markets
global land markets. *See* land markets
globalization, 24
GMAs. *See* Game Management Areas, Zambia
GOANA. *See* Grande Offensive Agricole pour la Nourriture et l'Abondance
Goba, 199–200. *See also* customary institutions, Zambia
Grande Offensive Agricole pour la Nourriture et l'Abondance (GOANA) (Senegal), 202–3
groundnut economy, Senegal, 137–38
group size
Senegal land titling rates and, 235–36, 297–98
Zambia land titling rates and, 190–91, 294–95, 306

Herbst, Jeffrey, 21, 74
hierarchical institutions, 14–19, 101–3, 230, 241–42
in British, French colonies, survival of, 126
land titling rates and, 104–5, 182–83, 185, 187–88, 243, 281
population density and, 187, 233–34
smallholder farmers and, 35–36, 193–98
state building, population density and, 187

hierarchical institutions, Senegal, 18–19, 230, 241
in colonial period, 101–2, 109–10, 124–30, 232–33
land titling rates and, 205, 231–38, 243, 296, 298, 312
population density and, 233–34
precolonial, 109–10, 112–15, 124–28, 213, 235–36, 296, 298
rental markets and, 239–42, 312
hierarchical institutions, Zambia, 18–19, 166–67
accountability in, 168–76, 179–83, 214, 230, 243
citizens and, 200
land titling rates, patterns and, 182–83, 185–98, 234, 243, 294–95, 301, 305–7
paramount chieftaincy systems, 121, 167, 170–73, 175–76, 179, 181, 188–89, 194–95, 281, 294
population density and, 187
precolonial, 109–11, 119–24, 166–70, 281
precolonial, legacy of, 166–70, 201
smallholder farmers, land titling of, and, 194–98, 301, 308–9
tenure security and, 197–98
HoC. *See* House of Chiefs, Zambia
horizontal accountability. *See* accountability, horizontal
House of Chiefs, Zambia (HoC), 162
households, in surveys
education level of, 249, 252, 256–57, 260, 263–65, 271–73, 300, 302, 308–9, 313, 315–16
migrant, nonmigrant, 262–64, 300, 303, 308–9
local, nonlocal, 257–58, 271–72, 300, 303, 308–9, 315, 322
wealth, 260–61, 263–65, 273, 299–302, 308–9, 313, 315
Senegal, 249–52, 257, 265, 273, 302, 315, 322
Zambia, 249–52, 260, 263–64, 273, 299–301, 308–9, 313, 316
hybrid authority, 27–28, 279. *See also* institutional pluralism

IAPRI. *See* Indaba Agricultural Policy Research Institute
IIC. *See* induced institutional change

Ila, 111–12. *See also* customary institutions, Zambia
incremental land titling. *See* piecemeal land titling
Indaba Agricultural Policy Research Institute (IAPRI), 32, 247–48, 293
indigénat policy, 129–31
induced institutional change (IIC), 33–34, 78–81, 229–30, 253, 272–75, 287
informal property rights. *See* property rights, customary
informational capacity, 21–22
infrastructure. *See also* railway
  Senegal, 229, 233–34, 237–38, 251–52, 264–66, 272–75, 297, 302, 312, 315, 323
  Zambia, 186, 189–90, 192–93, 237–38, 251–52, 260–66, 272–75, 295, 299–300, 306–9, 313
institutional change, 94
institutional multiplicity, 91–92. *See also* institutional pluralism
institutional pluralism, 33–34, 63–64, 71–72, 81–82, 289
  in British colonies, former, 59–65
  in French colonies, former, 60–63
  in Senegal, 60–63, 65
  in Zambia, 60–65
institutional syncretism, 27–28, 212. *See also* institutional pluralism
Islamic brotherhood institutions, Senegal, 303. *See also* marabouts
  in colonial era, 317–20
  customary institutions and, 204–5, 236–37, 317–18, 320–23
  differences among, 322, 324
  Khadrya brotherhood, 318, 321–22, 324
  membership in, 318
  Mouride brotherhood, 205, 236–37, 297–98, 318–26
  Tidjane brotherhood, 318–19, 321–22, 324

Kajoba, Gear, 253–54
Kaunda, Kenneth, 150–51
Kenya, 91, 135–36
Khadrya brotherhood, 318, 321–22, 324
kinship
  customary privilege and, 258–71, 313, 322–24
  with marabouts, 322–25

in Senegal, 259, 264–69, 271, 302–3, 322–25
in Zambia, 259–63, 267–69, 299, 302, 308–9
land conflicts, 5–6
land markets, 1, 78–81. *See also* biofuels
  global, 159–60, 206
  global investors, 6–8
  multinational land deals, 6–8
  Senegal, 2007–13, 206–8
  state interests and, 2–3
  Zambia, 2007–13, 157–61
land mass, Senegal and Zambia, 30
land policy, colonial
  British and French, compared, 129–31, 135–36, 138–49
  late colonial era, 139–47
  in Senegal, 130–31, 134–49, 153, 171
  in Zambia, 130–34, 139–44, 147–49, 154
land rights protests, 83–84
land tenure nationalism laws, 208
land titling. *See specific topics*
land titling, debates over, 57–58, 289–91
land titling, definition, 57. *See also* property rights, statutory
land titling, policy, 2, 7–8, 65–67, 130–52
land titling process, Zambia and Senegal, 67–68
land titling rates, 253, 293–98
  accountability and, 185
  hierarchical institutions and, 104–5
  population density and, 272–75
  for smallholder farmers, low, 247
land titling rates, Senegal, 237, 293
  district size and, 234, 296–98, 312
  group size and, 235–36, 297–98
  hierarchical institutions and, 205, 231–38, 243, 296, 298, 312
  infrastructure and, 229, 233–34, 237–38, 251–52, 264–66, 272–75, 297, 302, 312, 315, 323
  land values and, 229, 233–34, 237–38, 251–52, 264–66, 273
  nonhierarchical institutions and, 205, 232–36
  population density and, 233–34, 237–38, 273, 297, 312
  Zambia compared with, 243

land titling rates, Zambia, 247, 293–95
  customary authorities and, 188–89,
    194–98, 281, 294–95, 299–301,
    308–9
  district size and, 294, 306–7
  group size and, 190–91, 294–95, 306
  hierarchical institutions and, 182–83,
    185–98, 234, 243, 294–95, 301,
    305–7
  infrastructure and, 186, 189–90, 192–93,
    237–38, 251–52, 260–66, 272–75,
    295, 299–300, 306–9, 313
  land values and, 186, 189–90, 192–93,
    251–52, 261–66, 273
  nonhierarchical institutions and, 185,
    188–89, 194–96
  population density and, 186–87, 192–93,
    261–66, 268, 273, 295, 299, 306–9,
    313
  Senegal compared with, 243
  tenure security and, 197
land values, 78–81, 192–93, 201, 253,
    287–89
  infrastructure and, 186, 189–90, 192–93,
    229, 233–34, 237–38, 251–52,
    261–66, 273
  Senegal, 229, 233–34, 237–38, 251–52,
    264–66, 273
  Zambia, 186, 189–90, 192–93, 251–52,
    261–66, 273
Lands Act, Zambia (1995), 130–52
language groups, Zambia, 190–91
large scale land deals. *See* land markets
law, rule of, 22–23
Layenne brotherhood, 318
Lebou, 212–13. *See also* customary
    institutions, Senegal
legibility, of land, 21–22
Lewanika. *See* customary institutions,
    Zambia; Lozi
Liberia, 7
Lipton, Michael, 287–88
local councils, 68–69
  Senegal, 67–68
  Senegal, customary authorities and,
    69–71, 209, 247
  Senegal, NAC land deal and, 222–24, 226
  Zambia, 67–68
  Zambia, customary authorities and, 69,
    71, 247
Local Government Code, Senegal (1996), 151

locals, land titling and, 257–58, 271–72. *See
    also allochtone*; *autochtone*
  in Senegal, 303, 315, 322
  in Zambia, 300, 308–9
Lochner Concession, 119
Lozi, 111, 119, 181, 185, 190–91. *See also*
    customary institutions, Zambia
  British agreements with, 119–22, 143–44,
    149–50
  constitution of, 160–61
  Lewanika, 119
  Lewanika, territory of, 119–20
  Lochner Concession with, 119
  native reserve for, 133
Lunda, 111. *See also* customary institutions,
    Zambia
Lungu, 111–12. *See also* customary
    institutions, Zambia
Lusaka, Zambia
  customary authorities and expansion of,
    155–56
  land titling and distance from, 186–87,
    192–93, 260, 273, 294, 299, 306–9,
    313
Luvale, 166–67. *See also* customary
    institutions, Zambia

Madagascar, 7
Malawi, 60–61, 66, 83
Mambwe, 111–12. *See also* customary
    institutions, Zambia
Mamdani, Mahmood, 26–27
Mann, Michael, 21
marabouts, 303, 317–18
  in colonial era, 317–20
  contemporary, 320–25
  customary adaptation and, 325–26
  as customary authorities, 48–49, 205,
    320–25
  customary privilege and, 320–25
  differences among brotherhood
    institutions, 322, 324
  kinship with, 322–25
  in precolonial Senegal, 204–5, 317–20
Masla/massla, 70
Mbacké, 321–22
Mexico, 286
Migdal, Joel, 25
migrant, nonmigrant households, 262–64,
    300, 303, 308–9, 315, 322
mining, Zambia, 29–30, 119, 142–44, 158

Ministry of Finance, Senegal, 68
Ministry of Lands and Natural Resources, Zambia, 68
Mouride brotherhood, 236–37, 297–98, 318
  brotherhood communities compared with, 322, 324
  in colonial era, 318–19
  as customary authorities, 205, 236, 320–23
  in Touba, 319, 321, 325–26
Mozambique, 42–43
multinational land deals, 6–8. *See also* land markets

national domain land, Senegal, 50–52, 151–52, 202–3. *See also* customary land, Senegal
National Domain Law, Senegal (1964), 152, 204, 208, 242, 281–82
  customary control, de facto, under, 151–52
  in Dagana district, 217–19
  in Podor district, 218–19
  resistance to, 218–19, 231
  usage rights under, 151, 217–19, 239
National Land Commission, Senegal (NLC), 232
native, stranger and. *See allochtone*; locals, land titling and
native authorities
  native reserves, Zambia, 131–34, 139–42
  native treasuries, Zambia, 141–42
  native trust land, Zambia, 142–44
Ng'ong'ola, Clement, 66
Ngoni, 111, 121, 200. *See also* customary institutions, Zambia
NLC. *See* National Land Commission, Senegal
nonhierarchical institutions, 14–19, 35–36, 101–2
nonhierarchical institutions, Senegal, 233
  in Dagana, NAC land deal negotiations and, 224–25, 227, 242
  land titling rates and, 205, 232–36
  precolonial, 124–25, 213–14
nonhierarchical institutions, Zambia, 167
  accountability in, 169
  Bisa, 170–72, 177–79
  citizens and, 199–200
  Goba, 199–200
  hierarchical, differences from, 194–95
  land titling rates and, 185, 188–89, 194–96
  precolonial, 111–12, 166–67
nonlocal. *See allochtone*; locals, land titling and
nonlocals, land titling and. *See* locals, land titling and
nonmigrant households. *See* migrant, non-migrant households
North Eastern Rhodesia, 119–22, 142–44
North Western Rhodesia, 119–20, 122, 142–44
Northern Rhodesia, 140–42. *See also* British colonialism; North Eastern Rhodesia; North Western Rhodesia
northern Senegal. *See* Dagana district, Senegal; Podor district, Senegal
Nuesiri, Emmanuel, 45–46
Nyamnjoh, Francis, 41
Nyanja, 190, 295, 306

Obeng-Odoom, Franklin, 290–91
official chiefs. *See* customary authorities
Okoth-Ogendo, Hastings, 253–54
Osafo-Kwaako, Philip, 187
Ouedraogo, Hubert, 9–10

paramount chieftaincy systems. *See* customary institutions, Zambia
Parti Démocratique Sénégalais (PDS), 221
Parti Socialiste, Senegal (PS), 221
PDS. *See* Parti Démocratique Sénégalais
piecemeal land titling, 2, 7–9, 65–66, 71–72, 81–82
  in Senegal, 33–34, 67–68, 71, 229, 246
  state land authority, building, and, 78, 289
  in Zambia, 33–34, 67–68, 71
Platteau, Jean-Philippe, 79–80
pluralism, institutional. *See* institutional pluralism
Podor district, Senegal, 216–21, 230
  agriculture in, 219–21
  customary authorities, institutions, in, 216–19, 221–28, 230–31, 243
  customary property rights in, Dagana compared with, 239–40
  horizontal accountability in, 231
  land rentals in, 239–40
  land values in, 229
  NAC land deal negotiations in, 221–30

National Domain Law in, 218–19
partisan electoral politics in, 221
precolonial institutions in, 216–17, 231
Tidjane brotherhood in, 321–22
population density, 272–75
hierarchical institutions and, 187, 233–34
Senegal land titling rates and, 233–34, 237–38, 273, 297, 312
state building and, 187
Zambia land titling rates and, 186–87, 192–93, 261–66, 268, 273, 295, 299, 306–9, 313
precolonial boundaries, 127–28
precolonial institutions, Senegal. *See* customary institutions, Senegal; hierarchical institutions, Senegal
precolonial institutions, Zambia. *See* customary institutions, Zambia; hierarchical institutions, Zambia
precolonial state building, 16
privilege, customary. *See* customary privilege
privilege, in state, 107
property rights, 54–55. *See also* property rights, customary; property rights, statutory; usage rights
in colonial era, 116, 128, 135–36
enforcement and, 56–59
land rights, governance and, 130–38
political determinants of, 286–89
tenure security and, 57–58, 87–89
property rights, customary. *See also* customary land; customary land, Senegal; customary land, Zambia
cross-national extent of, 50–56
customary authorities enforcing, 56
customary authorities holding primary, 53
in Dagana, Podor districts, Senegal, 239–40
as informal property rights, 11–12
prevalence of, 250–51
secondary land rights, 54–56, 90, 254–55
Senegal, 3–4, 239–40
Senegal and Zambia, compared, 52–59
Senegal rental markets and, 239–42
statutory compared with, 57–59, 288–89
property rights, statutory, 1, 57–59, 288–89
customary privilege, differences in, and, 246, 275, 282, 289–90
definition, 57
demand for, 2–3, 28, 32–33, 79–80, 99–100, 105–6, 197, 246, 287–90

French colonial, 128, 135–36
in smallholder surveys, 250
supply of, 287–88
in Zambia, expanding, 183–84
PS. *See* Parti Socialiste, Senegal
Pulaar, 235–36, 258, 297–98

qualitative data collection, 32–33
Quranic schools, 249

railway
Senegal, 312
Senegal, colonial, 137–38
Zambia, 186, 189–90, 260, 299–300, 306–9, 313
Zambia, colonial, 120, 140–41, 143–44, 189–90
RALS. *See* Rural Agricultural Livelihoods Survey, Zambia
Ravalomanana, Marc, 7
regime type, in Senegal and Zambia, 30
rental markets, Senegal, 239–42, 296–312
revenue, government, 1–2, 76
Robinson, James A., 187
rule of law, 22–23
Rural Agricultural Livelihoods Survey, Zambia (RALS), 247–48
rural councils. *See* local councils
Rwanda, 50–51

Saloum, 112–15. *See also* customary institutions, Senegal; Serer
sanctioning, 215, 226
Sata, Michael, 176
schooling. *See* education
secondary land rights, 54–56, 90, 254–55
Senegal. *See specific topics*
Senegal River Valley, 219–20
senior chieftaincy systems. *See* customary institutions, Zambia
Serer, 258. *See also* customary institutions, Senegal
Shipton, Parker, 91
Sine, 112–15, 213–14. *See also* customary institutions, Senegal; Serer
Sirleaf, Ellen Johnson, 7
smallholder farmers, 32, 254–55, 293
in British colonies, 138
citizens, state, and, 246, 272–73, 276
costs for, of land titling, 253–54

smallholder farmers (cont.)
  customary institutions impacting, 36, 194–98, 252–57, 276
  customary privilege and, 246, 252–57
  education level of, 249, 252, 256–57, 260, 263–65, 271–73, 300, 302, 308–9, 315
  hierarchical institutions and, 35–36
  infrastructure and land titling of, 251–52, 260, 263–66, 272–75, 299–300, 302, 308–9
  state and, 246, 256–57, 272–73, 276
  surveys of, classical models and, 272–75
  surveys of, sample characteristics in, 249–52
smallholder farmers, Senegal
  in colonial era, 137–38
  crops of, 250, 266, 303, 315
  customary authorities, institutions and, 210, 245–69
  customary privilege of, 259–61, 264–69, 271
  gender and surveys of, 264–66, 303, 315
  households of, 249–52, 257, 265, 273, 302, 315, 322
  kinship of, 259, 264–69, 271, 302–3, 322–25
  land titling rates of, low, 247
  land titling resisted by, 245–69
  land titling sought by, 244–45
  land values and, 251–52, 273
  piecemeal land titling and, 246
  surveys of, 247–49, 252, 259–61, 264–69, 271, 302–3, 315
  tenure security of, 245, 267–68, 315
  wealth of, 265, 273, 302, 315
smallholder farmers, Zambia, 138, 244
  crops of, 250, 260, 262–63, 301, 308–9, 313
  customary authorities and, 163, 253–54, 259–60, 262, 276, 301, 308–9
  customary privilege of, 259–64, 267–69
  gender and surveys of, 260, 263–64, 300, 308–9, 313
  hierarchical institutions and, 194–98, 301, 308–9
  households of, 249–52, 260, 263–64, 273, 299–301, 308–9, 313, 316
  kinship of, 259–63, 267–69, 299, 302, 308–9
  land titling rates of, low, 247
  land values and, 186, 189–90, 192–93, 251–52, 261–66, 273
  surveys of, 32, 247–52, 259–64, 267–69, 299–301, 308–9, 313, 316

wealth of, 260–61, 263–64, 273, 299–301, 308–9, 313, 315
South Africa, 42–43, 290–91
Southern Rhodesia, 60, 140
Spear, Thomas, 115–16
state
  accountability, in customary institutions, and, 98, 174–76
  in colonial era, customary authorities and, 42
  colonial legacy and, 42, 47–48
  customary authorities and, 25–26, 42–44, 47–48, 72–77, 98, 275–76, 279–80, 282–86, 291–92
  customary institutions as alternative to, 282, 285
  fiscal capacity, 23–24
  interests of, 2–3, 12, 33–34, 72–78
  land markets and interests of, 2–3
  land titling promoted by, 7–8
  piecemeal land titling and, 78, 289
  power, resources of, 73
  power of, expanding, 74–77
  privilege in, 107
  revenue of, 1–2, 76
  smallholder farmers and, 246, 256–57, 272–73, 276
  substitution effect for customary authorities and, 282–86
  territorial, geographic reach of, 20–21
  trust in, 304, 316
state, citizens and, 198–200, 242, 246, 256–57, 272–73
  citizen engagement with state, 282–86
  citizen privileges, differences in, 257
  customary institutions and, 43–44, 98, 275–76, 282–86, 291–92, 316
state, Senegalese
  agriculture and, 202–3, 205–6, 211–12, 220, 242
  citizens and, 242, 246
  commercial agriculture promoted by, 202–3, 205–6
  customary adaptation and, 325–26
  customary authorities and, 29–30, 202
  customary institutions and, 204, 230, 242
  in Dagana, Podor, agriculture promoted by, 220
  interests of, 72–74
  land markets, transforming, and, 2007–13, 206–8

state, Zambian, 192, 281
    accountability, of customary authorities, and, 98, 174–76
    citizens and, 198–200, 246
    customary authorities and, 98, 156–57, 168–69, 174–76, 181–82, 198–201
    customary land and planning of, 158–59
    interests of, 72–74
state building, 1–2, 8–9, 14–15, 74–77, 278–79. *See also* state capacity
    customary authorities and, 156, 181–82, 200–1
    fragmented, land titling as, 20–25, 325
    hierarchy, population density and, 187
    land titling in, functions of, 20–24
    land titling records in, 31
    piecemeal land titling and, 78, 289
    precolonial, 16
    smallholder land titling and, 276
    uneven patterns of, 38
state capacity, 24–25, 36–37, 192, 288. *See also* competing explanations; state building
    citizens on, 256–57
    fiscal, 23–24
    informational, 21–22
    interests and, 33–34, 72–78
    land titling and increasing, 278–79
state property rights. *See* property rights, statutory
Statutory Instrument of 1865 128, 135–36
stranger, native and. *See allochtone*; locals, land titling and
succession disputes, 41
supply, of property rights, 287–88
Swidler, Ann, 255
Sy, Mouhamadou, 258

Tanzania, 64–65
tenure security, 57–58, 87–89, 289–91
    customary privilege and, 255–56, 261–71, 313, 315
    definitions of, 87–88
    fallowing and, 197, 268–70, 315
    hierarchical institutions, Zambia, and, 197–98
    land titling rates, Zambia, and, 197
    measurement of, 267–68
    reform for, 291
    of smallholder farmers, Senegal, 245, 267–68, 315

Thomson-Sharpe treaties, 120–22, 143
Tidjane brotherhood, 318–19, 321–22, 324
Tine, Ngone Diop, 70, 258
Tonga, 111–12, 166–67, 190–91, 295, 306. *See also* customary institutions, Zambia
Touba, Senegal, 319, 321, 325–26
Toucouleur. *See* Fouta Toro; Pulaar
Town and Country Planning Act, Zambia (1962), 159
transaction costs, 79–80
trust
    in customary authorities, 45–47, 304, 316
    in state, 304, 316
trust land, Zambia, 142–44
Tswana customary institution, Botswana, 18

Uganda, 83
unofficial chiefs. *See* customary authorities
Urban and Regional Planning Act, Zambia (2015), 159
urbanization, 6, 155–56
usage rights, 56–57. *See also* property rights
    in Dagana district, Senegal, 218, 239–40
    under National Domain Law, Senegal, 151, 217–19, 239
    in Senegal, 151, 217–40

vertical accountability. *See* accountability, vertical

Waalo, 112–15, 125–26, 216, 230, 235–36, 281–82. *See also* customary institutions, Senegal
Wade, Abdoulaye, 202–3, 221
wealth, of smallholder farmers
    in Senegal, 265, 273, 302, 315
    in Zambia, 260–61, 263–64, 273, 299–301, 308–9, 313, 315
West Africa, British colonies of, 138
White settlement, 51–52, 120, 128, 131–33, 135, 137, 139–44
within-country comparisons, of historical institutional structures, 17–18
Wolof ethno-linguistic group, 235–36, 258, 297–98
World Bank, 7–8, 66

Zambia. *See specific topics*
Zambia Development Agency (ZDA), 158

CPSIA information can be obtained
at www.ICGtesting.com
Printed in the USA
LVHW080214120922
728136LV00003B/69